HISTORY OF WOMEN IN THE UNITED STATES

HISTORY OF WOMEN IN THE UNITED STATES

Historical Articles on Women's Lives and Activities

Edited by Nancy F. Cott

Series ISBN 3-598-41454-4

1. Theory and Method in Women's History
   ISBN 3-598-41455-2 Part 1
   ISBN 3-598-41477-3 Part 2

2. Household Constitution and Family Relationships
   ISBN 3-598-41456-0

3. Domestic Relations and Law
   ISBN 3-598-41457-9

4. Domestic Ideology and Domestic Work
   ISBN 3-598-41458-7 Part 1
   ISBN 3-598-41475-7 Part 2

5. The Intersection of Work and Family Life
   ISBN 3-598-41459-5 Part 1
   ISBN 3-598-41476-5 Part 2

6. Working on the Land
   ISBN 3-598-41460-9

7. Industrial Wage Work
   ISBN 3-598-41461-7 Part 1
   ISBN 3-598-41693-8 Part 2

8. Professional and White-Collar Employments
   ISBN 3-598-41462-5 Part 1
   ISBN 3-598-41694-6 Part 2

9. Prostitution
   ISBN 3-598-41463-3

10. Sexuality and Sexual Behavior
    ISBN 3-598-41464-1

11. Women's Bodies: Health and Childbirth
    ISBN 3-598-41465-X

12. Education
    ISBN 3-598-41466-8

13. Religion
    ISBN 3-598-41467-6

14. Intercultural and Interracial Relations
    ISBN 3-598-41468-4

15. Women and War
    ISBN 3-598-41469-2

16. Women Together: Organizational Life
    ISBN 3-598-41470-6

17. Social and Moral Reform
    ISBN 3-598-41471-4 Part 1
    ISBN 3-598-41695-4 Part 2

18. Women and Politics
    ISBN 3-598-41472-2 Part 1
    ISBN 3-598-41697-0 Part 2

19. Woman Suffrage
    ISBN 3-598-41473-0 Part 1
    ISBN 3-598-41696-2 Part 2

20. Feminist Struggles for Sex Equality
    ISBN 3-598-41474-9

HISTORY OF WOMEN IN THE UNITED STATES

Historical Articles on Women's Lives and Activities

9. Prostitution

Edited with an Introduction by

Nancy F. Cott
Yale University

K · G · Saur
Munich · New Providence · London · Paris · 1993

Publisher's Note

The articles and chapters which comprise this collection originally appeared in a wide variety of publications and are reproduced here in facsimile from the highest quality offprints and photocopies available. The reader will notice some occasional marginal shading and text-curl common to photocopying from tightly bound volumes. Every attempt has been made to either correct or minimize this effect.

Library of Congress Cataloging-in-Publication Data

History of women in the United States : historical articles on women's lives and activities / edited with an introduction by Nancy F. Cott.

p. cm.

Includes bibliographical references and indexes.

Contents: 1. Theory and method in women's history -- 2. Household constitution and family relationships -- 3. Domestic relations and law -- 4. Domestic ideology and domestic work -- 5. The intersection of work and family life -- 6. Working on the land -- 7. Industrial wage work -- 8. Professional and white-collar employments -- 9. Prostitution -- 10. Sexuality and sexual behavior -- 11. Women's bodies -- 12. Education -- 13. Religion -- 14. Intercultural and interracial relations -- 15. Women and war -- 16. Women together -- 17. Social and moral reform -- 18. Women and politics -- 19. Woman suffrage -- 20. Feminist struggles for sex equality.

ISBN 3-598-41454-4 (set)

1. Women--United States--History. 2. Women--United States--Social conditions. I. Cott, Nancy F.

HQ1410.H57 1992

305.4'0973--dc20 92-16765

CIP

Die Deutsche Bibliothek - CIP - Einheitsaufnahme

History of Women in the United States: historical articles on women's lives and activities / ed. with an introd. by Nancy F. Cott.

- Munich ; London ; New York ; Paris : Saur.

ISBN 3-598-41454-4

NE: Cott, Nancy F. (Hrsg.)

Vol. 9. prostitution - (1993)

ISBN 3-598-41463-3

Printed on acid-free paper/Gedruckt auf säurefreiem Papier

K.G. Saur Verlag GmbH & Co. KG, Munich 1993

A Reed Reference Publishing Company

Printed in the United States of America

Printed/Bound by Edwards Brothers Incorporated, Ann Arbor

ISBN 3-598-41463-3 (vol. 9)

ISBN 3-598-41454-4 (series)

Contents

CONTENTS

Series Preface

In the space of one generation, women's history has become the fastest-growing area of scholarship in U.S. history. Since the resurgence of feminism in the late 1960s and 1970s, insistent questions about the historical meanings of "woman's place" have sowed and reaped a garden of scholarship. Where scholarly works used to be bare of mention of women, academic enterprise has now produced a vigorous growth of books and articles, bringing to light diverse women of every region, race, class and age. This research is marked by a renovating intent that refuses to accept as "human" history a history of men. Interest is lively and debate is stimulating and sought after: attendance at the Berkshire Conference on the History of Women rivals the size of the annual convention of the American Historical Association.

While books in women's history are daily increasing in numbers and strength, as in any fast-developing field the scholarly literature in the form of articles is most expansive and up-to-the-minute. All the history journals now publish articles on women's work, domestic settings, family relations, household matters, female politics and organizations and so forth, and new journals have sprung into being to concentrate on such topics. Women's historians publish in numerous regional and thematic history journals as well as in feminist outlets and in journals of other social science disciplines. This series brings together a collection of outstanding articles from the field, almost all written in the past twenty years and more than half published during the 1980s. It brings together, in volumes organized by topic, essays otherwise widely dispersed. These volumes reprint only articles that originally appeared in journals, not chapters of books; review articles are not included. Articles have been chosen for overall quality and for range. Each one was chosen for one or more of the following reasons: because it is the standard authority on its subject matter; represents an important statement on a topic by a recognized scholar; presages an important book to come; provides a first look at new evidence or new methods; or opens an untapped area or new controversy. Older articles have been reprinted if their data or interpretation have not been surpassed or if they marked an important stage in the historiography, even if since superseded.

The historical coverage of the series extends from the Revolutionary era to the 1960s. The articles themselves are dated from the 1940s through 1988. Volumes are organized by topic rather than time period. Within each volume, the articles are ordered chronologically (with respect to substance), so that the whole can be read as an historical overview. The only exception to this ordering principle is Volume One, on Theory and Method, in which the contents are arranged in order of publication. Within each volume there is an attempt to include articles on as diverse kinds of women as possible. None of the volume topics is regionally or racially defined; rather, all volumes are topically designed so as to afford views of women's work, family lives, and public activities which cut across races and regions. Any volume in the series stands on its own, supplying as full a treatment of a designated subject matter as the scholarly literature will provide. Several groupings of volumes also make sense; that is, volumes two through five all center around domestic and family matters; volumes five through nine consider other varieties of women's work; volumes nine through eleven concern uses and abuses of women's bodies; volumes twelve through fourteen look at major aspects of socialization; and volumes fifteen through twenty include organizational and political efforts of many sorts.

As a whole, the series displays in all its range the vitality of the field of women's history. Aside from imbuing U.S. history with new vision, scholarship in this area has informed, and should continue to inform, current public debate on issues from parental leave to the nuclear freeze. By bringing historical articles together under topical headings, these volumes both represent accurately the shape of historical controversy (or consensus) on given issues and make historians' findings most conveniently available for current reference.

Introduction

Prostitution is a form of women's work, an incarnation of social values and an element in sexual regulation. Recently, historians have begun to investigate the features of prostitution in the past not only for what these reveal about sexual morality and behavior—or about criminal statutes or city politics—but also for what they reveal about women's choices of occupation and sexual expression. This volume includes some earlier articles (written in the 1960s) in which historians were interested mainly in discussing the social values revealed in reformers' attitudes about prostitution. More recent work has more frequently focused on prostitutes themselves—their range of alternatives, their conditions of work, their health and life spans, their careers—and on interaction between prostitutes and others, whether reformers, clients, or bosses. Feminist historians have tried to avoid the assumption that prostitutes were necessarily and only victims—although some must have been—and have taken the approach that they were rational individuals participating in a limited range of choices available to poor women. If marriage (the other obvious choice) meant the likelihood of being tyrannized over by an unsympathetic husband, and did not bring sure economic support, and besides, was not offered to every woman, the other alternative to achieve economic survival was very likely to be menial, drudging work. To some extent, recent historians have tried to assimilate the history of prostitution with the history of other kinds of women's work: like other more "legitimate" employments, it was clearly identified as "women's" work; it required little training and promised little promotion; it was a way to earn a living—a higher income than typical forms of women's work provided, though likely for only a short time—but it ultimately kept women still dependent on men. On the other hand, prostitution by its very existence acknowledged women's bodies and sexual favors as commodities to be sold, as no other form of women's employment so openly did. The explicit sexual character of women's work in prostitution—and the high pay women could earn thereby—beg for analysis and explanation with reference to sexual mores, the accepted marital norms, the sexual objectification and sexual bargaining power of women.

Much of historians' investigation of prostitution has focused on the era around the turn of the twentieth century. "Bawdy houses," streetwalking, and other forms of prostitution had long been present, episodically, in the U.S.—ever since the seventeenth-century immigration of English men and women established centers of white population—and had been prosecutable as crime by municipal regulation. However, it was not until large aggregations of urban population appeared in the nineteenth century that prostitution came to be seen as a "social evil," and then only by self-selected groups of moral reformers (male and female), who believed that women were being victimized, men corrupted, and families and society undermined by the practice. Since historians have, by and large, been guided to study prostitution by the diligent, literate and record-keeping contemporary opponents of it, focused historical work begins with the appearance of such "moral reform" and "purity crusades." It was at the turn of the century, an era of mass immigration and rapid growth and multiplication of cities in the U.S., that commercialized sex received the most attention from reformers and thus has also received the most attention from historians. While criminal sanctions were attached to prostitution in most American locations, it was not until the late nineteenth century that enforcement became seen as a great social issue. Reformers agitated by tensions between rich and poor, between men and women, and between differing racial and ethnic groups that now crowded into American cities, focused on ending the "traffic in women" as a way to cleanse and revivify urban community. Besides the voluntary reform groups in existence, during the first two decades of the twentieth century dozens of municipal and state "vice commissions" were formed in many American locations to investigate and expunge "red-light districts." They were largely successful in breaking up such areas of virtual toleration, and criminalizing prostitution, and in the process brought to the fore a great deal of testimony about prostitution which historians have found revealing.

Perhaps the most accurate way to characterize recent historical study of prostitution, as shown in this volume, is to say that it embeds prostitution in social and economic history, in the history of relations between the sexes and relations between the classes, while attempting to maintain the point of view of prostitutes as subjects and agents of their own actions rather than mere objects of trade. Making regional and racial variations in conditions of prostitution a matter of inquiry, historians have shown how practices vary in tandem with demography, economic structure, and patterns of immigration. Historians have begun to reveal patterns of exploitation of Chinese and Japanese women imported to become prostitutes on the West coast, and details of multi-ethnic prostitution in mining towns and other male strongholds in white settlement of the "wild West." Emphasizing the similarities of prostitutes' lives to those of their workingclass sisters (as well as the differences between them), the new work has exploded myths of the prostitute's "life of ease" and indicated the pervasiveness and diversity of commercialized sex. In this light, both the history of prostitution and the history of women assume new aspects.

Prostitution

Disorderly City, Disorderly Women: Prostitution in Ante-Bellum Philadelphia

Marcia Carlisle

UNTIL THE MID-NINETEENTH CENTURY, the wards of Philadelphia were a disorderly mixture of the rich, middling and poor; of native and immigrant; of black and white. Amidst the rush of growth and change, there was little room for privacy, no premium on decorum. The city was an urban frontier; people were bound together in neighborhoods where they lived and worked, and as time and money permitted, played. Such boundaries as distinguished between races were evident and deepening. The modern city was to bring with it more rigid rules of behavior and formal standards that set groups off from each other. But this development was neither simple nor smooth. The reshaping of the old city was as much a reshaping of the people who lived in it as it was a recasting of the urban horizon. It was a struggle fought many times over between the old habits of some and the new priorities of others.

Prostitutes—or disorderly women as they were frequently called—were familiar figures in the landscape of the disorderly city. They moved freely and openly in parks, on the streets, and in places of amusement. Along with paupers and peddlers, they used public spaces to their own advantage. Like more substantial citizens, they sometimes came before local magistrates to complain of wrongs against them; on other occasions, they might have been brought before the bench as vagrants and thieves. They were "public women," symbols of longstanding sexual disorder, tolerated as necessary nuisances.

This essay attempts to re-create in ethnographic style the "disorderly" world in which prostitutes lived and to examine their lives and careers in the context of those of their peers among the laboring

For patient assistance in the preparation of this essay, I am indebted to the late Warren Susman, Judith Walkowitz, Alan Dawley, and Rachel Bernstein.

poor. To date, very little has been written about prostitutes in the early decades of the nineteenth century, prior to the time when prostitution emerged as the great "social evil." Evidence from this early period suggests that prostitutes were primarily public nuisances like noisy public houses and street fighting. Their disorderly occupation did not single them out for especially harsh treatment from city officials; nor did it isolate them from their peers. Their brothels were households in mixed neighborhoods, but their working environment included the streets, the parks, the theaters and local taverns. They were public women at a time when prostitution was less marked by extensive commercialization; prostitutes themselves were not the center of a social debate on sexuality and moral order. The epilogue explores one unsuccessful attempt in the 1830s to remove prostitutes from one of their traditional haunts, the theaters. This effort by concerned citizens intimates the kind of challenges prostitutes would later face as the modern city took form and public opinion about the profession changed.

The Disorderly City

William Penn's design for Philadelphia called for systematic development of the land between the Schuylkill and the Delaware Rivers. The growth was to follow a grid pattern of wide east-west streets cut by north-south streets running parallel to the two rivers. Development was to move inward—westward from the Delaware River and eastward from the Schuylkill River—meeting at Broad Street, the intended city center. But, in practice, the less accessible Schuylkill River frontage remained sparsely populated, while the area along the Delaware River grew crowded. The congestion that Penn so hated in European cities appeared in Philadelphia in spite of his plans for a city of spacious, symmetric blocks. The elegant city that he envisioned for country squires grew into a commercial city of merchants who lived and worked on bits of land close to the bustling ports from which they drew their livelihoods. They lived in large houses along the fronts of streets that Penn laid out; but behind them, in unplanned streets and alleys, lived the unplanned urban poor.[1]

[1] The description of Philadelphia geography is drawn in part from Emma Jones Lap-

In 1800, Philadelphia had a population of 81,000; by 1840, the city had 200,000 inhabitants. During those years of growth, disease and disorder were a part of life in the crowded city. Yellow fever scourged the city in 1803, in 1805, and again in 1820; influenza appeared in 1807; cholera, in 1832. In these years, death stalked through the small streets and back alleys and along the open boulevards. Disorder, however, was a daily occurrence.[2]

Up and down the narrow streets, courts, and alleys of Philadelphia there was disorder. Columns of the pennypress regularly carried accounts of incidents in such seemingly colorful locations as Gillis Alley, Nanny Goat Alley, Ram Cat Alley, and in Baker Street, Bedford Street, Small Street, and St. Mary's Street. One neighborhood's reputation for continual fighting and drunkenness earned it the name "Brickbat Row." In one month of 1836, a variety of residents of Sassafras Alley appeared in the Magistrate's Court. Amanda Smith was found drunk with a gang of boys collected around her, taunting her. Her neighbor, Catherine Deal, had to be brought in for disorderly conduct on the streets. Catherine Dawes called the watchman to protect her from her husband, Thomas, "a loafer who refused to work then came home to kick up a row." All the while, poor old "Lady McGuire," an insane widow, wandered the streets. Years ago, it was said, her husband had mistreated her, and she turned to drink. Now, her face, once "one of considerable beauty," was bloated. Without husband or property, she was a hopeless vagrant in the city of brotherly love.[3]

---

sansky, "South Street Philadelphia, 1762-1854: 'A Haven for Those Low in the World.'" (Ph. D. dissertation, University of Pennsylvania, 1975), chapter 1.

[2] Ibid.

[3] See the work of Dennis Clark on the Irish in Philadelphia, especially "'Ramcat' and Rittenhouse Squares: Related Communities'" in William W. Cutler, III, and Howard Gillette, eds., *The Divided Metropolis: Social and Spatial Dimensions of Philadelphia, 1800-1975* (Westport, 1980), 125-140. On the problem of changing notions of order and disorder, see Susan G. Davis, "'Making Night Hideous': Christmas Revelry and Public Order in 19th Century Philadelphia," *American Quarterly* 34 (1982): 185-199. On the violence in mid-nineteenth-century Philadelphia, see Michael Feldberg, *The Philadelphia Riots of 1844: A Study of Ethnic Conflict* (Westport, 1975) and David Johnson, *Policing the Urban Underworld: The Impact of Crime on the Development of the American Police, 1800-1887* (Philadelphia, 1979).

Contemporary accounts include *The Mysteries and Miseries of Philadelphia: A Sketch of the*

For an annual salary of $365, watchmen patrolled those crowded neighborhoods where the rough and respectable of the laboring population lived. Their charge in 1836, unlike their wage, had not changed since 1771. It was "to apprehend all nightwalkers, malefactors, rogues, vagabonds, and disorderly persons whom they shall find disturbing the public peace, or shall have cause to suspect of any evil design." With more than 2,000 licensed hotels and taverns in the city and county of Philadelphia, not counting the oyster cellars and other unlicensed "tippling shops" where rum was sold in small quantities, cheap liquor was often the fuel that sparked the fights that led to the watchman's troubles.[4]

The women of Philadelphia figured prominently in public records, both as victims of disorder and as violators of the public order. Some were, like Johanna Lee, "tidy looking white girl[s]." Lee was first arrested in February, 1837, for being drunk on the street; by November, 1839, she was described as "an incorrigible girl" who delivered her "customary shower of abuse" on the court before being sent to Moyamensing Prison for the eleventh time that year. Others, like mulattos Jane Green and Sarah Crosby, were among those women arrested for disturbing the peace with their "furious and sacreligious language."[5]

On numerous occasions women called the watchmen to restore order in the family. Frequently, however, the wives then refused to press assault charges in court. After Samuel Ross was charged by his wife with cruelty, she begged the judge "as is usual in such cases," the judge commented, not to send her husband to jail. When Michael Conway was charged by a neighbor with having beaten his wife, Ann, she testified that the fight was "a little bit of flogging, which she deserved." Although we may recognize the outlines of what we now describe as a "battered woman syndrome" in the actions of the women

---

Condition of the Most Degraded Classes in the City (Philadelphia, 1853), located at the Historical Society of Pennsylvania. Specific instances of disorder appear almost daily in the *Philadelphia Public Ledger* (hereafter *PPL*). See for instance, *PPL*, November 21, December 9, 22, 1836, January 13, 1837, May 4, 1839.

[4] Philadelphia City Councils, *A Digest of the Ordinances of the Corporation of the City of Philadelphia and the Acts of the Assembly Relating Thereto* (Philadelphia, 1834), 24; *PPL*, July 3, 1837.

[5] *PPL*, February 14, 1837, November 5, 1839, October 11, 1836.

who refused to press formal charges in court, their actions may also suggest something of the attitudes toward allowable disorder in the 1830s. If the occasion of the mistreatment was "all through liquor," as it often was, the women who suffered merely wanted immediate protection from physical abuse. Calling the watchman was protecting the family in a time honored way; putting the husband in jail was not.[6]

Evidence suggests that women of varying degrees of vulnerability and respectability used the Magistrate's Court as an arena for conflict resolution. Sometimes women used the court for protection from charges of having acted like prostitutes. This was the case for Widow Anderson, who successfully sued her brother-in-law when he spread the rumor that she slept with several men. Other times, prostitutes themselves used the court to press charges against those who preyed upon them. For instance, Susannah Gore, a known (white) prostitute, pressed charges against Joseph Smith, in whose house she was an inmate, for stealing a gold watch from her. He was found guilty of the larceny while Gore went away without court action against her. A madame, like any other bar or tavern keeper, could press charges against her patrons if they acted out of order. On one occasion, Mrs. Sarah Jaggers, who kept a house in New Market Street, charged a drunk customer with assault and battery. He was committed, solely on her word. Another woman, Susan M'Kane, took three customers to court when they created a ruckus in her house, breaking a clock, a punch bowl and assorted furniture. Later M'Kane appeared to charge another patron with assault. The man evidently had made what she felt were "disparaging remarks" about one of her "girls," and an argument followed. During the argument, the man pulled a knife, and M'Kane pulled two pistols. In the end, the court held them both accountable for charges of assault and battery. The focus of the court was the nature of the crime and not the moral standing of those involved.[7]

[6] Information on the issue of family violence is drawn from a daily reading of the *Public Ledger*, 1836-1838. For cases cited, see *PPL*, February 1, March 10, 1837. For more systematic research on domestic violence in mid-nineteenth-century London, see Nancy Tomes, "'A Torrent of Abuse': Crimes of Violence Between Working Class Men and Women in London, 1840-75," *Journal of Social History* 11 (1978): 328-45.

[7] For examples, see *PPL*, August 20, 1836, June 20, December 9, 1837. Gore's case

The Geography of Disorder

Indication of the place of prostitution in the disorderly city can be drawn from the information about the places prostitution was practiced. We know something of the trade from a surviving mid-nineteenth-century guidebook to Philadelphia brothels. Some brothels cited in the guidebook were adjacent to respectable working-class families in new working-class neighborhoods. Others were situated along the older waterfront area and in the notorious South Street corridor.[8]

The corridor stretched a quarter of a mile along the southern boundary of the city, an area in which Philadelphia's sizeable free black population lived. Described as "a haven for those low in the world," it was the site of inter-racial violence in 1834, 1835, 1838, 1842, and again in 1849. There, in the underbelly of the city, taverns with bright and lovely names but dark and dismal interiors beckoned to passers-by. Prostitutes, their neighbors, and customers drank in The Rising Sun, The Break of Day House, and The Morning Glory. Others flirted in taverns named The Girard, The Columbia, and The Tremont in mockery of the city's fashionable hotels. Duffy's Arcade—the underworld's Astor House—was on Baker Street, below Eighth Street in Moyamensing. According to a report in a Philadelphia newspaper, it was a large, frame building, renting eight-by-ten foot rooms, each of which was lighted by a square hole sawed in its door.[9]

Dandy Hall was a landmark of the old demi-monde. A three-story brick building, it was a hotel, dance hall, gambling "hell," and brothel. To get there, the curious traveler had to walk down Fourth Street below Shippen, then turn eastward on Plum Street, a small dark

---

appears in *PPL*, July 20, 1837. Cases about the madames appear *PPL*, October 5, November 18, 1837, November 24, 1838.

[8] *A Guide to the Stranger, or Pocket Companion for the Fancy, Containing a List of the Gay Houses and Ladies of Pleasure in the City of Brotherly Love and Sisterly Affection* (Philadelphia, 1848) located at the Library Company of Philadelphia. Other locations are drawn from Johnson, *Policing the Urban Underworld*; *The Mysteries and Miseries of Philadelphia*; and The Society of Friends, "Census of the People of Colour of the City and Districts of Philadelphia" (Philadelphia, 1848), which is located at the Historical Society of Pennsylvania. The research on the colored census was begun by Alan Dawley, who shared it with me. I am further indebted to Jeffrey Roberts for conversations about the urban development of Philadelphia.

[9] *PPL*, March 3, 1846; Lapsansky, "South Street Philadelphia." The contemporary was George G. Foster, "Philadelphia in Slices," George R. Taylor, ed., *The Pennsylvania Magazine of History and Biography* 93 (1969): 23-72.

alley. One mid-century journalist wrote that it was at the center of the most concentrated region of white prostitution in the city.[10]

There was some truth to that observation. A string of brothels extended down South Street and Bainbridge Street from the Delaware River to Eighth Street. However, the guide to the city's brothels identified the occupants of one house in the area as mulattos, "a swarm of yellow girls who promenade up and down Chestnut Street every evening, with their faces well-powdered." The census enumerator listed the same building as a "house of assignation," headed by Maria Burries and occupied by seven other women and one small child. The customers were merchants and merchants' clerks, the guidebook noted. They were part of the new urban culture, while Burries' neighbors—laborers, draymen, rag and bone men who lived in cellars—were symbols of long-standing poverty.[11]

There was another cluster of brothels at the corner of Twelfth Street and Pine Street, still another just to the west of Washington Square. These brothels were newer than those in the area around Dandy Hall; their numbers continued to grow as the decades passed. In the Pine Street area, one brothel run by Mrs. Louisa O'Neil was described as a "palace of love" and a resort for the best men in the community. Mrs. O'Neil lived with Francis O'Neil, a seaman, possibly her husband. One next door neighbor was an Irish grocer who had six children and $4,000 worth of personal property. Other neighbors included Elizabeth Hewett, a middle-aged madame who ran what the guidebook described as a "tolerable second-rate house," and Mary Yeager, a younger madame, who ran a "first-class house for first-rate boarders."[12]

Brothels also stood among the homes of respectable working people around Washington Square. Here Mary Shaw operated "a bed house, well-furnished and neat," and Isabella McDaniels ran what was described as one of the best assignation houses in the city. There were still other brothels between Arch and Vine on Eighth, Ninth, Tenth, and Eleventh Streets, north of a concentration of boarding houses on

[10] Foster, "Philadelphia in Slices," 38-41.

[11] *A Guide to the Stranger*; United States Census of Population, Characteristics of the Population, Pennsylvania, 1850.

[12] *A Guide to the Stranger.*

Market Street in which clerks and shop girls lived. This was a neighborhood of artisans' families. The guidebook described a brothel here operated by Josephine Somers, "an accomplished lady," as a "Temple of Venus." The census showed that the household, located near Wood and Eleventh Streets, was composed of Somers, thirty-six, and four white prostitutes ranging in age from twenty to twenty-seven; all were born in the United States. Nearby was "a good and safe second class" brothel run by Mrs. Eliza Thompson, a thirty-five-year-old black woman who boarded two black women, the child of one of them, and a black drover, Charles Thompson, possibly her husband.[13]

More tantalizing than conclusive, this evidence further suggests that the best houses were run by white women, slightly older than the women who boarded with them. Second-class houses were run by older women, and black women sometimes were among the boarders. What the descriptions and colorful designations show is that in the eyes of those who rated such houses, it was not the location of the brothel but the women who boarded there and the company they kept that determined the status of the house.

Sometimes brothels were merely lodging houses, like those west of Washington Square lining Walnut and Spruce Streets, an area populated by laborers, artisans, and a growing number of workers employed in area shops. The prostitutes who lived here solicited in nearby theaters or taverns and then brought customers to their rooms.

Prostitutes had displayed themselves from the third tier of the theater from the beginning of American drama. They came to the theater from the brothel-households in groups, often several hours before curtain time. Once there, they made contact with customers, old and new, in the upper gallery, to which there was a special entrance for their use. The other sections of the theater were visible from the upper gallery; but the upper level was not visible to people below, unless they turned around. Occasionally, however, prostitutes solicited in the pit, for which the admittance fee was the same as for the upper gallery. At times the women in Philadelphia were reported to have stood on the benches, blocking the view of others as they waved to men they knew in the first and second tiers.[14]

[13] Ibid.

[14] Claudia Johnson, "That Guilty Third Tier: Prostitution in Nineteenth Century Amer-

Prostitutes reportedly strolled slowly through the parks after lamps had been lighted in the evening. Solicitation also occurred along the busy streets of the business district in daylight. Two unlucky women, Harriet Robinson and Margaret Murdoch, "well dressed and of fair appearance," solicited the mayor and a friend as they were talking on Walnut Street one day in 1841. Others like Maria Walsh advertised themselves through their dress. When she was arrested, Walsh wore "a revealing calico dress" and bright copper earrings. She was also bonnetless, a mark of a public woman. Women who paraded the streets might be arrested for vagrancy, which carried a one-month jail term.[15]

A concerned contemporary was in some respects accurate when he complained that vice "was fearless of rebuke stalking with giant strides through our streets." Disorderly people did seem to act openly without fear. They did not concede that public spaces ought to be restricted to the use of those who acted with more decorum.[16]

The Public Women

From specific information for roughly one hundred prostitutes who lived in Philadelphia brothels from 1806 to 1818, it appears that they were primarily young and city-born. Fifty percent were between the ages of fifteen and twenty; another 29 percent were between the ages of twenty-one and twenty-five. Of the eighty-four women for whom place of birth is known, about half grew up in Philadelphia; another 8 percent grew up in New York City. Among the others, 14 percent were immigrants; a mere 3 percent were country women who had come to the city.[17]

---

ican Theaters," *American Quarterly* 27 (1975): 575-84. The tradition, according to Johnson, was well established in New York, Boston, Chicago, St. Louis, Cincinnati, Mobile, and New Orleans. Incidents in Philadelphia appear in *PPL*, February 2, August 10, 1837, December 1, 1838.

[15] Johnson, *Policing the Urban Underworld*; and *PPL*, September 8, October 31, 1841. For the dress code in Victorian England, see Judith Walkowitz, *Prostitution and Victorian Society: Women, Class and the State* (New York, 1980), 26.

[16] *PPL*, May 3, 1836.

[17] *Register*, Magdalen Society of Philadelphia, 1806-18; located at the Historical Society of Pennsylvania. Of the admissions to this rescue home, I used only those women who were cited as having come from a brothel. Such an approach limits the evidence but assures me that I have not included others who came to the home but did not live as prostitutes.

As a group, these young women shared certain similarities with the women who went to work in the Lowell Mills and women who later moved into industrial occupations. In the Lowell Mills, more than four-fifths of the early workers were between the ages of fifteen and thirty. Like Philadelphia prostitutes, they lived in communities of women and were paid in cash for their labor. However, they came to the mill because of active recruiting efforts of the agents of mill owners who went to the countryside to encourage them to come to the mills. The energy with which these women and their employers continually asserted their virtue might have been a reflection of their awareness that they shared, on the surface, some characteristics with women with whom they claimed to have nothing in common. For some observers going to work in the mill was like "going on the town." Both occupations exposed a woman to an independent way of life that ran counter to the developing ideals of true womanhood.[18]

Compared to other working women in their own neighborhoods, many prostitutes were well paid. Although evidence for income is difficult to locate in these early years, some houses charged $2 per visit. Other prostitutes would have received more, for the hierarchy of houses and inmates described above suggests a variation in price according to the status of the establishment. Even the lowest paid women would have received more than the majority of women workers. The favorable comparison is, however, as much commentary on the sorry state of women's wages as on the size of a prostitute's income.[19]

A prostitute's work, like that of others among the working population, was dependent on economic cycles. This shared dependence furnished the occasion for a comic broadside published in Philadelphia in 1834. *Support the Trade* appeared in bold letters across the top of the document. Below, the text began: "The present state of the currency and the failures of many of our most opulent merchants, have induced the undersigned to call a meeting of the 'Ladies of

[18] Thomas Dublin, "Women, Work and the Family: Female Operatives in the Lowell Mills, 1830-50," *Feminist Studies* 3 (1975): 30-39.

[19] For a discussion of women, work and wages, see Alice Kessler-Harris, *Out To Work: A History of Wage-Earning Women in the United States* (New York, 1982), chapters 2 and 3. The pamphlets Mathew Carey published about the oppression of working women in Philadelphia are cited in note 21.

Easy Virtue'" to discuss the suffering experienced by prostitutes as a consequence of the economic downturn. "Already we have felt the change," the broadside reported; should it continue, "one and all will be reduced to PENURY and WANT." The five hundred women alleged to have supported the appeal wished to send a delegate to Washington to investigate the money shortage: "Without MONEY, we cannot nor will not accomodate gentlemen with the LUXURY which our SEX ALONE CAN AFFORD." Humor aside, there was some truth to the appeal. Even if the broadside were a male's parody of the needs expressed by all laboring women, the broadside—despite its humor, perhaps because of it—identified with some accuracy the prostitutes' financial difficulties. The trade depended on cash; there is no evidence of bartering between prostitutes and their customers even in the turbulent 1830s when the economy was most unstable.[20]

There were also serious calls for relief from poverty for Philadelphia's women, like those issued in the 1830s by the crusading publisher Mathew Carey. In his pamphlet *Female Wages and Female Oppression* addressed to the "Ladies of the United States," Carey wrote that virtuous women were "in spite of their utmost industry and talents, and merits, actually driven to pauperism which grinds them down to the earth," because they were refused adequate wages for their labor. Like the "Ladies of Easy Virtue," the ladies to whom Carey addressed his pamphlet depended on the good will and hard cash of the men in the city. Virtue was a luxury some could not always afford or achieve. Sometimes it was weakness, but other times it was chance and circumstance that made some oppressed females starving seamstresses and others public prostitutes.[21]

Entry into prostitution was less orderly than recruitment to other occupations in which women received wages. Prostitution appears to have been one of the few trades a woman entered without references or recruitment if her traditional life course had been disrupted. Rachel Brooks, for example, became a prostitute after her marriage failed.

[20] *Support the Trade* (Philadelphia, 1834). Located at the Library Company of Philadelphia. This document was probably intended to mock the broadsides that called attention to the plight of working men in Philadelphia at this time.

[21] Mathew Carey, *Female Wages and Female Oppression*, No. III (Philadelphia, 1835); and Carey, *Essay on the Public Charities of Philadelphia* (Philadelphia, 1829); *PPL*, June 17, 1836.

Brooks married a man from Maryland at twenty, bore him four children (all of whom died), and contracted syphilis from him. In disgrace and despair, she returned to her native Philadelphia and lived as a prostitute until at twenty-seven she was too diseased to continue. Another woman, Christiana Phillips, became a prostitute when her husband deserted her. Sophia Smith, an Irish immigrant, was married, widowed, and "seduced" while a domestic servant before she was twenty years old. She then lived as a prostitute for six years until she landed in prison as a vagrant.[22]

Some women were, no doubt, misguided by those who abused the new "intelligence" offices where young women came for help in locating employment. According to one source, women applying at some of these offices were charged fees for worthless bits of information. With their money gone, they might have been introduced to someone who supposedly needed a servant or seamstress. But the women would be taken to a brothel to be kept, until they had no choice but to cooperate with their deceivers.[23]

Friends and relatives enticed some women into the trade. One young woman from New Jersey reported that she had been convinced by a friend who described "in glowing and attractive colors the pleasures of the life" to come to a brothel in Philadelphia. One thirteen-year old was lured into the life by a friend, a dancer at the Walnut Street Theatre, and by her parents, who ran the "Texas Oyster House." Still another young woman told a magistrate she had run away from an aunt who ran a bawdy house because she did not want to entertain men as her aunt wanted her to do.[24]

The careers of prostitutes were as varied as their beginnings. Some women, like Ellen Hughes, a resident of Sassafras Alley, started their careers when young. Ellen was a daughter of an army officer whose widow was thought to have "an indifferent reputation herself." Al-

[22] *Case Records*, Magdalen Society of Philadelphia. Early case records contain some biographical information. See Marcia Carlisle, "Prostitutes and Their Reformers in Nineteenth Century Philadelphia." (Ph. D. dissertation, Rutgers University, 1982). See also Steven Ruggles, "Fallen Women: The Inmates of the Magdalen Society of Philadelphia, 1836-1908," *Journal of Social History* 16 (1983): 65-82.

[23] *PPL*, August 17, 1836.

[24] *PPL*, June 2, 1836, May 28, 1839, Ezra Stiles Ely, *Visits of Mercy*, 2 vols. (Philadelphia, 1829-31), I, 87-88.

though at age thirteen Ellen was reported to have "superior personal charms," the "effects of prostitution and intemperance" were also visible. By the time she was fourteen, she appeared in court records as "a cyprian of ordinary caste." Another, Mary Ann Brown, "an insolent and abusive woman," was described in 1837 as "an old frail sister," and was reported to have been "on the town" for fifteen years. Still others, like Caroline Brown, tired of the life before that. Caroline Brown, described as a young and good-looking white woman, was first arrested in May, 1837. She was arrested again in January, 1839 for fighting in the Arch Street Theatre. She hanged herself in January, 1843, with a white muslin kerchief she had attached to the bedpost in her room in a South Street brothel.[25]

Sometimes coerced, sometimes fully aware of what they were doing, women continued to move into prostitution. Although first-hand accounts of how that move took place are rare, some insight might be drawn from the case of Harriet Sperry. Sperry, a seamstress, sued James Reed for bastardy. In her testimony, she described how she had come to have sex with Reed, accepted money from him at various times, but evidently did not think of herself as a prostitute. As the court reported her words, she said:

> I got introduced to him by a girl named Mary Fisher at the corner of Sixth and South Street. I had a slight conversation with him; he asked me if I would walk up? I said I did not care. We walked up as far as Mrs. King's house in Seventh between Pine and Spruce Streets. He said we will go in here. I said very well. He locked the door. I went upstairs. He followed me with a lamp. 'Twas there the child was got. We staid there about an hour. I saw him about a week afterwards in the same house, about two or three o'clock in the afternoon. I got there before him about a quarter of an hour. He then had connextion with me again. About a week afterwards I met him again at the same house and probably three or four times were all the times I had connextion with him. In regard to my age, I will be 18 on the 22nd day of next March. I did not know what kind of house he took me into but after the door was locked I found it to my sorrow. I could not make resistance; he put his hand or his handkerchief over my mouth. He gave me no

[25] *PPL*, June 22, 1836, September 1, 1837, May 12, 1836, October 23, May 16, 1837, January 11, 1839, September 21, 1842, January 7, 1843.

> money the first time. We were upstairs about one hour. I did not undress and go to bed. I did not the second and third times; I did not undress at all. I was never at a house of that kind before; the second time he gave me about $2; the third time he gave me about $2. I can't say for what.[26]

In further testimony, Harriet Sperry claimed she had thought Reed's conduct—but not, evidently, her own—that first evening "highly improper," and added "I only met him afterwards because I was afraid he would expose me." But other testimony presented Sperry as a woman who carried around "handfuls of shinplasters" (paper money) even though she was not known "to follow anything productive of money." Another witness, a woman bookfolder, testified that Sperry had set out to entrap Reed. "She told me if I would swear that he was the father of the child, she would give me handsome recompense." The testimony is noteworthy in that Sperry apparently did not believe accepting money for sex would alter her chances in her lawsuit. Reed was found not guilty, but the court ruled that he would pay the court costs—a further sign that the court found Reed partly responsible even in dealing with a woman he treated as a prostitute. The case, regardless of the "truthfulness" of Sperry's account, indicates central ambiguities about entry into prostitution and public response to it.[27]

From the narrative evidence of their lives, there is little to indicate that there was any glamour associated with the profession of prostitution. On the other hand, in spite of their often grim situations, prostitutes did not always see themselves as outcasts. One woman remarked that she did not consider herself "a great sinner." Another refused to believe she was a sinner at all because she had a good heart. With the firmness of a still proud woman, she maintained "I've done all I could and behaved as well as I knew how."[28]

Other women had few illusions about their lives. As one stated, "I ain't learn'ed in these things, but I hope I sha'nt go to a worse world than this." In 1810 another prostitute claimed "she had been seven years in the professional business, had never been caught before,

[26] Harriet Sperry's case appeared in the *Public Ledger* on December 14, 15, and 19, 1837.
[27] Ibid.
[28] Ely, *Visits*, vol. II, 420.

and since she took up the trade to get a living, she is determined to die in it." Another echoed similar sentiments when asked why she continued to prostitute herself. "I have never been taught to do any kind of work; I have few friends that will receive me; and I must proceed or perish with hunger." Such statements, though few, reflect both the absence of opportunities for women who needed to work to support themselves and their determination to survive in spite of the difficulties of this work.[29]

Prostitutes, like drunken husbands and contentious neighbors, contributed their share to the general disorder of the city. They were not arrested for prostitution, however. They were brought before magistrates for the same crimes as their neighbors: vagrancy, drunk and disorderly behavior, assault and battery. The legal definition of a prostitute as a woman who supported herself by the sale of sexual favors or who solicited sex resulted from the need of reformers in the early twentieth century to define prostitution as an act in order to make it a crime. In early nineteenth-century Philadelphia, such precision would have been as out of place as precise street addresses for the homes crowded into alleys and lanes.[30]

Frequently prostitutes appeared in court because they were accused of robbing their customers. As a crime, such theft may be compared to the persistent problem of petty theft among the servant class. It was common but not condoned. The crime was considered more serious if the alleged perpetrator were black, as the cases of Eliza Lennox and Maria Gray suggest. Eliza Lennox, a black prostitute, was accused of stealing a watch she said had been given to her as a deposit for a debt owed her. The man who was pressing charges against Lennox did not appear in court to testify. In most cases, especially in those of white women, when plaintiffs failed to appear the cases were dismised. But Lennox, a black, was committed to trial

[29] Ely, *Visits*, vol. II, 41, 22; I, 14.

[30] For relevant discussion of prostitutes later in the century, see Walkowitz, *Prostitution and Victorian Society*; Robert D. Storch, "Public Control of Street Prostitution in Victorian London: A Study in the Contexts of Police Action," in David Bayley, ed., *Police and Society* (Beverly Hills, 1977), 49-72; Christine Stansell, "Women, Children and the Uses of the Streets: Class and Gender Conflict in New York City, 1850-60," *Feminist Studies* 8 (1982): 309-35. See also Ruth Rosen, *The Lost Sisterhood: Prostitution in America, 1900-1918* (Baltimore, 1982).

by the judge. In a similar case, Maria Gray, a mulatto, was charged with robbery by John Roberts, a white man. He claimed she lured him into an alley. She claimed he offered her the money to go into the alley with him. According to the account in the newspaper, the court "was disposed to believe her story but as such cases of connection of the most revolting description between blacks and whites are of late not uncommon," Maria Gray was held to answer a larceny charge; she was unable to raise the $800 bail the court set.[31]

Recent research on the free black population in urban America between 1800 and 1850 demonstrates that blacks were not prosecuted disproportionately for drunkenness, fighting, gambling, and illicit sexual activities if they engaged in such disorder in their own neighborhoods. The unarticulated assumption seems to have been that such disorder was intra-racial. When inter-racial sexual activities came to the attention of the court, the cases evoked a special concern because of long-standing fears of miscegenation. Black prostitutes who sold sex to white men were a stark symbol of that reality.[32]

Further information about the relationship of prostitutes to each other and their neighbors can be drawn from reports of sporadic raids on disorderly areas of the city. Often, a motivating factor in a reform drive was the location of the disorder in relationship to potential city development. Thus the commissioners of Southwark were anxious to clear several notorious streets as a way to improve the business potential of the area. One policing effort in 1852 forced the evacuation of a series of "haunts" deemed public nuisances along Plum Street, long a center of low-life in the city. In 1854, Blackberry Alley was the target of a nine-house raid that resulted in the arrest of sixteen men and thirty-eight women. All were brought to jail for the night although

[31] Occasionally the "theft" was a dispute between the prostitute and the customer over what price had been agreed upon. There is also some evidence to show that prostitutes did use such games as the "panel routine" and the "angry husband" routine to get more money from their customers. *PPL*, November 24, 1838, September 13, 1836.

[32] Leonard Curry, *The Free Black in Urban America, 1800-1850* (Chicago, 1981). The history of racial violence in Philadelphia during this time period lends credence to the evidence in the *Public Ledger* about the especially harsh treatment of black prostitutes in the courts. In the case cited, the woman was essentially bound over because of the fears of racial mixing. Although no systematic study of such inter-racial sex for money exists, the evidence in Philadelphia suggests the need for one.

"every conceivable method was attempted by the proprietors of the houses and the male visitors to get released from custody."[33]

In the Blackberry Alley raid all of the proprietors arrested were women, several of whom owned the houses in which they lived and worked. For these women, prostitution was a business requiring enterpreneurial attitudes, business acumen, and the capital necessary to buy the buildings in which their businesses operated. The rapid growth and the absence of established municipal institutions in ante-bellum Philadelphia seems to have allowed disorderly women more opportunities for participation in various aspects of the trade. This possibility is reinforced by the experience of prostitutes and madames on the frontier. In Helena (Montana), in San Francisco, and on the Comstock Lode in Nevada, women controlled the business of prostitution and the property in which it was transacted until those areas became more "civilized."[34]

This evidence suggests that at certain times, at least, women rather than men controlled prostitution. In ante-bellum Philadelphia, the participation of men in the world of prostitution seems to have been limited to their roles as customers, supporting rather than profiting from disorderly women. Sometimes men lived in households in which prostitutes lived; and sometimes "fancy men," frequently gamblers, were associated with prostitutes. But there is little evidence that pimps controlled the women, the hours they worked, or the earnings they accumulated.[35]

The accounts of the raids on the brothel-household in the 1850s call to our attention the attempt by the authorities to get the women of the household to testify against the brothel-owners. In one raid a

[33] See for instance, *PPL*, October 22, 1841. For the raids on Plum Street, see *PPL*, June 3, 16, 28, 1852; for the raid on Blackberry Alley, see *PPL*, September 9, 1854. See also Roger Lane, *Policing the City: Boston, 1822-1885* (Cambridge, Mass., 1967).

[34] See the work of Paula Petrik, "Prostitution in Helena, Montana, 1865-1900," *Montana: The Magazine of Western History* 31 (1981): 28-41. See also Jacqueline Baker Barnhart, "Working Women: Prostitution in San Francisco from the Gold Rush to 1900." (Ph. D. dissertation, University of California-Santa Cruz, 1976) and Carlisle, "Prostitutes and Their Reformers."

[35] For a discussion of pimps with which I am in agreement, see Walkowitz, *Prostitution and Victorian Society*, chapters 1 and 10. For a discussion with which I disagree, see Marion S. Goldman, *Gold Diggers and Silver Miners: Prostitution and Social Life on the Comstock Lode* (Ann Arbor, 1981), chapter 5.

madame, Mary Lamotte, was arrested. Eight women lived in her house, all of whom were released on their word that they would testify against her. Similar offers were made to other boarders, although no follow-up story appeared indicating whether or not the proprietors were convicted. Against these sporadic policing efforts, both bawdy house owners and inmates had little protection except a common understanding that none of them would provide evidence, especially willing witnesses, necessary to prove a charge in court. Disorderly "Ladies of Easy Virtue" and saloon keepers alike used this strategy to frustrate authorities' efforts to force compliance with the wishes of those citizens who desired a more orderly city.[36]

Signs of What Was to Come

The 1830s brought an effort by some private citizens to enforce new standards of order and decorum. The theaters—long plagued by prostitutes—were one of their first targets. Citizens' complaints were numerous enough that in June, 1836 a grand jury presented the Walnut Street Theatre as a public nuisance. Outside the theater, passers-by had claimed they were regularly insulted. Inside, the audience was bothered by noise and shouting from the upper levels. In September the managers asserted that all was orderly. But beginning in February, 1837, a newspaper correspondent complained that prostitutes were again causing commotion by soliciting in the third tier and in the pit as well.[37]

"Billy Pitt" (as the letters in the series were signed) believed it was the duty of the theater managers to keep the pit free of prostitutes. He called on the newspaper, as a friend of morals, "to satisfy yourselves of these facts above asserted and then to aid public opinion in purging the best places for seeing and hearing in the whole theatre." In another letter, the correspondent reasserted his claim that the pit was increasingly "a place of assignation for prostitutes and young men and boys ripe for temptation." Theater managers countered that

[36] Lamotte's case appeared in the *PPL*, September 9, 1854; see the *PPL*, March 31, 1837 for the law under which the police operated. See also *Police Manual* (Philadelphia, 1835), Section 89. Roger Lane also cites the difficulties various mayors in Boston faced as they tried to deal with prostitution and other disorderly behavior. Lane, *Policing the City*.

[37] *PPL*, June 22, September 3, 1836, February 2, 1837.

respectable people sat there. The conflict then disappered from the paper.[38]

It reappeared several years later in August, 1839. An editorial reminded theater managers that it was illegal to sell liquor on their premises. The following day, the paper charged, as "Billy Pitt" had years before, that "loose women" plied their trade openly. According to the account, they "flaunt and flare without any regard to the proprieties of decorum," exposing virtuous women to the sight of "bold and unblushing hardihood in women." Although theaters were public places and prostitutes had long used them, the editors of the paper threatened a grand jury investigation if such activities continued. The author of the article further enlisted the aid of virtuous women to help "purge what should be a refined and chaste means of amusement" by boycotting the theaters until loose women were kept out.[39]

Virtuous women responded in another way, however, to the call for aid. They reached out to the prostitutes to help them. In 1847, a group of concerned women formed the Rosine Society to assist "their fallen sisters" to a better way of life. The organizers included several boarding house keepers, gentlewomen, wives of small businessmen and of clerks, all of whom vowed not to judge the women who worked as prostitutes but to help them find "more dignified labor." Their motto—"You shall support yourself honestly by the labor of your own hands"—reflected their purpose. The organizers criticized the only existing organization in Philadelphia dedicated to helping prostitutes, the Magdalen Society, because it was "under the superintendence of men" and was little more than a "magdalen prison." Although the initial enthusiasm waned by 1860 when the goals of the Rosine Society focused more on the moral rather than the economic welfare of women, the issue of prostitution remained on the feminist agenda throughout the nineteenth century. For many women the issue was one of sexual disorder in which men played a significant role. Prostitutes were public women who sold sex but the charge of "disorderly behavior" was hurled at many other women

[38] *PPL*, February 2, 21, 1837, May 12, 1836.
[39] *PPL*, August 31, September 12, 1839.

who attempted to move into the public sphere for a variety of other reasons.[40]

The work of the early female reformers probably had more lasting effect on their own lives than on the lives of the disorderly public women whose presence prompted them to action. Prostitutes remained part of what would come to be seen as persistent urban disorder. They lacked respectability in the eyes of some, but they held a place among the people with whom they lived and worked. In ante-bellum Philadelphia, they used the courts to settle disputes. They complained of wrongs against them and expected to be dealt with as others were. When times were good, they were lucky. When times were bad, they suffered as others did. Drink, disease and death were as much a part of their lives as they were of other people. In later years, links between commercialized prostitution and the leisure industry would reshape the trade and tie it to urban bosses, who, like prostitutes, were viewed as an urban problem. By then, the terms *public women* and *public houses* would no longer be used. Public interest came to define a new public order that did not include "those hordes of beggars, of unlicensed pedlars and hawkers, and prostitutes who nocturnally swarm in some of our more frequent streets and public walks." *Public* became a respectable word, but prostitution became a women's issue. A concern for public disorder was replaced by a concern for sexual disorder and inequality that threatened to undermine—more than prostitution did—the modern city.[41]

New York University MARCIA CARLISLE

[40] For the classic discussion of Jacksonian era women and the problem of prostitution and sexual disorder, see Carroll Smith-Rosenberg, "Beauty, the Beast and the Militant Woman: A Case Study in Sex Roles and Social Stress in Jacksonian America," *American Quarterly* 23 (1971): 562-84. For a more recent treatment of the effects of reform work on women reformers themselves, see Mary P. Ryan, *The Cradle of the Middle Class: The Family in Oneida County, New York, 1790-1865* (New York, 1981). For a discussion of the Rosine Society, see Carlisle, "Prostitutes and Their Reformers." The records of this society are located at the Historical Society of Pennsylvania. Those that are relevant to this discussion are *The Constitution and Address* (Philadelphia, 1847); and the *Annual Reports*, 1847-92. In order to determine the status of the reformers, I located as many as possible in the 1850 Census and in the local directories.

[41] *PPL*, May 3, 1836.

Strumpets and Misogynists: Brothel "Riots" and the Transformation of Prostitution in Antebellum New York City

By TIMOTHY J. GILFOYLE

Sometimes spontaneous, sometimes planned, the attacks on bawds and bawdy houses stemmed from the male desire to control women. Timothy Gilfoyle, a doctoral candidate at Columbia University, teaches at the Harry Van Arsdale Jr., Center for Labor Studies, Empire State College.

IN THE PAST three decades, historians have produced an impressive volume of work examining the composition, form and motives behind the riotous behavior of early American crowds and mobs. Nineteenth-century examinations of crowds, notably those of Gustav LeBon and Hippolite Taine in Europe and Joel T. Headley in New York, depicted collective violence as the behavior of bloodthirsty, irrational men seeking the destruction of civilized society. Inspired by the pathbreaking revisionist work of George Rudé, Eric Hobsbawm, and E. P. Thompson, most American historians now view crowd behavior, especially in the Revolutionary and preindustrial eras, as a beacon for raw, unfettered social equality and political fairness, a reaction against the arbitrary distribution of justice, and vindication of time-honored traditions. When perceived rights were ignored or violated, especially by agents of the state, rioting to redress grievences was a common resort.[1]

For their commentary on earlier drafts of this essay, I should like to thank Sigmund Diamond, Deborah Dugan, Kenneth Jackson, Mark Kaminsky, James Shenton, and especially Myra Sletson. I also thank the faculty of Empire State College and the New York City Municipal Archives, especially Kenneth Cobb and Idelio Garcia-Peña.

1. Joel T. Headley, *Great Riots of New York, 1712–1871* (New York, 1873), 66–110; George Rudé, *The Crowd in History* (New York, 1964, revised edition 1981); idem., *Paris and London in the Eighteenth Century: Studies in Popular Protest* (New York, 1970); idem., *Ideology and Popular Protest* (New York, 1980); Eric Hobsbawm, *Primitive Rebels: Studies*

The frontispiece of the fifth edition of an exposé-directory of New York City prostitutes in 1839. From the Collection of Leo Hershkowitz.

Historians of the early American republic concur that the tradition of "republican" violence continued into the early decades of the nineteenth century. For example, Leonard L. Richards found Rudé's model appropriate for antiabolition mobs. Most were "destructive," "discriminating," and "purposeful," and some included respectable, middle-class citizens. Similarly, Sean Wilentz concluded that such violence-prone groups followed the "rules of classic 'preindustrial' urban mobs by choosing their targets with care, attacking property, but not persons, and by taking advantage of every symbolic opportunity." Indeed, from handloom weavers in Philadelphia to day laborers in the building trades to antiabolitionist crowds in New York City, artisans and unskilled workingmen violently defended their occupations from industrial technology, changing market relationships, and racial or ethnic competition.[2]

In their efforts to understand early industrialization and class formation in the United States, historians have neglected important

---

in Archaic Forms of Social Movement in the Nineteenth and Twentieth Centuries (New York, 1959); E. P. Thompson, "The Moral Economy of the English Crowd in the Eighteenth Century," *Past and Present* 50 (1971), 76–136. For American examinations, see Dirk Hoerder, *Crowd Action in Revolutionary Massachusettes, 1765–1780* (New York, 1977); Edward Countryman, *A People in Revolution: The American Revolution and Political Society in New York, 1760–1790* (Baltimore, 1981), 36–71; idem., "The Problem of the Early American Crowd," *Journal of American Studies* 7 (1973), 77–90; Pauline Maier, *From Resistance to Revolution: Colonial Radicals and the Development of American Opposition to Britain, 1765–1776* (New York, 1972), chapter 1; Gary B. Nash, *The Urban Crucible: Social Change, Political Consciousness, and the Origins of the American Revolution* (Cambridge, Mass., 1979), chapter 11; Rhys Issac, "Dramatizing the Ideology of Revolution: Popular Mobilization in Virginia, 1774–1776," *William and Mary Quarterly* 33 (1976); Gordon S. Wood, "A Note on Mobs in the American Revolution," *William and Mary Quarterly* 23 (1966), 635–42; Arthur M. Schlesinger, "Political Mobs and the American Revolution, 1765–1776," *Proceedings of the American Philosophical Society* 99 (1955), 244–50.

2. Leonard L. Richards, *"Gentlemen of Property and Standing": Antiabolition Mobs in Antebellum America* (New York, 1970); Sean Wilentz, *Chants Democratic: New York City and the Rise of the American Working Class, 1788–1850* (New York, 1984), 264–65, 168–70. Examining Jacksonian era riots in Philadelphia, Michael Feldberg says that Pauline Maier's model applies because "actions was motivated ... by appeals of natural justice, constitutional rights, and the notion that community interests superseded private rights." See "Urbanization as a Cause of Violence: Philadelphia as a Test Case," in Allen F. Davis and Mark H. Haller, eds., *The Peoples of Philadelphia: A History of Ethnic Groups and Lower Class Life, 1790–1940* (Philadelphia, 1973), 53–70; idem., "The Crowd in Philadelphia History: A Comparative Perspective," *Labor History* 15 (1974), 323–36; idem., *The Philadelphia Riot of 1844: A Study in Ethnic Conflict* (Westport, Conn., 1975); idem., *The Turbulent Era: Riot and Disorder in Jacksonian America* (New York, 1980). David Grimsted argues that during the Jacksonian period rioting "regained its eighteenth century status as a frequent and tacitly accepted if not approved mode of behavior." See "Rioting in Its Jacksonian Setting," *American Historical Review* 77 (1972), 364. For other New York examples, see Ray Allen Billington, *The Protestant Crusade, 1800–1860* (New York,

exceptions to this model of reactive, limited collective violence. With at least one social group, such violence exceeded traditional restraints and frequently evolved into terror. From 1825 to 1857, at least fifty New York City brothels, "female boarding houses" and their residents were violently attacked. Especially during the 1830s, recurrent attacks upon females waxed into a popular sport, and public women became victims of terror. Violent acts transformed the behavior of prostitutes, the power of madams, and the role of prostitution in New York society. And in a larger sense, brothel riots reflected dramatic changes in urban politics, gender roles and male sexual aggression. Some attacks on prostitutes were personal, private vendettas; others were public, with large numbers of participants. Their unprecedented frequency and visibility evidenced increasing male resentment and misogyny against sexually-independent women and a desire to control them.[3] Outside the domestic sphere, *gender* was a justification for violence.

Historians have only scratched the surface in delineating patterns of violence against prostitutes. Europeanists like Lawrence Stone discovered seventeenth-century London apprentices plundering bawdy houses on Shrove Tuesday, ostensibly to remove temptation during Lent. Nancy Tomes has argued that nineteenth-century London prostitutes were "considered fair game for violence by working-class men." In antebellum Detroit, John C. Schneider found that violent incidents against the city's brothels centered around racial tensions between black prostitutes and German immigrants and desire by the latter for increased residential space. The most extensive examination, however, remains Jacques

1938), chapters 3, 4, 9; Linda K. Kerber, "Abolitionists and Amalgamators: The New York City Race Riots of 1834," *New York History* 48 (1967), 28–39; Paul O. Weinbaum, *Mobs and Demagogues: The New York Response to Collective Violence in the Early Nineteenth Century* (Ann Arbor, 1979); Amy Bridges, *A City in the Republic: Antebellum New York and the Origin of Machine Politics* (Cambridge, England, 1984), 72.

3. Records of brothel attacks are in the New York City District Attorney Indictment Papers, Court of General Sessions, New York City Municipal Archives and Records Center (hereafter DAP), and the New York *Sun*. In the former, the defendant was usually charged with "rioting" and not simply assault and battery. The indictment did not always describe the dwelling under attack as a house of prostitution, but in most cases, the individual proprietor appeared in other indictments for operating a disorderly house. Furthermore, the physical description of the attack, the interior arrangement of the house, and the behavior of the men and women involved frequently indicated that it was a house of prostitution.

On the transformation of antebellum work and class relations, see especially Wilentz, *Chants Democratic*; and Christine Stansell, "The Origins of the Sweatshop: Women and Early Industrialization in New York City," in Michael H. Frisch and Daniel J. Walkowitz, eds., *Working-Class America: Essays on Labor, Community, and American Society* (Urbana, Ill., 1983), 78–103. For a description and analysis of the spread of prostitution in antebellum New York City, see Timothy J. Gilfoyle, "The Urban Geography of Commercial Sex: Prostitution in New York City, 1790–1860," *Journal of Urban History* 13 (May, 1987).

Rossiaud's study of fifteenth-century French towns. Rossiaud attributed the rise in sexual violence to sudden changes in gender relations. Once a woman was violated by one man, others were entitled to the same. Women were either pure or whores. Thus, rape and attacks on public women became a means to acquire the privileges of manhood.[4]

Brothel attacks in New York City were not unique to the antebellum period. In Revolutionary New York, soldiers mistreated by "ladies of pleasure" sacked several whorehouses. In 1793, Philip Hone witnessed a remarkable attack on a house of ill-fame that included the dispersal "of 'Mother Carey's chickens,' the destruction of mahogany tables and looking glasses." Soon the "air was filled with feathers, and the street with rags and fragments," according to Dr. Alexander Anderson. The mob's excesses did not desist with "this Mother Damnable," and men "continued their riotous proceedings several successive nights, and many houses of ill-fame in other parts of the city were demolished and their miserable inmates driven naked and houseless into the streets." In 1799, a crowd of nearly one thousand gathered to destroy a Murray Street brothel but was thwarted by the timely intervention of the mayor and local magistrates. Two years later, a large assemblage of Haitians attacked Madame Volunbrun's reputed house of sin. Similarly, the disorderly house of William and Catharine Mackline on George Street was besieged by four men in 1807. Five years later, several hundred rioters tried to pull down a brothel on James Street.[5]

These incidents of mob action against prostitutes were sporadic, uncommon, and infrequent. In each instance, the mob sought to

4. Lawrence Stone, *The Family, Sex, and Marriage in England, 1500–1800* (New York, 1977), 616; Nancy Tomes, "'A Torrent of Abuse': Crimes of Violence Between Working-Class Men and Women in London, 1840–1875," *Journal of Social History* 11 (1978), 337; John C. Schneider, *Detroit and the Problem of Order* (Lincoln, Nebraska, 1980), 20–31, 121; Jacques Rossiaud, "Prostitution, Youth, and Society in the Towns of Southeastern France in the Fifteenth Century," in Robert Forster and Orest Ranum, eds., *Deviants and the Abandoned in French Society: Selections from the Annales* (Baltimore, 1978), 1–31. Despite his compelling argument and innovative use of sources, Rossiaud sometimes confuses fact and hypothesis, never conclusively showing that males attacked females for these reasons. In her essay, Tomes admits that she found very few attacks on prostitutes in her sampling of crimes. Finally, Marcia Carlisle, in "Prostitutes and Their Reformers in Nineteenth Century Philadelphia" (Ph.D. dissertation, Rutgers University, 1982), 31, argues that the absence of attacks on prostitutes from 1800 to 1840 was a reflection of their general acceptance and respectability. Yet, she admits factory girls and others were often mistaken for prostitutes and abused. More importantly, the failure to find a record of attacks may be the result not of social toleration, but of the lack of acceptance, and fear by prostitutes to publicly prosecute their violent opponents. If so, the dearth of violence in the public record may show *greater* disrespect and unacceptability of prostitution.

close a brothel and put it out of business. Rare was the personal assault or homicide. Such onslaughts originated from particular circumstances unrelated to prostitution itself—the castration and murder of a soldier, the seduction of the daughter of a popular ship pilot, or the murder of a fellow seaman in a whorehouse. These preindustrial attacks resembled the spontaneous "extrainstitutional," retributive actions described by Pauline Maier during the Revolutionary era. They were a recourse to justice when civil authority failed. To Philip Hone, perched in a tree over Madame Carey's house, they even had the quality of a spectator sport. Violence was inflicted only upon property, not upon individuals. As reactions to specific events, brothel attacks in the colonial and early republican eras were limited, isolated forays against the private property of misbehaving citizens. To paraphrase Bernard Bailyn, heads did not roll in brothel riots; mobs did not turn to butchery.[6]

After 1820, physical violence against prostitutes increased dramatically. As the ideology of "separate spheres" for the sexes grew in popularity, collective violence played an increasing role in intergroup relations.[7] Previously tolerated behavior by women was subjected to a new misogynist offensive. By inflicting pain upon individual prostitutes, certain males crossed a threshold and redefined the place of prostitution and thereby the boundaries of public sexuality in the antebellum city.

Assaults upon prostitutes appeared in three different forms during the mid-nineteenth century. Some attacks were vigilante acts by an individual or group perpetuating the traditional focus upon the brothel as an institution. The spontaneous individual attack was a second type. Short, quick, and angry, such violence frequently

---

5. Countryman, *A People in Revolution*, 41; Edward Bangs, ed. *Journal of Lt. Isaac Bangs, 1776* (Cambridge, Mass., 1890), 29–30; Allan Nevins, ed., *The Diary of Philip Hone* (New York, 1927), 339; Dr. Alexander Anderson Diary, October 14, 15, 1793, Columbia University; I.N. Phelps Stokes, *The Iconography of Manhattan Island, 1498–1910* (New York, 1912), V, 1301, 1370, 1550; DAP, Case of Jeanne Matharine Dronillan Volunbrun, October 9, 1801; People v. Perry, October 10, 1807. For other attacks, see DAP, People v. Varian, et al., April 11, 1812; People v. Rioters, July 9, 1814.

6. Bernard Bailyn, ed., *Pamphlets of the American Revolution, 1750–1776* (Cambridge, Mass., 1965), I, 581–84; Maier, *From Resistance to Revolution*, chapter 1; Schlesinger, "Political Mobs." Maier mentions similar attacks on brothels during the colonial period. For other examples of antiprostitution violence in the antebellum period, see Schneider, "Public Order and the Geography of the City: Crime, Violence, and the Police in Detroit, 1845–1875," *Journal of Urban History* 4 (1978), 193.

7. The literature on "the cult of domesticity" is voluminous. I have been most influenced by Nancy Cott, *Bonds of Womanhood: Woman's Sphere in New England, 1780–1835* (New Haven, 1977); Barbara Welter, "The Cult of True Womanhood," *American Quarterly* 18 (1966), 151–75; and Suzanne Lebsock, *The Free Women of Petersburg: Status and Culture in a Southern Town, 1784–1860* (New York, 1984).

resulted from a prostitute's refusal to submit to unusual sexual demands. Finally, the most significant variety of sexual assault was the "spree" or "row," a form of destructive, group male behavior, emblematic of the changing nature of antebellum violence.[8] These latter two varieties of aggression, shifting from institutional to individual objects of attack, reflected increasing male resentment against independent, autonomous women who refused to conform to the emerging "cult of domesticity."

Group vigilante action against prostitution—premeditated, well-designed, and organized—continued the colonial tradition of extrainstitutional violence. The men (and in one case, a woman) who instigated these attacks had clear plans of how to enter the house and specific intentions once inside. Repeated attacks by certain individuals, the circumspect behavior inside the brothel, the "respectable" backgrounds of some offenders, and the accusation by prostitutes that city officials encouraged certain assaults, suggest premeditation and calculation. The prostitute's property, not her person, took the beating. The tools of a prostitute's craft—her bed, furniture, glassware and crockery—were destroyed.

Several examples reveal the vigilantes' limited goals. Early one morning in 1842, Jane Williams's house was stoned and then forcibly entered by three men who simply destroyed her furniture.[9] Mary Wall admitted five potential customers to her house after they arrived in a hack one evening in 1833. After sitting down, they requested a drink and inquired about her glasses and decanters. Then, "one of them grabbed a fire shovel and commenced breaking ... all most [sic] everything on the sideboard...." Likewise, the four men who entered Mary Ann Davis's house on Centre Street "behaved in a very noisy and disorderly manner, breaking tumblers, cursing and swearing and when they were going away they took one of her decanters." Isaac Roberts celebrated Christmas in 1851 by leading forty men to Catherine Cauldwell's brothel on Lispenard Street, "to give a benefit." Once inside, Roberts gave orders to "ribbon everything" and his accomplices put tumblers in

8. Brothel "mobs" differ from the two types of anti-abolition mobs identified in Richards, *"Gentlemen of Property and Standing,"* 84–85, 112, 129. Unlike anti-abolition mobs, the size of the crowd and number of participants varied in both planned and unplanned attacks on houses of prostitution. Furthermore, planned assaults occurred without the support of local government officials. Finally, brothel riots were greater in number and continued over a longer period of time.

9. DAP, People v. Ford, September 28, 1842. The accused included William Ford, (bootcrimper, 22 Watts Street), John McCloster, and George Remus. See *Longworth's City Directory* (New York, 1842).

their pockets, broke a sofa and destroyed a piano stool. Before departing, they heaved stones through the front window.[10]

Such riotous assaults were well-planned. George Gale was indicted in four brothel attacks during a two-week period in 1831. In three of them, he was accompanied by his friend Bentley Curran. Forcibly entering Elizabeth Baker's establishment on several different occasions, they broke her windows, destroyed her stoop, and committed "many outrages of an ... offensive nature." Enoch Carter joined Gale at Phoebe Doty's brothel on Church Street one evening, when they began "cursing and swearing, kicking the furniture and taking lamps down, spilling the oil and threaten[ing] to knock her down ..."[11]

Individual assaults marked a second form of misogynist violence. Drunken, disorderly, and delerious males often exploded when a prostitute or madame denied them their heart's desire. John Evans, for example, was arrested for throwing stones at the house of Eliza Vincent after she "refused him admittance." One January evening in 1834, William Green traversed Church Street, hopping from groggery to brothel, his drunken enchantment terminating only after he broke the window of a house of ill-fame.[12] The rash, impulsive character of these attacks reveals that they were not directed at institutions, but at individuals.

Even personal acquaintance afforded little protection for vulnerable prostitutes. Murdered on 11 April 1836, Ellen Jewett was beautiful and popular, "the goddess of a large race of merchants, dealers, clerks and their instruments," and lived in Rosina Townsend's "City Hotel" brothel. No one was ever convicted of the bloody deed, but most contemporaries were convinced that her paramour, Richard Robinson, was guilty.[13] Jewett's murder was not an isolated act of violence by a prostitute's acquaintance. Early one summer morning in 1844, for example, Hannah Fuller was awakened by William Ford. After kicking in her door, he removed his boots and pants, carried her to the bed, and attempted "to ravish and ... carnally know her." Only the last minute intervention by the

10. DAP, People v. Valentine, March 11, 1833; People v. Kelso, et al., September 10, 1829; People v. Isaacs, March 19, 1852; A year later, Cauldwell still resided at the same address. See People v. Roberts, September 15, 1853.

11. DAP, People v. Gale, June 14, 1831.

12. *Sun*, September 3, 1833, January 22, February 11, 1834. Roberts was probably a prostitute because in other breaking and entering cases the newspaper coverage describes the victim as living in a "respectable" house or family. See *Sun*, February 12, 1834. This part of Anthony Street was also a major zone of prostitution from 1820 to 1850.

13. *Herald*, April 13, 15, 25, 28, 30, June 7, 9, 1836; George W. Walling, *Recollections of a New York Police Chief* (New York, 1887), 25; Nevins, *Diary of Hone*, 213; *National Police Gazette*, 26 August 1882.

watch prevented the rape. Fuller later dropped the charges because Ford was an "old friend."[14]

Women had even less protection on the street. Mary Smith, a Leonard Street prostitute, was walking home in 1832 after an evening at the Park Theatre when William Nosworthy seized the spritely grisette "in a grossly rude and indecent manner and raised her clothes so as to expose her nakedness to the passers by."[15] Such occasions, which became more frequent as mid-century approached, indicate that prostitutes were fair game for the aggression of frustrated males.

The final and most significant form of assault was the spree or row. Sprees were violent, illegal acts by young males, hoping, in part, to earn respect within their male subculture. These violent outbursts reflected deindividualization—the loss of inhibition and sense of individual accountability when part of a large group. Fueled by male camaraderie and substantial quantities of liquor, the spree, as Edgar Allan Poe aptly described it, was "the mad excess of a counterfeit hilarity—the joint offspring of liberty and of rum."[16]

Gangs of drunks on a rampage often moved from one saloon or brothel to another, becoming increasingly obnoxious and violent at every stop along a trail of bacchanalian indulgence. The arbitrary, unplanned, and unstructured behavior revealed a predeliction for intoxicated conviviality, not prudish outrage at the existence of prostitution. Some attacks, for instance, stopped just short of personal assault. In 1834, John Lawrence, Henry Flender and a dozen others attempted to break into several Chapel Street brothels, but settled instead for spattering the front doors with mud. On another occasion, Samuel Anderson, Charles Dykes, and their chums failed to break into a brothel on Anthony Street, retreating to the street and launching stones through the front windows. Finally, William Weed brought eight to ten accomplices "to take possession" of Eliza Swinson's Chapel Street brothel, but only stoned her "castle" after she locked them out.[17]

14. DAP, People v. Ford, August 10, 1844. Ford, however, was convicted of assaults on three police officers who arrested him.

15. DAP, People v. Nosworthy, March 12, 1832. Nosworthy was a leader in an unrelated attack on Mary Bowen's Leonard Street brothel.

16. Edgar Allan Poe, "The Mystery of Marie Roget," in *The Complete Tales and Poems of Edgar Allan Poe* (New York, 1938), 197; Allan Nevins and Milton Halsey Thomas, eds., *The Diary of George Templeton Strong* 5 vols. (New York, 1952), I, 22–24, 62, 84. See also W.J. Rorabaugh, *The Alcoholic Republic: An American Tradition* (New York, 1979), 150–61.

17. *Sun*, February 4, March 11, 1834; Police Court Papers, New York City Municipal Archives and Records Center (hereafter PCP), Box 7445, Stewart v. Anderson and Dykes, January 2, 1833.

Many sprees, however, evolved into scenes of sadistic terror. The three rioters who stoned Amanda Smith's house on Franklin Street also "destroyed her furniture, knocked her down, beat her on the face and head so as to blind her entirely, and after having knocked her down, kicked her." The invaders then beat her crippled son William "in a most shameful and outrageous manner." Witnesses testified that the same men forced their way into two other Orange Street brothels, "making a great noise and disturbance, breaking the furniture." Likewise, John Golding led four other men into Elizabeth Rinnell's Crosby Street house and demanded food, drink, money, and entertainment. After their drunken orgy, Golding assaulted and beat Miss Rinnell. On another occasion, Jane Williams refused to open her brothel door to a dozen men. Two then forced their way through a window, punched Williams in the head, went to the front door, admitted the remainder, and then stamped about the house. Similarly, when John Williams entered an Anthony Street brothel, he threw oil of vitriol in Mary Ann Duffy's face, severely scarring her. In 1836, seven men, upon entering Mary Gambel's Crosby Street brothel, "fell upon her with their fists." Their violence culminated when one attacker "drew a sword and stabbed her in the nose ... and left her face most shockingly cut and injured."[18]

The threat of rape was common in many brothel riots. Five men broke into Eliza Logue's Thomas Street house when she refused them admittance. After breaking the cookery and throwing a lamp at the head of a prostitute, they strangled Logue, and "threw her across the foot of a bed and endeavored by force and violence to have connection with her...." A nearby watch heard the commotion and prevented consummation of the act. In another instance, more than ten laborers from the Eleventh Ward broke into Eliza Ann Potter's Suffolk Street house, violently assaulted her and "threatened to pickle" and rape her before hastily departing.[19]

Since most sexually-related crimes go unreported, the brothel riots described above (most of which appeared in the prosecution papers of the district attorney) surely represented but a small portion of a widespread phenomenon.[20] Undoubtedly, numerous

18. Most of these cases are in the DAP. See People v. Samis, February 20, 1837; People v. Golding, February 11, 1842; People v. Mott, October 20, 1842; People v. Small, January 16, 1829; People v. Dikeman, et al., December 14, 1836.

19. DAP, People v. Timpson, April 11, 1842; People v. Henrietta, April 8, 1836; *Herald*, January 9, 1836.

20. Sociology of crime studies show that only 20 to 25 percent of sexual crimes are reported. See Rossiaud, "Prostitution, Youth, and Society," 6.

repeated assaults upon prostitutes produced significant changes in the structural development of nineteenth-century commercial sex. Specifically, prostitutes attuned to the increasing misogynist resentment resorted to three sources of protection: self-defense, the municipal government, and the "pimp." Several examples illustrate how working-class women, particularly prostitutes, employed physical violence to assert and protect their autonomy. For instance, the calendar of the Court of General Sessions in 1828 disclosed an unprecedented seventy cases of assault and battery by women.[21] In 1843, one angry prostitute stabbed a client in his chest on the steps of the Astor House. Only a deflection by his rib prevented the knife from piercing his heart. On another occasion, when John Briggs became uncontrollably drunk and disorderly in Phoebe Doty's and Moll Stephens's brothel, one prostitute tried to shoot him with a pistol. Similarly, Mary Gambel, upon being stabbed in the nose, scratched her assailant's face so badly that nearly a month later she was convinced that "he must [still] carry the marks with him."[22]

Antebellum prostitutes also used the law to protect themselves. By initiating legal proceedings against their aggressors, prostitutes utilized the machinery of the state to defend their interests and property rights, firmly entrenching their profession in the social fabric of the metropolis. Even streetwalkers sought legal redress when threatened or attacked. When a drunken male approached and kissed a prostitute promenading Broadway, she objected to his uninvited sexual advances and prosecuted him.[23] On another occasion, Jane Williams charged Jim Waters with assault after he struck her when she abandoned him on the street for another client. Unapologetic, Waters justified his actions: "I had no notion of letting her off," he insisted. "She wanted to go away with another fellow cause [sic] he was dressed a little better than I was."[24] Williams, unsatisfied, fully prosecuted her assailant. Instead of retreating to the domestic hearth, Williams and her sagacious compatriots asserted themselves through every means at their disposal.

Prostitutes were undoubtedly an exploited and marginal group in antebellum New York City. Historians Judith Walkowitz and Christine Stansell have nevertheless demonstrated how prostitution be-

21. *Niles Register*, July 19, 1828.

22. *National Police Gazette*, January 2, 1847; DAP, People v. Dikeman, et al., December 14, 1836; DAP, People v. Norman, November 23, 1843. Most interestingly, the prostitute in the Astor House stabbing, Lydia Brown, alias Amelia Norman, was acquitted of her crime.

23. *Sun*, May 5, 1834. She later dropped the charge when he apologized.

24. *Sun*, May 17, 1834.

came an increasingly viable alternative for working women affected by the industrialization process during the nineteenth century. Such women did not necessarily become outcasts from their laboring counterparts. Rather, their prostitution was often understood to be a temporary means of survival and adaptation.[25] Just as the extreme behavior of men in brothel attacks revealed a transformation in attitudes toward prostitution and the nature of male violence in antebellum society, the use of the legal system by prostitutes to defend themselves was equally important. These prostitutes did not see themselves as "fallen women." They publicly defended their personal integrity and private property instead of succumbing to violent intimidation, and they refused to act as fugitives from justice. They rejected a defensive, reticent posture when subjected to violent terror. By asserting their rights, they forswore surrender.

Forcing the resolution of these conflicts into a public forum, prostitutes turned the municipal government into their agent and protector. For example, they summoned the watch when attacked and prosecuted violators upon arrest. Some rioters even considered the watch a protector of the brothel. When Marshal Joseph L. Hays tried to arrest three men in the process of destroying Miss Robins's house of ill-fame, the culprits temporarily took him hostage too. Another time, Charles Taylor and Charles Jennings berated the watch who removed them from Adeline Miller's house, "saying it was a damned shame that watchmen should receive pay for protecting whore houses. . . ."[26] In court, prostitutes were outraged by the destruction of their property.[27] Rioters were thus compelled to repair the damage even when the judge knew about the illicit carnal activities of the plaintiff. Although the records of the district attorney provide no clue as to the final decisions in most cases, on at least eleven occasions the courts convicted the riotous defendants.[28] In other cases, men eluded conviction only because the prostitute dropped the charge.[29]

25. Christine Stansell, *City of Women: Sex and Class in New York 1789–1860* (New York, 1986), 169–92; Judith R. Walkowitz, *Prostitution and Victorian Society: Woman, Class and the State* (Cambridge, Eng., 1980), 14–20.

26. DAP, People v. Anderson, et al., January 12, 1829; People v. Lozier, et al., June 14, 1831. For corruption as early as 1815, see Ebenezer Burling to Humane Society (circa 1815), Society for the Suppression of Vice and Immorality Manuscripts, Reel 3, John Jay Papers, New-York Historical Society.

27. DAP, People v. Small, et al., January 16, 1829; People v. Gale, June 14, 1831; People v. Nosworthy, March 12, 1832; People v. Tuttle, January 15, 1834; People v. Graham and Cole, December 14, 1836; People v. Hyer, et al., December 17, 19, 1836.

28. *Sun*, March 11, 1834; DAP, People v. Small, January 16, 1829; People v. Chichester, May 11, 1836; People v. Hyer, December 13, 1836; People v. Thorp, et al., February 13, 1841; People v. Golding, February 11, 1842; People v. Timpson, April 11, 1842; People v. Isaacs,

In this ironic fashion, the state both defended and protected prostitution. Unlike later forms of legal intervention which sought to regulate, control, and hinder the independence of prostitutes, governmental power was invoked for their benefit.[30] When prostitutes exercised their property rights, the municipality was compelled to defend prostitution and prosecute its more violent enemies. Since antebellum government was primarily devoted to protecting the interests of taxpayers and private property, a bewildered municipality faced an unappealing, imperfect choice: suppress sexual deviancy, punish prostitutes and thereby violate their (and ultimately others') property rights or punish their male aggressors and tolerate the existence of prostitution. In the end, the state chose to defend property, and thus prostitution, at the expense of other laws and the puritanical sensibilities of many New Yorkers.

What sort of men were these "brothel bullies?" Ordinary laborers constituted 71 percent of those charged. Of the remainder, 9 percent were semiskilled laborers, 15 percent skilled artisans, and 5 percent white-collar professionals.[31] Most rioters lived in the same or adjacent ward as the prostitute they attacked. Less than a quarter lived in more distant areas of the city.[32] While most were

December 25, 1851; People v. Moody, et al., January 15, 1852.

29. DAP, People v. Samis, February 20, 1837; People v. Pearsall, December 6, 1832; People v. Ford, August 10, 1844. Marcia Carlisle and John C. Schneider found that antebellum Philadelphia and Detroit prostitutes also resorted to the legal system to defend their rights and property. See "Prostitutes and Their Reformers in Nineteenth Century Philadelphia," 36–40; Schneider, *Detroit and the Problem of Order*, 20–21.

30. Walkowitz, *Prostitution and Victorian Society*. On American efforts to regulate prostitution, see David C. Pivar, *Purity Crusade: Sexual Morality and Social Control, 1868–1900* (Westport, Conn., 1973), 51–71.

31. The term "brothel bullies" was used by George Templeton Strong. See Nevins, *Diary of Strong*, IV, 113. In the 50 known or suspected attacks on disorderly houses from 1825 to 1857, 132 individuals were indicted (a much larger number were arrested, but not recorded). At least 16 of these defendants were repeat offenders involved in two or more attacks. In identifying rioters, I used the city directory. If the individual was unlisted, I followed those occupations given in the indictment. The ward numbers and occupations recorded on the standard indictment form, however, tended to be inconsistent and unreliable. In many cases, the ward listed was *where* the crime occurred and contradicted other information on the indictment. Even when skilled occupations were given in the defendant's testimony, the indictment frequently listed him as "laborer." See DAP, People v. Tuttle, January 15, 1834; People v. Chichester, April 8, May 11, 1836; People v. Graham, et al., December 13, 14, 1836. The breakdown for 12 semiskilled workers was: grocers and saloon keepers - 7, boardinghouse keepers - 2, cartmen - 1, female dressmaker - 1, stable keeper - 1; for skilled workers: butchers - 5, river pilot - 1, ship carver - 1, baker - 1, tailor - 1, masons - 3, printer - 1, binder - 1, bootmaker - 1, bootcrimper - 1, caulker - 1. (Three others had several listed for the same name, but all were either skilled or professional occupations); and for 7 white collar or professional workers: clerks - 2, engineer - 1, attorney - 1, City Hall or mayor's official - 3.

32. The wards and addresses of the rioters were based, firstly, on city directories, and

working-class laborers, brothel rioters crossed class lines. In 1831, for example, attorney James Lozier joined his neighbor, grocer Charles Taylor, and two others in attacking Adeline Miller's Elm Street brothel.[33] The instigators of these assaults, therefore, were not simply disenchanted "rabble," parts of unruly mobs, professional criminals, or clearly-defined deviants, but "respectable" elements of society as well. Indeed, their behavior was tolerated and sometimes condoned by neighbors and the municipality.

These brothel riots depart in several ways from the earlier forms of pre-industrial collective violence described by Rudé and others. First, much violence was inflicted on the persons, not simply on the property. While some assaults were planned and had political motives, many were virtually spontaneous forms of terror. Third, unlike those who attacked such agents of the state as soldiers, tax collectors or government officials, who often fought back with greater ferocity than the mob, brothel bullies faced little physical opposition from a protective authority defending their victims. Finally, since prostitution always existed in New York, preservation of it as an institution was an unlikely motive behind their behavior.[34]

Why then did men choose to act with such violence toward prostitutes? Historians Christine Stansell and Amy Gilman Srebnick have shown how antebellum society grew increasingly restless over the public activities and accessibility of working women in general.[35] Contemporaries feared that women in public places risked destructive physical harrassment. "There are strange things said of attacks upon females in the streets of New York,... if alone," reported *Niles Register* in 1831. Philip Hone bemoaned that some outrage occurred nightly by "young ruffians who prowl the streets insulting females." Even George Templeton Strong was selective in his remorse. When nineteenth-century feminists en-

secondly, on the ward given in the standard indictment. The breakdown was: 113 total defendants with a known address or ward, 39 from the same ward, 47 from an adjacent ward, and 27 from another part of the city.

33. DAP, People v. Lozier, et al., June 14, 1831. The occupations and addresses for the participants were: James Lozier, attorney, 65 Division Street; Charles Taylor, grocer, 64–66 Division Street; Jeremiah Dodge, ship carver, 264 Rivington Street; Charles B. Jennings, unknown. See *Longworth's City Directory* (New York, 1831).

34. For a convenient classification scheme on pre-industrial riots, see Rude, *Paris and London*, 18–23.

35. Stansell, "Women, Children, and the Uses of the Streets: Class and Gender Conflict in New York City, 1850–1860," *Feminist Studies* 8 (1982), 309–35; Amy Gilman Srebnick, "The Murder of Mary Rogers: Identity, Sex and Class in Mid-Nineteenth Century New York City" (paper delivered to the American Historical Association Annual Meeting, New York City, December 29, 1985.)

couraged women to wear bloomers and speak before public audiences, Strong confessed he was "glad to see them respectfully pumped upon by a crowd of self-appointed conservators of manners and morals." In his opinion, the "strumpets of Leonard and Church streets are not *much* further below the ideal of womanhood than these loathsome dealers in clack, who seek to change women into garrulous men without virility."[36] For women, the message was clear—get off the streets, stay in the home.

36. *Niles Register.* January 8, 1831; Nevins, *Diary of Hone*, 435, 451. For examples of

FIFTH EDITION—WITH MANY ADDITIONS.

PROSTITUTION EXPOSED;

OR, A

MORAL REFORM DIRECTORY,

LAYING BARE THE

Lives, Histories, Residences, Seductions, &c.

OF THE MOST CELEBRATED

COURTEZANS AND LADIES OF PLEASURE

OF THE CITY OF NEW-YORK,

Together with a Description of the Crime and its Effects,

AS ALSO OF THE

Houses of Prostitution and their Keepers,

HOUSES OF ASSIGNATION,

THEIR CHARGES AND CONVENIENCES,

AND OTHER PARTICULARS INTERESTING TO THE PUBLIC.

BY A BUTT ENDER.

NEW-YORK:

PUBLISHED FOR PUBLIC CONVENIENCE,

1839.

The title page, above, and sample entries, opposite, of an 1839 directory of New York City prostitutes. From the Collection of Leo Hershkowitz.

> *Old Screech.*
>
> This (the only name by which this stinking old buster is known,) has been worn out in public service for the last three years. She received this name from the fact of the wretched noise she makes while pursuing the duties of her profession. She has no regular place of living, but grubs it at the markets, and takes her company up into alleys.
>
> *Jane Fickell,*
>
> Has been on the town about 3 months; has no regular place of residence, but usually carries her company to Aunt Betsy's House of Assignation, next door but one to the cor. of Walker-street, in Orange; she is only 14 years of age, and is remarkably small; one would suppose from appearances that she was ill-suited to that occupation, and would meet a speedy death. Her seduction affords another instance of a most depraved spirit; her mother had but lately married a second husband, the indulgence of whose brutal propensities on this unfortunate girl, has cast her on an unfeeling world to seek a livelihood by prostitution.
>
> *Rachel Lloyd,*
>
> A fair damsel but lately broke in, about 17 years of age, formerly of 14 Elizabeth-st. Seduced by a Dry Goods clerk in Chatham-st. and now kept by a milliner's son in Pearl-st.

The increasingly prominent role played by prostitutes in urban social life was a second factor. Outside the home, prostitutes were among the most visible women in the industrializing antebellum city. After 1820, the geographic expansion of prostitution and the appearance of at least four red-light districts reflected the rise of a new sexuality and the commercialization of sex.[37] One newspaper complained that "a new code of ethics" had emerged by 1836 glamorizing the prostitute with her gold watch, splendid earrings and embroidered stockings, at the expense of "a poor hardworking

attacks on women, see *Tribune*, March 13, 1844, March 27, May 1, 1846. Nevins, *Diary of Strong*, II, 129–30.

37. Gilfoyle, "The Urban Geography of Commercial Sex."

man, who sticks to one woman, ... his wife." Indeed, by 1825 madams like Maria Williamson were successful enough to own several brothels and actively engage in New York's lucrative real estate market. Others like Rosina Townsend, Adeline Miller, and Julia Brown were public figures appearing on the front pages of the penny press, in the diaries of the city's gentry, and in guidebooks sold at corner newstands.[38] The *Herald* asked when "was there ever found an instance of the open and shameless defence [sic] of the character of a public prostitute?" Why, indeed, had leading prostitutes become models "of truth and virtue?"[39] At a time when gender roles were in the initial stage of redefinition and the "cult of domesticity" was gaining ground, the behavior of some prostitutes was a vivid counterpoise.

From 1820 to 1840, women had greater control and influence over prostitution than at any other time. Low wages in the factory and the household made prostitutes the best-paid women workers in the nineteenth-century city. And the willingness of many prostitutes to prosecute their violators in the public arena illustrated their personal faith and confidence in their own individual rights. The sporadic, infrequent attacks prior to 1830, the sharp decline after 1840, and the sudden and unprecedented rise in violent abuse between 1832 and 1838 make those years a watershed in the transformation of attitudes regarding prostitution, sexuality, and women. Clearly, some men found the increased economic and social power of prostitutes threatening. And others intended to shape and control commercialized sex, resorting to terror when necessary.

Simultaneously with the sudden rise in brothel riots, America experienced an increase in male communal drinking. According to W. J. Rorabaugh, such group forms of intoxication were commonplace after 1820 and endowed the participants with feelings of liberty and independence while inducing a sense of equality. The group drinking binge was an ideological inebriation; to be drunk was to be free. Liquor, therefore, increased the American male's

38. *Herald*, 23 June, 1836. For front page stories, see the *Herald* and *Sun*, April 13–30, 1836, June 7–20, 1836, and *The Whip*, July 9, 1842, copy in DAP, People v. Wooldridge, July 14, 1842. Maria Williamson appears in New York City Land Title Registrations, Pre-1917 Conveyance Records, Office of City Register, liber 137, page 25, May 15, 1819; and Record of Assessments, Fifth Ward, 1820–1825, New York City Municipal Archives and Records Center. On the popular attention given to prostitutes, see Nevins, *Diary of Strong*, I, 114, 133; II, 270; Robert Taylor Diary, February 14, April 4, 17, November 17, 18, 20, 21, 22, 23, December 5, 6, 17, 1846, January 6, 1847, New York Public Library.

39. *Herald*, June 26, 1836.

sense of autonomy.[40] Brothel sprees were an extension of such drunken displays of egalitarianism. Participants unleashed pent-up male frustration by attacking a visibly independent, autonomous, and sometimes materially-successful woman. Whereas a vigilante attack on a house of prostitution was a public protest, a spree was a source of fun. As mock-heroic skirmishes of pride and violation, such attacks were an aggressive form of misogynist, masculine recreation, a means to assert male perogative and supremacy at the expense of a hapless, unprotected, vulnerable prostitute. The spree was an illusion of power for powerless men.[41]

Political control over the profits of prostitution was a final motivating force in some brothel attacks. In 1836, John Chichester and his politically-connected gang attacked at least three bordellos. Entering Jane Ann Jackson's Chapel Street brothel with bats, they destroyed windows and shutters, and threatened to cut Miss Jackson's throat. Chichester's consorts then broke into Eliza Ludlow's house and forced her to serve brandy, and concluded their guzzling by tossing the glasses in the fire. Then they "abused the inmates of the house," burnt a rug, broke a bench by hurling it at a prostitute, and threatened to toss one woman out the window.[42] Similarly, Thomas Hyer's gang raided at least four brothels from 1836 to 1838. Upon breaking into Ellen Holly's house in 1836, they grabbed one inmate, and "by the most forcible and violent means," gang raped her. Despite conviction for the deed, a year later Hyer led the same culprits into Mary Banta's house, destroyed her tableware, and knocked an inmate unconscious. Within the next two decades, Hyer's pugilistic habits were rewarded with the American heavyweight boxing championship, political alliances with Nativist Bill Poole, Democrat Mike Walsh, and Republican William Seward, and control of the prostitution, saloons and gambling dens along Mercer Street.[43]

40. W.J. Rorabaugh, *The Alcoholic Republic: An American Tradition* (New York, 1979), 150–52, 161.

41. David Grimsted similarly argues that Jacksonian rioters attacked groups less powerful and influential than they were. Their victims tended to be "the oppressed, the unpopular, and the unprotected." See "Rioting in Its Jacksonian Setting," 392–93.

42. People v. Chichester, May 8, 11, 1836. One of Chichester's accomplices, John Boyd, only four years earlier broke into Mary Bowen's Leonard Street domicile with a gang of fourteen males and destroyed her furniture. See PCP, Box 7445, People v. Boyd, et al., December 18, 1832. The Chichester gang is mentioned in Samuel Prime, *Life in New York* (New York, 1847), 180; *Herald*, April 15, 25, 1836; Herbert Asbury, *The Gangs of New York* (New York, 1927), 29; Weinbaum, *Mobs and Demagogues*, 151, 155. Their headquarters was at 44 Bowery.

43. DAP, People v. Hyer, December 17, 1836; People v. Roberts, et al., January 10, 1838. Among Hyer's accomplices was Abraham Vanderzee, who earned a position on the police

While motives were less evident in other attacks, the participants had significant political connections. For example, rioters who destroyed Jane Weston's, Sarah Ferguson's, and Adeline Miller's belongings were white-collar workers and skilled laborers, allegedly acting on orders from Justice Bloodgood and Street Inspector Daniel McGrath.[44] In 1834, Phoebe Doty accused William H. Tuttle, a clerk for the mayor, and John L. Martin, a tavernkeeper, of attacking her bawdy house, during which they "commenced a work of outrageous and disorderly conduct... by squirting upon them... dirty water..." On a separate occasion, Andrew R. Jackman, a City Hall officer and future city assessor and common school trustee, and seven other skilled workers broke into Mary Adams's Thirteenth Ward establishment. While inside they accosted an inmate, wrapped her up in a straw mat, and rolled her down the stairs.[45]

In antebellum New York, gangs like those led by Hyer, Chichester and others played critical roles in the distribution of power and early formation of the political machine. As Amy Bridges argues, wealthy elites in New York concentrated on national and state issues. Local concerns and grass-roots organization were left to a new political animal—the career politician, who employed gangs to keep opponents away from the polls, guard ballot boxes and enforce political conformity. Hyer, for example, was allied to the Nativist "Bowery B'hoys" who, according to Alvin Harlow, were not as vicious as rival Five Points gangs and had a tendency "toward the political rather than the purely savage or criminal."[46]

---

force when it was created in 1844. See D.T. Valentine. *Manual of the Corporation of the City of New York* (New York, 1846), 59. Hyer's gang operated out of saloons at 42 and 50 Bowery. On Hyer and Poole, see *Tribune*, March 10, 12, 1855; Asbury, *Gangs*, 87–100; Frank Moss, *The American Metropolis* (New York, 1897), II, 397. On Hyer's alliances with Walsh and Seward (whom he supported at the 1860 Republican convention), see Wilentz, *Chants Democratic*, 328; Alvin F. Harlow, *Old Bowery Days: The Chronicles of a Famous Street* (New York, 1931), 301, 306.

44. DAP, People v. Graham, December 13, 14, 1836. The five arrested included: James Graham, age 21, clerk, 53 Lumber Street; William C. Rider, age 19, bartender, 505 Pearl Street; Henry Bertholf, age 25, mason, 76 Amos Street; James Cole, age 19, engineer, 38 Hubert Street; George Mayne, age 21, printer, 29 Madison Street. McGrath was listed as a street inspector in *Longworth's City Directory* (New York, 1835), 47.

45. DAP, People v. Tuttle, January 15, 1834; People v. Ryerson, et al., December 10, 1834. *Longworth's City Directory* (New York, 1834) lists the following occupations and addresses for the accused: John K. Ryerson, tailor, 28 Ludlow Street; Joseph B. Smith, butcher, 64 North (Houston) Street; Samuel Hill, butcher, 51 1st Street; James Johnson, butcher, 86 Delancey Street; Andrew Jackman, City Hall officer, 101 Elizabeth Street; Jacob Vogle, butcher, 50 1st Street. Charles Kemp and Henry Avis were not listed. Jackman was listed as a Eleventh Ward Common School trustee in 1843 and a city assessor in 1846. See D.T. Valentine, *Manual of the Corporation of the City of New York, 1842–43* (New York, 1843), 75; idem., *Manual* (New York, 1846), 47.

Tom Hyer. Collections of the New-York Historical Society.

While the ward-based, career politician controlled votes, he lacked money. In order to establish a secure financial base, ward politicians resorted to bribery and extortion of neighborhood proprietors of saloons, gambling dens, and houses of prostitution in return for ignoring laws outlawing or regulating such activities. As prostitution became a significant revenue source for the local political boss, gangs were probably used as a means to control and police brothel keepers and their inmates. Employing terror, politically-organized gangs restructured prostitution into a male-con-

46. Bridges, *A City in the Republic*, 73–77, 126–36, 152–53; Harlow, *Old Bowery Days*, 188, 205, 296–301.

trolled institution and established a financial foundation for the political machine for the remainder of the century. After 1880, it was commonplace for one-time gang leaders and political allies like "The" Allen, "Big Tim" Sullivan and Martin Engel to dominate important institutions of commercial sex.[47]

This mixture of violence and politics gave rise to a new participant in commercial sex—the "pimp." American historians have erroneously attributed the appearance of pimps and male-control of prostitution to greater police harassment after 1890. But as brothels were attacked with increasing frequency during the 1830s, men for the first time were hired to provide protection. Both brothel keepers and prostitutes admitted that men lived in their houses of prostitution to provide physical protection or perform services such as buying groceries, repairing the house, or serving the guests. Even streetwalkers were not exempt from this trend. By the 1850s, a visible, well-established system of pimps existed in New York. When Mayor Fernando Wood instigated a campaign against streetwalkers in 1855, pimps appeared with them in court. Commonly referred to as "Broadway Statues," pimps and their associates stood in front of the "monster" hotels along New York's best-known avenue. These "scamps have the audacity to address [women] without ceremony," complained one reporter, "and if their advances are received with indignation,... the wretches apologize and plead mistake." The corner of Broadway and Broome Street was a notorious hangout for pimps waiting for prostitutes to hand over their earnings before returning to work.[48] By the mid-nineteenth century, pimps were a standard feature of New York prostitution. They remain so today.

For the nineteenth-century female, prostitution was the quintessential symbol of male sexual coercion. By 1840, such coercion had escalated to dangerous levels of physical abuse and intimidation. If assumptions about women were expressed within structures

47. On "The" Allen's gang associations and involvement in prostitution, see *National Police Gazette*, 28 August 1880. On Sullivan, see Harlow, *Old Bowery Days*, 505–22.

48. *National Police Gazette*, December 8, 1866, June 8, 1867; *Tribune*, 28, 29 March 1855. *McDowall's Journal* reported that boarding houses acting as fronts for parlor houses usually employed one man for such purposes. See *McDowall's Journal*, May 1833; PCP, Box 7448, Bennett v. Pearce, November 9, 1835; DAP, People v. Shannon, April 19, 1836; People v. Smith, July 25, 1840; James MacCabe, *The Secrets of the Great City* (Philadelphia, 1868), 290. This evidence contradicts Christine Stansell's and Ruth Rosen's thesis that pimps and male dominance of commercialized prostitution did not appear until after 1890 and greater police harassment. See Rosen, *The Lost Sisterhood: Prostitution in the Progressive Era, 1900–1918* (Baltimore, 1982), 33, 40; Stansell, *City of Women*, chapter 9. Jacques Rossiaud found prostitutes with pimps in fifteenth-century France. See "Prostitution, Youth and Society," 18.

of feeling rather than in bodies of well-defined ideas, as Christine Stansell argues, then antebellum brothel riots were most emblematic of a new misogynist attitude toward prostitutes and women in public life. Bypassing older, traditional limits of collective protest and crowd behavior, antebellum males resorted to terror. Gender became a sufficient cause for violence.[49] On one level, individual antebellum males believed they had the right to control, if not physically coerce, prostitutes and other public women. Efforts to extend male power over autonomous and sexually-independent women, however, met with defiance. Through self-defense and utilization of the legal system to defend their property, prostitutes protected themselves. Ultimately, the final victor in this struggle was the local, ward politician. As Tammany Hall emerged as the political reckoning force of Gotham, violent gangs allied to neighborhood machine representatives used force and terror to restructure commercial sex and insure male control over the profits of prostitution.

49. Ellen Carol DuBois and Linda Gordon, "Seeking Ecstasy on the Battlefield: Danger and Pleasure in Nineteenth-Century Feminist Sexual Thought," *Feminist Studies* 9 (1983), 7-25.

PROSTITUTION AND POLITICS IN ANTEBELLUM NEW ORLEANS

Richard Tansey
University of Texas

During the antebellum period, prostitution was a major industry which enhanced New Orleans's image of old world charm and sexual mystery. Thousands of visitors joined local citizens in seeking out the pleasures of New Orleans bordellos. In providing sexual pleasures for male customers, many city residents reaped economic dividends through the operations of these illicit houses. Large landlords fattened their purses by renting dwellings to harlots, while retail storeowners sold clothes and fancy goods to these women. Some lawyers collected lucrative fees for defending clients accused of moral turpitude or keeping a brothel. Managers of large ballrooms grew rich by entertaining their guests with prostitutes, and off-duty policemen earned extra income by working as private watchmen in these establishments.

New Orleans in the 1850s was in a transition period. Merchants sought public funding for railroad growth and greater economic diversification of the city's trade structure, and they placed less reliance on the river trade. During the 1850s, merchants led two reform drives for abolishing harlotry in their city, because they opposed the economic viewpoint of traditional prostitution cliques. From the reformers' perspective, harlotry was not merely a moral evil; this vice represented the most visible and sordid part of an antiquated economic structure which prevented New Orleans from keeping pace with her rivals in controlling the South's trade. Reform businessmen complained that wealthy landowners amassed large fortunes by renting to prostitutes and speculating in undeveloped lots, but refused to contribute personal funds to railroad projects or to endorse city tax measures for these improvements. Large property holders preferred the low real estate taxes which characterized the river economy instead of the inflated property taxes which merchants proposed for building the new railroad empire for New Orleans. City merchants tried to persuade voters that the river economy favored by land speculators and harlotry forces was no longer a viable means for maintaining the city's economic dominance. Increasingly after 1850, New Orleans was losing significant parts of her Mississippi River commerce to New York City, Memphis, and Charleston railroads. Confronted with the challenge of aggressive urban competitors, New Orleans merchants urged the construction of major railroad arteries radiating north and west from the city. The scarcity of private investment capital in Louisiana compelled New Orleans merchants to engage in political activities for raising public revenue on behalf of new railroad ventures.

Merchants composed the driving force in both the Third Municipality anti-harlotry campaign and the 1854-1856 Know-Nothing upsurge. Third Municipality business leaders throughout the 1840s suffered under the hands of a Democratic municipal council which refused any requests for allocating tax funds to improve the levee area or to build railroads connecting this district with Florida or western Louisiana. During these years, the Third Municipal Council was content to approve only light tax rates on land speculators and to defeat anti-vice statutes against brothels. Third Municipality reformers hoped that by destroying the ring of harlots, landlords, and corrupt politicians, they could attract new businesses and homeowners.

During the tumultuous years between 1854 and 1856, Know-Nothing businessmen carried on the anti-harlotry crusade for both economic and political reasons. Know-Nothing candidates focused on law and order issues for healing the division between their business and labor followers. Know-Nothing merchants, realizing that their economic program of increased railroad expenditures and higher property taxes might alienate their blue-collar partners, emphasized in their campaign speeches the urgency for arresting prostitutes, thieves, murderers, and vagrants. Once elected on the law and order platform, Know-Nothing aldermen faced the difficult task of allocating limited city funds for economic and moral improvements. By providing several million dollars for new railroad construction, merchant aldermen depleted most of the city's revenue and were thus unable to implement their anti-crime program. By 1858, Know-Nothing labor groups, disgusted with the business orientation of the incumbent city council, dissolved their partnership with Nativist businessmen. Ironically, Know-Nothing labor leaders joined forces with prostitution cliques in supporting the old economic order for low property taxes and reliance on the river traffic against merchants' demands for railroads and higher property taxes.

I. THE OLD ORDER

The commercial trade of New Orleans created an annual influx of sixty thousand seamen and riverboat workers seeking pleasure and housing accommodations. A severe shortage of hotel rooms inflated boarding costs from one to two dollars per day, an expense which few sailors earning a monthly salary of fifteen to eighteen dollars and steamboat deckhands earning a monthly income of thirty to forty-five dollars could absorb.[1] Many transient working class men frequented brothels to obtain cheaper sleeping quarters, as well as to satisfy their sexual needs.

Sailors' boarding house runners swarmed around the levee where they greeted arriving seamen with the appealing offers of prostitutes and moderately priced rooms. Fierce competition among boarding houses kept a ceiling on the fees which these establishments charged their lodgers. The daily rates in such houses ranged from ten cents to a dollar depending on the quality of the house. As attractive as the cheap room rates was the practice among sailors' boarding house keepers of furnishing rooms to penniless seamen in exchange for the privilege of receiving advance wages of these men on their next job assignment.

Unemployment and low wages among female workers in New Orleans produced a class of women willing to sell sexual services. Women jobseekers entered a labor market where men were displacing women in such traditional female jobs as flower sellers and market vendors and were competing against women for domestic servant positions. Foreign-born and teenage women encountered the greatest difficulty in obtaining employment. Because native-born adult females probably had superior job skills and references, immigrant and adolescent females received the least desirable positions. Trapped in jobs with low wages and poor working conditions, many Irish and German women considered alternative employment. The average salary for a female servant varied between eight and twelve dollars a month, but sometimes declined to five dollars.[2] Unemployed or underpaid women presented easy targets for ballroom and brothel keepers who offered them a dollar or a dollar and a half per evening as well as free drinks to work as prostitutes.

Less visible than brothel and sailors' boarding house managers was a small coterie of elite landlords. Large landlords often eschewed

---

1. Henry M. Emery v. Ship Martin, United States District Court (doc. no.—6,210) filed, 17 June 1845. Regional Branch of the National Archives at Fort Worth, Texas; Ferman Sweed et als v. Ship Wabash, Ibid. (doc. no.—6,203) filed, 23 May 1845; Maxwell, Wright and Company v. Winter Latimer, Fourth District Court (doc. no.—5,371) filed, 13 January 1852. In 1846, the city of New Orleans created six local courts; the First District Court was the criminal court, and the remaining five bodies handled civil cases. All the civil courts cited in this paper are stored in the New Orleans Public Library.

2. Mary McDermot v. Dr. L. Johnson, Third District Court (doc. no.—4,671) filed, 5 August 1852; Mary Clark v. Mr. and Mrs. Simon, Ibid. (doc. no.—14,707) filed, 22 March 1860; *New Orleans Daily Crescent*, 4 December 1850; *New Orleans Louisiana Courier*, 15 September 1846 and 24 January 1851.

sinking substantial amounts of money into constructing homes for middle-class families. Instead of building homes for middle-income tenants, affluent landlords earned greater profits by erecting cheaper quarters for prostitutes and charging these women exorbitant rents. While demanding excessive rents, some landlords promised their tenants protection from police harassment. An 1852 contract between Lucinda Pattan, a madam, and John Brandy, a landlord, included the following penalty clause:[3]

> John Brandy does oblige himself that if the occupant has to move on account of complaints made by the Police or city authorities or any other persons, The said John Brandy will pay the Occupant of the herein mentioned house the sum of five hundred dollars for damages for being obliged to remove from the said house.

Middle class critics signaled out the millionaire John McDonogh for his hábit of leasing dwellings to prostitutes in decent neighborhoods.[4] Opponents accused this long-time landlord of blockbusting activities in fashionable residential areas where he bought a single home and then rented the premises to a brothel keeper. During the exodus from the deteriorating neighborhoods, McDonogh purchased the remaining dwellings for a fraction of their value. Content with the lucrative income from such rental units, McDonogh neglected to repair and maintain his property holdings. Railroad enthusiasts, disgusted with McDonogh's slumlord tactics, assailed him for his refusal to contribute money for new economic projects. Moreover, McDonogh opposed any increase in real estate taxes for financing railroad expansion. Merchants claimed that raising property taxes was the only practical means for underwriting the costs of railroad construction. Mercantile

---

3. This criminal case is one of the few criminal cases in which any testimony is given. Most prostitution and other criminal cases between 1840 and 1861 contain no testimony about the specific events which occurred in the alleged offense. State v. Lucinda Patton, First District Court (doc. no.—8,444) filed, 24 January 1853. All the pre-Civil War criminal court cases and docket books are stored in the New Orleans Criminal Court Building at the corner of Broad Street and Tulane Avenue.

4. On 2 May 1851, the *New Orleans Daily Delta* wrote: "The houses on the south side of Girod street between Camp and Magazine belong to the estate of John McDonogh—as well as several between Magazine and Tchoupitoulas streets—all of which are brothels and drunkeries," In a letter to the same journal on the proceeding day, 'H' stated that "John McDonogh preferred letting his houses to disorderly people, prostitutes etc. as it depreciated the property adjoining, and he could buy it lower as few people would buy or improve in such a neighborhood." In describing McDonogh's success, the *New Orleans Picayune* commented "when a man desires to become rich, he must corrupt the high, oppress the poor, and look to God to sustain him." Sarah Seawright, *New Orleans* (New York City, 1973) 84; *New Orleans Daily Delta*, 1 and 2 May 1851; *New Orelans Picayune*, 2 January 1851.

leaders argued that any further increase of taxes on the business community would weaken their ability to compete against New York traders. In the eyes of many businessmen, McDonogh's lack of economic vision symbolized the regressive forces impeding the development of a diversified economy based on the twin arteries of railroad and river trade.[5]

The political strength of landlords and brothel managers sheltered them from the vengeful hands of reform elements. Official tolerance of harlotry stemmed from the failure of the Whig and Democratic Parties to challenge the financial power of real estate barons and from the recognition that brothels often influenced the decisive votes in a close election. Prostitution forces enhanced their political influence by bloc support of individual candidates, such as A. D. Crossman, a Whig printer who became mayor of New Orleans between 1846 and 1854. Before his ascendancy as mayor, Crossman was chairman of the First Municipality police committee. While serving on this board, he ingratiated himself with brothel operators by supporting a ballroom license system and the creation of an understaffed police force incapable of suppressing bordellos. In the spring of 1846, Crossman narrowly won the mayor's race by receiving 2,989 votes (41%), while his two Democratic rivals split their party's votes with A. J. Guirot receiving 2,743 ballots (37%) and E. Montegut receiving 1,614 votes (22%).[6]

The slender margin of victory inclined Crossman to continue his leniency towards large brothels and ballrooms, while suppressing small and poor bordellos. During this tenure in office, he issued licenses to large ballrooms, while denying the requests from managers of smaller brothels. The concentration of licenses in the hands of large ballroom operators provided them with a measure of immunity which the smaller competitors did not enjoy. Although the license only allowed the holder to conduct a regular dance hall and did not officially entitle him to engage in harlotry, the police rarely raided a licensed ballroom where ladies-of-the-evening pursued their trade.

During the 1850 Third Municipality vice campaign, reformers ac-

---

5. A. F. Righton to John McDonogh, 2 February 1845, John McDonogh Manuscripts, 1845-1850, Howard Tilton Library, Tulane University; P. S. Warfield to John McDonogh, 2 December 1846, Ibid.; Mrs. C. Walker to John McDonogh, 8 October 1848, Ibid.; P. A. Fox to McDonogh, undated, John McDonogh Miscellaneous Manuscripts, Undated, Howard Tilton Library, Tulane University.

6. *New Orleans Louisiana Courier*, 27 May 1840; 2 January 1845; 2 and 11 April 1846; 30 March 1848; *New Orleans Bee*, 16, 18-20 January 1845; 10 June 1845; 18 November 1845; 30 January 1846; 6-9 April 1946; 6 August 1846; 19 July 1851.

cused Crossman of visiting and soliciting votes in disreputable ballrooms.[7] Reformers pointed out that Crossman ordered an occasional raid on small bordellos in order to give the illusion that he was enforcing the anti-prostitution laws. Crossman again incurred the wrath of his opponents in 1851 when he approved the reappointment of a First Municipality policeman charged with assault on a respectable merchant. Admitting that the accused corporal had not stood trial, this Whig mayor refused to take disciplinary action, since the policeman allegedly controlled over three hundred ballroom votes. As an executor of the deceased John McDonough's estate, Crossman angered vice reformers by continuing McDonogh's custom of leasing dwellings to prostitutes in decent neighborhoods.

Among the ballroom managers prospering under Crossman's administration was Salvador Viosca. In 1840, this Spanish-born immigrant operated a small coffeehouse. Several years later, his diligent efforts on behalf of Democratic candidates led to his appointment as a tax collector in one of the Fruit Markets. Viosca's Democratic orientation did not stop him from supporting Whig candidates sympathetic to his interests. The meteoric rise of this once humble grog shop keeper increased to the point in 1850 where Viosca owned real estate assessed at $25,000 and managed two large ballrooms—the Globe Ballroom in the First Municipality and the Whitehall Establishment in the Third Municipality.[8] With few exceptions, the police did not crack down on Viosca's ballrooms where prostitution and gambling flourished, since the unnamed owner of the Globe Ballroom occupied a seat on the city council. In operating the Whitehall Establishment, Viosca developed strong ties to powerful economic and political forces in the Third Municipality. Viosca paid an annual rent of $3,500 for leasing the Whitehall Ballroom. He frequently borrowed money from Pelanne Brothers, a blacksmith firm, and bought large quantities of liquor on credit from Joseph Lavata, a grocer.[9] To increase his

7. *New Orleans Daily Orleanian*, 16 October 1850 and 6 January 1852.

8. In both 1851 and 1853 Salvador Viosca ran an unsuccessful candidate for tax collector in the First Municipality. J. E. Maignon v. S. Viosca et al, Third District Court (doc. no.—4,007) filed, 13 December 1851; Joseph Lanata v. Salvador Viosca, Fifth District Court (doc. no.—5,289) filed 17 November 1851; Adeline Davis v. Salvador Viosca, Ibid. (doc. no.—5,375) filed, 13 December 1851; Pablo Gelpi v. Salvador Viosca, Ibid, (doc. no.—5,398) filed 22 December 1851; 1850 United States Census, Fourth Ward, First Municipality, p. 300; *New Orleans Louisiana Courier*, 11 June and 23 July 1840; 8 June and 14 December 1843; 17 May 1848; 10 June and 23 July 1851; 21 July and 11 September 1853; *New Orleans Bee*, 11 January 1849; *New Orleans Daily Orleanian*, 7 December 1850; *New Orleans Daily Delta*, 19 January and 25 June 1851.

9. As a blacksmith firm, Pelanne Brothers sold large amounts of iron railing for fences and road and bridge construction materials to the city, as well as to private

income, Viosca subleased part of Whitehall to the Polar Star, and Odd Fellows' Lodge, whose Grand Noble was J. L. Fabre, deputy sheriff of Orleans Parish.

II. THE THIRD MUNICIPALITY VICE CAMPAIGN

Although prostitution existed in a majority of the city's wards, this vice was concentrated in the Third Municipality. Under the lenient policy of Peter Seuzeneau, the Democratic recorder in this district, land speculators erected cheap dwellings and leased these premises to brothel keepers for excessive sums. In response to Seuzeneau's official tolerance towards harlotry, merchants led the movement in 1850 and 1851 to defeat this Democratic incumbent and replace him with a candidate pledged to eradicate this vice. Business leaders laced their campaign speeches with the assertion that prostitution and uncontrolled land speculation were important reasons why the Third Municipality's economy languished behind the aggressive growth which characterized the Second Municipality.[10] Reform advocates especially denounced the presence of numerous bawdy houses which discouraged hundreds of families and business firms from moving into the Third Municipality where real estate prices were substantially lower than in the more densely populated First and Second Municipalities. The small rate of in-migration by "respectable" people contributed to the Third Municipality's condition of being the least economically developed area in the city. Reform businessmen noted that their district had no banks, insurance companies, first-rate hotels, large-scale factories, wholesale firms and groceries, and dry good stores for serving the needs of its almost twenty thousand residents.

An analysis of the 1850 and 1860 New Orleans census supports the reform businessmen's contention that the Third Municipality was

---

customers such as the St. Louis Cathedral. For instance, between 24 June 1850 and 3 April 1852, the First Municipality Surveyor's Office made forty-seven payments amounting to $31,115.60 to the Pelanne Brothers. According to the 1858 city tax records, the Pelanne Brothers owned $62,500 in land, $650 in slaves, and $3,000 in capital (total of $66,150). Surveyor's Office, Journal of Expenditures, First Municipality, 24 June 1850-3 April 1852. New Orleans Public Library; 1858 New Orleans Tax Records, Second District, p. 181. New Orleans Public Library; Joseph Lanata v. Salvador Viosca, Fifth District Court (doc. no.—5,260) filed, 11 November 1851; City Council Proceedings of the Board of Aldermen, 12 May 1857. New Orleans Public Library; Contract between Wardens of St. Louis Cathedral and Pelanne Brothers, Joseph Cuvillier, public notary, 17 February 1854, vol. 61, no. 101; Copartnership Agreement, Joseph Lisbony, public notary, 10 July 1860, vol. 23, no. 219.

10. *New Orleans Daily Orleanian*, 1 July 1849; 19 January, 16 and 26 March, and 23 April 1851.

economically underdeveloped.[11] Although this district in 1850 contained 20 percent of the city's inhabitants, the Third Municipality had only 5.9% of the Crescent City's merchants and brokers. Since the 1850 census takers did not inquire into the personal wealth of local citizens, it is impossible to compare the economic status of merchants operating in the various districts. Fortunately, the 1860 census provides information on both the real and personal wealth of New Orleans residents. Between 1850 and 1860, the number of merchants in the Third Municipality jumped from ninety-two to one hundred and fifty-one. By 1860, this district was the home of 12% (instead of the 5.9% in 1850) of the merchants who lived in the original three districts which composed New Orleans before the 1852 consolidation with Lafayette (see Tables I and II). Despite this growth, the average Third Municipality merchant in 1860 was less affluent than his counterpart in the other districts of the city. The average Third Municipality merchant in 1860 owned $6,103 in real and personal wealth, as compared to his rival in the First District who owned $18,300. In sum, during the 1850 decade, the Third Municipality business community was increasing in number, but lacked the financial resources of its more prosperous competitors in other regions of the city. The lack of economic power hurt Third Municipality businessmen's chances of defeating the strong alliance of wealthy landlords and brothelkeepers.

Several reform and anti-reform petitions written during the period illustrate how merchants and other socio-economic groups in the

TABLE I

1,551 Merchants and Brokers in 1850 New Orleans*

	FIRST DISTRICT	SECOND DISTRICT	THIRD DISTRICT
Number	458	1,001	92
Average Real Estate Holding	$3,772	$3,407	$2,441

* After the 1852 consolidation, the Second Municipality became the First District. The First Municipality became the Second District. The Third Municipality was called the Third District. The city of Lafayette became the Fourth District.

Sources for Tables I-VIII are the 1850 United States Census and city directories for the 1850 decade.

11. See Manuscript Census Returns, Seventh Census of the United States, New Orleans, Orleans Parish, Louisiana, Free Schedules, National Archives Microfilm Series, M—432, rolls 235-8; See Manuscript Census Returns, Eighth Census of the United States, New Orleans, National Archives Microfilm Series, M—653, rolls 415-22.

TABLE II

1,567 Merchants and Brokers in 1860 New Orleans

	FIRST DISTRICT	SECOND DISTRICT	THIRD DISTRICT	FOURTH DISTRICT
Number	604	493	151	328
Average Real Estate Holding	$ 6,762	$ 7,466	$4,236	$10,313
Average Personal Estate	$11,538	$ 6,464	$1,867	$13,272
Average Total of Real and Personal Wealth	$18,300	$13,930	$6,103	$23,585

Third Municipality reacted to the issue of prostitution. In 1849, the Third Municipality Council received two petitions concerning harlotry.[12] Reform oriented citizens signed one of the petitions with the request that Recorder Peter Seuzeneau suppress bordellos and disreputable ballrooms, while pro-harlotry supporters signed the other document asking the police to continue their hands-off policy towards prostitution. Disenchanted with the negative image which harlotry gave their district and the myopic economic decisions of previous municipal councils which opposed public funding of railroad and levee projects, merchants and manufacturers assumed a prominent role among reform petitioners, hoping to create a more congenial environment for business expansion (see Tables III and IV). A minority of merchants supported prostitution. For the most part, they were individuals who sold liquor, oysters, and other goods to ballrooms and brothels. Unlike most Third Municipality merchants, they evinced little interest in expanding the cotton and sugar trade of their district.

Professional men added their names to those of merchants in signing the anti-harlotry document. According to medical authorities, prostitution was a major cause of the high incidence of venereal disease in this city. Some doctors feared that brothels along the Third Municipality waterfront spread yellow fever and cholera, since these bordellos attracted a large influx of transient sailors and riverboat

12. These two petitions were published in the *Daily Orleanian*, the official newspaper for the Third Municipality, but they, as almost all petitions, were not printed in the Third Municipality Resolution and Minute Books. *New Orleans Daily Orleanian*, 21 June and 6 July 1849.

TABLE III

1849 Third Municipal Petitions

OCCUPATION	ANTI-HARLOTRY		PRO-HARLOTRY	
1. Merchant	6	(6%)	3	(2%)
2. Manufacturer	3	(3%)	0	(0%)
3. Professional	11	(12%)	0	(0%)
4. Lawyer	1	(1%)	0	(0%)
5. Clerk	2	(2%)	0	(0%)
6. Ship or River Captain	7	(8%)	0	(0%)
7. Shipping Agent	2	(2%)	0	(0%)
8. Shopkeeper	6	(6%)	27	(21%)
9. Coffeehouse Keeper	4	(4%)	7	(6%)
10. Skilled Worker	13	(14%)	10	(8%)
11. Semi- or Unskilled Worker	4	(4%)	8	(6%)
12. Political Officeholder	6	(6%)	3	(2%)
13. Other	5	(5%)	14	(11%)
14. Unknown	25	(27%)	57	(44%)
	95	(100%)	129	(100%)

TABLE IV

1849 Third Municipality Petitions

WEALTH (1852 TAX RECORD)	ANTI-HARLOTRY		PRO-HARLOTRY	
1. $1-$500	4	(4%)	5	(4%)
2. $501-$1,000	6	(7%)	4	(3%)
3. $1,001-$2,000	4	(4%)	2	(1.5%)
4. $2,001-$5,000	5	(5%)	7	(5%)
5. $5,001-$10,000	5	(5%)	2	(1.5%)
6. $10,001-$25,000	3	(3%)	1	(1%)
7. Over $25,000	0	(0%)	2	(1.5%)
8. None	68	(72%)	106	(82%)
	95	(100%)	129	(100%)

workers who often carried diseases from other ports.[13] No evidence exists by which we can measure the impact of prostitution on mortal-

13. John Duffy, *The Sword of Pestilence: The New Orleans Yellow Fever Epidemic of 1853* (Baton Rouge, 1966): 103, 107, 127, 139, 162.

ity and morbidity rates, but a look at the coroner's records sheds light on the comparative mortality rates among the four districts in New Orleans. According to the coroner's records between January 1, 1852, and June 8, 1854, the Second District had the highest rate of deaths attributed to various fevers. The Second District had 2.83 deaths per thousand from cholera, yellow fever, and other fevers, while the Third District (Municipality) had the second highest rate of 1.85 deaths per thousand. The First and Fourth Districts had 1.4 and 1.1 deaths per thousand (see Table V). Besides having a high death rate due to fevers, the Third Municipality had the highest rates of deaths attributed to intemperance and drowning. Perhaps because of his concern over the ravage of disease and alcoholism among sailors, C. W. Whitall, an Episcopal minister, signed the 1849 anti-prostitution petition.[14] Later, he established a Seamen's Mission in order to rescue sailors from the moral and health hazards of local brothels.

Ship and riverboat captains put their signatures on the reform petition. As employers, they complained about the drunkenness and lazy habits which their laborers acquired in bordellos. They maintained

TABLE V

Mortality Rate Per Thousand
For New Orleans Between January 1, 1852 and June 8, 1854*

CAUSE OF DEATH	FIRST DISTRICT	SECOND DISTRICT	THIRD DISTRICT	FOURTH DISTRICT
Cholera	.8% (37)	1.22% (41)	.75% (15)	.31% (4)
Yellow Fever	.48% (22)	1.01% (34)	.3% (6)	.79% (10)
Typhus	.02% (1)	.12% (4)	.15% (3)	0.00% (0)
Other Fevers	.1% (5)	.48% (16)	.65% (13)	0.00% (0)
Total for Above Fevers	1.4% (65)	2.88% (95)	1.85% (37)	1.1% (14)
Intemperance	.9% (42)	.65% (22)	1.00% (20)	.32% (4)
Homicide	1.4% (65)	.72% (24)	.65% (13)	.32% (4)
Infanticide	.04% (2)	.09% (3)	.0% (4)	0.00% (0)
Drowned	1.35% (62)	1.52% (51)	3.62% (72)	.4% (5)

* Sources: New Orleans Coroner Records and the 1850 United States Census.

14. Another reason for C. W. Whitall's opposition to harlotry was that the Louisiana Ballroom operated near Reverend Whitall's Episcopal Church located at the corner of Esplanade and Victory streets. Ibid., pp. 78 and 81; *New Orleans Daily Orleanian*, 21 June and 19 July 1849.

that brothel and boarding house keepers who furnished rooms to sailors and deckhands were partially responsible for their workers' demand for higher wages and refusal to honor their labor contracts.[15] Stevedores, who employed longshoremen to load and discharge vessels, also complained about the negative influence of brothels on their workmen. Stevedores were displeased when their employees took periodic breaks without permission to visit brothels. Many bordello keepers earned handsome profits by selling liquor and other pleasures to levee workers.

In addition to ship captains and stevedores, many skilled workers advocated the suppression of bordellos. As family men and homeowners, artisans opposed the existence of brothels in their neighborhoods, because such illicit establishments reduced their property's value and threatened the moral fiber of their families. Both middle and working class families had good reason to fear the disrupting influence which prostitution had on their family life. An examination of 153 New Orleans divorce cases reveals that in twenty of these proceedings (13%) either a wife became a prostitute or a husband violated his marital vow by visiting a brothel.[16]

Shopkeepers represented the only group which overwhelmingly endorsed the pro-harlotry petition. Many of these retail operators sold food, clothing, jewelry, shoes, and other fancy goods to prostitutes. In contrast to the expansionary vision of cotton and sugar merchants, retail stores feared major economic alterations. Progressive changes would attract the powerful wholesale and retail firms in the First and Second Municipalities to move into the underdeveloped Third Municipality. The arrival of new competition threatened to destroy the existing small retail firms. According to reform critics, many retail stores survived because of Recorder Seuzeneau's laxity towards prostitution and theft.[17] Retail firms often depended on purchasing stolen goods from river and levee robbers who sold these items at ten to twenty percent of their market value. Sometimes, thieves had their headquarters in brothels where they received shelter and sanctuary in exchange for a percentage of their earnings. In their vituperation against shopkeepers and bordello managers for encouraging thieves to plun-

---

15. Patrick Meagher v. Spencer Field and Company, Third District Court (doc. no.—6,910) filed, 30 November 1854.

16. I randomly pulled these 153 divorce cases for the years between 1845 and 1860 from the Third, Fourth, Fifth and Sixth District Court Records, stored in the New Orleans Public Library.

17. *New Orleans Daily Orleanian*, 25 May 1850 and 14 May 1851.

der the Third Municipality's waterfront, merchants observed that the heavy incidence of river thefts induced ship captains to dock their vessels elsewhere in New Orleans.

The prostitution question caused a division among coffee house proprietors. With twenty-three hundred drinking establishments vying against each other for business, many New Orleans coffee houses employed prostitutes in order to entice male customers away from their competitors. In the Third Municipality, coffee house owners also lamented that they suffered under an inequitable tax system. From 1836 to 1851, coffee house and boarding room establishments paid over $362,000 in tax levies, but merchants contributed less than $23,000.[18] Already highly taxed and struggling in a competitive trade, many coffee house proprietors opposed reform plans of raising real estate taxes and suppressing prostitution.

A dissenting group of coffee house managers supported the reform drive. Coffee houses and cabarets, catering to families and "respectable" patrons, frowned upon the influx of harlots into their neighborhoods, because the close proximity of prostitutes induced customers to avoid their places of business. Unlike some coffee house managers who railed against the yearly two hundred dollar tax on all drinking houses, reform-oriented coffee house proprietors expressed concern that Recorder Seuzeneau was allowing many of their competitors to avoid paying this tax imposition. Perhaps, one motive why certain "respectable" coffee house groups joined the anti-harlotry movement lay in the hope that this campaign could eliminate their dishonest rivals by enforcing uniform tax measures on all drinking places.

Although public petitions reveal the social strata composing the anti-prostitution elements, such documents disclose limited insights into the occupational profile of pro-prostitution cliques. Lawyers, politicians, and landlords had economic ties to harlotry, but such groups tended to avoid any publicity about their convert working arrangements with brothel keepers. Obviously, these men had little to gain by attaching their signatures to public petitions. Through an analysis of a list of forty-five persons furnishing bail for bordello operators in the First District Criminal Court between 1846 and 1861, we can supplement our knowledge of the links between brothels and

---

18. According to the *Daily Orleanian*, coffeehouses and boarding houses paid $362,817.54 in municipal taxes between 1 June 1836 to 31 July 1851. During the same period, merchants paid only $22,815.94. Day Book of Receipts and Expenses of the Third Municipality, 11 May 1850 (pp. 93-96). New Orleans Public Library; *New Orleans Daily Orleanian*, 18 September 1851.

their hidden partners.[19] Although the cases appearing in the Criminal Court were sent from all areas of New Orleans, it is plausible to infer that the persons posting bail for brothel keepers in this court had similar occupational interests as those supporting harlotry in the Third Municipality.

Not unexpectedly, shopkeepers constituted the principal stratum which was most likely to sign the 1849 pro-harlotry petition (21%) and to put up bail for brothel keepers in the First District Court (22%). Coffee house managers were three times more apt to post bail for a brothel keeper (18%), than they were to endorse an open petition (6%). Bondsmen, moreover, included three stable keepers who operated carriage and cab companies to transport tourists and sailors to see the charms of New Orleans, including local bawdy houses. While no lawyer signed the pro-prostitution declaration, two attorneys acted as bondsmen on behalf of local brothel keepers in the criminal court. An inquiry into the job background of bondsmen appearing before the First Criminal Court underestimates the role of lawyers in protecting prostitution cliques. Newspaper stories suggest that attorneys were instrumental in defending and arranging bail for brothel managers in recorder courts where the majority of harlotry cases were handled.[20] In sum, a coalition of shopkeepers, coffee house proprietors, landlords, lawyers, stable owners, and brothel managers supported prostitution and the *economic status quo* against the "progressive" alliance of merchants, doctors, ministers, shipping interests, "respectable" coffee house owners, and skilled artisans who favored the abolition of prostitution and the construction of new railroads.

Candidates selected by the reformers during the 1850 and 1851 municipal elections were pledged to the tenets of the "Association for Good Government." This reform coalition called for the elimination of prostitution, improvements along the Third Municipality levee area, and railroad expansion.[21] James Phillips, an iron foundry owner,

---

19. I used New Orleans city directories and census returns to find the occupational background of these forty-five bail bondsmen. Of the ten of these bondsmen whose political affiliations are known, all belonged to the Democratic Party.

20. *New Orleans Daily Orleanian*, 7 February 1849 and 24 January 1852.

21. In the 1850s the Third Municipality was vying against the First and Second Municipalities to obtain the terminus and depot of the New Orleans, Jackson and Great Northern Railroad. B. F. Flanders, P. G. Collins, F. B. LeBeau, and other Third Municipality politicians and businessmen hoped that this railroad would be built along the Madisonville route and thus end in their district. They pointed out that the Jackson Railroad could save money by linking with the Pontchartrain Railroad which was already constructed. Third Municipality business leaders, moreover, labored on behalf of the New Orleans, Opelousas, and Great Western Railroad which had its terminus in Algiers, directly across the Mississippi River from the Third Municipality. The Opelou-

and three other signers of the 1849 anti-harlotry petition ran as candidates on the reform slate. Merchants and manufacturers exercised considerable influence among reform politicians, composing twenty-two percent of the reform candidates, while constituting only four percent of the non-reform officeseekers. (See Tables VI and VII). The reform ticket reflected a coalition of dissident Whigs and Democrats wishing to challenge the Democratic Party's hegemony over the Third Municipality.

Throughout the campaigns, F. B. LeBeau, the owner of the largest cotton press in this district, and W. C. C. Claiborne, a director of the Pontchartrain Railroad, denounced Recorder Seuzeneau for his protection of local brothels.[22] In the eyes of his detractors, Seuzeneau

TABLE VI

OCCUPATION	REFORM		ANTI-REFORM	
1. Merchant	5	(16%)	1	(2%)
2. Manufacturer	2	(6%)	1	(2%)
3. Professional	2	(6%)	2	(4%)
4. Lawyer	4	(13%)	12	(24%)
5. Clerk	0	(0%)	0	(0%)
6. Ship or River Captain	0	(0%)	0	(0%)
7. Shipping Agent	3	(9%)	0	(0%)
8. Shopkeeper	3	(9%)	1	(2%)
9. Coffeehouse Keeper	2	(6%)	2	(4%)
10. Skilled Worker	2	(6%)	4	(8%)
11. Semi- or Unskilled Worker	0	(0%)	1	(2%)
12. Political Officeholder	3	(9%)	14	(28%)
13. Other	4	(13%)	8	(16%)
14. Unknown	2	(7%)	4	(8%)
	32	(100%)	50	(100%)

sas Railroad hoped to link New Orleans with Western Louisiana and Texas. Third Municipality Council Resolution, passed on 20 December 1851, 1851 Third Municipality Resolution Book. New Orleans Public Library; *New Orleans Daily Orleanian*, 14 February, 1, 9, 15, 16, and 20 April, 1 May, 8 July 1851, and 2 January 1852.

22. As one of the leaders of economic expansion in this municipality, F. B. LeBeau had unsuccessfully tried to build a cotton factory in his home district. In 1850 and 1852 LeBeau along with other shareholders in the Pontchartrain Railroad bought $100,000 worth of stock in the Jackson Railroad in order to succeed in locating this railroad's terminus in the Third Municipality. *New Orleans Daily Orleanian*, 23 November 1849 and 18 April 1851; Sale of stock, Adolphe Mazureau, public notary, 31 October 1850, vol. 37, p. 600; Sale of Stock, Ibid., 14 December 1850, vol. 37, p. 770.

TABLE VII

1850-1851 Third Municipality Candidates—Wealth
(1852 Tax Records)

	REFORM	ANTI-REFORM
1. $1-$500	2 (6%)	6 (12%)
2. $501-$1,000	2 (6%)	4 (8%)
3. $1,001-$2,000	3 (9%)	6 (12%)
4. $2,001-$5,000	4 (13%)	6 (12%)
5. $5,001-$10,000	3 (9%)	5 (10%)
6. $10,001-$25,000	5 (16%)	0 (0%)
7. Over $25,000	1 (3%)	1 (2%)
8. None	12 (38%)	22 (44%)
	32 (100%)	50 (100%)

had perjured himself in the First District Court by falsely swearing that several infamous whores were respectable women. An alleged reason for Seuzeneau's leniency toward brothels was the charge that houses-of-ill-fame employed the relatives of many policemen serving under this Democratic officeholder. In addition, J. C. Prendergast, the reform editor of the *Daily Orleanian* argued that almost every Third Municipality brothel had a gambling table whose profits financed the election campaigns of Seuzeneau and fellow Democrats.[23] Hoping to shed a less jaundiced light on his tolerance towards prostitution, Seuzeneau commented in his campaign speeches that the license fees for brothels generated revenue for public schools and Charity Hospital.

As a prominent merchant and reform councilman who labored industriously for the construction of a railroad linking New Orleans to Texas, B. H. Payne challenged Seuzeneau's statement regarding the

23. During the 1849 and 1851 period, J. C. Prendergast used his journal to articulate ideas and goals of the Third Municipality anti-harlotry campaign. In a civil case in 1851, John McGinnis, editor of the *New Orleans True Delta* stated: "I look upon Mr. Prendergast as a very superior phenomenon in the management of a newspaper. I know him as a practical printer in all its details, as a writer and as a man capable of managing a newspaper Editorially and its operative department. I believe he has no superior; from my knowledge of the [newspaper] business I doubt if he has an equal for sobriety of habits and indefatigable industry. . . ." J. C. Prendergast v. P. O. Reilly, Third District Court (doc. no.—3,297) filed, 31 March 1851: J. C. Prendergast v. Patrick O'Reilly, *Ibid.* (doc. no.—3415) filed 16 January 1851; Paul Villars v. J. C. Prendergast, *Ibid.* (doc. no.—13,518) filed, 28 May 1859.

use of the ballroom fees for school funding.[24] This reform business leader stated that less than twenty percent of the funds collected under the ballroom tax went into the school treasurer. Moreover, he stressed that the Third Municipality schools did not need revenue collected from the ballrooms, since the state legislature allocated sufficient revenue to cover the operating costs of this district's schools. Throughout the 1840s, Payne and other merchants had been unsuccessful in their pleas to the Third Municipality Council for allocation of public funds for railroad construction and revitalization of the levee area which was languishing under the neglect of incompetent port officials.[25] It appears that during the 1850 and 1851 elections, merchants supported the anti-prostitution forces for two reasons—first, because they believed prostitution hurt the Third Municipality's economic growth, and secondly, because prostitution represented one of the few issues by which they might obtain a majority of the seats on the municipal council.

In appealing to the business community, reform spokesmen hammered away at the need to remodel the waterfront in order to increase the Third Municipality's trade. While describing the levee area, one reform editor wrote that "Heretofore, the wharves when the business season terminated were permitted to fall into decay—were never cared for or examined into; consequently nearly every season, new wharves had to be erected at an immense expense to the [Third] municipality."[26] Reform candidates promised to maintain the wharves year round in order to avoid the need of rebuilding these structures every year. Reform officeseekers, also, advocated the elimination of levee fees assessed on all cargo arriving in this district to encourage ship and steamboat captains to dock in the Third Municipality. Moreover, merchants were angry that under Seuzeneau's Democratic administration, they did not receive grain from the midwest markets, because Third Municipality port officials refused to set aside landing space for steamboats and flatboats carrying this trade to New Orleans.[27] To remedy this situation, reform politicians pledged that if elected, they would reserve three wharves for midwestern river vessels.

In contrast to the permissive Democratic Party policy towards har-

---

24. *New Orleans Louisiana Courier*, 12 December 1846; *New Orleans Daily Orleanian*, 6 and 20 June 1849; 8 March and 7 December 1850; and 2 April 1851.

25. *New Orleans Daily Orleanian*, 16 and 25 February, 23 March, 3 May, and 13 September 1850.

26. Ibid., 28 August 1850.

27. Ibid., 23 March 1850.

lotry, reform politicians promised to prosecute landlords guilty of renting to prostitutes and to impose heavy taxes on real estate speculators. A salient difference between reform and non-reform candidates was that twenty-five percent of the reform nominees owned property valued at $10,000 to $25,000, as compared to ten percent of the opposition (see Table VII). The property holdings of reform aspirants, however, were modest in contrast to the immense wealth of absentee landlords, like John McDonogh whose personal assets included sixteen hundred lots in the First and Third Municipalities.[28] McDonogh's habit of leasing to prostitutes combined with his policy of holding on to huge tracts of underdeveloped land in the Third Municipality irritated reform leaders who proposed new street and sidewalk taxes to compel McDonogh to sell his unused lots. Acting on the assumption that railroad improvements would increase their business opportunities and property values, reformers favored higher real estate taxes to finance railroad growth—a measure antithetical to the interests of McDonogh who preferred a low tax rate for expanding his real estate empire. In addition, reform candidates promised to compel McDonogh and other land speculators to pay one hundred percent of their taxes instead of allowing them to pay fifty percent or less of these levies as Democratic tax collectors had permitted.

Besides raising property taxes, reformers were eager to reduce unnecessary public spending. B. F. Flanders, a prominent supporter of the Opelousas and Great Western Railroad who tried unsuccessfully to persuade the Third Municipality Council to act favorably on the 1849 anti-harlotry petition and who in 1851 appeared as a witness against Salvador Viosca indicted in the criminal court for brothel keeping, led reformers in their demands for a reduction in the number of policemen, street commissioners, tax collectors, and other appointed officials.[29] A more streamlined municipal bureaucracy suited

28. According to one letter to the editor in the *Daily Orleanian* on 2 April 1851 ". . . the principal reason, in my opinion, why it is this [Third] municipality does not improve like the others. It is owing chiefly to lot or land speculators. A large portion of the lots is held on speculation; the owners will neither use, improve, or sell them. . . . Yet worse than all, these speculators pay neither State nor Municipal tax upon at least one-half of what they own. And why? Because it is not assessed; and even of what is assessed, there are portions from which no municipal tax is collected." This anonymous writer singled out John McDonough as a glaring example of a land speculator who avoided paying the bulk of taxes on his real estate holdings. *New Orleans Daily Delta*, 30 April, 2 May 1851; *New Orleans Daily Orleanian*, 2 April 1851.

29. In the 1851 trial against Salvador Viosca for brothel keeping, B. F. Flanders, F. B. LeBeau, J. C. Prendergast, P. G. Collins, B. H. Payne, and other Third Municipality reformers testified against Viosca. I checked the B. F. Flanders personal papers

reformers' needs, since they hoped to channel tax revenue into railroad and levee projects instead of funding a bloated police department which interfered too frequently in election contests. Reformers' policy of entrenchment also jeopardized the careers of many lawyers who joined the Democratic Party in hope of obtaining an elective or appointed position in the local government. Although three to four hundred attorneys resided in New Orleans, newspaper stories maintained that only thirty legal firms monopolized the trade, handling two-thirds of the legal work in the city. To make matters worse for Third Municipality attorneys, their district had the highest ratio of lawyers to merchants and brokers than any other area of town (1 lawyer: 4.5 merchants and brokers, as compared to the First and Second Municipalities which had 1:9 and 1:10 respectively.)[30] Moreover, the business community in the Third Municipality was too small and weak to provide adequate work for more than a few law firms. Suffering from a scarcity of private employment, it was no surprise that lawyers composed twenty-four percent of the anti-reform candidates in 1850 and 1851 who sought to defeat the reform platform with its demand of reducing the number of municipal jobs for lawyers and policemen.

Reform groups selected P. G. Collins to spearhead their 1850 election campaign for running against Recorder Seuzeneau. As one of the supporters of the 1849 anti-prostitution petition, Collins reflected the economic impetus behind the reform drive. He was a cotton pickery

---

at the Louisiana State University archives. Flanders' papers contain almost no material for the pre-Civil War Period. Flanders was a prominent governor in Louisiana during Reconstruction. State v. Salvador Viosca, First District Court (doc. no.—5,932) filed, 30 January 1851; *New Orleans Daily Orleanian*, 21 June 1849; 22 April and 13-16 May 1851, and 11 March 1852.

30. In both 1850 and 1860, the Third Municipality (District) had the highest ratios of lawyers to merchants and brokers. According to the 1850 Census, there were forty-five lawyers to 458 merchants and brokers (1:10) in the First District; 105 lawyers to 1001 merchants and brokers (1:9.5) in the Second District; and twenty lawyers to ninety-two merchants and brokers (1:4.5) in the Third District. According to the 1860 Census, the ratios of lawyers to merchants and brokers were: 1:5.9 in the First District; 1:8 in the Second District; 1:4.4 in the Third District; and 1:9.9 in the Fourth District. Despite the increase in the number of businessmen in the Third District over the 1850 decade from ninety-two to 151, the high ratio of lawyers to merchants remained the same (1:4.5 and 4.4). Many lawyers in the Third District probably contemplated moving to the American First District which was the fastest growing commerical area and the leading economic district in the city. However between 1850 and 1860, despite the increase of merchants in the First District from 458 to 604, while the number of merchants in the Second District shrank from 1,001 to 493, the ratio of lawyers to businessmen in the First District rose from 1:10 to 1:5.9. A higher ratio of lawyers to merchants in the First District made it harder for lawyers in the Second and Third District to find lucrative employment in this economically expanding district.

manager and a member of the Business Committee of the Jackson and Great Northern Railroad Company.[31] In his role as director of the Irish Union Immigrant Society, this Irish-born reformer was familiar with the exploitation of immigrant women by brothel keepers. Throughout the election contest, Collins accused Seuzeneau of being an arch supporter of prostitution and white slavery. Afraid of the effectiveness of his rival's verbal assaults, Seuzeneau on the election day of April 21, 1850, withdrew the police from the First Ward poll and bribed a mob composed of boarding house runners and ruffians dressed in red shirts from Gallatin Street brothels to stuff the ballot box with Democratic votes.[32] Not satisfied with stuffing the ballot box on election day, the Seuzeneau forces ordered a Democratic police lieutenant to lead a crowd in an attack on the reform *Daily Orleanian* which had published stories concerning the recent election day vandalism.[33]

Despite the extra-legal tactics by their opponents which deprived them from controlling the Third Municipality Council, reformers embarked on a two part program aimed at securing convictions against brothel managers in the criminal court and for preparing a new slate of candidates in 1851. Reform hopes received a boost in January, 1851 when Judge John C. Larue convicted three Third Municipality brothel keepers.[34] During the trials, Larue called for the dismissal of Recorder Seuzeneau because of his malfeasance and protection of bordellos. Rebuffing the defendants' argument that ballrooms should exist, since taxes levied on them supported Charity Hospital, Larue retorted angrily that "it were better that the bodies of a thousand men should perish than that the soul of one should be corrupted."[35]

Several months later, Recorder Seuzeneau shrewdly called Judge Larue's bluff by sending him several harlotry cases, including a brothel keeping charge filed by P. G. Collins and other reformers against Salvador Viosca.[36] When Larue had convicted the three bordello operators in January 1851 he had confronted three recently ar-

---

31. Francois Lacroix v. P. and L. Collins, Third District Court (doc. no.—3,857) filed, 7 October 1851; P. G. and L. E. Collins v. James P. Freret, Ibid. (doc. no.—5,286) filed, 26 March 1853; *New Orleans Daily Orleanian*, 6 June 1849; 13 April 1850; 13 Feburary and 8 March 1851; 14 March and 2 June 1852.

32. *New Orleans Daily Orleanian*, 23-27 April and 12 May 1850.

33. Ibid., 11-12 May 1850.

34. State v. H. Dirker, First District Court (doc. no.—5,929) filed, 31 January 1851; State v. Dink and [A] Hayse, Ibid. (doc. no.—5,930) filed, 31 January 1851.

35. *New Orleans True Delta*, 13 and 16 March 1851; *New Orleans Daily Orleanian*, 13 March 1851; *New Orleans Commercial Bulletin*, 28 February 1851.

36. Although filed on 30 January 1851, this case went to trial on 19 May 1851. Between 1845 and 1861 the judges and juries in the First District Court convicted few of

rived German immigrants who possessed no property and had few political connections. The Viosca case presented Larue with a more difficult task. The defendant was a wealthy Democrat with strong political affiliations. Since Larue had previously chastised Viosca for permitting slaves to visit his Globe Ball Room, reformers expressed optimism for a conviction of this Spanish-born resident. However, over reformers' objections, Larue dismissed the charge against Viosca with the unconvincing explanation that he had no law for convicting brothel keepers. He was unable to justify his previous conviction of the three German brothel operators, while dismissing the suit against Viosca. By refusing to try Viosca, Larue apparently allowed political expedience to outweigh philosophical consistency. Larue, an ambitious figure who became in 1856 president of the Orleans Parish Democratic Committee avoided alienating influential members of his party by not prosecuting Viosca.[37]

Despite political and legal reversals, the reform coalition captured control of the Third Municipality Council in the 1851 spring election. They immediately passed an ordinance prohibiting harlotry under a heavy fine, but their inept dealings with the police led to the nonenforcement of this law.[38] Although the reform council raised policemen's monthly salary from thirty to forty dollars, it demoralized the police force by reducing the sixty-four man department to thirty

---

the persons indicted for keeping a brothel. Of the sixty persons indicted for brothel keeping during these sixteen years, only eight (13%) were convicted. In dismissing the charges against Salvador Viosca, Judge Larue was repeating the usual method for processing brothel keepers. In forty-eight (80%) of the sixty cases, the case was filed with no further action taken or a judgement of *nolle prosequi* was entered for the accused. In the remaining four cases, juries found three persons innocent, and there was one mistrial. First District Docket Books, 1 January 1846 to 31 December 1861. State v. Salvador Viosca, First District Court (doc. no.—5,932) filed, 30 January 1851.

37. In lamenting Larue's decision to drop the charge against Viosca, J. C. Prendergast of the *Daily Orleanian* wrote: "No law for punishing brothel keepers!—It cannot be, and we advise the Judge [Larue] to scrutinize the codes more closely." *New Orleans Louisiana Courier*, 2 September 1856; *New Orleans Daily Orleanian*, 20 May 1851; *New Orleans Picayune*, 18 November 1856.

38. For the changes in handling prostitution between the Democratic and Reform Third Municipality Councils between 1847 and 1851, see the following resolutions and ordinances adopted by this body: "Ordinance Concerning Public Balls," Third Municipal Council Ordinance Book, 26 May 1847. New Orleans Public Library; Resolutions passed on 26 June, 10 July, 13 August, 21 September, 6 November, and 15 November 1847, 1847 Third Municipality Resolution Book; Resolutions passed on 20 January, 7 February, 20 April, and 31 May 1848, 1848 Third Municipality Resolution Book: Resolution passed on 20 April 1849, 1849 Third Municipality Resolution Book; Resolutions passed on 31 May, 26 September, and 26 November 1850, 1850 Third Municipality Resolution Book; Resolutions passed on 24 April and 19 June 1851, 1851 Third Municipality Resolution Book; *New Orleans Daily Orleanian*, 8 April, 14-16 May 1851.

officers. The reform program stalled, as disgruntled police officers refused to suppress brothels. Policemen preferred the bribes and gratuities of the bordellos to the financial frugality of the reformers.

III. NATIVISM AND PROSTITUTION

Hampered by police intransigence, the Third Municipality reform drive came to an abrupt halt in 1852 when the consolidation of the city transferred power from the three separate municipal bodies to a general council.[39] Many Third Municipality business reformers, drawn by the promises of railroad expansion and suppression of vice, joined merchants from other areas of town in shifting their allegiance to the Know-Nothing (Nativist) movement. Within the Know-Nothing ranks, merchants occupied the most dominant position, as they composed twenty percent of the Nativist candidates nominated between 1854 and 1856, compared to only six percent for labor. (See Table VIII). An unexpected crisis during this period was a major reason for the high level of mercantile participation in Know-Nothing politics. From August 1854 to July 1855 local journals noted that the low level of water in the Mississippi River severed trade between New Orleans and upper river cities. In February 1855 one editor exclaimed that "Nearly two thirds of the cotton crop has yet to be received at New Orleans and probably three-fourths to seven-eights of all Western produce has yet to come forward."[40] At the close of the 1854-1855 fiscal year, local financial observers revealed that the city's business community had suffered a seventeen million dollar (12%) decline in the receipts of southern and midwestern produce at New Orleans as compared to the 1852 period.[41]

The cessation of river trade in the 1854-1855 business year highlighted New Orleans's need to diversify its trade structure by building

---

39. Leon Cyprian Soule's account of the Know-Nothing ascendancy in New Orleans is perhaps the best current account of this movement. This paper agrees with many of Soule's points, but it differs in that Soule overlooked the economic reasons why the Know-Nothing merchants failed to implement their law and order program and neglected to focus on the ties between prostitution and working class Nativists. Leon Cyprian Soule, *The Know-Nothing Party in New Orleans: A Reappraisal* (Baton Rouge, 1961); W. D. Overdyke, *The Know-Nothing Party in the South* (Baton Rouge, 1950); Roger W. Shugg, *Origins of Class Struggle in Louisiana: A Social History of White Farmers and Laborers during Slavery and After, 1840-1875* (Baton Rouge, 1939); Robert C. Reinders, *End of an Era: New Orleans, 1850-1860* (New Orleans, 1964).

40. *New Orleans Daily Crescent*, 1 February and 16 April 1855; *New Orleans Picayune*, 7 January 1855.

41. *New Orleans Semi-Weekly Creole*, 5 May 1855; *New Orleans Picayune*, 6 September 1856; *Memphis Daily Appeal*, 27 February 1855.

railroads to tap midwestern and Texas markets. Nativist candidates capitalized on the depressed economic condition by soliciting votes with the promise of increased public funding for railroads. In line with this strategy, Know-Nothings selected J. W. Breedlove as their mayoral candidate, because he was a popular merchant and railroad supporter whose personal life was unblemished.[42] Nativist leaders selected Breedlove over A. D. Crossman, the incumbent Whig mayor, since they feared that Crossman's ties to brothels alienated respectable voters. Nativist newspapers were eager to use the prostitution issue as a weapon against Democratic officeseekers. A few days preceding the March 27, 1854, election, the *Picayune* espoused the Nativist demand for a purge against harlots.[43] Sensationalizing a recent incident in which a harlot had assaulted a respectable lady, this paper urged husbands to protect their female relatives by voting for the reform ticket.

Besides offering an effective weapon against Democratic rivals, the prostitution issue gave Know-Nothing leaders a means of achieving

TABLE VIII

1854-1856 Candidates—Occupations

	KNOW-NOTHING		DEMOCRATS	
1. Merchant	33	(20%)	14	(9%)
2. Manufacturer	4	(2%)	3	(2%)
3. Professional	15	(9%)	13	(8%)
4. Lawyer	27	(16%)	42	(26%)
5. Clerk	5	(3%)	5	(3%)
6. Ship or River Captain	0	(0%)	0	(0%)
7. Shipping Agent	3	(2%)	1	(1%)
8. Shopkeeper	14	(8%)	9	(5%)
9. Coffeehouse Keeper	1	(1%)	3	(2%)
10. Skilled Worker	11	(6%)	10	(6%)
11. Semi- or Unskilled Worker	0	(0%)	0	(0%)
12. Political Officeholder	23	(14%)	19	(12%)
13. Other	12	(7%)	13	(8%)
14. Unknown	20	(12%)	29	(18%)
	168	(100%)	161	(100%)

42. Leon C. Soule, *The Know-Nothing Party in New Orleans*, p. 53; *New Orleans Louisiana Courier*, 18 March 1854.
43. *New Orleans Picayune*, 25 March 1854.

intra-party unity between clashing mercantile and labor factions. By emphasizing the crack down on harlots, murderers, thieves, and other criminals, Nativist leaders apparently hoped that they could reduce the friction caused by disagreements between merchants and blue-collar groups over economic issues. Although composing the bulk of Nativist voters, laboring men feared the consequences of underrepresentation among their party's candidates and office holders. They were uneasy about the possibility that a merchant dominated city council might restrict its approval to bills favoring railroad and street improvements, while ignoring working class requests for improved fire and police protection, as well as larger water supplies.[44] In particular, labor leaders expressed concern that a merchant-oriented city council might increase real estate and occupational taxes on workers for defraying the expenses of railroad and street construction.

To solidify the bonds between labor and mercantile factions, Nativist party bosses proclaimed the benefits which a vice crusade could have for all the city's inhabitants regardless of their class position. According to Nativist spokesmen, the eradication of prostitution promised to make more housing available and to preserve the property value in decent residential areas.[45] Previously, brothel managers often had been able to outbid families for medium priced dwellings, a scarce commodity in a town where builders found it more profitable to construct either elegant homes for the rich or hovels for the poor. The presence of a brothel in a respectable neighborhood caused the value of surrounding houses to plummet by twenty-five to fifty percent.[46]

In an effort to placate a tax conscious electorate, Know-Nothing politicians implemented a program for reducing the costs of incarcerating prostitutes. Under former Whig and Democratic administrations, recorders had no regular policy for fining harlots. Reversing this trend, Nativist recorders imposed heavy fines on women convicted under the prostitution statute. As the leading Know-Nothing journal, the *Daily Crescent* published fines levied on harlots to demonstrate publicly that Nativist officeholders were fulfilling their campaign pledges. According to this newspaper's figures, recorders before the Nativist ascendancy had only extracted about $600 from prostitutes

---

44. Ibid., 19 March 1854 and 30 January 1855; *New Orleans Daily Delta*, 10 August 1854 and 10 June 1855; *New Orleans Daily Crescent*, 21 July 1856.

45. *New Orleans Picayune*, 3 and 14 May 1857 and 12 August 1858.

46. Ibid., 7 September 1856; *New Orleans Daily Crescent*, 4 November 1858 and 8 January 1859.

from January 1, 1851, to May 1, 1855, while Know-Nothing recorders collected $3,187 in fines during an equivalent period of time between May 1, 1855, and December 31, 1859.[47]

Nativist policemen exploited the racial fears and prejudices of white citizens who opposed miscegenation in local brothels. Congratulating police officers in December, 1855, for apprehending sixty-two slaves and free blacks for attending a soiree at the Globe Ballroom where whites were also present, the *Picayune* declared that "These balls where white and colored people indiscriminantly mix and mingle stand foremost among our city's curses."[48] From the journal's perspective, "unlawful assemblages of the character in question have long enjoyed a most unaccountable impunity in the Second and Third Districts, and it is high time that such degrading amalgamation should be prohibited by the law's strong arm."[49] During their tenure, Nativist watchmen enlisted public support by arresting Emeline Gibson and other free black madams noted for keeping brothels where the inmates ignored racial taboos.[50]

47. No city records exist by which we can confirm the accuracy of the *Daily Crescent*'s claim of increased fines against prostitution. In the Journals of Receipts and Expenditures between 1852 and 1860, money collected as fines was not broken down into various categories. Although having a slight majority in the city council in March 1854, the Nativists did not have complete control of the city council and the police until the spring of 1855. Through its control of the police, Know-Nothing recorders and aldermen increased the amount of criminal and civil fines and the amount of money collected under the ballroom tax. Significantly, Know-Nothings collected more revenue from fines and ballroom licenses, even though they reduced the police from five hundred to two hundred and fifty men. By licensing the ballrooms which prostitutes attended, the merchant-oriented Nativists increased city tax revenue between 1855 and 1857. By not licensing these establishments, the city would have lost tax dollars. (The data for 1852 is incomplete)

	BALLROOM TAX	FINES	TOTAL
1853	$1,150	$ 6,549	$ 7,699
1854	$1,520	$14,732	$15,852
1855	$8,645	$23,088	$31,733
1856	$5,685	$17,948	$23,633
1857	$7,035	$24,927	$31,962

Leon C. Soule, *The Know-Nothing Party in New Orleans*, p. 64; *New Orleans Picayune*, 8 March 1854; Treasurer, Journal of Receipts and Expenditures, 1852-1856; Ibid., 1856-1860. New Orleans Public Library.

48. *New Orleans Picayune*, 24 December 1855.

49. Ibid., 24-25 December 1855.

50. State v. Emeline Gibson, fwc, First District Court (doc. no.—5,136) filed, 4 June 1850; State v. Emeline Gibson, fwc, Ibid. (doc. no.—8,562) filed, 21 February 1852; State v. Emeline Gibson, fwc, Ibid. (doc. no.—12,398) filed, 10 June 1857; *New Orleans Daily Crescent*, 17 May 1855; *New Orleans Bee*, 17 May and 11 October 1855.

The police raids on poor and racially-mixed brothels represented a token effort by the police authorities to control prostitution. The city police lacked adequate manpower for suppressing prostitution. With a shortage of public revenue, the Nativist city council had to chose between economic and moral reforms, and the council resolved this dilemma by voting for increased funding of railroad projects, while refusing to increase the undersized police force.[51] In the spring of 1854, the city council decided to increase the operating capital of the Jackson Railroad from two to six million dollars. To cover the cost of this new railroad program, the Nativist council escalated the tax rate on real estate, small shops, and coffee houses. Besides passing these regressive tax measures, the council sidestepped demands for increasing taxes on merchants and banks with the explanation that such legislation created an unfavorable business climate. Despite paying a disproportionate share of the tax revenue, workers received few dollars from the city council for alleviating their long standing problems of an inadequate water supply, poor fire and police protection, exorbitant housing costs, and inflationary food prices.[52] Workers expressed more anger, after the merchant-dominated city council decreased public school funding and reduced the number of policemen from 500 to 250 under the guise of eliminating non-essential services.[53] The reduction of police personnel meant the police had even fewer men for monitoring prostitution activities and protecting blue-collar neighborhoods.

Several events occurred which led working-class Nativists to suspect that their merchant allies were more interested in economic than moral reforms. According to newspaper reports, Nativist policemen appointed by the merchant-controlled city council had extensive ties to the shadowy underworld of prostitution. In exchange for police

51. Instead of increasing the number of policemen as one would expect of a party elected on a law and order platform, Know-Nothing aldermen reduced the five hundred man police department under the Democratic rule to two hundred and fifty to three hundred men. Even with five hundred men, the police department still lacked adequate manpower for patrolling the city streets. With a department cut in half, police officers had even less chance to arrest criminals. In July 1855 the merchant-controlled Nativist city council reduced the amount of money allocated to public schools by lowering the amount of money the city provided for each pupil during a year from twenty to nineteen dollars. Treasurer, Journal of Receipts and Expenditures, 30 November 1854 (pp. 426-27); City Council Proceedings of the Board of Aldermen, 23 December 1856 (pp. 171-73); Ibid., 30 December 1856; Ibid., 28 October 1856; *New Orleans Picayune*, 8 March 1854; 8 July 1855; and 9 December 1855.

52. *New Orleans Picayune*, 25 December 1858; *New Orleans Daily Delta*, 10 August 1854; *New Orleans Daily Crescent*, 25 April 1855.

53. *New Orleans Picayune*, 9 December 1855; *New Orleans Daily Crescent*, 8 July 1855.

protection, bordellos furnished bribes to the higher echelons in the police department, while employing subordinate officers as private watchmen.[54] One police lieutenant scorned public opinion by openly consorting with an Irish prostitute.[55] More serious than the personal transgressions of policemen was the decision by Know-Nothing recorders not to enforce statutes against landlords guilty of leasing their property to ladies of questionable character. As a result of the corrupt practices of recorders and policemen, several small-scale riots occurred in which working and middle class homeowners destroyed houses of prostitution. In late August 1855, for example, the Apollo Street residents rose up *en masse* and forcibly evicted the inmates of Mary Charles' brothel.[56]

Fearing the spread of violence, the Nativist city council searched for a compromise to appease reform and prostitution groups. Aldermen refused to overhaul the police department for political and financial reasons. Incumbent aldermen depended upon police officers to solicit votes for them, often in ballrooms and brothels. Moreover, city council members opposed enlarging the police force to the point where officers could control prostitution activities because of the drain on city revenue which was needed to fund the merchants' pet railroad and street paving projects. While on the one hand constrained by the business community's tightfisted policy, Nativist aldermen on the other hand had to respect the wishes of wealthy landlords who leased their property to harlots. Working and middle class homeowners constituted a third interest group which demanded increased police protection and a suppression of brothels in their neighborhoods. Walking a tightrope between the competing factions, the city council adopted the Lorette Ordinance in 1857.[57] The new statute pleased businessmen by imposing heavy taxes on brothels, while the legislation promised middle-income residents the abolition of single-story bordellos in most city wards. City legislators extended the hand of peace to brothel owners by legalizing harlotry in multi-story buildings throughout the town.

Unhappy with the tax and zoning provisions in the Lorette Ordi-

54. *New Orleans Picayune*, 24 November and 6 December 1855.

55. *New Orleans Louisiana Courier*, 16 and 18 September 1857.

56. Mayor's Complaint Book, 10 and 15 July, and 2 August 1856. New Orleans Public Library; *New Orleans Bee*, 27-29 August 1855.

57. City Council Proceedings of the Board of Aldermen, 29 July, 14 November, and 6 December 1856; Ibid., 17 March 1857; "Ordinance Concerning Public Balls, Theatres, and Public Exhibitions," Ordinances of Common Council, 8 December 1856. New Orleans Public Library; "An Ordinance Concerning Lewd and Abandoned Women," Ibid., 10 March 1857.

nance, rich landlords challenged the legality of the new bill.[58] Landlords objected to the ordinance's tax clause requiring them to pay an annual levy of several hundred dollars on each brothel. Even more significantly, landlords of one-story dwellings were irate at losing their lucrative trade with prostitutes. Under the new law, they had to tear down the shanties which they previously rented to lewd women and build more expensive rental units for attracting middle class tenants. In erecting the new houses, landlords faced the prospect of paying higher property taxes and street paving fees.

Dissatisfied landlords jumped at the chance of testing the validity of the Lorette Ordinance in May 1857 when the police arrested sixty-two prostitutes for violating the recently passed statute. Prostitution landlords hired W. J. A. Roberts, A. G. Semmes, and A. P. Field as attorneys to defend their renters.[59] Among his arguments, Roberts alleged that the Lorette Ordinance violated a citizen's right to rent to whom he pleased and illegally voided contracts already in effect between a renter and his tenants. The Second District Court Judge, after hearing the case, ruled in favor of the harlotry groups by declaring the Lorette Ordinance unconstitutional.

Enjoying few benefits and bearing most of the costs of merchant sponsored legislation, Nativist labor groups withdrew from their partnership with businessmen.[60] Instead, they ironically joined prostitution factions to oust merchants from control in the Know-Nothing Party. In 1858, rebuffed by labor elements in his party, Charles Waterman, the incumbent mayor, along with hundreds of other businessmen bolted the Nativist organization and supported an independent ticket. A. G. Semmes, the well-known prostitution lawyer, acted as president of the Know-Nothing convention which nominated Gerald Stith, a printer, to oppose B. Beauregard, the choice of the Independents.[61] Successful in his bid for the mayor's seat, Stith repaid his political debts to prostitution supporters by appointing some of their members to the police force, especially those from the Third

58. State of Louisiana v. J. L. Fabre, Recorder of Second District of New Orleans and Officers, Justices of the Peace, Third District Court (doc. no.—9,823) filed, 27 June 1857; *New Orleans Bee*, 2 May 1857.

59. State of Louisiana in relation to Catherine Yager, Sophia Harper, and Augustine Lambert, Third District Court (doc. no.—14,185) filed, 7 December 1859; Miguel Valory v. City of New Orleans, Fifth District Court (doc. no.—10,788) filed, 23 February 1856; *New Orleans Louisiana Courier*, 8 October 1857 and 5 August 1860; *New Orleans Bee*, 19 November 1855 and 6 June 1859; *New Orleans True Delta*, 27 October 1859 and 20 April 1860.

60. Leon C. Soule, *The Know-Nothing Party in New Orleans*, pp. 93-94.

61. Semmes and Hill v. Matilda Phillips, Fifth District Court (doc. no.—11,989) filed, 4 December 1857; *New Orleans Bee*, 25-28 May 1857 and 25 May 1858.

Municipality—Antoine Cambre, a signer of the 1849 proharlotry petition and manager of the Louisiana Ballroom, Benjamin Leggett, a prominent brothel manager, and St. John Ducoing, the police lieutenant who led the mob assault on the *Daily Orleanian* in 1850.[62] The employment of such prominent brothel supporters suggests the important role which the Third Municipality bawdy houses had in electing Stith's labor ticket. After a decade of struggle, antiprostitution forces found that they had achieved few significant victories over their foes when Stith appointed well known prostitution men to the police force and adopted a lenient policy towards this vice.[63]

CONCLUSION

The failure of Third Municipality and later Know-Nothing reformers highlights the political and class barriers permitting prostitution to thrive despite its opponents' efforts. Police intransigence and an unexpected city consolidation thwarted the Third Municipality reform drive. Although serving only a brief tenure, Third Municipality councilmen pursued a strategy copied by succeeding Nativist mercantile leaders. In the 1850-1851 period, Third Municipality reformers reduced unnecessary spending and slashed the number of public employees, while funneling most of the tax revenue into levee and railroad projects.

By reducing the police force in half, reform aldermen denied police officials an adequate number of men for suppressing prostitution. Fortunately for the Third Municipality reform coalition, their reign in office was too brief for most voters to realize that they had funded economic improvements at the expense of moral reform.

Having a longer tenure in power, Nativist aldermen after 1852 were unable to hide their political priorities. Like their Third Municipality predecessors, they slashed the number of municipal employees and

62. According to Leon C. Soule, the American Party's victory on 7 June 1858 depended upon their success in the Third Municipality (District). Soule writes: "The American party again carried the third district. It was said that the Know-Nothings sent vagabonds claiming to be Irish and German citizens into the back precincts 'to lie, bully, and intimidate voters.' The district had been 'overawed' in the election. Had the Independents carried it, they probably would have won the election." Leon C. Soule, *The Know-Nothing Party in New Orleans*, pp. 102-3; *New Orleans Louisiana Courier*, 28 May 1852 and 19 June 1860; *New Orleans Bee*, 1 July 1858, 15 March, 24 December 1859, and 12 June 1860; *New Orleans Daily Orleanian*, 20 January 1852; *New Orleans Daily Crescent*, 26 May 1852; *New Orleans Daily Delta*, 7 January 1857.

63. During the 1858 New Orleans Nativist Convention, A. G. Semmes and his followers nominated J. L. Fabre to run as this party's candidate for the recordership of the Second District. Fabre in 1850 subleased part of Salvador Viosca's Whitehall Establishment. *New Orleans Bee*, 27 September and 1 October 1859.

policemen in hope of providing more revenue for an expanded railroad system. Unlike Third Municipality reform aldermen who served in office for about a year, Know-Nothing merchants held the reins to the city government between 1854 and 1858. At the end of these four years, enough voters perceived that in distributing the limited city dollars, merchant aldermen allocated business community's railroad and street paving plans, but ignored most middle and working class requests. By reducing the city police force from five hundred to two hundred and fifty, the city council removed any chance that the police could control harlotry.

Finding their alliance unsatisfactory, Nativist labor groups in 1858 dissolved their partnership with Mayor Charles Waterman and his business supporters. They formed a new alliance with prostitution cliques. By aligning with brothel keepers and landlords, working-class Nativists relinquished any hope of expelling bordellos from decent neighborhoods. The new coalition, however, allowed labor leaders to obtain control of the mayoral and city council seats. The labor dominated general council did not respond favorably to merchants' request for increased subsidies to railroads.[64] Moreover, labor-oriented aldermen reduced occupational and real estate taxes. By doubling the police force to five hundred men, the city council furnished more watchmen to protect blue-collar areas which had received little protection under Mayor Waterman's rule.

The retrenchment policies of Nativist labor politicians against merchant economic reforms was rooted in working men's belief that such changes were inimical to their needs. Blue-collar groups had to choose between the new economic order emphasizing railroad growth or the old economy characterized by low property taxes and dependency on the river trade. Labor leaders were not antirailroad *per se*, but they refused to bear the brunt of the taxation for financing railroad expansion. Moreover, laboring men felt that they might enjoy few of the benefits and most of the disadvantages of railroad expansion which inflated property taxes. Workers experienced a hundred percent increase in their rents during the 1850s when landlords passed on increased costs to their tenants.[65] In addition, skilled craftsmen had

---

64. In fact, Mayor Stith and other labor members of the New Orleans Board of Tax Supervisors reduced the amount of city dollars flowing into public financing of railroad growth by reducing real estate taxes which was the main source of tax revenue for railroad growth. Stith and his blue-collar companions did not change the tax rate on real estate, but reduced the assessed values on large tracts of urban real estate. *New Orleans Picayune*, 16 July 1858.

65. *New Orleans Daily Crescent*, 31 January 1856.

no guarantee that they would benefit from new jobs created by railroads and industrialization. Local employers often imported northern artisans to fill these positions. During the 1860 spring, fifty carpenters went on strike against the New Orleans Jackson Railroad Depot to protest the replacement of southern employees by northern workers.[66] Preferring the security and low tax rates of the old river oriented economy, Nativist laborers and brothel keepers cast their ballots for Gerald Stith who rewarded his prostitution supporters by adopting a soft line towards this vice, while pleasing white workers by expelling hundreds of out-of-state free black laborers who were illegally residing in New Orleans.[67]

66. Ibid., 10 March and 12 July 1860.

67. In 1858, Mayor Stith apparently ordered his police to increase the number of arrests of out-of-state free blacks illegally residing in New Orleans. Between 1 November 1853 and 30 June 1856, the police arrested 8.5 black men and two free black women per month. In 1857, these figures remained stable, as nine free black males and 2.1 free black females were apprehended for this offense. By 1858, the monthly average jumped to 21.4 and five arrests for free black males and females respectively. (These arrest figures were published monthly in the *New Orleans Daily Crescent.*) *New Orleans Bee*, 27 September and 1 October 1859.

Joel Best

Careers in Brothel Prostitution: St. Paul, 1865–1883

According to the 1870 manuscript census of St. Paul, Minnesota, Mary E. Robinson kept a house of ill fame. Her household contained ten prostitutes, two female servants, and one male servant. Robinson was a forty-four-year-old widow, with $2,000 in personal property and $75,000 in real property. Her brothel at 18 W. Eighth Street was notorious:

> . . . the leading and, so to speak, the fashionable resort for men of easy virtue, and the abiding place of the more select among the "soiled doves" of the city. . . . The reputation of the establishment has extended far and wide, and its existence was well known to every citizen of St. Paul.

In addition to her brothel, Robinson owned her personal residence next door, as well as other property throughout the city. In 1874, after operating her brothel for over eight years and accumulating over eighty arrests on charges of keeping a house of ill fame, she announced her retirement and sold the brothel's contents at public auction. "A woman of more than ordinary ability," she remained in the city, actively pursuing her real estate interests.[1]

Robinson appears to fit one of the stock roles in the history of Victorian prostitution: the shrewd madam who saved her earnings, invested wisely, and retired to a life of comfort. Few women took this career path, but authorities disagree over whether the typical prostitute died in misery or returned to respectability. Sanger, drawing on his pre-Civil War survey of 2,000 New York prostitutes, argued that women entered prostitution in fashionable brothels and proceeded through a series of progressively shabbier

Joel Best is Professor of Sociology at California State University, Fresno.

An earlier version of this article was presented at the 1980 meeting of the Society for the Study of Social Problems. The article has benefited from the comments of B. R. Burg, Barbara S. Heyl, David F. Luckenbill, and John Modell.

0022-1953/82/040597-23 $02.50/0

1 *St. Paul Pioneer*, Nov. 11, 1869; May 13, 23, 1874; *St. Paul Pioneer Press*, Oct. 6, 1875; Feb. 14, 1877.

establishments, dying, on the average, within four years. Finnegan's recent study of York streetwalkers supports Sanger; she concludes that women entered prostitution because they were poor and that they found drink, disease, and destitution, rather than opportunities for improvement. This model, also advanced by Victorian moralists, holds that prostitutes' lives inevitably led to misery and death. In contrast, Acton, Victorian England's leading authority on vice, believed that most prostitutes "return sooner or later to a more or less regular course of life." Similarly, Walkowtiz and Walkowitz suggest that in south England "prostitution was . . . a part-time or seasonal activity, or a stage in their lives that they would pass through." In this model, women drifted into and out of prostitution according to their circumstances, many eventually leaving vice for respectable employment or marriage. Although the majority of prostitutes remained poor, they were not doomed to special misery and a few even were upwardly mobile.[2]

The sociological concept of the deviant career can clarify the issues in this debate. Becker, in an influential essay, defined career as "the sequence of movements from one position to another in an occupational system made by any individual who works in that system." Adapting the concept for the study of deviance, Becker outlined four stages in the deviant career: committing a deviant act; acquiring a deviant perspective; being caught and labeled; and joining a deviant group. Becker's essay became the standard statement of the interactionist or labeling theory of deviance, but other sociologists, Sagarin among them, have criticized his description of the deviant career for being overly rigid. Lemert notes that, whereas respectable bureaucracies structure the careers of their members, deviants are faced with more options. In short, career patterns can vary within a deviant group; although some individuals may take common pathways into, through, and out of deviance, others may blaze new trails. The single-minded models of prostitutes' careers ignore the options open to the

2 William W. Sanger, *The History of Prostitution* (New York, 1972; orig. pub. 1858); Frances Finnegan, *Poverty and Prostitution* (Cambridge, 1979); William Acton, *Prostitution* (New York, 1968, orig. pub. 1870), 72; Judith R. Walkowitz and Daniel J. Walkowitz, "'We Are Not Beasts of the Field,'" in Mary Hartman and Lois Banner (eds.), *Clio's Consciousness Raised* (New York, 1974), 193. Cf. Ruth Rosen, "Introduction," in Rosen and Sue Davidson (eds.), *The Maimie Papers* (Old Westbury, N.Y., 1977), xi–xliv.

women. In nineteenth-century St. Paul, the deviant careers of the women engaged in brothel prostitution followed diverse routes.[3]

Studies of prostitution in late nineteenth-century America have three principal limitations: they often focus on cities with large, notorious vice districts, e.g., San Francisco or New Orleans; they lean heavily on anecdotal accounts about elite brothels; and they frequently derive the bulk of their information from a single source, e.g., one manuscript census, thereby making the analysis static. As a consequence, they cannot describe typical career patterns in prostitution.[4]

This article attempts to circumvent these limitations. It examines brothel prostitution in St. Paul over nearly twenty years, from 1865 to 1883. As a river city, St. Paul had a regional reputation for vice, but its "under the hill" district was far smaller than the Barbary Coast or Storyville. The city grew rapidly during this period, from 10,401 in the 1860 federal census to 41,473 in 1880, but the sex ratio was nearly balanced (49.5 percent of the population was female in 1870). There was no severe shortage of women to inflate the demand for prostitution. In contrast to the famous vice districts in major seaports and on the frontier, prostitution existed on a modest scale in St. Paul. In this respect, it was typical of many other cities. St. Paul's prostitutes made career choices—to enter or leave vice, to move from brothel to brothel and city to city, and between the statuses of madam and prostitute—which were available to prostitutes elsewhere. The picture which emerges is one of women in motion, choosing among the

3 Howard S. Becker, *Outsiders* (New York, 1963), 24–39; Edward Sagarin, *Deviants and Deviance* (New York, 1975), 137–138; Edwin M. Lemert, *Human Deviance, Social Problems, and Social Control* (Englewood Cliffs, 1967), 51. For introductions to interactionist studies of deviance and sociological writings about careers, see Earl Rubington and Martin S. Weinberg (eds.), *Deviance* (New York, 1978; 3rd ed.); Barney G. Glaser (ed.), *Organizational Careers* (Chicago, 1968). Paula Petrik, "Prostitution in Helena, Montana, 1865–1900," *Montana*, XXXI (1981), 28–41; Neil Larry Shumsky and Larry M. Springer, "San Francisco's Zone of Prostitution, 1880–1934," *Journal of Historical Geography*, VII (1981), 71–89; Al Rose, *Storyville, New Orleans* (University, Ala., 1974).

4 See for example, Curt Gentry, *The Madams of San Francisco* (New York, 1964); Marion S. Goldman, "Sexual Commerce on the Comstock Lode," *Nevada Historical Society Quarterly, XXI* (1978), 98–129; Lucie Cheng Hirata, "Free, Indentured, Enslaved: Chinese Prostitutes in Nineteenth-Century America," *Signs, V* (1979), 3–29; Carol Leonard and Isidor Wallimann, "Prostitution and Changing Morality in the Frontier Cattle Towns of Kansas," *Kansas History*, II (1979), 34–53.

available career paths, within the confines posed by the community's economy and morality and the underworld's structure.[5]

MADAMS, BROTHELS, AND INMATES Prostitution in St. Paul was not restricted to the city's brothels. Some prostitutes claimed that they were legitimately employed, often in the needle trades. In the 1880 census, the two young women living with George and Sarah Kimball—a notorious couple with a long history of arrests for managing brothels—listed themselves as dressmakers. This alibi was common enough that the city's leading newspaper sometimes used "plain sewing" as a euphemism for prostitution. Cigar stores provided another common cover for vice: "In front of the dirty little shanties, a beggarly display of cigars and fruits is made while behind is a sitting room containing some gay furniture and a wheezy organ, or jingling piano is found, while several asthmetic [*sic*] painted females are prepared to sing or play cards." Although "sewing girls" and "cigar stores" existed, brothels housed the major portion of the city's prostitutes. A physician, lecturing about venereal disease in 1874, estimated "that there were six regular houses in St. Paul with thirty-six inmates, and six irregular ones, such as cigar stores, with nine inmates who have rooms by themselves, and from forty to fifty 'kept women.'" Three years later, there were eight brothels with fewer than fifty inmates, but reformers argued that "there are in the city several hundreds of prostitutes, who are working an inexplicable evil." This vague figure probably exaggerated the proportion of prostitutes outside the brothels. In 1883, Mayor Christopher D. O'Brien stated that the city had twelve regular brothels with sixty-four inmates, nine other houses with three to six inmates each, and "the usual number of the lower grades of disreputable women. . . ." Brothels played the most prominent role in St. Paul's demimonde because city politics let them operate openly.[6]

Although St. Paul lacked a formally designated vice district, most brothels were concentrated in two areas. Downtown they clustered along and near four blocks of Fifth Street, running from

5 Philip D. Jordan, *Frontier Law and Order* (Lincoln, Nebraska, 1970), 126–131; *idem*, *The People's Health* (St. Paul, 1953), 243–252; Frank J. Mead and Alix J. Muller, *History of the Police and Fire Departments of the Twin Cities* (Minneapolis, 1899).

6 *Pioneer*, July 24, 1870; Mar. 10, 1874; *Pioneer Press*, Jan. 21, 1878; Aug. 9, 1883; *Minneapolis Tribune*, Dec. 23, 1874.

Cedar to Silbey. The establishments "under the hill" were on or near Eagle Street, a few blocks southwest of downtown. Both neighborhoods offered other forms of vice; in addition to brothels and "cigar stores," they contained notorious saloons, gambling "hells," and assignation houses. Public drunkenness and fights were commonplace. By 1882, the district "under the hill" was patrolled by a special officer as well as a regular patrolman. Not all brothels were in the vice districts; Robinson's house was located about two blocks north of the downtown area and other houses were on the outskirts of the city.[7]

From 1865 to 1883, St. Paul's city government adopted a *de facto* system for regulating prostitution within the city. Prostitution was illegal under both state law and city ordinance, but enforcement took the form of arresting each of the city's madams at monthly intervals and fining them according to the number of inmates in their houses—in effect, taxing their operations. This system was openly acknowledged by city officials and the newspapers often covered the madams' courtroom appearances. As a consequence, Robinson and her colleagues were familiar figures. There was no need to keep the brothels secret. At the same time, the police and courts prohibited streetwalking, levying heavy fines or jail sentences against independent prostitutes whose activities were visible to the public.[8]

The system of regulation distinguished between madams and the inmates who worked in their brothels. After 1867, madams before the police court (later the municipal court) were charged with keeping a house of ill fame, whereas inmates ordinarily faced charges of visiting a house of ill fame. Although the same charge, violating ordinance No. 10, was made against both categories of women before 1868, the fines were different; madams paid from $15 to over $100, prostitutes only $10. Madams also were distinguished by their regular, monthly appearances in the city's courtrooms, where they were charged and fined. On some occasions, the inmates appeared in court with their madam, sometimes being charged separately, but often as a "family." The inmates' appearance was required; brothels were charged a fixed fee plus an additional sum for each inmate. Typically, a madam was fined

7 *Pioneer Press*, July 24, 1882.

8 *Pioneer*, Apr. 22; July 30, 1870; June 13, 1872; Feb. 4, 1874; *Pioneer Press*, Jan. 11, 21, 1878.

$25 plus $10 per prostitute. In other months, the madam appeared in court unaccompanied, paying a single, larger sum, which sometimes took into account the number of prostitutes in her house. Regardless of the system of fines adopted by the court in a given month, the madam apparently paid all of the fines for her brothel.[9]

As a consequence of this policy, madams can be identified by their regular appearances in the court records. If a madam is defined as a person who was, on at least three occasions during one calendar year, either charged with keeping a house of ill fame or charged with violating ordinance No. 10 and fined more than

9 Sources for court records vary over the period: irregular reports of the city justice and the chief of police appeared in *Proceedings of the St. Paul City Council*, 1866–1870; a manuscript ledger of arrests (hereafter arrest ledger), located in the office of the St. Paul Chief of Police, 1869–1870, 1872–1874; official minutes of the city council, published periodically in the *St. Paul Press*, 1871–1872; the criminal dockets, St. Paul Municipal Court (Ramsey County Records Center, section 6, shelf 4, vol. A–Z), 1875–1883. For two gaps in these sources—June, 1870 through June 1871, and Nov., 1874 through Apr., 1875—mention of specific arrests in the *St. Paul Pioneer* served to compile a partial record.

These different policies produced records of varying detail, particularly in the arrest ledger. On some of the occasions when both madams and prostitutes were charged, the names of the inmates in each brothel were listed beneath the madam's name, giving a *structured record*:

Madam 1	Prostitute 4
Prostitute 1	Prostitute 5
Prostitute 2	Prostitute 6
Prostitute 3	etc.
Madam 2	

On other months, both categories of names were listed, but the women in each category were grouped together, producing a *categorical record*:

Madam 1	Prostitute 2
Madam 2	Prostitute 3
Madam 3	etc.
Prostitute 1	

But during most months, the prostitutes were not charged individually, and only the madams appeared in *primary records*:

Madam 1
Madam 2
Madam 3
etc.

Since primary records appear in the vast majority of months under examination, more is known about the madams than about their inmates. For a detailed account of one court session where a structured record was produced, see *Pioneer*, Apr. 22, 1870; for sessions producing primary records, see *Pioneer Press*, Apr. 7; June 2, 1881; Jan. 3, 1883.

$10, then forty madams can be identified between November, 1865 and May, 1883. Demographic information is available for nineteenth of these women. Thirteen reported being born in the United States; one each was born in England, Scotland, Ireland, Germany, and Sweden, and one madam's birthplace was not given. Nine reported being single, seven said that they were married, and there was no information about three. Of the women who reported being married, at least two lived with their husbands in the brothel; one husband, George Kimball, and not his wife Sarah, sometimes faced charges of keeping a house of ill fame. Unlike the stereotypical middle-aged madam, the women were young; age at first known arrest as a madam ranged from twenty to forty, with a median of only twenty-six. Similarly, the age at the last known arrest as a madam ranged from twenty-two to forty-eight, with a median of twenty-eight. The madams were mostly native-born, single, and in their twenties.

The forty madams accumulated 1,029 arrests for prostitution, including arrests as madams, brothel inmates, and independent prostitutes. The number of known arrests per woman ranged from 3 to 109, with a median of 15.5 (and a mean of 25.7). Sarah Kimball and her husband George had only seventeen arrests, but they spanned a sixteen-year period, 1866–1881. This spotty record may reflect their location well away from downtown and the police. Then, too, the Kimballs may have drifted in and out of brothel-keeping; in various city directories, George was listed as a painter, glass stainer, and laborer, while Sarah was once recorded as doing washing and ironing. Kate Hutton's career was nearly as long (1867–1881) and more consistent, with 109 arrests over almost fifteen years. Annie Oleson had the most consecutive arrests; she was charged in sixty-two of the sixty-three months from May, 1875 to July, 1880. Although her record is exceptional, twenty-one madams had at least ten arrests in one twelve-month period. The city's records, although incomplete, reveal considerable stability in the madams' careers.[10]

10 Demographic information was drawn from the manuscript census schedules for the federal censuses of 1860, 1870, and 1880, and the state census of 1875, in the cases of nine madams. Three others were described in the register of prostitutes kept at the back of the arrest ledger. Where the women could not be located in either the census schedules or the register, information was taken from the arrests recorded in the ledger proper (for the remaining seven cases). When madams appeared in more than one of these sources, the

The brothels themselves displayed even greater stability. Addresses are known for thirty-two of the madams. Often, one madam succeeded another in managing the same brothel; altogether, the forty women operated twenty houses. Thirteen establishments had a single madam; Robinson, who ran her brothel for over eight years, had the longest tenure. At the other extreme, the "Lookout," at 1 Jackson Street, operated for ten years under eight madams. One brothel was especially stable: it operated at 94 Washington Street from 1865 to 1883 under the management of four madams; when the original house burned down in 1876, another was built on the lot within a year. The number of brothels in operation rose steadily throughout most of the period, as did the city's population. Five were in operation in 1866, seven in 1870, ten in 1874, and thirteen the following year, dropping to ten in 1878 before reaching fourteen in 1880.[11]

Brothels displayed different patterns of operation. Several moved from one building to another.[12] When Lou Adams registered with the police in September, 1873, she gave her address as 14 Washington Street, "under the hill" near several other brothels. Six months later, she had moved to 11 Nash Street—located in a respectable neighborhood—but neighbors' complaints drove her out. By the end of 1874, her brothel was located downtown, near Cedar and Third, her third address in sixteen months. Some madams bought their buildings and rented them to their successors. Kate Hutton bought the house at 7 Hill Street in 1869 and

---

information frequently differed from one source to the next. In such cases, the census was taken as the most reliable source, with the register second, on the grounds that details about the women were more likely to be recorded accurately on these occasions than in routine appearances before the police or municipal court.

11 Many of the madams had other arrests, particularly for drunkenness or disorderly conduct. The women's activities were considered newsworthy; 37 of the 40 appeared in newspaper articles and some, such as Robinson, were the subjects of dozens of stories.

12 Addresses were gathered from St. Paul city directories, 1865–1884, the register of prostitutes kept at the back of the arrest ledger, and newspaper articles. Twenty-eight of the madams appeared in city directories during years when they operated brothels (the directories usually gave no occupation for the women); 4 madams were located through other sources. The process was complicated by St. Paul's irregular method for numbering houses and by the decision to renumber buildings in the middle of the period studied. Sanborn's St. Paul insurance atlases for 1875 and 1885 were used to locate buildings and determine when a house had been renumbered. Although the precise addresses of the remaining 8 madams are not known, at least 3 ran houses "under the hill." These figures include all 40 madams, treating those without known addresses as having their own firms. A firm was presumed to be in operation throughout the period from first to last known arrests, unless there was evidence to the contrary.

ran the establishment until 1875. She left to live with her lover and Maggie Morse took over for a year, presumably paying rent to Hutton. When the latter returned, Morse moved into the rebuilt house at 94 Washington Street, establishing one of the "finest" brothels in the city. By 1879, she was in turn renting her building to Jennie Bateson. In two cases, brothels merged: Florence Campbell ran the brothel at 93 Eagle Street from 1870 to 1877, and during the latter part of this period, Hattie McBride operated a "cigar store" at 71 Robert Street. When Campbell became ill McBride moved to take over the Eagle Street house.[13]

Although St. Paul's madams and their brothels remain visible in historical records, less can be determined about the brothels' inmates. Besides the madams, several hundred other people were arrested on prostitution charges between 1865 and 1883, including madams of minor, short-lived establishments, brothel inmates, independent prostitutes, pimps, servants, and customers. Unfortunately, it is frequently impossible to determine the category in which an individual belongs. In particular, since visiting a house of ill fame was an all-purpose prostitution charge, brothel inmates cannot be distinguished from independent prostitutes or those in "cigar stores." Positive identification of brothel inmates is only possible in two sources: structured arrest records, where prostitutes were listed beneath their respective madams, and manuscript census schedules. The most detailed series of structured arrest records appeared in the arrest ledger between April and October, 1873; sixty-one prostitutes were listed as brothel inmates during these months. Inmates from six brothels appeared in census schedules; three brothels in 1870, two in 1880, and one in the state census of 1875 contained a total of thirty inmates. Two women appeared in both the structured records and a census schedule to bring the total to eighty-nine inmates identified from both sources.

Demographically, the inmates resembled the madams.[14] Their ages ranged from sixteen to thirty, with a median of

13 Arrest ledger; *Pioneer*, Nov. 7, 1869; Mar. 10–14; Dec. 2, 1874; *Pioneer Press*, Aug. 24, 1876; Nov. 14, 1877; Jan. 21, 1878; Feb. 4, 1880.

14 Where information about a prostitute appeared in two sources, the rules described in footnote 10 were followed: census data were considered most reliable, followed in order by the listing in the arrest ledger's register, and information recorded under an arrest. There was one exception: since the arrest ledger's register recorded the woman's age when she first arrived in the city, arrest records were taken as the more reliable measure of the ages of women working in the brothels.

twenty-two; twenty-three were under twenty-one, fifty-one were between twenty-one and twenty-five, and ten were over twenty-five (ages were unrecorded for five women). Of the fifty-six for whom marital status is known, fifty-five were single. Over three fourths were native-born: United States—sixty-seven; Canada, Ireland, and Sweden—three each; Germany—two; England, France, and Italy—one each; with eight unknown. Census schedules gave the state of birth for twenty-four native-born women; eighteen of these (75 percent) came from only five states—Minnesota, New York, Wisconsin, Illinois, and Pennsylvania. (The same states accounted for 79 percent of the native-born residents in the 1880 federal census of the city.) Compared to their madams, brothel inmates were slightly younger, somewhat less likely to be married, but about equally likely to have been born in the United States. If geographical and cultural differences are taken into account, this pattern resembles those found in other studies of nineteenth-century prostitues.[15]

Brothels fluctuated in size from month to month, but a typical establishment had four to six inmates in residence, plus the madam. Sometimes brothels were small; the Kimballs had only two "dressmakers" living with them in 1880 and Cora Webber had only one prostitute (as well as a handful of other men and women) in her house in 1870. At the other extreme, Robinson had ten inmates with her in 1870 and Hattie McBride had nine in 1880.[16]

In sum, the structural context for brothel prostitution in St. Paul from 1865 to 1883 is relatively clear. The police supervised

15 U.S., Census Office, Tenth Census, *Statistics of the Population of the United States* (Washington, 1883), I, 536–537. All 40 madams and 89 inmates were apparently white. Occasional newspaper reports mention black prostitutes, but never in the context of the established brothels. By 1880, blacks accounted for barely 1% of St. Paul's population. Cf. *Pioneer*, May 29, 1867; July 23, 1870; *Pioneer Press*, July 7, 1877.

Two-thirds of Nashville's prostitutes were born nearby in Tennessee, Kentucky, or Alabama. Virginia City's prostitutes were slightly older than St. Paul's; the median age for whites was 26, suggesting that some women moved west to the frontier when they became older and less competitive in the urban marketplace. Oriental prostitutes were concentrated in the far west. Cf. Goldman, "Sexual Commerce"; Hirata, "Chinese Prostitutes"; Yuji Ichioka, "Ameyuki-san: Japanese Prostitutes in Nineteenth-Century America," *Amerasia*, IV (1977), 1–21; David Kaser, "Nashville's Women of Pleasure in 1860," *Tennessee Historical Quarterly*, XXIII (1964), 379–382.

16 The 1873 city directory counted, by sex, the number of inhabitants in each dwelling. Five brothels appear, with 5 to 13 women apiece—figures including the madam and any live-in help.

the brothels, but let them operate openly. Most firms, located in well-etablished vice districts where brothels could attract customers with minimal interference, sometimes operated from the same building for several years. The brothels were small, managed by women who often had stable careers as madams. The women involved in brothel prostitution, both as madams and inmates, were typically in their twenties, single, and native-born. Within this structure, however, these women experienced fluid careers, finding their way into the world of vice, changing locations and sometimes status, and ultimately leaving prostitution.

ENTERING PROSTITUTION Most sociologists studying deviant careers focus on the initial step—becoming deviant. For theoretical and practical reasons, it is important to ask why some people turn to prostitution or other deviance. Interactionist studies of deviant careers argue that, in addition to committing their first deviant acts, individuals entering deviance must modify their definition of self, redefining deviance as an appropriate activity and justifying their involvement in it. For some, deviance may be a defense against a threat, whereas others may seek adventure through deviance; in any case, entry into deviance involves assessing options and, ultimately, choosing deviance.[17]

Other explanations assign the individual a less active role in the process of becoming deviant; in these models, the person becomes a pawn of outside forces. Nineteenth-century sexual ideology favored explanations which denied that prostitution was a calculated choice. Medical and scientific literature, as well as popular writings, minimized female sexuality and emphasized women's innocence and purity. Since purity was woman's essence, prostitution represented a fundamental contradiction—purity depraved. This contradiction accounts for the choice of explanations for prostitution favored by nineteenth-century moralists. Reformers pointed to the white slave trade's role in ruining young girls; innocents were said to be abducted and forced

17 For general discussions of the process of becoming deviant, see: John Lofland, *Deviance and Identity* (Englewood Cliffs, 1969), 39–205; David Matza, *Becoming Deviant* (Englewood Cliffs, 1969); Rubington and Weinberg, *Deviance*. Most sociological studies of prostitutes' careers focus on this initial stage: James K. Bryan, "Apprenticeships in Prostitution," *Social Problems*, XII (1965), 287–297; Diana Gray, "Turning Out," *Urban Life and Culture*, I (1973), 401–425; Barbara S. Heyl, *The Madam as Entrepreneur* (New Brunswick, 1979).

to enter brothels, or they were tricked into beginning a "life of shame." Other contemporary explanations suggested that women could be overcome through a weakness in their character: loving "not wisely but too well," they were seduced; permitted to read novels, they were corrupted by false, romantic ideas; or, proud and greedy, they longed to wear fine clothes. Yet nineteenth-century newspaper stories revealed the inadequacy of these explanations and the ideology which lay behind them.[18]

St. Paul's newspapers shared the fascination with women's descent into vice, but they offered little support for claims that abduction or trickery led women into prostitution. Prostitutes occasionally accounted for their "fall" in this fashion and their stories sometimes were believed. However, investigations usually revealed that these stories were fraudulent attempts to gain sympathy; only five cases were substantiated, and only one of these involved an established brothel.[19]

Although there was limited support for romantic explanations for women's entry into prostitution via abduction, trickery, or seduction, such incidents lay outside the general pattern. In newspaper accounts, the most common pathway into vice involved a calculated decision, reflecting the available opportunities for women in the city. Some young women saw prostitution as a means of escaping unhappy family lives. Others, probably the majority, entered prostitution because it was one of the few occupations in which a woman could earn a comfortable living. Working-class women were otherwise largely restricted to employment in the needle trades or domestic service—careers which paid notoriously little. The 1880 census listed 3,081 St. Paul women in selected occupations; two categories—tailors, dressmakers, and milliners and domestic servants—accounted for 77 percent of their jobs. Although there were reports of prostitutes whose parents were respectable or even wealthy, most women

18 Cf. Peter Cominos, "Late Victorian Sexual Respectability and the Social System," *International Review of Social History*, VIII (1963), 18–48, 216–250; Deborah Gorham, "The 'Maiden Tribute of Modern Babylon' Re-examined," *Victorian Studies*, XXI (1978), 353–379; David J. Pivar, *Purity Crusade* (Westport, Conn., 1973); several of the essays in Hartman and Banner, *Clio's Consciousness*.

19 *Pioneer*, Dec. 31, 1867; Mar. 4; Aug. 30, 1870; Nov. 21, 1871; Aug. 19, 1873; Feb. 25, 1875; *Press*, Aug. 17, 1873; *Pioneer Press*, Oct. 29, 1875; Nov. 1, 1878; Jan. 28–30; Oct. 26, 1879; Jan. 2–4, 26; Oct. 27, 1880; May 9, Aug. 22, 1882. Cf. Barbara J. Berg, *The Remembered Gate* (New York, 1978), 177–182.

chose prostitution because it offered one of the few chances for a more comfortable life.[20]

One story, well designed to shock the Victorian reader with its theme of vice as a calculated choice, appeared repeatedly in the newspapers. In its simplest version, an adolescent girl enters a brothel. Her relatives enlist the aid of the police, who find her and offer her a chance to return to her family. She refuses, sometimes remaining defiant even when threatened with jail. This story, which appeared in seventeen different cases, caused reporters some discomfort. Faced with a woman's clear, calculated choice of prostitution, the image of female innocence could not be maintained; instead, the young women were characterized in harsh terms: "The girl's action is explicable only on the grounds of precocious perversity. . . ."[21]

Not every adolescent girl who tried to enter a brothel was admitted; madams discouraged or turned away some young applicants. Moreover, there were other routes into prostitution. Some women were born to the scarlet—daughters of madams or inmates; others may have started out as servants in the brothels. Some older women, who were already married, entered brothels. One woman left her husband of eleven years, a Minneapolis policeman, to enter Sarah Mason's house. Sometimes the husband played a more direct role; one young woman fled Minneapolis, joining her sister in a St. Paul brothel, after her husband tried to force her to prostitute herself. Other reports mentioned women who were married to their pimps, but did not say whether they entered prostitution under their husbands' direction.[22]

MOBILITY IN PROSTITUTION Once an individual embarks on a deviant career, new options become apparent: the individual may learn new skills, develop contacts with other deviants, or become aware of additional opportunities within deviance. Different pathways were open to St. Paul's prostitutes. For economic as well

20 U.S. Census Office, Tenth Census, *Report on the Social Statistics of Cities* (Washington, 1887), pt. 2, 901; *Pioneer Press*, May 18; June 13, 1883. On the conditions of domestic servants, see David M. Katzman, *Seven Days a Week* (New York, 1978).

21 *Pioneer*, Jan. 12; Aug. 31; Dec. 31, 1867; Aug. 12, 1869; Jan. 10–11, 1871; Feb. 15, 1874; Mar. 12, 1875; *Pioneer Press*, July 20, 1875; Apr. 19, 1876; Jan. 30; Apr. 22, 1878; Feb. 1, 16, 18; Aug. 14; Sept. 20, 1879; Sept. 4, 1881; Dec. 6, 1882.

22 *Pioneer*, Apr. 22, 1870; Aug. 23, 1872; *Pioneer Press*, Jan. 21, 1878; Jan. 21, 1881; May 18, 1882.

as personal reasons, most prostitutes kept moving. Geographical mobility, from one city to another or between brothels in the same city, was very common. In addition, some women were upwardly mobile within the world of vice, changing status from brothel inmate to madam.[23]

Movement to and from St. Paul was commonplace. For some women, moving to the city was part of the process of becoming a prostitute; a typical pattern had a young woman leave her home town, travel to St. Paul and take a low-paying but respectable job as a waitress or domestic, and then enter a brothel after a few months. The news stories about parents hunting for their young daughters spoke of girls from Faribault, Shakopee, Mankato, and other towns in Minnesota and Wisconsin. Others moved to St. Paul after becoming prostitutes; the register of prostitutes kept by the police was unsystematic, but it occasionally listed the places of origin or, less often, the destination of women leaving St. Paul. Although some of these women may have been newcomers to vice, many probably came from brothels elsewhere. Many entries named towns in Minnesota or the surrounding region, but some women were on the move to or from major cities in other states. Only one woman's origin was listed as outside the country—Norway. Sometimes madams deliberately imported inmates; in 1867, Robinson brought four prostitutes from Chicago, although they left St. Paul after a couple of weeks, complaining that the customers were not as wealthy as those in Chicago.[24]

In most cases, the women probably had their own reasons for moving. Some prostitutes were ordered to leave the city and just as St. Paul authorities drove some women away, others came to the city fleeing officials elsewhere. But not all pressure to move came from the authorities. When fire struck Chicago's vice district, 500 prostitutes fled, some to St. Paul. Although newspapers were more likely to cover these dramatic stories, most women probably moved on simply because the opportunities seemed better elsewhere. The proximity of Minneapolis made it especially

23 There is no general sociological statement about the middle stages of deviant careers. The most detailed study describes compulsive gamblers: Henry R. Lesieur, *The Chase* (Garden City, 1977). On career shifts among prostitutes, see Paul J. Goldstein, *Prostitution and Drugs* (Lexington, Mass., 1979); Heyl, *Madam*.

24 Arrest ledger; *Pioneer*, Sept. 4, 1867.

easy to shift cities. Police raids or rumors of a crackdown occasionally led women to move across the Mississippi into the other jurisdiction.[25]

Once in St. Paul, brothel inmates often moved from one establishment to another. Reasons for changing houses varied: at least one inmate regularly alternated between two brothels; some left at the madam's orders; on other occasions, madams were angry when inmates left, particularly if the prostitute attracted customers.[26]

Mobility between cities and within St. Paul gave brothels shifting populations. Madams might remain at one address for years, but most inmates moved on after a few months, particularly if the brothel was not under stable management. Tables 1 and 2, drawn from the arrest ledger's structured records for April to October, 1873, illustrate the high rate of turnover. Brothel A, shown in Table 1, was run by a madam who controlled her house for several years. A total of twelve prostitutes were arrested as inmates of Brothel A, with between one and seven arrests apiece. In addition, one of these women was arrested in another brothel during this period. A second prostitute had an arrest as an independent, i.e., she was not arrested on the same day as the brothel inmates and was presumably working on her own. If we assume that all of its inmates were arrested, Brothel A fluctuated in size from four to seven inmates; counting the madam, between four and six of the women arrested each month had been there the previous month. This reflects a reasonably stable population within the establishment; occupants tended to be in residence from one month to the next.[27]

By contrast, Table 2 shows the arrest pattern in a second, less stable house. Brothel B had four madams during the seven-month period, with control passing from A who had managed the house for six months, temporarily into the hands of B and C, before D took over for about a year. Six other women were arrested as inmates of Brothel B; none had more than five arrests in the seven months. This establishment had considerable turn-

25 *Press*, Feb. 12; July 19, 22; Aug. 27, 1874; *Pioneer Press*, Apr. 29, 1875; Nov. 8, 1878; Dec. 21, 1878; Mar. 13; May 4, 1879; Oct. 22, 1882; Apr. 17; July 25, 1883. *Pioneer*, July 19, 1870; Apr. 15; Aug. 19, 1873; Feb. 8, 1874.

26 *Pioneer*, Apr. 21; Dec. 31, 1867; May 10, 1870; Nov. 21, 1871; Aug. 23, 1872; *Pioneer Press*, Dec. 12, 1880.

27 *Pioneer*, May 10, 1870; 1870 manuscript census; city directories for 1868, 1870.

Table 1 Arrests within Brothel A, April–October, 1873

WOMAN	DATE OF ARREST							ARRESTS PER PERSON
	APRIL 10	MAY 13	JUNE 12	JULY 11	AUG. 13	SEPT. 10	OCT. 4	
A	K	K	K	K	K	K	K	7
B	V	V	V	V	V	V	D	7
C	V	D		D	D	D	D	6
D	V	V	V			O	O	3
E	V	V	V					3
F	V	V		V				3
G		V	V	V	V	V		5
H	I	V	V			V	V	4
I			V	V				2
J				V				1
K				V				1
L					V	V		2
M						V	D	2
Total	6	8	7	8	5	7	5	46

(Totals include only arrests within Brothel A.)

K = Arrest for "Keeping a House of Ill Fame," fined $20.

V = Arrest under this madam for "Visting a House of Ill Fame," fined $10.

D = Arrest under this madam for "Visiting a House of Ill Fame," dismissed.

O = Arrest under another madam for "Visiting a House of Ill Fame."

I = Arrest for "Visiting a House of Ill Fame" but not listed under a madam (on an odd day of the same month).

over; the number of occupants who remained in the brothel from one month to the next ranged from only one to three. Whereas Brothel A was a relatively large, relatively stable establishment, Brothel B was smaller and considerably less stable.

The cumulative impact of shifting populations, even in the relatively stable brothels, was to repopulate the city's houses every few months. Although the data are limited because brothel inmates were not arrested systematically during most months, comparisons can be drawn between the summers of 1873 and 1874. Table 3 includes all women arrested as madams or brothel inmates during these months. It confirms that madams were more likely to have stable careers than their inmates. Six of the ten women arrested as madams during the summer of 1873 were also arrested in 1874; two had been downwardly mobile and their 1874 arrests

Table 2 Arrests within Brothel B, April–October, 1873

WOMAN	DATE OF ARREST							ARRESTS PER PERSON
	APRIL 9	MAY 13	JUNE 12	JULY 10	AUG. 13	SEPT. 10	OCT. 4	
A	K							1
B		K	V					2
C	V	V	K	K				4
D	V	V			K	K	K	5
E		V	V	V	V		V	5
F		V						1
G			V	V	V	V		4
H	O_1	O_1		V	I	O_2	O_2	1
I					V	V		2
J						V		1
Total	3	5	4	4	4	4	2	26

(Totals include only arrests within Brothel B.)

K = Arrest for "Keeping a House of Ill Fame," fined $15.

V = Arrest under this madam for "Visiting a House of Ill Fame," fined $10.

O = Arrest under another madam for "Visiting a House of Ill Fame" (subscripts denote different brothels).

I = Arrest for "Visiting a House of Ill Fame" but not listed under a madam (on an odd day of the same month).

were for prostitution, but four continued to hold the status of madam. Even discounting the two downwardly mobile madams, the retention rate for madams was 40 percent. In contrast, only twelve of the fifty-two women arrested as prostitutes in the summer of 1873 were arrested one year later—a retention rate of only

Table 3 Prostitutes and Madams Arrested during the Summers of 1873 and 1874

STATUS	TOTAL ARRESTED IN		
	1873	1874	BOTH
Madams	10[a]	9	4
Prostitutes	53	49[a]	12
Total	63	58	18[a]

a Includes two women who were arrested as madams in 1873 and as prostitutes in 1874. Note that they are included in the total for "Both."

23 percent. Further, this table ignores intracity mobility; many of the inmates still in town after a year might have moved to other firms.[28]

The high turnover among brothel inmates reflected the nature of the market for vice. Nineteenth-century madams argued that customers demanded variety. Symanski accounts for the high turnover rates in Nevada's legal brothels by identifying four functions of turnover: minimizing social friction among the brothel's staff; giving prostitutes a variety of customers and colleagues; supplying customers with a variety of prostitutes; and reducing the risks of a customer becoming emotionally involved with a prostitute. Presumably, most of St. Paul's prostitutes moved on for similar reasons.[29]

Geographical mobility was a feature of nearly every prostitute's career, but social mobility was less common. The major step within the demimonde was from independent prostitute or brothel inmate to madam, from paying a keeper a portion of one's earnings to collecting from one's "boarders." This pathway was not open to every woman, but a substantial number took it. At least thirteen of the forty madams had spent time as an independent prostitute or brothel inmate in St. Paul and, given the gaps in the inmates' arrest records, the proportion may have been much higher. Some madams may have opened houses without having served as prostitutes, but the evidence is insufficient to establish this. A better index of opportunities for mobility is that only four of the sixty-one brothel inmates arrested from April to October, 1873, went on to manage brothels in St. Paul within the next ten years. Some women may have moved on to run houses in other cities, but former inmates would be most likely to open firms in a city with which they were familiar, particularly in St. Paul, where both the general population and the number of brothels were expanding and the authorities were not repressive. This suggests that perhaps a tenth of all prostitutes were upwardly mobile.

Downward mobility from madam to prostitute was less common, but it did occur. One woman, Frank Livingston, operated a brothel in St. Paul in 1886. She moved to Minneapolis

28 Arrest ledger for June–Sept. of 1873 and 1874. The former period had structured records, the latter categorical records.

29 *Press*, Aug. 26, 1871; Richard Symanski, "Prostitution in Nevada," *Annals of the Association of American Geographers*, LXIV (1974), 371; Gentry, *Madams*, 146.

for a time, then returned to St. Paul where she had several arrests for visiting a house of ill fame (i.e., she was no longer a madam). At least two other madams stayed in St. Paul and were downwardly mobile, becoming brothel inmates or independent prostitutes.[30]

LEAVING PROSTITUTION The final stage in the deviant career often is hidden because ex-deviants try to divorce themselves from their past to avoid stigma. Sociological studies of deviant careers emphasize the reforming influence of formal social control programs featuring punishment, treatment, or interaction with other ex-deviants; little is known about individuals who find their own pathways out of deviance. Yet most nineteenth-century prostitutes left vice on their own after a few years; no inmate in St. Paul reported being over thirty. Even if the women lied, they could not hope to remain in prostitution long; each year made them less attractive, less competitive in their marketplace. Finding that the great majority of New York prostitutes were under twenty-five, Sanger concluded that a typical career led the women through a series of increasingly disreputable brothels, until they died within a few years. Nineteenth-century newspapers embellished this theme; the death of a prostitute contrasted nicely with the surface glitter of her life, offering an obvious moral for newspaper readers.[31]

St. Paul's newspapers gave detailed reports of the deaths of several prostitutes. These accounts suggest the array of risks faced by madams and brothel inmates. One inmate died from the complications of an abortion. Fights and other disorders broke out frequently in the brothels. Although there were no reports of women dying in these incidents, some suffered serious injuries. Suicide attempts were common.[32]

30 *Pioneer*, July 18, 1868.

31 On the process of leaving deviance, see Lofland, *Deviance and Identity*, 209–295; Robert A. Stebbins, *Commitment to Deviance* (Westport, Conn., 1971); Rubington and Weinberg, *Deviance*, 461–508. There is no sociological study of the process among prostitutes, but see the remarks in Jennifer James et al., *The Politics of Prostitution* (Seattle, 1977; 2nd ed.), 44.

32 *Pioneer*, Aug. 30, 1870; July 28; Nov. 11–12, 1871; *Pioneer Press*, Nov. 13, 1875; Apr. 1, 1876; Apr. 19, 1879; Aug. 26–27; Nov. 9–10, 1881; Feb. 9, 1882; Jan. 7, 1883. The newspapers also occasionally reported suicides or suicide attempts by customers who had fallen in love with brothel inmates: *Pioneer*, Apr. 5; Oct. 1, 1872; *Pioneer Press*, Apr. 3, 1881.

Prostitution was a hard life and many women turned to drink or drugs. Drunkenness was an everyday occurrence in the brothels, contributing to the frequent disorders. The testimony at the Robinson arson trial, which offers a glimpse of a typical evening in a brothel, revealed that several of the inmates had been drinking or were drunk. Many prostitutes preferred using morphine or laudanum; they accounted for most of St. Paul's narcotics users. Alcohol and drugs probably contributed to deaths by natural causes. At least four madams died from disease—three before they were thirty-five. Unfortunately, the newspapers were less likely to cover brothel inmates' or independent prostitutes' deaths from disease. The annual reports of the Magdalen Home, however, describe three deaths of prostitutes, including a former inmate of Henrietta Charles' brothel, who entered the home and found salvation. Obviously, the Home's officers were especially likely to relate tales demonstrating the effectiveness of their good works; there were no reports of deaths of unrepentant women.[33]

Deaths from violence and disease are consistent with the Sanger thesis of inevitable decline, but they are not sufficient proof that most prostitutes died after short careers. The newspapers mentioned eleven deaths of madams or prostitutes but, as the women passing through the city's brothels must have numbered several hundred, far more must have died if Sanger were correct. One method of testing his thesis is to compare brothel inmates with independent prostitutes. If Sanger were correct, women worked in better brothels when they entered prostitution, before moving down to "cigar stores" and independent prostitution. As a consequence, inmates should have been younger than other prostitutes. Yet an examination of the arrest ledger's entries in 1873 and 1874 shows no difference in the ages of the two groups. Eleven independent prostitutes were located, with a median age of twenty-one (range eighteen–twenty-seven), compared to twenty-two for brothel inmates. Similarly, five women had one or two arrests for keeping a house of ill fame (suggesting that they operated minor establishments); their median age was twenty-seven (range eighteen–thirty-five)—the same as the forty madams in mid-career. A further challenge to Sanger's thesis

33 *Pioneer*, May 10–13, 1870; *Pioneer Press*, May 27; Sept. 30, 1874; Jan. 24; Oct. 25, 1875; Nov. 14, 1877; Apr. 23, 1878; Oct. 25, 1879; Feb. 19, 1882.

appears in the pattern of inmates' movements between brothels. Although Robinson's house ranked above her rivals' brothels, inmates often worked for another firm before joining Robinson. From April to October, 1873, six inmates moved from rival brothels to Robinson's house; two of the women each worked in two other firms before moving to Eighth Street. Contrary to Sanger's claim, prostitutes did not always move down to shabbier establishments.[34]

Furthermore, some prostitutes and madams left vice for respectable or quasi-respectable lives. They retired, married, or took up legitimate work. Their numbers are difficult to estimate because they left few records; most tried to conceal the facts of their past to avoid hostility from respectable citizens and, once they were no longer "women of the town," newspapers ignored them.

Retirement on one's savings was an option open to the frugal. Robinson's resources were substantial and Lilly Thompson was said "to have a large number of United States bonds carefully laid away, besides a good sized bank account." If they owned their buildings, madams could turn over the firm to a successor and collect rent; Hutton, Morse, and Oleson all retired in this fashion.[35]

Marriage probably offered a more common route out of prostitution. Some marriages were unsuccessful; one woman returned to vice and later killed herself. Others married and dropped from sight: "a nolle prosequi was entered, as the defendant had left the business, got married, and was respectable." Newspaper stories hinted that prominent men frequented the brothels and sometimes fell in love with the inmates, but the papers were too discreet to publish the details of a marriage between a respectable man and a madam or prostitute, making it impossible to trace the women once they entered respectable lives.[36]

Still other women entered respectability through a deliberate

34 Only women who had no arrests on days when brothels were "pulled" were defined as independent prostitutes, i.e., a woman who was arrested on an odd day in one month but had other arrests in later months on days when madams were arrested was assumed to have joined a brothel. Comparison groups are the 40 madams and 89 inmates discussed above.

35 *Pioneer*, Apr. 23, 1870; *Pioneer Press*, Aug. 24, 1876; Feb. 4, 1880; Nov. 10, 1881.

36 *Pioneer*, Jan. 16; Mar. 19–23, 1872.

effort to reform. The Home of the Good Shepard and the Magdalen Home admitted prostitutes as well as other fallen women. The court sentenced some to serve a term in the Home of the Good Shepard; St. Paul lacked other facilities for incarcerating women during much of this period. Other prostitutes entered the homes because they were pregnant, angry with their lovers, or sincerely interested in reform. The homes' regimen consisted largely of religious instruction and training for domestic service. The annual reports of the Magdalen Home contained accounts of successes—prostitutes who found religion and left the home for marriage or respectable employment. Others' experiences ended in failure; they returned to vice. The *Pioneer* mocked one inmate who returned to the brothel: "Black gowns and a quiet respectable life do not possess the charms for the little siren, that pinchbeck jewelry, flashy clothing and panniers do."[37]

Respectable society's refusal to admit former prostitutes made attempts at reform more difficult. A fallen woman's stigma was not easily shed. After Robinson confined herself to legitimate real estate ventures for four years, a newspaper reminded its readers about her past. Reports from the Magdalen Home speak of more serious setbacks. One woman left the Home to work as a domestic but, when her employers learned about her past, they discharged her: ". . . she left the house at 10 o'clock at night, without shelter or friends, after ten months of faithful service and earnest strivings to do right."[38]

Nineteenth-century authorities described typical careers in prostitution but, like other popular explanations for deviance, their accounts treated the women as passive—pawns of age, disease, and procurers. In contrast, the sociological concept of the deviant career suggests that prostitutes typically confronted similar problems and chose similar methods of solving them. Although prostitutes' careers did not duplicate one another, the women tended to travel down similar pathways. Madams and brothel inmates actively shaped their own careers: they typically entered vice

37 John E. Forliti, "The First Thirty Years of the Home of the Good Shepard, St. Paul, Minnesota, 1868–1898," unpub. M.A. thesis (St. Paul Seminary, 1962), 52–54; *Pioneer*, Dec. 19, 1868; May 27, 1874; *Pioneer Press*, Oct. 29, 1875; Oct. 20, 1877; Sept. 29, 1878; Apr. 1; Oct. 25, 1879; Oct. 15, 1880.

38 *Pioneer Press*, Oct. 20, 1877; Dec. 21, 1878; Oct. 15, 1880.

because it offered a higher income and more independence than the other jobs open to them; they sought better opportunities by constantly moving from place to place; some inmates became entrepreneurs, opening their own brothels; and, of those whose fates are known, as many returned to respectability through retirement, marriage, or reform as died at an early age.

In seeking to control their own careers, prostitutes, like respectable men and women, were active participants in the fluid urban scene of the nineteenth century. The city's social structure shaped career paths. For St. Paul's prostitutes, the demand for vice, the limited opportunities for respectable work for women, the police department's policy of regulating brothels through regular arrests, and the stigma which followed the women back into respectability provided part of the context within which careers developed. The individual's choices—to enter or leave vice, to move on to another place or up to another status—took this context into account. The same process shaped respectable careers.

Discovering patterns among people's lives is a central task for social history. Studies of occupational mobility or marriage age assume that individuals' life decisions reflect the social structure, that coherent collective patterns emerge from personal assessments of opportunities and risks. The concept of career offers a framework for such analysis. By examining the impact of changing social structure on career contingencies, historians can better understand the lives of ordinary people, both within and outside deviance.

HISTORICAL PERSPECTIVES ON THE STUDY OF FEMALE PROSTITUTION

FRANCES NEWMAN and ELIZABETH COHEN
with PATRICIA TOBIN and GAIL MACPHERSON

ABSTRACT

This paper surveys the twentieth-century evolution of the study of female prostitution in order to understand the significance of recent innovations in analysis and remediation. The paper identifies and summarizes four schools of interpretation: 1) late Victorian moralistic, biological determinism; 2) progressive reform before and after World War I; 3) academic sociology from the 1930s; and 4) psychoanalysis from the 1940s. Each of these approaches emphasizes a single aspect of the prostitute's situation. The earliest of this work attributed her moral degradation to bad genes. The progressives blamed her plight rather on poor social supervision and education and sought reform. Shifting focus from the individual to society, sociologists examined the function of prostitution and applied such concepts as deviance, role, and gender. Followers of the psychoanalytic tradition returned their attention to the individual, in whose mind they sought memories of early experience to account for pathological behaviour.

This paper represents a collaboration between the disciplines of psychology and history. The present authors include a social historian and a doctoral candidate in clinical and developmental psychology, assisted by two graduate students in school psychology. We assembled to review the literature on prostitution with the aim of providing an intellectual context for a particular clinical study (Newman & Caplan, this issue) on the backgrounds and psychodynamics of adolescent female prostitutes as compared with other delinquents. It soon became clear that prostitution was so broad a topic and had so long been a subject of serious commentary that we decided to limit our review to our own society and to the twentieth century, the locus and era most pertinent to our concerns.

In preparing this review we read a smorgasborg of sources, ranging from late Victorian newspaper tracts on the pursuit of purity, vice commission reports of the 1910s, and sober, sociological examinations of the role and function of the pimp, to accounts of the hypnoanalysis of prostitutes and racy, contemporary articles on "hand whores" and massage parlours. Through this variety of material we have tried to trace the roots of the current, interdisciplinary, interactionist approach to the scientific study of prostitution that focuses on the development and recruitment of the young girl. Four schools of writing emerged as particularly important in this context: The Victorian biological and moral traditions still current in the early twentieth century; the social reformism of the progressives before and after World War I, academic sociology from the 1930s; and the psychoanalytic literature after World War II.

Twentieth-century western Europeans and North Americans initially considered prostitution a biological or social phenomenon to be managed, stamped out, or punished, depending on the moral and political attitudes of the observers. This simplistic view gradually changed, as we will see, to a finer-grained examination in which the complexities of prostitution—including the social institutions that support the behaviour, the contribution of the familial and developmental antecedents of the prostitute, and her conscious and unconscious motivations—were all taken into account. This refinement culminated in the understanding that prostitution is not a unitary phenomenon, but that, for example, variation in intra-occupational status accounts for widely different ways of life (Exner, Wylie, Leura & Parrill, 1977; Barry, 1979).

Among the many themes in the literature a few stand out. First, in scientific literature and serious writing, the change in the view of prostitution paralleled a change in the society's view of the proper place of women and their sexuality. At the end of the nineteenth century "good" women were regarded as essentially asexual, passive, and biologically "immobile"; they might fall or be pulled from grade by either bad genes or bad company. As the twentieth century progressed, women were increasingly regarded as legitimately sexual creatures, though the "whore-madonna" split is still evident today in popular attitudes and even some scientific thinking.

A second theme is that, as the study of prostitution developed in this century, the focus shifted not only from society to the individual, but also more specifically to the entrance into prostitution of the young girl. Although early psychoanalytic writers emphasized the importance of infantile and adolescent development, most studies of prostitutes dealt only with adults' characteristics and circumstances.

Third, with evolving views of prostitution, implications for action and remediation changed. Biological determinists considered prostitutes bad women for whom there was no hope; reformers wanted to save them; academic sociologists ignored the issue; and psychoanalytic thinkers spoke maiinly in terms of intrapsychic rearrangements. Our conclusions will explore some current views on remediation.

Before beginning this selective history of the scientific study of prostitution in the twentieth century, a word about definitions is in order. The most common definition of prostitution is "sexual acts performed for material gain and without emotional involvement." Nevertheless, in the light of the predominant twentieth-century view that "good" women are not overtly sexual, some confusion persists regarding the use of the term "prostitute." Obviously sexual women have frequently been called deviant or delinquent. The line between deviance or delinquency in this sense prostitution is very fine indeed, particularly in the case of young females who, when their sexual behaviour has appeared unconventional, have often been labelled "tarts" or "hookers". An example from the experience of one of the authors illustrates this habit. A 12-year-old was lectured by her male school principal about her provocative behaviour with the boys in her class. Carol, as we will call her, had been teasing Ricky by saying that "some day I'll go to bed with you". Ricky advanced this taunt to the principal as his reason for hiding Carol's shoes in the classroom. "She keeps promising, but she never does it," Ricky complained. The principal told Carol that girls who make deals with boys are called hookers. "That makes you a hooker, doesn't it?" he concluded.

This examination of the literature is restricted to prostitution in its sense of sexual acts performed impersonally for money. Although we have not considered the subtleties of dowry and other social and psychological phenomena that may be interpreted as relating to prostitution, it is important to keep in mind the wide range of behaviour that may be embraced by that term. We will now outline the history of the study of prostitution and then consider current approaches to both analysis and remediation.

HISTORICAL BACKGROUND

As the twentieth century opened, the Victorian moralistic view of the prostitute as a fallen woman shared currency with a biologically deterministic interpretation. Associated with Cesare Lombroso, a nineteenth-century Italian criminologist primarily concerned with the study of physical and ethnic characteristics of criminals and criminal "types", and evident in the work of the Danish sociologist Tage Kemp in the 1930s, and others even later, this scientific approach reduced the explanation of criminality—of which prostitution was the primary form for females—to a single dimension (Lombroso, 1903/1958; Kemp, 1936; Klein, 1980). Buttressing their claims with measurements and statistics, these writers argued that in criminals, genes prescribed socially destructive behaviour as truly as they did body types and mental defects. Furthermore, in female miscreants the power of biology loomed awesome indeed, for the same intellectual tradition, rooted in nineteenth-century science, regarded women in general, let alone prostitutes, as weak, indecisive, and foolish. Thus, the prostitute, both as a woman and as a criminal, was the hapless creature of her genes, doomed to hurt society and herself unless she was isolated and restrained. Where "nature" made the criminal, there was little hope for human will to effect change and little chance of redemption.

The next innovation in the understanding of prostitution came during the great progressive crusade for social reform in the early decades of this century. Not accidentally, the "social evil"—as the progressives called it—figured among their most urgent concerns. During the years before the First World War, North American society faced major adjustments in the role and image of its women, specifically their assumption of legitimate sexual appetites and of paid employment outside the home. The reformers focused on the prostitute, as the embodiment of both female sexuality and paid work, in an unconscious attempt to reconcile their own ambivalence regarding women's changing social position (Connelly, 1979). The progressives' accommodation took the form of a campaign, on the one hand, to eradicate prostitution as an institution, yet, on the other, to help the prostitute as a person to a more acceptable and salubrious way of life. This two-pronged attack on the problem added new dimensions to the previously moral, biological view.

Progressive writing about prostitution favoured polemic over analysis. Nevertheless, the fact-crowded, scantily-interpreted reports from the vice commission of several large American cities between 1910 and 1920 and the highly coloured expositions of the "white slave traffic" both reflected changed ideas (e.g., Vice Commission of Chicago, 1911; Bell, 1910; Addams, 1912). First, the authors presented prostitution as an economic enterprise, a well-organized business benefitting many others besides the women who were its sales force. More important were alterations in the image of the prostitute herself. No longer a moralized literary type nor an anonymous biological grotesque, she acquired a personal history detailed in the reformers' believed case reports. Moreover, although while the prostitute continued to be considered vulnerable, passive and weak, her lapse was now said to derive largely from her youth and her social circumstances. This literature, even where its facts documented many counter-examples, ignored all prostitutes except the mythologized "white slave". She, too young freed of supervision and inadequately tutored, her internal controls not yet able to replace external ones, fell prey to the lures of the city—among them, ice cream parlours and ferry boat excursions—where she was trapped by a seasoned seducer. According to this scenario, the young prostitute's actions deserved condemnation, but her character did no need to be inherently evil. Rather she was a victim of society and changing times; in her possible rehabilitation the progressives firmly believed.

Those progressives who sought to reform prostitutes rather than prostitution, stepped further and more carefully in delineating the social context of recruitment into the trade. Their data subverted some of the favourite biological theories of the time, although the authors did not always acknowledge the implications of their own results. Studies by various, now little-remembered workers in social rehabilitation were commonly burdened with vague definitions of the sexual delinquent, of whom the prostitute was one scarcely distinguished variety. This definitional confusion—the offspring of the general ambivalence about sexuality and woman's place—encouraged the blurring of moral absolutes about good and bad behaviour. The data assembled in these reports about groups of delinquent girls touched age, size, mental health, ethnic and geographic background, and family pathology. These categories reflected the typical preoccupations of the era: urbanization and immigration, and their effects on collective and personal security and well-being (Kneeland, 1913; Bingham, 1923; Feldman, 1968). The principal direction of these investigations pointed to the individuality of every delinquent or prostitute and eschewed deterministic explanations based only on one factor. Some writers of the 1920s (Thomas, 1969; Seagrave, 1926) wrestled with the biological approach, but in the end they seem to have set it aside in preference for a pluralistic view which allowed social circumstances considerable influence but not control over a girl's actual movement into prostitution.

The progressives—while believing that reform must include not only the elimination of the institutions sustaining moral failure but also the recovery of individual prostitutes—said little about the psychology of that undertaking. With time, however, writers of the reformist tradition began to debunk the myth of the "white slaves" and to talk about how girls might be attracted, rather than forced, into prostitution (Reckless, 1933). The analytical consequences of that shift of perspective escaped notice until many years later, when writers picked up the theme of the ways in which young girls might find partial fulfillment of their needs in prostitution and the fast life.

From the 1930s the consolidation of sociology as a modern discipline brought another perspective to prostitution. Abandoning morality and the impulse to work directly upon society, and adopting instead a stance of objectivity and aloofness, academic sociologists set out to describe and explain social beings and their institutions through the use of measurement, statistics, and a satchelful of new concepts including structure, function, roles and norms. Sociologists postulated that people's needs varied with their social niches and that social arrangements, including prostitution, persisted because they worked to fulfill some such needs. Early on, as in the much-cited and often reprinted 1937 article of Kingsley Davis, "The sociology of prostitution", this approach addressed the most general questions: How did prostitution fit into society as a whole, and how did it serve the requirements of its many participants—clients, wives, pimps, as well as the prostitutes themselves? Davis scarcely considered the prostitute's background and recruitment, which so concerned the progressives. After undermining arguments for the primacy of economic desperation as a motive, Davis took some glee in reversing the standard query, "Why do some women become prostitutes?" and asked instead, "Why do not more women become prostitutes?" Implied but unexplored in this remark lurked the notion that for at least some women prostitution better served some sexual, social, or psychological needs than did more conventional ways of life. Later sociologists of prostitution, narrowing their focus from global society to the sub-culture of deviance with its own organization, values, and mores, pursued this idea with greater precision. The perspective, however, tended to remain that of an outsider and, at best, a sympathetic voyeur (e.g., Murtagh & Harris, 1957; Limoges, 1967).

Followers of the psychoanalytic tradition, the last of the major areas we examined, regard prostitution as a form of sexual aberration—of both women and the men who frequent them. Typically, however, it is the prostitute rather than the client who has been the focus of studies of prostitution. Without detailing psychoanalytic theory, let us agree that it is essentially concerned with the individual as a psychological being and in particular as shaped by repressed infantile sexual wishes and desires. To examine prostitution, one must therefore have access to unconsious processes not evident on ordinary scrutiny. Here lies room for interpretation, inference, and subjectivity. Here, too, appears the assumption that the individual is not conscious of what motivates here. So, of course, there is little effort to understand the *conscious* meaning for the prostitute or her own behaviour. While psychoanalysis centres clearly on the person rather than on society or institution, it is deterministic and leaves little room for conscious individual manoeuvre. The "causes" of prostitution—or the motives of the prostitute—are regarded as unconscious homosexual desire, unconscious hatred of men, and unconscious wishes to punish mother for her "unavailability". Furthermore, though psychoanalytic writers usually acknowledge the contribution of unhappy and distorted early experience, they conceive of remediation only in terms of intrapsychic change.

One psychoanalytic writer, Edward Glover, who published his *Psychopathology of prostitution* in 1945, exemplified this pattern of thought. However, he not only acknowledged the importance of the early history of the young prostitute but also discussed the reciprocal aspect of prostitution: The psychopathological demand of a (married) man who, unable in adulthood to resolve the infantile oedipal split between erotic love and aim-inhibited, idealized love, has become impotent with his wife or social equal and can perform sexually only with "deteriorated" sexual objects. This concept of the deteriorated or devalued sexual object is important for current theory, particularly with respect to how a young girl experiences herself, and it will be discussed again later.

Although Glover's principal concern, like that of others working the the psychoanalytic tradition, was the motivation for women whose sexual commerce brought them to the attention of the legal system and social agencies, he felt it useful to differentiate among styles of prostitution. He distinguished the "drab prostitute", or streetwalker, from the "flourishing professional", or "call girl", as she is known today; the "gold digger"; the "enthusiastic amateur"; and the impulsive adolescent. Following up the logic of this series of types, he pointed out the consequences of our society's constraints on female sexuality in general, such that all women may be construed in one way or another as prostitutes. In this context he noted, for example, dowries and marriage contracts.

A relatively recent development in psychoanalytic thought—the ego-analytic theory associated with Anna Freud, Hartmann, and Kris in the 1940s and more recently with Erik Erikson—is focused on the mechanism and functions of the Ego or self, rather than on the Id or impulses. The contribution of this theory is considerable, for here is a way in which to understand the individual as an active participant in, if not creator of her own life and life choices.

THE CURRENT VIEW

Recent statistics, both Canadian and American, reflect an increase in what many social critics consider one of the most alarming and self-destructive activities within North American society—juvenile prostitution. The current scientific approach to prostitution, which began to emerge around 1970, is characterized by:

1) a focus on the individual's interaction with society;
2) a view of society as modifiable;
3) an assumption that the prostitute is neither simply victim nor simply villain but is instead an active participant in the construction of her life and lifestyle insofar as she is capable, given her particular set of strengths and weaknesses;
4) an assumption that much of the prostitute's deviant behaviour is motivated by the same needs that everyone else in society has, namely, the needs for love, a sense of self-worth, competence, and power;
5) a focus on understanding how sex-role and gender expectations contribute to female prostitution; and
6) a special emphasis on the complexity of the process by which the adolescent female enters into prostitution.

Jennifer James and her colleagues at the University of Washington are perhaps the major proponents of this new approach. It is interdisciplinary and makes appropriate and instructive use of the techniques and accumulated knowledge from the range of the social sciences. In a series of studies, James and her colleagues have examined: The early sexual experiences (including rape and incest) of young prostitutes; disturbed and unsupportive parental relations; and economic and social influences that have combined to create within a particular individual in a particular society the identity, role and occupation of prostitute. In 1980, James, Boyer, Withers and Haft summarized this work in *Perspectives on prostitution*, a handbook designed for use by street-workers, counsellors, legal professionals, and all those actively involved in working with prostitutes.

Among the social factors examined by recent researchers is a theory of "sexual labeling", which James, Davis and Vitaliano (1980) use to explain young girls' "drift into deviance." They postulate that as a result of some early sexual experiences these girls come to label themselves, or are labelled by others, as prostitutes. They suggest that this is partly because young girls in North America have been taught that they should not be sexually active, and so early sexual experiences are often interpreted as signs of promiscuity or depravity. Karen Rosenblum, a sociologist, suggested in 1975 that females in general are supposed to balance their sexuality delicately: They are supposed to be attractive and pleasing to males but only under certain, carefully designated circumstances. A young girl who has been unduly stressed or deprived can easily fall into an exaggeraton of some part of that role—the sexual availability part. Majorie Brown (1979) has recently investigated the experiences that might predispose a girl to deviant sexual activity. She finds that these include early sexual experiences and adolescent promiscuity. She also explicates the way that treatment by law enforcement agencies tends to perpetuate this situation. Similarly, Nanette Davis (1979) examines the development of a deviant identity and cites early sexual experiences and stigmatization by parents, peers, and significant others (such as school teachers) as precursors of sexual precocity. In addition, she identifies factors that may attract adolescents to "the life", including needs for excitement, companionship, and money; all of these are promised by the "glamourous" street life. The young recruit hopes (unconsciously) that they will fill up the inner emptiness felt by her early deprivation. The same quest for excitement in the street life was found by Newman and Caplan in 1980 in their study of girls charged with prostitution who had suffered early emotional deprivation (Newman & Caplan, 1980 and this issue). Recent investigators, then, have undertaken to deal with the "problem" of juvenile female prostitution in its complexity. They have sacrificed theoretical simplicity for a broader, more comprehensive, and potentially more useful approach.

Our own approach to the study of juvenile prostitution is based upon a model proposed by Newman and Caplan in 1980. One purpose of this model is to acknowledge that biological, familial, socioeconomic, psychosocial, and psychosexual factors may be important in the development of a deviant identity and potentially dangerous lifestyle. At the same time, a major ingredient of the model is the view that the normal adolescent struggles actively to forge an identity, a sense of power, and a means of access to the goods and rewards offered by society. The adolescent prostitute is seen in the sample context, not as a passive victim who is flawed beyond redemption by unfortunate circumstances, nor as a villain acting blindly on the urgings of infernal, inner drives. The proposed model integrates material from recent investigators into a developmental pathway that is uniquely focussed on the process of ego-development, including the ego's strengths, weaknesses, defenses, and resources and the nature of the ego identity. The latter is crucial to an understanding of how a girl comes to have a deviant self-concept.

IMPLICATIONS FOR ACTION

Current perspectives on prostitution are concerned with the experience of the prostitute and with the meaning of the activity for those who engage in it, as well as with the social institutions, forces, and supports that influence the life and choices (and lack of choices) of the prostitute. The combination of these two perspectives has important implications for intervention and remediation. Respect for the individual who has made a particular adjustment to the society in which she lives—as a devalued sexual object in a society which values women primarily as sexual objects—requires that attempts be made to demonstrate other ways to fulfill important needs and goals without violating and devaluing the integrity of her experience. In addition, an understanding of the social systems that influence and control the individual leads to a commitment to social change in the form of decriminalization of prostitution and of more enlightened attitudes toward women in general.

REFERENCES

Addams, J. *A new conscience and an ancient evil.* N.Y.: Macmillan, 1912.

Barry, K. *Female sexual slavery.* Englewood Cliffs, N.J.: Prentice-Hall, 1979.

Bell, E.A. *Fighting the traffic in young girls, or, war on the the white slave trade.* Chicago: n.p., 1910.

Bingham, A.T. Determinants of sex delinquency in adolescent girls based on intensive study of 500 cases. *Journal of Criminal Law and Criminology*, 1922-1923, 494-586.

Brown, M. Teenage prostitution. *Adolescence*, 1979, 665-79.

Connelly, M.T. *The response to prostitution in the progressive era.* Chapel Hill: Univ. of North Carolina Press, 1979.

Davis, K. The sociology of prostitution. *American Sociological Review*, 1937, 2, 744-55.

Davis, N. Prostitution: Identity, career, and legal-economic enterprise. In J.M. Henslin & E. Sagarin (Eds.) *The Sociology of Sex.* N.Y.: McGraw-Hill, 1979.

Exner, J.E., Wylie, J., Leura, A. & Parrill, T. Some psychological characteristics of prostitutes. *Journal of Personality Assessment*, 1979, 41, 474-85.

Feldman, E. Prostitution, alien woman and the progressive imagination, 1910-1915. *American Quarterly*, 1968, 20, 192-206.

Glover, E. *The psychopathology of prostitution.* London: Institute for the Study and Treatment of Delinquency, 1945.

James, J., Boyer, D., Withers, J. & Haft, M. *Perspectives on prostitution.* Judicial Advocates, 1980.

James, J., Davis, N. & Vitaliano, P. *Female sexual deviance, a theoretical empirical analysis.* Unpublished manuscript, Univ. of Washington, 1980.

Kemp, T. *Prostitution: An investigation of its causes, especially with regard to hereditary factors.* Copenhagen: Levin & Muhksgaard, 1936.

Klein, D. The etiology of female crime: A review of the literature. In S.K. Datesman & F.R. Scarpitti (Eds.) *Women, Crime and Justice.* N.Y.: Oxford Univ. Press, 1980.

Kneeland, G.J. *Commercialized prostitution in New York City*. N.Y.: Century, 1913.

Limoges, T. *La prostitution à Montréal: Comment, pourquoi certaines femmes deviennent prostituées.* Montreal: Editions de l'Homme, 1967.

Lombroso, C. *The female offender*. N.Y.: Philosophical Library, 1958. (Originally published, 1903).

Murtagh, J.M. & Harris, S. *Cast the first stone*. N.Y.: McGraw Hill, 1957.

Newman, F., & Caplan, P.J. Juvenile female prostitution as gender-consistent response to early derivation. Presented to Institute of Canadian Psychological Association's Section on Women and Psychology, Calgary, 1980, and this issue.

Reckless. W.C. *Vice in Chicago*. Chicago: Univ. of Chicago Press, 1933.

Rosenblum, K. Female deviance and the female sex role: A preliminary investigation. *British Journal of Sociology*, 1975, 26, 169-85.

Seagrave, M. Causes underlying sex delinquency in young girls. *Journal of Social Hygiene*, 1926, 12, 523-29.

Thomas, W.I. *The unadjusted girl*. Montclair, N.J.: Patterson-Smith, 1969.

Vice Commission of Chicago. *The social evil in Chicago*. Chicago: Gunthrop-Warren Printing Co., 1911.

The White Slave Traffic Act: Historical Impact of a Federal Crime Policy on Women

Marlene D. Beckman

ABSTRACT. When Congress passed the White Slave Traffic Act, legislators were strongly influenced by early twentieth century progressive era reformers, who sought to rid the country of commercial prostitution. The statute was directed at the elimination of the business of securing women and girls and selling them outright or exploiting them for immoral purposes. Instead, it was used to prosecute the voluntary and ordinary immoralities of people and to punish the women "victims" whom the law was designed to protect.

On June 25, 1910, Congress passed the White Slave Traffic Act, known as the Mann Act. Progressive era reformers used the catchwords "white slavery" to promote the vision of women held in bondage against their will, of mysterious druggings and abductions of helpless young girls, and of unexplained disappearances of innocent and naive immigrants forced into lives of prostitution and vice. Yet, just several years later, law enforcement officials relied on the White Slave Traffic Act to arrest, prosecute and send to prison a man and a woman who traveled from Jersey City to spend the weekend in New York.

This paper will show how the White Slave Traffic Act was misapplied. The Mann Act was to be directed at the elimination of the business of securing women and girls and selling them outright or exploiting them for immoral purposes. Instead, it was used to prose-

Marlene D. Beckman, U.S. Department of Justice, Washington, D.C. I acknowledge Dr. Claudine SchWeber, Criminal Justice Department, State University College at Buffalo, for getting me started and Wendy Williams, Georgetown University Law Center, for keeping me going.

cute the voluntary and ordinary immoralities of people and to punish the women "victims" whom the law was designed to protect.

DEVELOPMENT AND EXPANSION OF THE WHITE SLAVE TRAFFIC ACT

The White Slave Traffic Act made it a federal crime to engage in prostitution in interstate commerce. The act provided heavy penalties for transporting or in any way aiding, abetting or causing the transporting in interstate or foreign commerce of "any woman or girl for the purpose of prostitution or debauchery, or for any other immoral purpose."[1]

In more than one sense, the name "White Slave Traffic Act" remains a misnomer.[2] First, the act makes no distinction as to the race or the color of the female whose transportation is a violation of the law. Second, in many instances the "victims" willingly consented to the practices in which they were engaged. Nonetheless, Congress gave the act its name because the central purpose of it was to halt what many believed was a serious and widespread practice: foreign-born commercial procurers taking innocent young girls and women by force and holding them captive with threats to their lives, a practice held to resemble black servitude in its exploitative and barbarous nature.

The legislators were influenced by what was taking place in the country. In no period of U.S. history did the custodians of morality direct more serious attention to the eradication of prostitution than during the first two decades of the twentieth century known as the progressive era.[3] The energetic outburst against white slave traffic grew out of the progressive's view that women were naturally chaste and virtuous, and no woman became a whore unless she had first been raped, seduced, drugged or deserted. The image of the prostitute, developed by reformers, was of a lonely and confused female. In the search for explanations of what could have led girls so to degrade and ultimately destroy themselves, the progressive formula maintained that female prostitutes were passive victims of social disequilibrium and the brutality of men. This conception of female weakness and male domination left no room for the possibility that prostitutes might consciously or aggressively choose their activities.[4]

A review of the historical development of the Mann Act reveals two themes. First, Congress intended the act to apply only to commercial vice and those cases where there was evidence of coercion.[5] Second, the act was not intended to apply to ordinary prostitution, control of which remained within the police powers of the states.[6] Instead, Congress intended to supplement local authority by reaching interstate transportation for commercial purposes. Despite this clear congressional intent, inclusion in the statute of the words "any other immoral purpose" had an unforeseen effect: the prosecution of noncommercial sex as a federal crime.

In the 1917 case, *Caminetti* v. *United States*, the U.S. Supreme Court first upheld convictions under the act where there was no evidence that the women were prostitutes, that their actions were involuntary, or that the defendants derived any profit except their own pleasure. In *Caminetti* two men voluntarily accompanied by two women traveled from California to Reno, Nevada, for the weekend. The five-justice majority, relying on the plain meaning of the words "any other immoral purpose," upheld the convictions on the grounds the Mann Act applied to voluntary acts of immorality, even when no commercial intention or business profit was shown.[7]

While opportunities to overrule *Caminetti* subsequently presented themselves, the Court continued to rely on this landmark case. In 1946 it reaffirmed the *Caminetti* holding in *Cleveland* v. *United States* by finding that "other immoral purposes" applied to a Morman who, in practicing polygamy, had frequently transported his wives across state lines.[8] Cases such as *Cleveland* show that the clause "any other immoral purpose" was so broad, it could be used to reach any conduct that fell within the popular understanding of immorality. For a time, the federal courts relied on the controversial immoral status concept to become a censor of the nation's sexual morals. The term "other immoral acts" was held to apply to the interstate transportaton of a woman to work as a chorus girl in a theatre where the woman was exposed to smoking, drinking and cursing;[9] a dentist who met his young lover in a neighboring state and shared a hotel room to discuss her pregnancy;[10] two students at the University of Puerto Rico who had sexual intercourse on the way home from a date;[11] and a man and woman who lived together for four years and traveled around the country as man and wife while the man sold securities.[12]

The activity prohibited by the Mann Act was transportation of "any woman or girl" in interstate commerce. On a plain reading of the act, Congress intended the woman who was to engage in sexual conduct to be treated as the person "transported" and the persons who accompanied her or assisted in her transportation were to be prosecuted as "transporters." Only the latter were targeted by the act's criminal sanctions. The courts, however, went beyond the law's objectives.

While two early cases established that a woman could not be an "accomplice" to the offense of transporting herself from one state to another for immoral purposes, the Court held that the woman may be indicted for *conspiracy.*[13] A woman could have conspired to "commit an offense against the United States" within the meaning of the federal statute, although the objective of the conspiracy was her own transportation in interstate commerce for the purpose of prostitution. The extension of the law of conspiracy to include the woman would, the Court reasoned in the 1915 case of *United States* v. *Holte*, prevent victimization of men. The spectre of blackmail, whereby a woman would lure a man to cross a state line with her and then, by threatening to notify authorities, extort money from him, moved the Court to find a way to prosecute the woman, the language of the act notwithstanding. The woman could now be punished for blackmail or for malicious prosecution. Justice Holmes, writing for the majority in *Holte*, made clear the Court's position:

> We think that it would be going too far to say that the defendant could not be guilty in this case. Suppose, for instance, that a professional prostitute, as well able to look out for herself as was the man, should suggest and carry out a journey within the Act of 1910 in the hope of blackmailing the man, and should buy the railroad tickets, or should pay the fare from Jersey City to New York, she would be within the letter of the Act of 1910, and we see no reason why the act should not be held to apply. We see equally little reason for not treating the preliminary agreement as a conspiracy that the law can reach, if we *abandon the illusion that the woman always is the victim.*[14]

In the 1932 case of *Gebardi* v. *United States*, the Court looked again at this issue and held that for the woman to fall within the ban of the Mann Act, she must at least aid or assist someone else in transporting or procuring transportation for her, and such aid and assistance must be more active than mere acquiescence.[15] This retreat from the broader implications of the earlier *Holte* decision may be explained on the ground that the *Gebardi* Court was confronted with a woman whose only immoral action was acquiescence to interstate transportation, as opposed to the situation in *Holte* in which the woman was actually a prostitute. The facts of *Gebardi* made the need for establishing limits to the *Holte* principle apparent. In fact, the *Gebardi* Court's conclusion was consistent with the contemporary view that women's criminality was due primarily to their economic and psychological dependence on men. It was also more attuned to the act's original philosophy than was the *Holte* decision.

ENFORCEMENT OF THE MANN ACT

In 1969 William Seagle, a commentator on the Mann Act, asserted that the critics of the Mann Act who had made a "bogey law" out of its sweeping potentialities had failed to consider the selectivity that prosecuting officials exercised in the enforcement of the act. Seagle maintained that although the decisions of the courts had allowed wide latitude to law enforcement authorities, U.S. Attorneys had taken little advantage of this latitude; rather, absent commercial vice, they prosecuted only those cases involving highly aggravated circumstances.[16] The evidence, however, contradicts the Seagle theory. Official circulars issued by the U.S. Department of Justice reveal that the Attorney General, concerned about "federal courts allowing themselves to be turned into ordinary police courts," cautioned prosecutors to use their discretion in noncommercial cases. Nevertheless, my review of the official files of individuals convicted under this law suggests that U.S. Attorneys did not exercise the desired restraint.[17] F.B.I. statistics obtained for this project also confirm the finding.[18]

After *Caminetti* established, in 1917, that commercialism was not an essential element of a Mann Act violation, the Attorney General issued a circular outlining the elements of aggravation required for prosecution in noncommercial cases. The guidelines restricted prosecution in noncommercial cases to "those cases involving a fraudulent overreaching, or involving previously chaste, or very young women or girls, or (when State laws are inadequate) involving married women (with young children) then living with their husbands . . . ." The guidelines further provided "that blackmail cases should, so far as possible, be avoided; and that whenever the women herself voluntarily and without any overreaching, has consented to the criminal arrangement she, too, if the case shall seem to demand it, may be prosecuted as a conspirator." These guidelines represented a significant departure from the congressional intent, articulated in the legislative history, to punish only the procuror or transporter of an unwilling victim of commercial vice.[19]

These instructions were re-issued every year from 1917 to 1932.[20] During the 15-year period, the U.S. Attorneys continued to prosecute individuals engaged in strictly personal sexual escapades that in no way involved either commercial gain or exploitation of innocent victims. The evidence presented here cannot be explained by an occasional error on the part of federal prosecutors in judging the circumstances of a particular case to be "aggravated."

A more likely explanation for this overzealous enforcement was the emergence, at the same time, of the Federal Bureau of Investigation (F.B.I.) as a national police force. As one of the first laws to create a "federal" crime, the Mann Act allowed the new crime-fighting office to prove its mettle. F.B.I. agents were encouraged to present to U.S. Attorneys for a decision on prosecution those complaints which alleged interstate transportation but failed to indicate the existence of prostitution.[21] Further, agents actually filed complaints against victims charging them with conspiracy in order to keep them in custody. If the victim later cooperated, she was not prosecuted on a charge of conspiracy because U.S. Attorneys viewed her as a valuable witness. Arrests of women were thus used to induce them to testify against their male "transporters."[22]

In 1932, one month after the *Gebardi* case was decided, the Attorney General altered the guidelines for prosecution for the first time since *Caminetti*. The Attorney General advised that as a result of the *Gebardi* decision, "a woman, by consenting to go and voluntarily going from one state to another with a man, with a view to immoral relations with him, does not violate the conspiracy statute." He instructed U.S. Attorneys to drop from their list of priorities the prosecution of "the woman herself who voluntarily and without any overreaching has consented to the criminal arrangement."[23] Thus, although before *Gebardi* U.S. Attorneys prosecuted women for conspiracy under the Mann Act whether commercial prostitution was involved, the only cases indicting women after *Gebardi* did involve prostitution, albeit sometimes only on an extremely limited scale. Women engaged in prostitution for a short time in order to earn a few dollars for support could hardly be considered models of the commercial vice that concerned Congress when it passed the Mann Act in 1910.[24]

THE WOMEN IN ALDERSON

After 1927, female violators of the Mann Act were sent to the Federal Industrial Institution for Women in Alderson, West Virginia, which was opened that year as the first and only federal prison exclusively for women. Prior to 1927, female federal prisoners were housed in state correctional facilities. Early records of the women incarcerated for Mann Act violations support the hypothesis that the objectives of the White Slave Traffic Act were thwarted in two ways: 1) by prosecuting individuals who were not involved in commercial vice, but rather engaging in ordinary sexual behavior and 2) by prosecuting the female "victims" of a law designed to "protect" women.

The author examined the records of 156 women committed to Alderson for Mann Act violations between the years 1927 and 1937. This sample represents 87% of the total number of women committed for Mann Act violations during this period.[25] The women were divided into four groups based on the extent of commercial vice associated with their offense.[26]

1. Group one consists of those women with no prostitution or commercial activity of any kind connected with their arrest (n=36, 23%). For the most part, these women were traveling with men across state lines, and either one or both of them was married to someone else. One predominant pattern involved single women traveling with men they loved and hoped to marry, but who turned out to be already married; both the woman and the man were arrested as co-conspirators when the man's wife turned them in.
2. Group two includes those women whose prostitution was incidental to their interstate travels with a man, who was sometimes their husband (n=25, 16%). A common pattern here involved a woman who, at the man's insistence, engaged in isolated instances of prostitution to earn enough money so that they could complete their journey.
3. Group three is composed of women involved in commercial prostitution (n=23, 15%). Typically, such women worked in a brothel or house of ill-repute, and were arrested when they solicited at a hotel, and in so doing crossed the state line. These women had become prostitutes to earn enough money to support themselves.

4. Group four is comprised of women who, themselves often prostitutes, were arrested for aiding or securing transportation for another woman to cross state lines for prostitution (n=72, 46%). At one extreme was the madame who actually ran the brothel and recruited new workers; at the other was the woman who wrote a letter to a friend back home suggesting that she might do well to come north and join her in her illegal activity. In one case, a woman was sentenced to 18 months because she gave a friend's name to her boyfriend for this purpose. A factor in this indictment may also have been the fact the woman and her boyfriend were, at the time of the arrest, living together as man and wife.

The women in group one were not involved in commercialized vice and further did not fit the profile of the "aggravated" non-commercial cases that had been established by the Attorney General as targets for federal prosecution. On the contrary, most of these cases contain no hint of commercialism nor of the aggravating circumstances required by the prosecution guidelines. Excerpts from the personal history files of two women in group one are illustrative.

> Viola had known Blake since she was eight years old—he owned a tin shop and she worked in his office, sending out bills and answering the phone. A friend of his came to the shop by the name of Thomas. He was 24 years old and married, but not living with his wife. Viola became infatuated with Thomas. Her family objected to her working for Blake and she finally left home. Blake told her that he was going to close his shop and go away with Loretta and suggested that she go along with Thomas. Viola agreed and they left Pittsburgh and went as far as Fredericksburg, Virginia where they stayed all night, Loretta and Blake registering as man and wife, and Viola and Thomas as man and wife. The next two days they took turns driving and sleeping. The fourth day they decided to separate; she had had quite enough of the trip and wanted to go home. While the two men were willing to send the girls home, Loretta didn't want to be discarded, so she telephoned the police and reported that they were being beaten. All four were arrested and charged with Mann Act violations.
>
> When Elizabeth was 15, she secured employment as a domestic in order to get away from an unhappy home. There

> were nine children in all, and as long as Elizabeth stayed at home, she had to wash, iron and cook for her brothers and sisters only to get unkind words in repay for her efforts. Elizabeth left home and went to live with a maternal aunt who sympathized with her. While she was staying with this aunt, she met and fell in love with a man named Steve. He proposed to her but postponed the date of marriage. Steve asked Elizabeth to accompany him on his business trips to deliver liquor. She did and stayed with him at a hotel as his wife. They made 11 trips until they were both arrested on the road in Fairmont, West Virginia. It was then that Elizabeth first learned that Steve was married and that his wife had turned them in.

Overall, the women in group one cannot be described as fitting the profile of aggravated noncommercial cases. Fifteen of the 36 women are under 20 years of age, 14 are in their 20s, and 7 others are in their 30s. The majority, or 25 of the 36 women, had been married at an earlier time. Only 9, however, were married and living with their husbands at the time of their offense; 13 were separated and 3 were divorced. Only 14 had any children at all and, in 2 of those cases, the children were grown and no longer dependents.[27]

This prosecutorial "indiscretion" in noncommercial cases slowed down only after 1932 when the Attorney General directed U.S. Attorneys to drop women as targets in noncommercial cases. As indicated in Figure 1, after *Gebardi*, women were committed in only five noncommercial cases; in three instances the man involved left behind a wife and children; in the fourth case the woman had an illegitimate child with the man; and in the fifth case, the couple were prosecuted for Mann Act violations only after they were apprehended for holding up a gas station. Women in group two—those women to whom prostitution was incidental to their interstate travels—were still being sent to prison but also in smaller numbers. Eighteen of the 25 in this group were convicted before *Gebardi*, while 7 were convicted following *Gebardi*.[28]

Across all 4 groups, the average age is 28 years with the most pronounced age cluster in the 24 to 30 year old bracket. This is a significant departure from the progressive era stereotype of prostitutes as girls whose youthfulness, naivete and inexperience with the world betrayed them. Also, extending across the entire sample, 107 (69%) were not living with a husband; the majority were separated or divorced. Significantly, few of the women had any dependent

Table 1a - Description of Mann Act Violators by *Number* and Group for Years 1927-1937

	Marital Status[1]			Age			Race		Citizenship		Education		IQ[2]		Children[3]			Prior[4] Convictions		Sentence (Yrs)		Region Where[5] Prosecuted		
Group	S	M	Div	16-19	20-29	30+	W	Blk	USA	Other	None-8th	9th+	50-75	76+	0	1-2	3+	None	1+	1-1½	2-5	South	Midwest	Other
1(N=36)	11	9	16	15	14	7	35	1	36	0	32	4	25	11	22	8	6	33	3	28	8	27	7	2
2(N=25)	7	6	12	5	18	2	25	0	24	1	15	10	13	12	17	7	1	19	6	20	5	19	6	0
3(N=23)	7	7	9	2	19	2	22	1	23	0	16	7	17	6	22	1	0	16	7	18	5	17	3	3
4(N=72)	13	27	32	2	28	42	68	4	67	5	59	13	47	25	42	26	4	38	34	35	37	28	22	22
Total (N=156)	38	49	69	24	79	53	150	6	150	6	122	34	102	54	103	42	11	106	50	101	55	91	38	27

Table 1b - Description of Mann Act Violators by *Percent* and Group for Years 1927-1937

	Marital Status[1]			Age			Race		Citizenship		Education		IQ[2]		Children[3]			Prior[4] Convictions		Sentence (Yrs)		Region Where[5] Prosecuted		
Group	S	M	Div	16-19	20-29	30+	W	Blk	USA	Other	None-8th	9th+	50-75	76+	0	1-2	3+	None	1+	1-1½	2-5	South	Midwest	Other
1(N=36)	31	25	44	42	39	19	97	3	100	—	89	11	69	31	61	22	17	92	8	78	22	75	19	6
2(N=25)	28	24	48	20	72	8	100	—	96	4	60	40	52	48	68	28	4	76	24	80	20	76	24	—
3(N=23)	30	30	40	9	82	9	96	4	100	—	70	30	74	26	96	4	—	70	30	78	22	74	13	13
4(N=72)	18	38	44	3	39	58	94	6	93	7	82	18	65	35	58	36	6	53	47	49	51	38	31	31
Total (N=156)	24	31	45	15	51	34	96	4	96	4	79	21	65	35	66	27	7	68	32	65	35	58	24	17

1. Women separated and widowed were counted in divorced category.
2. Women whose IQ was too low to test were counted in 50-75 category.
3. Children were often not dependent on their mother at time of her arrest, i.e., grown-up, living with father, living with other relatives. The number of women with any dependent children included: Group 1-12, Group 2-6, Group 3-1, and Group 4-19.
4. Prior convictions were usually for such related offenses as prostitution, running a house of prostitution, liquor law violations, and vagrancy.
5. States counted in southern region: Alabama, Arkansas, Florida, Georgia, Louisiana, Mississippi, North Carolina, South Carolina, Tennessee, Texas, Virginia, and West Virginia. Midwestern states included: Illinois, Indiana, Iowa, Michigan, Minnesota, Missouri, Ohio, and Wisconsin.

FIGURE 1 - NUMBER OF MANN ACT CASES THAT RESULTED IN COMMITMENTS TO ALDERSON BEFORE AND AFTER *Gebardi* in 1932, by Group.

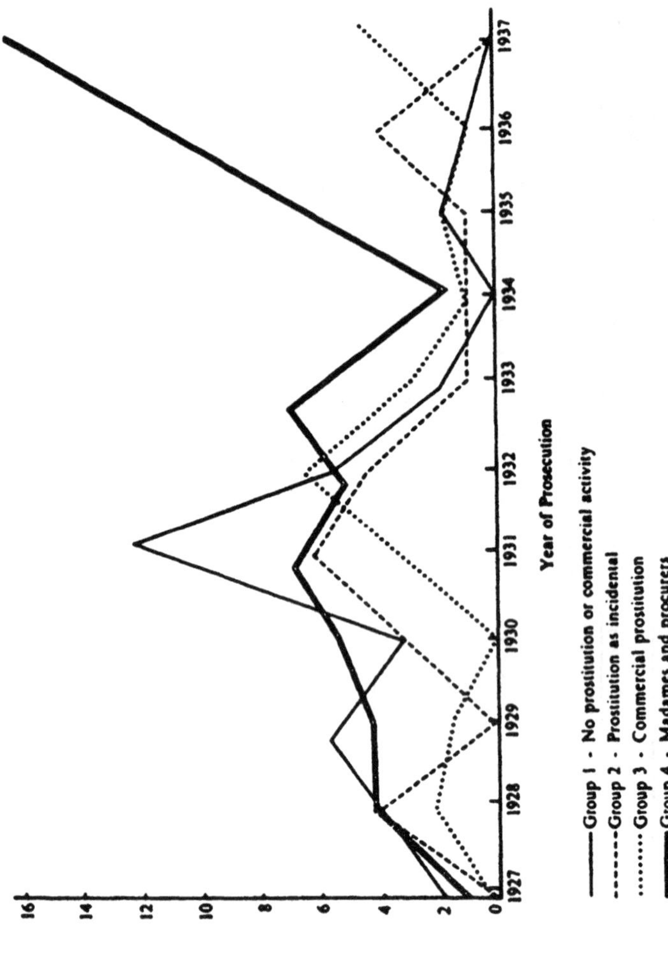

children. Of the total 156 women, only 38 had dependent children at the time of their arrest; aside from 9 with 3 or more dependents, 8 had 2 dependent children, and the remaining 21 had 1 dependent child. Almost all these women received low scores on the Binet Simon IQ test routinely administered by prison officials with 102 (65%) scoring below 76. Thirty-four (21%) went beyond the eighth grade in school.[29]

In contrast to the disproportionately black prison population in this country today, 150 (96%) of the women in the sample are white. Of the six black women, one became infatuated with a white fireman who took her from Montgomery, Alabama, to Columbus, Ohio, where they lived as man and wife until they were arrested. The second was the illegitimate daughter of a white prostitute mother and black father; she too became a prostitute to support her lover. The remaining four black women were madames—one was 63 years old.[30]

Despite the anxiety over "widespread prostitution by alien women," only six women were not U.S. citizens and of those, five were procurers. The sixth was a Mexican woman who most closely resembles the lawmakers stereotype of a "victim." The woman did not speak a word of English and was forced to commit acts of prostitution by her boyfriend, who held her captive by pocketing the money she earned and in return gave her gifts of inexpensive jewelry. Not only did this woman receive a prison sentence, she was also deported.[31]

Overall, the family histories of these women reveal deprived life experiences. Typically, the woman left home at an early age (i.e., 13 or 14) to enter a bad marriage or take on a menial job in the city. She sought to escape abusive parents who had forced her to quit school, or desolate rural surroundings. In many cases, her father or mother died when she was very young, and she had to take care of the surviving parent and a large number of even younger siblings. Most of these women were unskilled and had little education. They were, for the most part, law-abiding individuals. Only 16 women of a total of 84 in the first 3 groups had any prior convictions.[32] The following three case histories exemplify this pattern:

> When Leota's father became deputy sheriff in 1926, he began to drink liquor, deserted his family several times and repeatedly beat his wife and children. Leota's mother did washing, ironing and sewing in order to support herself and

the children. Leota made good grades and wanted to complete high school, but her father would not allow her to continue school after she was fourteen. Leota did the housework and took care of her younger brother and sister while her mother worked. Several times her father left the family without food and money and would be gone for weeks at a time. In 1928 he lost his position and took work now and then on the highway. He would come home at all hours and if supper was not ready, he would threaten to kill his wife. One night Leota heard her father threaten to kill her mother if she didn't get the salt shaker for him. After her mother got it, he threw his plate full of hot food at her. Leota ran to a neighbor's house and called the police who came and put her father in jail. When he was released on bond, he beat Leota and the other children every-time he came home from work. When Leota's sweetheart came and found her in tears, he begged her to marry him. She consented and left for Louisiana to get married since it took several days to get a license in Texas. Leota admits having immoral relations on the road. As soon as Leota's father learned that she was going to get married, he notified the police. She was arrested two weeks later.

Betty is the 7th of 15 children. Her childhood was very unhappy due to the family's poverty and her father's drinking liquor. Three siblings starved to death when they were infants. The father was never very ambitious and never provided a good home. Her parents and their five small children live in a one room shack and are considered "white trash." Betty finished the 5th grade and then ran away from home because her father was drunk and beat her often. She went to a tourist camp and worked for $10.00/week making beds and running errands. She sent this money to her mother and prostituted for her spending money. Betty has prostituted since she was 12 years of age. She was only 16 years old at the time of this arrest.

Ruby's mother died in childbirth when Ruby's father refused to call a doctor. He seemed repentant for a short while, then deserted the children. Ruby and her two young brothers shifted for themselves. Ruby had been going with a man by the name of Elmer. He was married, but separated from his wife and was expecting to divorce. After Ruby's father deserted the children, Ruby completed the 8th grade by living with Elmer's

> mother and working for her room and board. Elmer asked her to take a trip with him to Stubenville, Ohio promising that they would be gone only a few days. His mother thought it was okay for Ruby to go. Ruby had immoral relations with Elmer and lived with him for several days. When Elmer's wife learned that Elmer had taken Ruby across the state line, she reported it to the F.B.I. and they were both arrested for Mann Act violations.

In sum, the evidence shows that the women committed to Alderson for Mann Act violations were neither the helpless, naive, exploited "white slaves" of the Progressive Era imagination nor the independent, economically sophisticated, self-determining women the *Holte* Court believed them to be. The truth is somewhere in between. In reality, the female "violators" of the Mann Act were "victims" of their own hard lives and the morals of the time.

THE PRESENT STATUS OF THE MANN ACT

Law enforcement authorities have become less enthusiastic about enforcing a law which has grown increasingly unpopular with changes in sexual mores over the years. The U.S. National Archives and Records Service has prepared a historical narrative of the White Slave Traffic Act, based on extensive review of F.B.I. headquarters records. The narrative reports that:

> In 1962 the Department of Justice prohibited U.S. Attorneys from prosecuting noncommercial cases without express approval of the Criminal Division. The F.B.I. followed suit relying on local authorities to handle routine cases and concentrating on "organized commercialized prostitution." It is currently a low priority in F.B.I. field offices.[33]

Nonetheless, men and women are still being sent to prison for Mann Act violations. According to federal prison system records, 439 defendants were committed to federal prisons between 1970 and 1982 for violations of the act, 35 of whom are women. Although a review of the records of all 35 women most recently convicted is beyond the scope of this paper, it is reasonable to assume from post-*Gebardi* trends that these women more closely resemble the violators whom Congress had in mind when the statute was enacted. While these women are more likely to be madames or procurers of other women for prostition, they are not any more likely than their predecessors to be part of an organized white slave ring. Moreover, even though the Mann Act has decreased in use as a penal law, Congress has breathed new life into it. In 1978 the act was amended to make the interstate transportation of minor boys for sexual purposes a crime.[34] Whether this recent expression of legislative intent to protect young males will result in the same kinds of distortions by courts and enforcement agencies remains to be seen.

REFERENCES

1. The White Slave Traffic Act, ch. 395, 36 Stat. 825 (1910) (codified as amended at 18 U.S.C. §§ 2421-2424 (1976 and Supp. V 1981), includes this provision: "That any person who shall knowingly transport or cause to be transported, or aid or assist in obtaining transportation for, or in transporting, in interstate or foreign commerce . . . any woman or girl for the purpose of prostitution or debauchery, or for any other immoral purpose, or with the intent and purpose to induce, entice, or compel such woman or girl to become a prostitute or to give herself up to debauchery, or to engage in any other immoral practice; . . . shall be deemed guilty of a felony, and upon conviction thereof shall be punished by a fine not exceeding five thousand dollars, or by imprisonment of not more than five years; or by both such fine and imprisonment, in the discretion of the court."

2. According to Vern and Bonnie Bullough, *Prostitution: An Illustrated Social History* (New York: Crown Publishers, Inc., 1978), p. 245, the term "White Slavery" is often attributed to Clifford G. Roe, an Assistant State's Attorney in Illinois and a leader in the fight against involuntary prostitution. Roe supposedly used the term at the beginning of the twentieth century when he became involved in a case in which a girl had thrown a note from a house of prostitution. She had written: "Help me—I am held captive as a white slave." The incident may have occurred, but the term predated Roe's use. The term also comes from the English translation of the French term, "Traite des Blanches," trade in whites, used in Paris in 1902 at a conference of 15 European nations to discuss the problem of international trade in women and children. At an earlier international conference on the Negro slave trade, the French had used the phrase "Traite des Noires," trade in blacks, and the reference to white trade was used to contrast the later conference with the earlier one. The British Government translated the French term as "White Slave Traffic or Trade," and in the United States, this translation was usually abbreviated to "White Slavery."

3. E. Feldman, "Prostitution, the Alien Woman and the Progressive Imagination," *American Quarterly* 19 Summer (1967) 2, part I: 200, reports that between 1890 and 1900 the *Reader's Guide to Periodical Literature* lists 36 entries under the separate subject of "Prostitution"; between the years 1910 and 1914 entries climbed sharply to 156 and then dropped to 41, 1915-1924.

4. Alan Block, "Aw! Your Mother's in the Mafia: Women Criminals in Progressive New York," in *The Criminology of Deviant Women*, ed. Freda Adler and Rita Simon (Boston: Houghton, Mifflin, 1979), p. 180.

5. On December 10, 1909, the immigration commissioner made a personal appearance before Congress to testify about the prosecutions initiated by immigration agents against pimps and procurers. In his introduction the Commissioner referred to the importing and harboring of alien women and girls for immoral purposes and the practice of prostitution or the

so-called "white slave traffic" as the most pitiful and revolting phase of the immigration problem. The commissioner painted a lurid picture of the capture of young girls who were subsequently forced into lives of squalor and prostitution.

Eleven days after the commissioner's testimony, Representative Mann reported from committee the bill that Congress subsequently enacted as the White Slave Traffic Act. The purpose of the bill as stated in the House report includes the following: "[The Act] does not attempt to regulate the practice of voluntary prostitution, but aims solely to prevent panders and procurers from compelling thousands of women and girls against their will and desire to enter and continue in a life of prostitution." Representative Mann defined the term "white slave" to include "only those women and girls who are literally slaves—those women who are owned and held as property and chattels. . . those women and girls who, if given a fair chance, would, in all human probability, have been good wives and mothers and useful citizens."

6. Representative Mann emphasized that the intent of Congress was "not to interfere with or usurp in any way the police powers of the states." He stated that "the punishment of the practice of prostitution or the keeping of houses of ill-fame, or other immoral places, in the several states, are matters wholly within the powers of the states. . . ." This distinction made by Representative Mann between the aims of the act and "ordinary prostitution" was an important one. Power to enact this legislation was derived from the commerce clause and extended only to interstate criminal activity. Mann and others justified this early interstate crime by analogizing the transportation of women (who, if the rhetoric is to be taken at face value, were viewed as passive, nonvolitional victims) to the interstate transportation of goods for commercial purposes.

7. 242 U.S. 470, 485 (1917). Factors unique to the circumstances of *Caminetti* may have led to the prosecution and conviction of the defendants. First, the interstate weekend was not a casual affair, but rather the culmination of the seduction of two young women, aged 19 and 20, by married men in a situation not entirely free from coercion. The men had apparently concealed their marital and parental status from the women. When the women discovered the truth, the men allegedly induced the women to take the trip to Reno by telling them that their wives would prosecute them in the juvenile court if they were found out. Second, the case had political overtones. Representative Mann and his Republican colleagues were eager to direct national attention to the fact that one of the seducers was Drew Caminetti, the son of the Democratic commissioner of immigration.

8. 329 U.S. 14 (1946).

9. *Athanasaw* v. *United States*, 227 U.S. 326 (1913).

10. *Carey* v. *United States*, 265 F. 515 (8th Cir. 1920).

11. *Jarabo* v. *United States*, 158 F.2d 509 (1st Cir. 1946).

12. *MacKreth* v. *United States*, 103 F.2d 495 (5th Cir. 1939).

13. *United States* v. *Holte*, 236 U.S. 140 (1915); *Diggs* v. *United States*, 220 F. 545 (1915).

14. *Holte* at 145 (emphasis added).

15. 287 U.S. 112 (1932). The *Gebardi* Court left open the question of just how much activity over and above mere acquiescence would bring the woman's conduct within the ban of the statute.

16. William Seagle, "The Twilight of the Mann Act," 55 *American Bar Association Journal* 643 (1969).

17. U.S., Department of Justice Circular No. 647, issued January 26, 1917. From the beginning, the department has advised district attorneys: "As to specific cases, the Department must rely upon the discretion of the District Attorneys who have firsthand knowledge of the facts, and opportunity for personal interviews with the witnesses, and who will thus be able to ascertain what circumstances of aggravation, if any, attend the offense, the age and relative interest of the parties, the motives of those urging prosecution, and what reasons, if any, exist for thinking the ends of justice will be better served by a prosecution under Federal law than under the laws of the State having jurisdiction."

18. 1939 and 1940 are the only years for which conviction statistics contain a breakdown

of defendants and victims by both age and sex and whether commercial activity was involved. Fiscal year 1939 data show that out of a total of 425 cases, 88 did not involve commercial interstate activity. In 1940, the total cases numbered 415, of which 106 were not commercial interstate situations.

19. U.S., Department of Justice Circular No. 647, issued January 26, 1917.

20. For example, U.S., Department of Justice Circular No. 986, issued August 5, 1919; U.S., Department of Justice Circular No. 2027, issued April 19, 1929.

21. F.B.I. Policy Memorandum No. 66-6200-31 issued September 15, 1949, and titled "Policy and Procedure: White Slave Traffic Act," p. 10.

22. *Ibid.* at 41.

23. U.S., Department of Justice Circular No. 2347, issued December 14, 1932.

24. With regard to convictions of women F.B.I. data show that in fiscal year 1939 of a total of 429 defendants *committed* for commercial trafficking, 93 were female; out of 88 defendants *committed* where there was no evidence of commercialism, 6 were women. In 1949, of the 357 defendants *committed* for commercial trafficking, 49 were female, and out of 106 defendants committed where there was no commercialism, none were female. No sex comparison data is available for the years prior to the *Gebardi* decision.

25. This particular 10-year span was selected because of the special interest in noting the after-effects of the 1932 *Gebardi* case on subsequent convictions of women. There were a total of 179 Mann Act commitments to Alderson during this period. Twenty-three records were unavailable (i.e., missing or incomplete); therefore the study deals with the 156 cases for which information is available.

26. Although this information is self-reported, there are two checks on accuracy. First, the inmate had already been sentenced and was incarcerated and therefore had little to gain by being untruthful to institutional social workers. Second, the information reported was corroborated by a description of the circumstances of the offense completed by the prosecuting official and included in the inmate's file for later determination of parole eligibility.

27. U.S., National Archives, Department of Justice, Bureau of Prisons, Record Group Number 129, Alderson Inmate Case Files, 1927-1940.

28. *Ibid.*

29. *Ibid.*

30. *Ibid.*

31. *Ibid.*

32. *Ibid.*

33. Brief for Plaintiff at Appendix X, Vol. II, Category 31, n.p., *American Friends Service v. Webster*, No. 79-1655 (D.D.C., Appendix filed Jan. 8, 1982). This appendix is an appraisal of the records of the F.B.I. submitted to the court by the National Archives and Records Service.

34. Pub. L. No. 95-225, § 3, 92 Stat. 7, 8-9 (1978) (codified at 18 U.S.C. § 2423 (1982)).

Free, Indentured, Enslaved: Chinese Prostitutes in Nineteenth-Century America

Lucie Cheng Hirata

In societies undergoing rapid industrialization, prostitution serves a double economic function. It helps to maintain the labor force of single young men, which is in the interest of the capitalists who would otherwise have to pay higher wages to laborers with families to support. In addition, prostitution enables entrepreneurs to extract large profits from the work of women under their control and thus accumulate considerable capital for other investments. Further, in multiracial areas, prostitutes of minority or colonized groups can also provide cheap labor themselves. Chinese prostitutes in the nineteenth-century American West performed all three functions as free agents and as enslaved and indentured workers.

After the formal abolition of black slavery, the capitalist mode of production predominated in nineteenth-century America. However, aspects of slavery persisted in varying degrees among racial minorities, for example, in contract labor and in Chinese prostitution in California. White prostitution on the American frontier quickly moved from a pre-capitalist form of organization to one characterized by either a partnership between madam and prostitutes or a relationship of employer and

This paper is part of a research project on "Asian American Labor before World War II" organized by the Asian American Studies Center at UCLA. I am indebted to Edna Bonacich, Alex Saxton, Gerald Surh, Peg Strobel, Don Nakanishi, and three anonymous reviewers for their helpful comments on an earlier draft. Special thanks to Gary Okihiro, who gave editorial assistance; to Paul Nakatsuka, who extracted part of the data from the census manuscripts; and to the Mormon Temple Library in Los Angeles, the Bancroft Library, the Library of Congress, and the National Archives for permission to use their collections. I wish also to acknowledge a grant from the UCLA Academic Senate which made this research possible. Parts of this essay are summarized and incorporated in my "Chinese Immigrant Women in Nineteenth-Century California," in *Women of America*, ed. C. Berkin and M. B. Norton (Boston: Houghton Mifflin Co., 1979).

[Signs: *Journal of Women in Culture and Society* 1979, vol. 5, no. 1]

wageworker. Chinese prostitution, in contrast, remained a semifeudal organization until the twentieth century. While sexual prejudice obscured the exploitative nature of prostitution as a business, a sense of racial superiority at first led whites to condone Chinese female slavery.[1] In addition, the linkages between the emigrant societies in China and the Chinese community in California helped to perpetuate the precapitalist relations in prostitution. Chinese prostitution also provided Chinese entrepreneurs one of the few opportunities to accumulate capital in a hostile society.

This paper will examine the social history of Chinese prostitution within the context of conditions in nineteenth-century China and the economic development of California. It will focus on Chinese prostitution as an economic institution and on the Chinese prostitute as a particular class of labor, earning direct or indirect profits for a complex web of individuals. Furthermore, it will seek to explicate the double oppression by race and sex and the lethal exploitation of Chinese prostitutes both as part of the working class in America and as sacrificial victims for the maintenance of patriarchy in semifeudal China.

Conditions Leading to the Importation of Women for Prostitution

Victimized by population pressure, landlord oppression, and foreign imperialism, many peasant families in nineteenth-century China lived on the edge of subsistence.[2] In a number of communities, particularly in Fujian and Guangdong, where emigration to distant lands was feasible, a large proportion of the male population left home in search of employment.[3]

In times of natural disaster and war, families often resorted to infanticide, abandonment, mortgaging, or selling of children.[4] Females, whose labor was less valuable than that of males, were frequently the first victims of extreme poverty. Furthermore, in patriarchal and patrilineal Chinese society, the family that raised a girl would not benefit from her labor and she could never carry on the ancestral line.

1. Later on, when anti-Chinese sentiment grew into a widespread movement, the slavery aspect of Chinese prostitution was emphasized in anti-Chinese rhetoric (see, e.g., California Senate, *Chinese Immigration* [Sacramento: State Office, 1878] [hereafter known as California Senate]).

2. F. Wakeman, *Strangers at the Gate* (Berkeley: University of California Press, 1966), pp. 117–56; K. Hsiao, *Rural China* (Seattle: University of Washington Press, 1967).

3. T. Chen, *Emigrant Communities in South China* (New York: Institute of Pacific Relations, 1940); Hsiao.

4. Hsiao, pp. 311–411; A. Smith, *Village Life in China* (New York: Greenwood Press, 1899), pp. 258–316; P. Ho, *Studies on the Population of China* (Cambridge, Mass.: Harvard University Press, 1959), pp. 58–62.

One remunerative solution for relieving the family of its female members was prostitution: the family did not have to provide for the girl's upkeep and her sale or part of her earnings could help support the family. The importance of this for the survival of the family is seen in the report of a Qing dynasty official, that ten family members were dependent for their sustenance upon every prostitute in Canton.[5]

The discovery of gold in 1848 along the Sacramento River brought thousands of immigrants from many countries to California.[6] Mining was an exclusively male activity; few of the men brought families with them because, among other reasons, mining involved moving from place to place seeking the most productive site. Among the first female arrivals were prostitutes of varying racial and national origins.[7] In San Francisco, where miners from nearby sites congregated during the winter and where immigrants gathered before they went into the mining areas, prostitution became a lucrative business. It was not uncommon for successful prostitutes to use their earnings to finance the miners or to invest in other pursuits.[8] The tremendous sexual imbalance (shown in table 1) and the lack of alternative employment made prostitution a major occu-

Table 1

Sex Ratio of Chinese and Total Population in California, 1850–1970

	Chinese*	Total*
1850	39.450†	1.228.6
1860	1.858.1	255.1
1870	1.172.3	165.4
1880	1.832.4	149.3
1890	2.245.4	137.6
1900	1.223.9	123.5
1910	1.017.0	125.4
1920	528.8	112.5
1930	298.6	107.6
1940	223.6	103.7
1950	161.9	100.1
1960	127.8	99.5
1970	107.0	96.9

SOURCES.—Ratio for Chinese from 1860 to 1960 based on California Department of Industrial Relations, *Californians of Japanese, Chinese, and Filipino Ancestry* (San Francisco: State Office, 1965); 1970 data based on U.S. Bureau of the Census, *Historical Census of the United States*, Bicentennial ed. (Washington, D.C.: Government Printing Office, 1975).

*Males per 100 females.

†There were only two Chinese women in 1850.

5. D. Chen, *Zhong-guo fu-nü sheng-huo-shi* (Shanghai: Shang-wu, 1928), p. 296.

6. J. Borthwick, *The Gold Hunters* (New York: Book League, 1929).

7. D. Smith, *Rocky Mountain Mining Camps* (Lincoln: University of Nebraska Press, 1967).

8. Ibid.

pation for women. This relationship between a surplus of males, limited employment opportunities for women, and the demand for prostitution in developing areas is well documented by Boserup.[9]

The demand for prostitution in San Francisco was partially met by Chinese women from Hong Kong, Canton, and its surrounding areas. Canton, opened up as a treaty port under the guns of Western imperialism, and Hong Kong, ceded to the British after the Opium War, were the first cities where a large number of foreigners arrived, and from them the early Chinese prostitutes came.[10]

Only a few women crossed the Pacific on their own in search of better compensation for their labor in prostitution. Usually the family, not the girl, arranged the sale. Girls often accepted their sale, however reluctantly, out of filial loyalty, and most of them were not in a position to oppose their families' decision. In addition, the sheltered and secluded lives that women were forced to live made them particularly vulnerable to manipulation, and many were tricked or lured into prostitution.

An important but unexplored facet of the relationship between patriarchy and prostitution in the Chinese case is its role in perpetuating Chinese sojourning abroad and in its support of the migrant labor system in America. The Chinese patriarchal family system discouraged or even forbade "decent" women from traveling abroad. In addition, the anti-Chinese sentiment and violence in California was often cited by immigrant Chinese merchants as a major reason for not bringing their families.[11] These two factors discouraged the emigration of Chinese women, who would have made possible a stable Chinese community in America. The failure of the Chinese to form families that would reproduce the work force locally prolonged the use of the Chinese by American employers as a migrant labor force.

Further, the patriarchal system required the preservation of the relationship between the men who went abroad to seek work and the families they left behind. It was common practice for the emigrant male to marry before his departure to insure that a wife be at home to fulfill his filial duties and with luck to give him a male descendant. These married women in the emigrant communities of China and Hong Kong, as noted by Chen Ta and Watson, were under more watchful eyes than their counterparts in nonemigrant communities.[12] The relatives were

9. E. Boserup, *Women's Role in Economic Development* (London: Allen & Unwin, 1970).

10. Y. Wu, *Er-shi-nian mu-du guai-xian-zhuang* (Hong Kong: Guang-zhi, 1903), pp. 238–43; X. Chen, *Dan-min di yan-jiu* (Shanghai: Shang-wu, 1946), pp. 124–28; U.S. Congress Joint Special Committee to Investigate Chinese Immigration, *Report* (Washington, D.C.: Government Printing Office, 1877), p. 286 (hereafter cited as U.S. Congress); O. Gibson, *Chinese in America* (Cincinnati: Hitchcock Printers, 1877), p. 134.

11. Zhong-guo ko-shang hui-guan, "Letter," *Tung-ngai san-luk* (February 8, 1855).

12. T. Chen; J. Watson, *Emigration and the Chinese Lineage* (Berkeley and Los Angeles: University of California Press, 1975).

charged with the duty of keeping the women of the emigrants "pure," and in return the emigrants were obliged to send their earnings to support their families. This arrangement permitted the preservation of the Chinese family at home and the perpetuation of the Chinese emigrant laborer's sojourning role in America. The emigrants, whenever they could afford it, returned to China to sire a child. If the child was a boy, he eventually joined his father in America. This arrangement recirculated Chinese labor in the migrant labor system; and the home villages of China reproduced the labor force, in terms of procreation and child rearing, for work in America.

Chinese prostitution was an integral part of that arrangement. While patriarchy prohibited the emigration of "decent" women, it did not forbid the emigration of prostitutes. The emigration of Chinese prostitutes helped to stabilize and preserve the family because Chinese emigrant males could thereby avoid liaisons which might lead to permanent relationships with foreign women. On the other hand, the earnings of Chinese prostitutes in America helped to support their families in China. One such prostitute sent back as much as $200 or $300 after seven months in San Francisco.[13]

The phenomenon of Chinese sojourning and the use of Chinese as migrant labor could not be attributed to poverty, patriarchy, and prostitution alone. Equally, if not more important, was the racist hostility of white society. In addition, like the European colonists who often made sure that the African laborer's wife and children did not follow the man to his new workplace,[14] American capitalists paid low wages to Chinese men to deter their women from crossing the Pacific. (The same phenomenon is observed in Western Europe today.[15]) Some whites in California advocated the importation of more Chinese laborers and not their women so they would not establish a permanent population here; others advocated the importation of more Chinese prostitutes who could meet the sexual demands of Chinese men and thus lessen the threat they perceived to white womanhood.[16] Similar arguments were later advanced by whites in Australia vis-à-vis Japanese prostitutes.[17]

Despite these mutual economic and social advantages, profit was undoubtedly the major reason for the creation and maintenance of the traffic in prostitution. Two distinct periods of Chinese prostitution in California corresponded with two types of relations in profit making: (*a*)

13. Wang Ah-so's letter to her mother in *Orientals and Their Cultural Adjustment*, ed. Fisk University, Social Science Institute (Nashville, Tenn.: Fisk University Social Science Institute, 1946), p. 34 (hereafter cited as Fisk University).

14. Boserup, p. 76.

15. S. Castles and G. Kosack, *Immigrant Workers and Class Structure in Western Europe* (London: Oxford University Press, 1973).

16. "Editorial," *Out West* (1911), pp. 355–56; U.S. Congress, pp. 141, 652.

17. R. Evans, " 'Soiled Doves': Prostitution and Society in Colonial Queensland," *Hecate* 1 (July 1975): 6–24.

the initial period of free competition, during which the prostitute was also the owner of her body service; and (*b*) a period of organized trade, during which the prostitute was a semislave and other individuals shared the benefits of her exploitation.

Period of Free Competition: The Self-employed Prostitutes and Small Entrepreneurs

The brief period of free competition (ca. 1849–54) was characterized by individual initiative and enterprise. Like their white counterparts, a number of Chinese prostitutes during this period were able to accumulate sufficient capital to leave the profession. Some returned to China as relatively affluent members of the business community. Others remained in America and either continued in prostitution as brothel owners or invested in other businesses.

Among the first Chinese female residents in America allegedly was a twenty-year-old prostitute from Hong Kong who landed in San Francisco late in 1848.[18] A free agent serving a predominantly non-Chinese clientele during a period of affluence, she accumulated enough money to buy a brothel within two years and retired the widow of a wealthy Chinese man.[19]

Other free-agent prostitutes during this initial period emigrated under different circumstances. A popular social novel in the late Qing dynasty period told of a Cantonese prostitute brought to San Francisco by her American paramour when she was eighteen. After seven years, she returned to Hong Kong with approximately $16,300, married a Chinese laborer, and opened a store specializing in foreign goods.[20]

This period of free competition among owner-prostitutes did not last long. Few Chinese prostitutes could afford the transportation expenses or had the business know-how to take advantage of the situation. Still, the affluence of the male residents and the extreme imbalance of the sexes suggested that a considerable sum of money could be made in the business. That prospect attracted Chinese entrepreneurs, who organized various aspects of the business; specialization occurred and a monopoly developed by 1854 under the control of the Chinese secret societies.

The Period of Organized Trade

In contrast to the first phase, the second period of Chinese prostitution in California (ca. 1854–1925) was characterized by a widespread

18. C. Gentry, *Madams of San Francisco* (New York: Doubleday & Co., 1964).

19. S. Wu, *Mei-guo Huo-qiao bai-nian ji-shi* (Hong Kong: by the author, 1954); Gentry; C. Lee, *Days of the Tong Wars* (New York: Ballantine Books, 1974); Borthwick.

20. Y. Wu, pp. 238–43.

organization of the trade with a network of specialized functions extending across the Pacific to Canton and Hong Kong. The persons chiefly responsible for this trade were the procurers who kidnapped, enticed, or bought Chinese women; the importers who brought them into America; the brothel owners who lived by their exploitation; the Chinese highbinders who collected fees for protecting them from other highbinders; the police who collected monies for keeping them from being arrested; and the white Chinatown property owners who leased their land and buildings for exorbitant rents.

The process by which brothels in San Francisco obtained their inmates was complex. The owner of a brothel recruited workers either by taking a trip to Canton or Hong Kong or by securing them through an agent or importer. A West Coast newspaper reported that agents of California brothels regularly went about China buying girls and young women. These agents received a regular circular or "price current" from San Francisco giving them information concerning the state of the market and the maximum prices which could be paid to derive an acceptable profit.[21]

Luring and kidnapping were the most frequent methods of procurement, particularly after 1870. When the agents did not find enough females to fill their orders, they sent subagents into rural districts to lure or kidnap girls and young women and forward the victims to them at the shipping ports.[22] Quite frequently those individuals who did the luring were returned emigrants from that community. The baits used included promises of gold, marriage, jobs, or education.[23] Sometimes the victims were invited to see the big American steamer anchored at the docks, and while they were enjoying the tour, the boat would sail off to San Francisco.[24] More often, kidnapping was carried out by force, and the victims were sometimes daughters of relatively well-to-do families.[25]

A number of women came to San Francisco under a contractual arrangement similar to that described in the Chinese contract coolie system.[26] The contract involved body service for a specified time, and if the prostitute succeeded in fulfilling the terms of service, she could, theoretically, get out of the business. Families, rather than women them-

21. *Eureka West Coast Signal* (January 6, 1875).

22. C. Holder, "Chinese Slavery in America," *North American Review* 165 (1897): 285–94.

23. C. Shepherd, "Chinese Girl Slavery in America," *Missionary Review* 46 (1923): 893–98; Fisk University, pp. 31–35; U.S. Industrial Commission, *Report*, 21 vols. (Washington, D.C.: Government Printing Office, 1901), 15:783–90 (hereafter cited as U.S. Industrial Commission).

24. Shepherd, pp. 896–97.

25. C. Dobie, *San Francisco's Chinatown* (New York: Appleton-Century Publishers, 1936), p. 69.

26. Z. Chen, "Shi-jiu shi-ji sheng-xing di qi-yue Hua-gong-zhi," *Li-shi Yan-jiu* 79 (1963): 161–79.

selves, participated in these transactions. Most Chinese women, who could not read or write, could easily be duped into affixing their thumbprint to any document by the agent or party who was the beneficiary of the contract.

In the organization of the trade, importation was a separate activity from that of procurement. Importers received the women from the recruiting agents, arranged for their passage, and handed them over to the brothel owners upon arrival in the United States. Although other secret societies were known to have engaged in the traffic of women,[27] the Hip-Yee Tong was clearly the predominant importer during the third quarter of the nineteenth century. It was estimated that between 1852 and 1873, the Hip-Yee Tong alone imported 6,000 women,[28] or about 87 percent of the total number of Chinese women who arrived during that period. The Hip-Yee Tong charged a $40 fee to each buyer, $10 of which were said to have gone to white policemen.[29] The Hip-Yee netted an estimated $200,000 between 1852 and 1873 from the import business.[30]

The traffic in women became more difficult after the passage of the code which allowed the commissioner of immigration to prevent certain classes of people, including "lewd or debauched" women, from immigrating to California,[31] and the enactment of the Page Act of 1875. The immediate effectiveness of these laws in reducing the number of female arrivals is unclear, but the statutes did subject women to close scrutiny both in Hong Kong and San Francisco and eventually made it more expensive to import women. These added expenses took the form of bribes which had to be paid to various U.S. consulate and customs officials.

The American consulate in Hong Kong was charged with the initial examination of Chinese women to determine if they were "lewd or debauched." If the consul's office was convinced of their good character, it would stamp the women's arms and send them to the harbor master, who would do the same. Only then would the women be allowed to purchase tickets and board the steamer.[32] The certificate with the woman's photograph issued by the consulate was mailed to the collector of customs at San Francisco. Women without appropriate documentation were refused landing and often had to wait more than twenty-four hours before they were cleared.[33] This procedure was subject to abuse by cor-

27. R. Park and H. Miller, *Old World Traits Transplanted* (New York: Harper & Bros., 1921), p. 164; R. Lee, *The Chinese in the United States of America* (Hong Kong: Hong Kong University, 1960).

28. Gibson (n. 10).

29. *Alta California* (December 14, 1869).

30. Gibson.

31. *Statutes of California and Amendments, 1873–74* (Sacramento: State Office, 1875).

32. *Alta California* (August 27, 1873).

33. U.S. Congress, pp. 387–920.

rupt consular officials, who could be convinced of a woman's good character with money or could refuse to certify a woman's good character without money. It was discovered in 1879 that Consul Bailey's office received $10–$15 for every woman shipped to the United States during his tenure in Hong Kong.[34]

Americans on this side of the Pacific also benefited materially from these new statues. As noted by the U.S. Supreme Court, the 1873 code was subject to a variety of abuses: "It is hardly possible to conceive a statute more skillfully framed, to place in the hands of a single man the power to prevent, entirely, the vessels engaged in a foreign trade, say with China, from carrying passengers, or to compel them to submit to systematic extortion of the grossest kind." The commissioner, noted the Court, could arbitrarily designate immigrants as paupers, idiots, convicted criminals, or prostitutes and deny them entrance on that basis.[35]

These regulations benefited white lawyers as well as the customs inspector. Some lawyers colluded with the Chinese importers in obtaining habeas corpus decrees to allow the landing of Chinese women headed for the brothels.[36] Although a number of these women were legal immigrants, some probably sought the help of American lawyers because U.S. customs officers were dissatisfied with their documentation.

The Chinese Exclusion Act of 1882 allowed only women who were native born, married, or born overseas to domiciled merchants to immigrate to the United States. Accordingly, enterprising Chinese developed elaborate arrangements to continue the traffic in women. Chinese agents in the United States instructed agents in China to coach the emigrant women in responding to questions by the immigration authorities. These coaching papers, circulated in Hong Kong and Canton, included eighty-one questions on subjects ranging from standard personal details to the geography of San Francisco.[37]

Each successive law placing additional restrictions on Chinese immigration provided more opportunities for corruption. People soon found that U.S. immigration inspectors and interpreters could easily be persuaded to accept bribes to render favorable decisions and interpretations of the law.[38] As the rules became more severe, the investigation of the immigrants' status took longer to complete, and the immigrants were subjected to greater indignities, pain, and suffering. Beginning in 1891 and particularly after 1910, Chinese men and women were detained at Angel Island while waiting to be cleared. Most stayed at least

34. M. Coolidge, *Chinese Immigration* (New York: Henry Holt & Co., 1909), p. 419.

35. U.S. Congress, p. 1165.

36. U.S. Industrial Commission, p. 762; Gibson, pp. 146–54.

37. U.S. Senate, *Chinese Exclusion* (Washington, D.C.: Government Printing Office, 1902), pp. 470–72 (hereafter cited as U.S. Senate).

38. H. Lai, "The Chinese Experience at Angel Island," *East/West* 10 (1976): 7–9; R. Dillon, *The Hatchet Men* (New York: Coward-McCann, 1962), p. 290.

three or four weeks, while others waited under very austere living conditions for months or even years while their cases were being fought in the courts.[39]

As importation became increasingly complex and expensive, the Hip-Yee Tong gradually lost its monopolistic control over the traffic. Because of the increasing complexity and costs of importing prostitutes, the price for their delivery skyrocketed. After 1870, for example, girls who originally sold for $50 in Canton now brought $1,000 in San Francisco.[40] And in the 1890s it was reported that as much as $3,000 in gold was paid for a single Chinese female in San Francisco.[41]

Still, the importation of women continued primarily because it provided large profits. In the 1890s a shoe manufacturer and tong leader, Fong Ching, alias Little Pete, was well known for, among other things, his ingenuity in importing women for prostitution. Besides bribing customs officials and paying both white and Chinese men $30 each for bearing false character witnesses, he used fairs and expositions held in Chicago, Atlanta, and San Francisco to import women. For example, during the Midwinter Fair in Golden Gate Park he imported over a hundred women ostensibly to perform at the fair. They ended up in brothels after spending only a brief time at the fair. San Francisco newspapers reported that Little Pete netted $50,000 through his female imports.[42]

Other methods employed by the tongs to land Chinese women were smuggling in women attired as boys, hiding them in buckets of coal, and concealing them in padded crates billed as dishware.[43] The cost of smuggling a woman into the United States may have been as high as $2,500.[44] When customs officials at San Francisco began enforcing the law, women were brought in through Portland, Oregon, Canada, or Mexico.[45]

Eventually, however, faced with the dwindling supply of females in China,[46] the nearly prohibitive costs and difficulties of procurement and importation, and the loss of prostitutes from brothels in San Francisco to other cities and mining towns, the tongs were forced to look for their supply locally. Whereas local Chinese women were supplementary to

39. Lai.

40. A. McLeod, *Pigtails and Gold Dust* (Caldwell, Idaho: Caxton Printers, 1948), p. 18.

41. U.S. Industrial Commission, p. 763.

42. Dillon, pp. 319–21.

43. U.S. Congress, p. 599; C. Wilson, *Chinatown Quest* (Stanford, Calif.: Stanford University Press, 1950), p. 87; D. Gray, *Women of the West* (Millbrae, Calif.: Les Femmes Publishing, 1976), p. 69.

44. U.S. Senate, p. 124.

45. Holder (n. 22).

46. The establishment of orphanages and children's welfare organizations was partly responsible for the decline (see Ho [n. 4], pp. 58–62).

overseas recruitment previously, after 1882 they became the major source of new supply.[47] It was reported that, in just one week in February 1898, eight women were kidnapped for prostitution.[48]

The Life and Economics of Prostitution

After the women had been transported to Chinatown, they were housed in temporary quarters known as "barracoons" to await their distribution. One barracoon reputedly held up to 100 women.[49] Those who had been imported for specific customers left when their owners paid the passage fare and the $40 fee. The others were carefully dressed and displayed before the bidding.[50] Well-to-do Chinese in San Francisco purchased the cream of this lot as concubines or mistresses. The remainder fell into two categories: the best went into higher-class brothels reserved only for the Chinese, while the rest were sold to inferior dens of prostitution which served a racially mixed clientele.[51]

The distinction between higher- and lower-grade brothels was one of both class and race. Chinese men generally felt that the most degrading thing a Chinese woman could do was to have sexual relations with a white man.[52] However, because of their comparatively low fees of twenty-five to fifty cents, the lower-class prostitutes were visited by whites and Chinese alike, while higher-class prostitutes had an exclusively Chinese clientele. Thus, the lower-grade prostitutes tended to attract the poorest laborers, teenage boys, sailors, and drunkards. They were often mistreated by their owners as well as their customers. A few brothel owners, for example, occasionally even beat some of them to death,[53] and white men often forced them to engage in aberrant sexual acts.[54] Prostitutes in mining camps served both Chinese and white clients and were often more harshly treated than their counterparts in San Francisco.[55]

The lower-grade prostitutes lived in rooms usually not larger than 4 x 6 feet, often facing a dimly lit alley.[56] "Bright cotton hangings hung

47. *Alta California* (January 31, 1875); *San Francisco Bulletin* (March 28, 1876); Y. Zhang, *San-zhou ri-ji* (n.p., 1896), chap. 5.

48. Dillon.

49. McLeod, p. 178.

50. Holder (n. 22), p. 292.

51. Dobie (n. 25), p. 195.

52. Dobie, pp. 242–43; California Senate, p. 213.

53. Dobie, p. 61; A. Genthe, *Pictures of Old Chinatown* (New York: Moffat, Inc., 1909), p. 52.

54. California Senate, pp. 28, 99, 176; Dillon, p. 46.

55. *Sacramento Bee* (June 5, 1876); S. Lyman, *Chinese Americans* (New York: Random House, 1974), p. 94.

56. U.S. Congress, p. 192.

in the doorways leading off from the main room or were sometimes used to break a larger room up into smaller compartments."[57] These rooms were sparsely furnished, usually with only a bamboo chair or two, a washbowl, and hard bunks of shelves covered with matting and set against the wall. The door, normally the only opening to the outside, was invariably covered with bars or a heavy screen behind which the woman would stand and call to passersby.[58]

The prostitutes who only served Chinese generally lived in upstairs apartments and had more or less long-term, regular customers. Very often the prostitute's client was also her owner. It is not always accurate to characterize them as prostitutes, for some may have been concubines while others may have lived in polyandry.[59] These higher-class prostitutes were often attractive and expensively adorned. Although they may have appeared to be well treated, they were nevertheless chattel, "one day loaded with jewels, the next day to be stripped and sold to the highest bidder, if it were the desire of their masters."[60]

Neither lower- nor higher-class prostitutes received regular wages, but the latter were sometimes asked to entertain at parties given by tong leaders and Chinese merchants, and they were permitted to keep the jewelry, silk, and cash gifts given to them by their customers. This is perhaps how some prostitutes were able to send money to their parents in China.[61]

The exploitative relations between the prostitute-worker and the procurer and brothel owner are clear. The capital outlay—kidnapper's fee, passage, bribes, legal fees—was miniscule compared with the profits from the woman's labor as a prostitute. For example, the cost of her passage would have been around $50 if she traveled in the same manner as the Chinese male laborers, and at the most $150 if she had comfortable accommodations, no doubt extremely rare.[62] The kidnapper's fee was once reported at $185.[63] And although we do not have data on the exact amount of bribes and legal fees, it seems safe to say that these did not usually exceed $100, though they became increasingly larger as restrictions on Chinese immigration grew.

The most profitable way of importing a woman, from the procurer's point of view, was to lure the woman to go with him or her voluntarily to

57. Dobie, p. 243.

58. McLeod, pp. 182–83; U.S. Congress, p. 192.

59. Cases of polyandry among the Chinese in San Francisco and Californian interior towns were reported by Henry K. Sienkiewicz, "The Chinese in California," *California Historical Society Quarterly* 34 (1953): 307.

60. McLeod, p. 183.

61. Fisk University, p. 34.

62. J. Kemble, "Andrew Wilson's Jottings on Civil War California," *California Historical Society Quarterly* 32 (1953): 209–24; 303–12.

63. Holder (n. 22), p. 292.

America. In one such case, the procurer, after painting a glowing picture of life in California and paying $98, obtained the consent of a girl's mother to permit her daughter to emigrate. Upon arrival, the procurer sold the girl for $1,950, a net profit of at least $1,700. This girl continued to bring in profits for her owner by laboring two years and averaging no less than $290 per month. At the end of the two years she was resold for $2,100.[64] The brothel owner's gross income from her labor as a prostitute and from her resale was about $9,060; even if she was kept at a higher standard of living and if we deduct the cost of her purchase, the brothel owner's net profit was no less than $5,000 in two years.

Besides kidnapping and luring, Chinese women entered American brothels under a system of contract mentioned before. Although this was on the surface the least exploitative form of Chinese prostitution, it was in fact devised to mask those features which permitted the procurers, importers, and brothel owners to derive considerable profits without any real advantage to the prostitute or indentured worker. The contracts were drawn up in appealing terms: they offered the contractee free passage to America, an advance of over $400, and a limited period of labor of about four and a half years. The contract system seemed all the more attractive considering that females were often sold for about $400 at the time.

In reality, though, the contract system offered very little advantage over the outright sale or slave system and was, in a number of ways, more brutal because it raised false hopes. First, the length of a prostitute's career, as noted before, was about four or five years. Thus, as far as the brothel owner was concerned, a prostitute was useful only for about four years, the period of the contract. Second, the terms of the contract specified that the person must work a minimum of 320 days, failing which the contract period could be extended to one additional year. Third, the contract prostitute would have less incentive to run away because of her limited period of labor. Fourth, her family was discouraged from redeeming her because the repurchase price included an exorbitant interest.[65] And finally, even after a woman had served out her contract, there were cases in which she continued in servitude and was not released.[66] The following is a translation of one such contract:[67]

> The contractee Xin Jin is indebted to her master/mistress for passage from China to San Francisco and will voluntarily work as a

64. U.S. Industrial Commission, p. 783; Shepherd (n. 23), pp. 892–95; Fisk University, pp. 31–35.

65. U.S. Industrial Commission, p. 783; G. Leong, *Chinatown Inside Out* (New York: Barrows Mussey, 1936), p. 231; Wilson (n. 43).

66. *Alta* (April 14, 1870); California Senate, p. 99.

67. S. Wu (n. 19), p. 92; McLeod (n. 40), p. 177.

> prostitute at Tan Fu's place for four and one-half years for an advance of 1,205 yuan (US$524) to pay this debt.[68] There shall be no interest on the money, and Xin Jin shall receive no wages. At the expiration of the contract, Xin Jin shall be free to do as she pleases. Until then, she shall first secure the master/mistress's permission if a customer asks to take her out. If she has the four loathsome diseases, she shall be returned within 100 days; beyond that time the procurer has no responsibility. Menstruation disorder is limited to one month's rest only. If Xin Jin becomes sick at any time for more than fifteen days, she shall work one month extra; if she becomes pregnant, she shall work one year extra. Should Xin Jin run away before her term is out, she shall pay whatever expense is incurred in finding and returning her to the brothel. This is a contract to be retained by the master/mistress as evidence of the agreement. Receipt of 1,205 yuan ($524) by Ah Yo. Thumb print of Xin Jin the contractee. Eighth month 11th day of the 12th year of Guang-zu (1886).

Thus far, a total of four such contracts have been discovered, the earliest dated 1873 and the latest 1899.[69]

A fourth way in which Chinese women entered San Francisco brothels was through outright purchase; in this case the women were no more than slaves. Initially, the average capital outlay for a woman brought over in this way amounted to no more than $600: the purchase price, the cost of passage, and the expenses associated with importation. But as immigration restrictions became more severe and the complexity of the importation system grew, the cost of buying and importing a prostitute likewise increased. The purchase and importation of a seventeen-year-old prostitute named Tsoi Ye illustrates this process. Tsoi Ye was sold in Hong Kong in the 1880s for a little over $400. She was resold by the procuress to a tong man for $882, who in turn entrusted a Chinese sailor to bring her over. After she was landed successfully, she was resold to a brothel for $1,800 in gold.[70] Despite the high cost, it is clear that brothel owners found it profitable to purchase women at such prices due to their potential earnings as computed above.

If the kidnapped woman was sold during the later decades of the nineteenth century, the importer could receive between $1,000 and $3,000. If, however, the importer was also a brothel owner, the kidnapped woman would labor in his or her brothel. From the information on hand, we are able to venture some conservative estimates of her

68. Although not specified in the contract, I suspect that the currency used was Mexican silver dollars. One Mexican dollar was equivalent to approximately US$0.48 in the mid-nineteenth century.

69. The other three contracts can be found in California Senate, 1877, p. 128 and 135, and U.S. Industrial Commission, p. 771.

70. U.S. Senate, pp. 227–28.

earnings. The lowest grade of prostitutes received twenty-five to fifty cents per customer. According to the literature on prostitution in general, an average full-time prostitute-worker receives four to ten customers per day,[71] and the average career life of such a prostitute is estimated at four to five years.[72] This means that, at an average of thirty-eight cents per customer and seven customers per day, a lower-grade prostitute would earn about $850 per year and $3,400 after four years.[73] Since women in lower-class brothels were generally kept at subsistence levels,[74] the cost of maintaining them probably did not exceed $8 per month or $96 per person each year.[75] The profits for the owner of a prostitute, then, even one of the lower grade, were considerable.

If a lower-grade prostitute earned an average of $850 a year, and if we assume that the average brothel in 1870 contained nine prostitutes (see table 2), the owner's gross annual income would have been about $7,650. In 1873, Chinese owned only 7 percent of the 153 major pieces of property in Chinatown, and as late as 1904, they owned only 8 percent of the 316 major parcels listed.[76] White landlords, many of whom were prominent citizens of San Francisco, owned most of the real estate in Chinatown, and they extracted high rents from brothel owners, often double or treble the rent they received from whites.[77] According to the Bureau of Labor Statistics, the average rental per month of a flat consisting of three to six rooms in San Francisco was $14.[78] The Chinese brothel owners probably had to pay no less than $28 per month or $336 a year. If the rent and maintenance of the women are deducted from the gross income, the owner would still have received an annual profit of no less than $6,000. Even if we added other expenses such as protection fees paid to the police and taxes extorted by the tongs from brothels not owned by their members, the profit which the brothel owner received would still compare very favorably with the less than $500 average annual income of other occupations in which he or she might engage.[79] Other commentators' estimates of the income of brothel owners make this look conservative. For instance, Cameron, a contemporary San

71. K. Xie, *Mai-yin zhi-du yu Tai-wan chang-ji wen-ti* (Taipei: Da-feng, 1972), p. 352.

72. W. Sanger, *The History of Prostitution* (New York: Eugenics, 1939); McLeod, p. 183.

73. The contracts examined indicate that a prostitute had to work a minimum of 320 days per year. An absence of more than fifteen days would subject her to a penalty of having to work one additional month, and menstruation disorder was limited to one month's rest per year.

74. Dobie (n. 25), p. 243.

75. B. Lloyd, *Lights and Shades of San Francisco* (San Francisco, 1876).

76. Dillon (n. 38).

77. E. Robbins, "Chinese Slave Girls," *Overland Monthly*, n.s., 51 (1908): 100–102; California Senate, pp. 106, 155, 197.

78. California Bureau of Labor Statistics, *Biennial Reports, 1887–1888* (Sacramento: State Office, 1888), p. 104.

79. U.S. Bureau of the Census, *Historical Statistics of the United States: Colonial Times to 1970* (Washington, D.C.: Government Printing Office, 1975), p. 165.

Table 2

Number and Size of Chinese Brothels in San Francisco, 1860–80

Size	1860	1870	1880
1	3	2	13
2	13	2	19
3	9	4	29
4	20	12	14
5	7	18	7
6	13	13	3
7	6	10	6
8	6	20	1
9	8	15	0
10	3	10	2
11	2	15	1
12	1	12	1
13	0	7	0
14	0	2	0
15	0	5	1
16–20	0	10	3
21–25	1	2	0
26–30	1	0	1
31–35	1	0	0
Total	94	159	101
$\bar{M}$ size of brothel	5.9	9.0	4.3

SOURCES.—Computed from unpublished census manuscripts for San Francisco for 1860, 1870, and 1880 (available from the National Archives).

Francisco reformer, stated that the average Chinese prostitute usually made between five and six dollars per day; one prostitute estimated that she made $278 per month, while another claimed to have made $318 per month.[80]

The exploitation of Chinese prostitutes was not limited to sex alone but also included their labor as semiskilled workers. Many sources indicate that in the daytime, when business was slack, women in the brothels sewed buttonholes and pantaloons and worked on shirts, slippers, men's clothing, and women's underwear.[81] The work was farmed out by sweatshops which subcontracted with the manufacturers. Since these female operatives probably did not receive payment for this extra work, the brothel owners and sweatship owners reaped a handsome profit.[82]

There were still other forms of exploitation. Besides the tax levied on brothel owners who were not tong members, the tongs imposed a weekly tax of twenty-five cents on every Chinese prostitute. If any woman refused to pay, they promised to use "harsh measures" to col-

80. U.S. Industrial Commission, p. 786; Leong (n. 65); Fisk University, p. 36.
81. California Senate, pp. 146, 154; U.S. Congress, pp. 211, 1169; Dobie (n. 25), p. 243.
82. U.S. Congress, p. 1170.

lect.[83] These harsh measures included whipping, torture by fire, banishment to brothels in the mining regions, and finally, shooting and killing the victim.[84] Blackmailing Chinese prostitutes was another method employed by the tongs to extort money. Members of a tong, noted one report, "went around among Chinese prostitutes and told them that a new chief of police had come in, and unless he received a handsome present, would shut up the houses. They collected from one and a half to five dollars from each one, and it was divided among the members of that society."[85]

Owners of brothels sometimes also owned opium dens and gambling joints.[86] A number of prostitutes were addicted to opium and/or gambled excessively.[87] The owners often encouraged these addictions so that the loans needed to feed them would increase the prostitutes' debts.[88] Desperate women committed suicide by swallowing raw opium or drowning themselves in the bay.[89]

The best thing that could happen to these women was to be redeemed and married. Occasionally a white male fell in love with a brothel inmate and married her after having paid the owner.[90] However, most of the men who married prostitutes were Chinese laborers. Chinese working people did not attach the same stigma to prostitution as whites did. One reason might have been that prostitutes in China were generally not seen as "fallen women" but as daughters who obeyed the wishes of the family. Although prostitution was not considered an honorable profession, particularly among the gentry, women who were able to get out of it were usually accepted in working-class society. Furthermore, the fact that there was such a shortage of Chinese women in San Francisco during this period would have tended to relax the sex mores that men might have held.

Apparently, quite a few women in San Francisco were able to leave the brothels, although not without struggle, and often at tremendous risk. Throughout the mid-nineteenth and the early twentieth centuries, reports of such instances abound.[91] Typically, a woman ran away to a mission, the police station, or her lover, with the hired tong soldiers in pursuit. The lengths to which the tongs would go in recapturing a run-

83. *Alta* (March 26, 1873).

84. *Alta* (December 4, 1870); U.S. Congress, pp. 110, 211.

85. California Senate, p. 213.

86. Ibid., pp. 164–66.

87. M. Stabler, "A Bit of Blue China," *Out West*, n.s., 3 (1911): 256–59; U.S. Congress, p. 96.

88. U.S. Congress, p. 96; California Senate, p. 99.

89. California Senate, pp. 99, 180; *Alta* (July 6, 1876); Y. Fu, *You-li Mei-li-jia guo tu-jing You-ji-lei*, vol. 5 (n.p., 1889).

90. *San Francisco Chronicle* (April 1, 1877).

91. "Bancroft Scraps," an unpublished collection of newspaper clippings (Bancroft Library, University of California, Berkeley), vols. 6–9 (1862–81); Wilson (n. 23).

away prostitute indicated her value to her owner. The tongs often kidnapped the escaped woman or even used the American courts to get her back by filing a charge of theft, claiming the woman had absconded with some clothes or jewelry. After the police had located the woman, the tongs would hire white lawyers to arrange for her bail and then return her to the brothel.[92] If that tactic failed, they placed public announcements on Chinatown walls, warning others who might assist her escape and offering rewards for her capture.

The tongs also offered rewards for the capture of the prostitute's male accomplice; sometimes such rewards ran into the thousands, depending on the value of the woman. If the male accomplice paid the sum asked for the woman's redemption, then the couple was left alone, but very often the man could not pay the exorbitant amount that the tong required. There are stories which tell of such men and women fleeing the San Francisco area in disguise or hidden in wooden boxes.[93] However, the tong network of informers reached even into rural communities. Telegraphs between Chinese men in Marysville, Downieville, San Francisco, and other places reveal that such a system operated at least during the 1870s.[94]

As further insurance against the escape of a prostitute, tongs gave the local police a retainer fee. Until 1877, a Special Police Force was engaged in a quasi-official capacity as peace officers in Chinatown. They received no set wages but derived their income from the Chinese residents. Normally, the "Chinatown Specials" collected fifty cents a week from each prostitute,[95] and they admitted that whenever there was a crackdown on prostitution, their income was reduced.[96] Tongs also made payments to City Hall to secure its agreement not to interfere.[97]

As mentioned before, a prostitute's work life in the brothels was normally four to five years, not surprising in the absence of sound medical care. The abundance of Chinese advertisements of "secret formulas" for curing syphilis and gonorrhea during the period testifies to the prevalence of such diseases.[98] Although some doctors blamed the Chinese prostitutes for spreading the diseases to the white population, it was pointed out by other physicians that these illnesses were equally, if not more, prevalent among white prostitutes in San Francisco.[99]

92. California Senate, p. 120.

93. *San Francisco Bulletin* (June 11, 1878).

94. *California Chinese Chatter* (San Francisco: Dressler, Inc., 1927).

95. California Senate, p. 166.

96. Ibid., p. 158.

97. Ibid., p. 113.

98. Bancroft Library has in its collection of Chinese immigration pamphlets advertisements for such secret formulae ("Chinese Immigration Miscellaneous," unnumbered boxes, Bancroft Library, University of California, Berkeley).

99. U.S. Congress, p. 142.

When a woman was no longer profitable as a prostitute, she might work as a cook or a laundry woman for the brothel.[100] If she was hopelessly ill, she would be left to die by the brothel owners.[101] Although, in general, the remains of the Chinese male laborers were shipped back to their place of nativity for burial, few cared about the remains of these working women. The *Alta* reported in 1870 that the bodies of Chinese women were discarded and left on the streets of Chinatown.[102]

Chinese prostitutes were mostly young women between the ages of sixteen and twenty-five. The year 1870 stood out as a watershed in that there were proportionately more younger prostitutes in that period than in either 1860 or 1880. Table 3 shows that close to 46 percent of the women were under twenty years of age in 1870, which was 12 and 23 percentage points higher than the 1880 and the 1860 aggregates, respectively. Since a great majority of the Chinese prostitutes were of child-bearing age, a natural question arose as to the mobility of their children.

The children of prostitutes, particularly female ones, were likewise exploited by the brothel owners. Table 4 shows the number, place of nativity, and residence of Chinese children living in San Francisco. The data reveal a significant trend: in the 1860 census, proportionately more children lived in brothels than outside brothels; in 1870, an even number of children lived in brothels and outside; and finally, in 1880, the situation was reversed with many more children living outside than inside. The overrepresentation of girls over boys in the brothels for all three decades was probably due to the owner's practice of retaining girls to do household chores and his or her intention to recruit them into prostitution. It is probably safe to say that native-born children living in brothels were almost invariably the children of prostitutes. But most of the children of prostitutes somehow managed to escape the clutches of the brothel. In 1880, nearly thirty years after the first large-scale importation of prostitutes, only seven of the 435 prostitutes in San Francisco were native born (table 3). In general, children moved away from the brothels and into the wider society (table 4).

Some of these children were placed into mission homes and with families of Chinese Christians.[103] Others might have returned to China or moved to the American interior. For those who remained in San Francisco, the occupational distribution of native-born Chinese females in the 1880 manuscript census gives a clue as to their destinations. Of the 250 U.S.-born women who were not classified as prostitutes, 227 were

100. U.S. Industrial Commission, p. 778; Gray (n. 43), p. 69.
101. *San Francisco Chronicle* (December 5, 1869).
102. *Alta* (October 9, 1870).
103. M. Slingerland, *Child Welfare Work in California* (New York, 1915), pp. 98–99.

Table 3

Age and Nativity of Chinese Prostitutes in San Francisco, 1860–80

	1860			1870			1880			
	Foreign Born	U.S. Born	%	Foreign Born	U.S. Born	%	Foreign Born	U.S. Born	Total	%
15 and under	8	0	1.4	16	1	1.1	18	4	22	5.0
16–20	122	0	21.9	637	0	44.7	125	2	127	29.2
21–25	105	0	18.9	416	0	29.2	129	1	130	29.9
26–30	165	0	29.7	215	0	15.1	86	0	86	19.8
31–35	64	0	11.5	70	0	4.9	32	0	32	7.4
36–40	64	0	11.5	34	0	2.4	20	0	20	4.6
41–45	19	0	3.4	14	0	1.0	8	0	8	1.8
46–50	6	0	1.1	18	0	1.2	8	0	8	1.8
51 and over	3	0	.6	5	0	.3	2	0	2	.5
Total	556	0	100.0	1,425	1	100.0	428	7	435	100.0

SOURCES.—See table 2.

Table 4

Chinese Children in San Francisco by Sex, Nativity, and Place of Residence, 1860–80

	Live in Brothels			Live Outside		
	Male	Female	Total	Male	Female	Total
1860:						
U.S. born	5	23	28	0	0	0
Foreign born	3	12	15	7	2	9
Total	8	35	43	7	2	9
1870:						
U.S. born	98	74	172	71	57	128
Foreign born	34	48	82	79	34	113
Total	132	122	254	150	91	241
1880:						
U.S. born	24	26	50	203	198	401
Foreign born	11	27	38	89	114	203
Total	35	53	88	292	312	604

SOURCES.—See table 2.

housewives, while the rest were students, apprentices, housekeepers, and seamstresses. Although certainly not all native-born women were offspring of prostitutes, a number of them clearly were. It is not incorrect to say, therefore, that the daughters of some indentured and slave prostitute-workers managed to become wage laborers and housewives.

Extent and Distribution of Chinese Prostitutes in San Francisco

The exact number of Chinese prostitutes in California and San Francisco during the nineteenth century is not known. Although several contemporary estimates are available, their tremendous variation indicates low reliability. Fortunately, we are not solely dependent on impressionistic accounts. The recently released manuscript censuses for 1860, 1870, and 1880 contain social and demographic information on individuals which makes it possible to estimate the numbers and to construct a statistical profile of Chinese prostitutes for these decades.

A tabulation of the census schedules of 1860 revealed that there were 2,693 Chinese residents in San Francisco, 654 or 24 percent of whom were women. Eight of these were laundry/washerwomen; five, gardeners; five, fisherwomen; three, laborers; four, storekeepers; two, clerks; and one, a tailoress; the remainder had no occupation listed.

Eliminating from the last category (*a*) those women living in households with a man with or without children, (*b*) those living in households with more than one man, and (*c*) girls under twelve years old, we have 556 women whose occupations might be said to have been prostitution. This figure represents 85 percent of the Chinese female population in San Francisco, and it is probably a reasonable estimate.

Since "prostitution" was used as an occupational category in the 1870 and 1880 census manuscripts, we have simply followed the designation of the census taker to identify Chinese women engaged in prostitution during those two decades. Obvious distortions may arise from this procedure. Although the census enumerator was instructed to record what was reported to him or her by the interviewee, a language problem could lead to guessing by the census worker. It is also reasonable to assume that the census taker was probably biased toward designating a woman a prostitute because of popular racist beliefs or an inability to distinguish between concubinage and prostitution. On the other hand, the interviewee was probably inclined not to state that she worked as a prostitute even if she really did. Since these biases run in opposite directions, they tend to neutralize each other.

A tabulation from the 1870 census schedules yielded 2,018 Chinese women in San Francisco, of whom 1,426 or 71 percent were recorded as prostitutes. From these figures, we can see that while the percentage of women in San Francisco engaged in prostitution declined relative to the total Chinese female population, the actual number of prostitutes more than doubled.

Between 1870 and 1880, Chinese prostitution became one of the salient issues in the anti-Chinese movement in California. During the two legislative hearings on Chinese immigration, one conducted by the California State Senate in April 1876 and the other by the U.S. Congress in October of the same year, numerous individuals testified on the extent of Chinese prostitution in San Francisco.[104] These estimates contradicted one another and revealed the witnesses' political biases and self-interests. Because of those contrasting interests, the estimates of Chinese prostitutes in San Francisco differed widely, ranging from 200 to 2,700. In neither hearings did witnesses or legislators cite the census figures.

A tabulation of the manuscript census for San Francisco in 1880 yielded 2,058 Chinese women, of whom 435 or 21 percent were recorded as prostitutes. Although this figure was probably an underestimate, other sources suggest that it was not too far afield. The San Francisco police testified in the congressional hearings of 1876 that, as a result of several raids on Chinese prostitution a few months before the

104. California Senate; U.S. Congress.

hearings, many prostitutes left the city for inland towns.[105] Later, in 1885, the San Francisco Board of Supervisors reported that there were 567 professional prostitutes in Chinatown.[106]

From the statistics presented, we see the dramatic increase in the number of prostitutes between 1860 and 1870, and the dramatic decrease in both the number and percentage of prostitutes between 1870 and 1880. These figures suggest that the heydey of Chinese prostitution in San Francisco was around 1870, and its precipitous decline occurred just before 1880.

Although Chinese prostitutes served a racially mixed clientele, they were physically concentrated in a few blocks in Ward Four, where Chinatown was located. Outside of Chinatown, in 1860, some brothels were found in three other wards, but in 1870, Chinese brothels were found in only one other ward. Data on the distribution and size of brothels (table 2) clearly confirms that the years around 1870 were the heydey of organized prostitution. There were more prostitutes, more and larger brothels, and a heavier concentration of brothels in a very small area. The data also suggest the idea that this was the period when small businesses were consolidated or liquidated by big enterprises.

Decline of Organized Prostitution

Several converging factors account for the decline of oganized prostitution in San Francisco. First, the female supply in South China dwindled, making families less willing to sell or mortgage their daughters and increasing the difficulty of procuring prostitutes. Second, the Chinese Exclusion Act of 1882 greatly reduced the number of prospective prostitutes and made their importation harder. The decline in the annual number of Chinese women immigrants—from an average of 304.6 between 1854 and 1882 to an average of 107.6 between 1883 and 1904—testifies to the effectiveness of the Exclusion Act,[107] despite the ingenious evasive methods devised by the importers, tongs, and brothel owners. The skyrocketing value of prostitutes in America and the increase in kidnapping in California after the 1880s also reflect the decline in Chinese women entering the United States for the purpose of prostitution.

Local conditions in San Francisco and California after the 1880s similarly led to the decline and eventual demise of this organized phase

105. U.S. Congress, p. 192.

106. San Francisco Board of Supervisors, *Special Committee Report on Chinatown* (San Francisco, 1885), p. 9; California Bureau of Labor Statistics, *Biennial Reports, 1887–1888* (Sacramento: State Office, 1888), p. 108.

107. Coolidge (n. 34), p. 502.

of prostitution. These included the more balanced sex ratio of the California population (see table 1); the availability of other sources of supply; the move of Chinese labor from migrant to stationary industries; the desire of capital to maintain a stable, cheap labor force; the change from sojourning to settlement or return; the increased alternatives for women's labor;[108] intra-tong conflicts and the struggle between the tongs and the allied forces of the Chinese consulate and the Six Companies; the enforcement of codes directed against Chinese prostitution; the arrival of white Victorian women and the establishment of white families in California; and finally, the crusade of the white missionaries for the abolition of Chinese prostitution.

The Six Companies, led by Chinese merchants, had their financial basis in Chinese laborers and trade. They supplied labor, collected membership fees, served as bankers for the immigrants, and sold provisions to the laborers.[109] The secret societies, which controlled the gambling, opium, and prostitution businesses, challenged the traditional authority of the Six Companies and competed with the merchants for the laborers' dollars. Their opposition sharpened during the 1880s, partly because the increase in local kidnapping related to prostitution alienated the Chinatown elites, who had families with them.[110] The more money laborers spent in San Francisco tong-controlled businesses, the less they had to spend in the merchants' shops or to send home to their families.[111] Since many emigrant communities in China depended on remittances, the Chinese consulate and the Qing government were also concerned.[112] In addition, the merchants knew that American families would not patronize the growing number of legitimate restaurants, stores, and curio shops in Chinatown if it was seen as a vice district.[113] The fierce competition among secret societies for the control of gambling, opium, and prostitution during the last few decades of the nineteenth century also contributed to their decline.[114]

Moreover, the heyday of Chinese prostitution in San Francisco cor-

108. V. Nee and B. Nee, *Longtime Californ'* (New York: Pantheon Books, 1973); J. Hooks, *Women's Occupations through Seven Decades* (Washington, D.C.: Women's Bureau, 1947); B. Liu, *Mei-guo Hua-qiao shi* (Taipei: Li-ming, 1976).

109. S. Lyman, "Conflict and the Web of Group Affiliation in San Francisco's Chinatown, 1880–1910," *Pacific Historical Review* 43 (1974): 473–99.

110. Dillon (n. 38); I. Light, "From Vice District to Tourist Attraction," *Pacific Historical Review* 43 (1974): 367–94; Liu; Lyman, "Conflict and the Web of Group Affiliation."

111. Q. Liang, *Xin-da-lu you-ji jie-lu* (Shanghai: Zhong-hua, 1936), p. 110.

112. T. Chen (n. 3); Hsiao (n. 2); G. Li, *Huan-you di-qiu xin-lu* (n.p., 1877); D. Li, "Zao-qi Hua-ren yi-Mei ji An-ji-li tiao-yue qian-ding," *Lien-ho Shu-Yuan Xue-bao* 3 (1964): 1–29; Liu.

113. Light.

114. E. Gong and B. Grant, *Tong War!* (New York: Brown, Inc., 1930); Dillon (n. 38); C. Reynolds, "Chinese Tongs," *American Journal of Sociology* 40 (1935): 610–23; C. Lee (n. 19).

responded with the period of mounting agitation against Chinese labor in general. And although prostitutes consisted of no more than 6 percent of the Chinese population in California, they were singled out for attack by the politicians. Chinese prostitution not only threatened the health of white men, claimed those politicians, but Chinese prostitutes serving as slave labor took away sewing and other jobs from white women.[115] Between 1866 and 1905, at least eight California codes were passed, all aimed at restricting the importation of Chinese women for prostitution and the suppression of Chinese brothels. Although white prostitution was equally if not more prevalent, these were additional and specific laws directed only against the Chinese. Chinese prostitutes, if caught, were sentenced to a fine of $25 to $50 and a jail term of at least five days.[116]

Both the Chinese consulate and the Six Companies saw prostitution as one of the major causes for the anti-Chinese movement in California. Further, both were concerned about the economic loss and image of the Chinese, so they actively collaborated with the American authorities in identifying and deporting Chinese prostitutes.[117] In reality, however, since Chinese prostitution was not the reason for the anti-Chinese movement, their action did not thwart the hostility; but their efforts did bring about a temporary decline in the organized traffic.

The increasing arrival of white women immigrants to San Francisco throughout the second half of the nineteenth century transformed the city from a frontier society with a fluid, predominantly male population to a more stable society with families. Smith accurately pointed out that the status of prostitutes declined with the advent of the Victorian ladies from the East Coast concerned with the preservation of the family, whose Puritan morality led them to crusade against prostitution in general and Chinese prostitution in particular.[118] In 1873, the interests of the Victorian ladies in San Francisco found expression in the Women's Occidental Board. Reportedly alarmed by the immorality of the traffic in women and the sinfulness of the prostitute's sexual activity, Margaret Culbertson and her successor Donaldina Cameron set out to rescue the Chinese slaves.[119] Although clergymen like Gibson and Loomis also crusaded against prostitution, Cameron was always singled out as the bravest and cleverest savior of Chinese females. She was said to have rescued approximately 3,000 girls during her forty-year career,[120] although Cameron herself testified in 1898 that, twenty-three years after

115. California Senate; U.S. Congress; U.S. Senate.
116. California Senate, p. 163.
117. Gibson (n. 10); Liu (n. 108).
118. D. Smith (n. 7).
119. Robbins (n. 77); Wilson (n. 23); Gray (n. 43), pp. 67–74.
120. Gray, p. 74.

the establishment of the Mission Home, about 600 girls had been rescued.[121]

Missionaries thought that every slave girl or prostitute would rather live at 920 Sacramento Street, but Chinese women did not always prefer this alternative, particularly if the brothel owner did not mistreat them too badly.[122] Most women who ran away from brothels to seek the protection of the Mission or the police cited cruelty, such as flogging and beating, as the reason for their escape.[123] The Mission established strict rules for the activities and behavior of the runaways and trained them in "motherhood" and "industrial skills." The rule against idle hands extended to cooking, cleaning, and maintaining the Mission, and even to the use of the women in hard labor. Cameron was known to have contracted with fruit growers in Northern California for the labor of Mission residents. She often sent twenty or thirty Chinese women from the home to work from four to eight weeks in the fields. It is not difficult to see why many prostitutes refused to run away to the Mission Home, or why a number of women who had been "rescued" by the missionaries later escaped from their saviors.[124]

There can be no doubt, however, that as a result of the efforts of Cameron and others like her, many prostitutes became wives and lived normal family lives. A few of these women became Christians and joined in missionary work. Many white women, perhaps including Cameron herself, were motivated by a sense of moral superiority. The more they saw Chinese women as helpless, weak, depraved, and victimized, the more aroused was their missionary zeal. Saving the Chinese slave girls seemed to have become the "white woman's burden."[125]

Conclusion

Rotenberg observed that "the heavy emphasis on the 'sinful' nature of the prostitute's sexual activity has obscured her role as a worker."[126] This paper has argued that prostitution is a form of labor. In the case of the individual owner-prostitute, she is a free agent, in possession of her own sexuality, offering it in the market in exchange for a fee from her clients. But the prostitute can be ruthlessly exploited by others who own

121. U.S. Industrial Commission, p. 788.

122. Wilson.

123. *Alta* (July 31, 1873).

124. Wilson, pp. 85, 125; *Alta* (May 28, 1876).

125. Gray (n. 43).

126. L. Rotenberg, "The Wayward Worker: Toronto's Prostitute at the Turn of the Century," in *Women at Work*, ed. J. Acton, P. Goldsmith, and R. Shepherd (Toronto: Canadian Women, 1974), pp. 33–69.

her sexuality and/or expropriate her earnings. The institution of Chinese prostitution was characterized by many layers of exploitative relations. Men and women, Chinese and white, reaped benefits from their oppression. The development of Chinese prostitution as a large enterprise in nineteenth-century California was related to both material and ideological conditions in the two countries; to the need for cheap labor in California and the economic underdevelopment of China; and to white racism and Chinese patriarchy.

Department of Sociology
University of California at Los Angeles

Sexual Commerce on the Comstock Lode

by Marion Goldman

> True she was a woman of easy virtue. Yet hundreds in this city have had cause to bless her name for her many acts of kindness and charity. That woman probably had more real, warm friends in this community than any other.[1]

THUS, THE CITY ATTORNEY of Virginia City, Nevada eulogized Julia Bulette, a fancy woman brutally murdered in 1867. Even during an era of ostensibly rigid morality, prostitutes throughout the American frontier were regarded as important community figures, to be both loved and hated, envied and despised. While most nineteenth century media focused on the bleak aspects of prostitution, often moralizing against it, they also offered glimpses of a zestful, dangerous lifestyle contrasting with the stark existence of respectable working class and poor women.

The luxuries of the fast life were only available to a small number of women at the top of the status structure within prostitution, yet verbal portraits of prostitutes tend to concentrate on the few exceptional women who had golden careers and temporarily amassed fortune and fame.[2] Both scholars and artists have devoted a disproportionate amount of time to high status prostitution, encouraging the belief that "prostitution comes perilously close to getting something for nothing."[3] However, for every one of Matt Dillon's Miss Kittys or Bob Dylan's Lilys, there were hundreds of prostitutes who lived and died in poverty.

While some recent writing on commercial sex has debunked the glorification of women of the night, glamorous prostitutes continue to appear in the popular media.[4] The spirited, independent frontier dance hall girl is the perfect consort for the wandering cowboy, just as the hooker with the heart of gold serves as an ideal foil for the lone vice squad cop. The survival of myths glorifying prostitution is particularly evident in dramatizations of the American frontier, where "men were men, and women were women," when the latter could not be ladies. This article will examine the daily lives and social relations of Comstock prostitutes with the hope of clarifying the general myths surrounding prostitution and contributing to an emerging history of working and lower class women.

Prostitutes are among the many American women whose images have suffered both intentional and unintentional distortion because of pervasive assumptions about female inferiority. They are sometimes described as having entered the fast life because of free, individual choice or because of personal maladjustment. This analysis blames victims for their

---

Marion Goldman is an Assistant Professor of Sociology at the University of Oregon. She received her Ph.D. from the University of Chicago. Currently she is writing a book on the sociology of prostitution, using data from the Comstock Lode as a source for grounded theory. The author wishes to thank Professor Neal Ferguson of the History Department, University of Nevada, Reno, for his advice on historical method and his useful criticism.

"X" marks the spot of Virginia City's main bawdy district. This photograph was taken about 1900, after the Comstock had settled into a considerable decline. Many buildings from the boom period still stood, however, and this panorama is one of the few providing a good view of D Street from the North end of town.

own fate, ignoring the importance of social structure in fashioning people's lives. Complementing the themes of choice and psychological compulsion, the common emphasis on high status prostitution describes fantastic material and intrinsic benefits actually available to few, if any, prostitutes. This second focus on rewards denies victimization itself, transforming oppression into privilege.

Descriptive accounts of prostitution emphasizing free will and benefits from the fast life tend to dismiss the structural factors creating both the supply and demand for impersonal sex. Prostitution is not an anomaly, but is rather an integral part of American social organization and an extreme case of women's subjugation within this society. It is far beyond the scope of this article to examine the manner in which structural variables of class, sex, and race have interacted to shape three centuries of sexual exchange in the United States. However, a detailed examination of prostitution on the Comstock Lode provides some insight into more general relationships between social structure and prostitution, as well as specific information about the mining frontier.

The Comstock Lode

Hundreds of prostitutes joined miners in rushing to the great sister silver mining towns, Virginia City and Gold Hill, which stood atop the fabled Comstock Lode in western Nevada.[5] During prosperous periods the towns were almost contiguous; and while Gold Hill had its own small commercial district, it was essentially a working class suburb of Virginia City. Thus, the two will be treated as one community, with downtown Virginia City as its social center.

The Comstock was the quintessential boomtown, growing from a collection of rude shanties to a sophisticated city of almost 20,000 in slightly more than a decade.[6] At the beginning of the first boom in 1860, there were 2,379 men and only 147 women, but the ratio of men to women was soon decreased by respectable women accompanying their husbands to the new city, and by many prostitutes adding the Comstock to their trade circuit from San Francisco through the California gold towns. By 1870, both ladies and painted women were an integral part of the community, and some of them expected to remain on the Comstock for the rest of their lives. However, despite the addition of large numbers of reputable women, prostitution was always legally condoned.

The Comstock was a unique community, and its enormous wealth from the mines and large population made it an exaggerated case of the frontier phenomenon. Nevertheless, it resembled well established metropolitan areas in its size, density, ethnic heterogeneity, and class structure.[7] Although some conditions on the Comstock crossed the invisible boundary between the normal and the pathological in American society, most of that crossing was an exuberant extension of general social trends. Examination of the city's economic and cultural development illuminates and clarifies the similar, but more complex structural patterns contributing to the growth of American prostitution in the last half of the nineteenth century.

Although the Comstock began in chaos, with miners staking indiscriminate claims, it soon developed a class structure similar to the industrial East. The absence of industrial diversification kept local economic and social life in constant flux, depending on the condition of the mines, and when the ore pinched out the community was all but abandoned. However, as long as the mines produced profit the Comstock was controlled by a small upper class. Silver mining demanded intensive capital for exploration, construction, and operation, and a small number of capitalists joined together in financial and industrial monopolies dominating the Lode during its most productive years.[8]

The community's upper class included the mine and ore mill owners and superintendents, stock brokers, wealthy merchants, and politicians. A small number of independent professionals were also included in the social and civic activities of this group. Merchants, restaurant and hotel owners, mining engineers, assayers, and independent craftsmen made up the middle class. The large working class primarily consisted of miners, along with men employed in other industries related to mining and in service establishments, such as boarding houses, restaurants, and reputable saloons.

Much of the working class immigrated from England and Ireland, and in Nevada in 1870, 44.2% of the population was foreign born, as compared with only 14% of the entire U.S. population.[9] In 1875, more than half of the Comstock's residents had not been born in the United States. Men came from all parts of the world seeking their fortunes in the fabled mines and the community surrounding them. Many left their wives behind or were single, and they provided a ready market for prostitutes. However, the scarcity of women was not the only economic factor contributing to the demand for fancy women.

The market economy embraced every area of social life on the Comstock, mediating between people and nature, people and their own labor, and people and each other. The nature and conditions of work under industrial capitalism forced people to think of themselves and others as objects to be used instrumentally. This alienation contributed to men's need to seek out harlots and also permitted them to rationalize their patronage by transforming sexuality into another commodity.

While a larger proportion of upper and middle class men brought wives to the Comstock, some of them still patronized prostitutes.[10] Whether married or unmarried, most men from these classes visited the hurdy houses, bawdy theaters, and brothels at some time. These irregular institutions were simply a part of the men's social lives, and the gaudy balls and masquerades attended by prostitutes were practically irresistible.[11] However, the bulk of prostitutes' patrons appear to have come from the working class.

On the Comstock, working people labored and lived under extremely harsh conditions. Some single working men shared tiny rooms with bunks stacked as in ships' cabins and no outside windows, for which they paid $40 to $60 a month including meals.[12] In some cases two sets of miners on different shifts shared the same room, with one group sleeping while the others worked. Men living in these rooms could do little more than sleep in them, and they spent their leisure hours on street corners and in saloons, gambling rooms, or bawdy houses.[13]

The vice districts not only provided "a home away from home," but also offered a necessary release from tension generated by the danger inherent in working in the mines. Between 1863 and 1880 there were three hundred mining fatalities, and when the mines were in full operation there was an average of a serious accident every day.[14] Without access to sexual partners miners may have been unwilling and/or unable to go back underground each successive day, and this may be one reason why mine owners never supported campaigns to close down or limit the location of bawdy districts.

Women and the Economy on the Comstock Lode

Respectable women in the Comstock labor force lived and worked under somewhat better conditions than miners. Domestics often resided with their employers, and other working women frequently roomed with private families. However, women's work was by and large menial, difficult, long and ill paid. Working women were in a curious position, since their participation in the public sphere of production and services made their respectability problematic to begin with.[15] Most could only attain full respectable status by finding husbands and withdrawing into their own families of procreation, yet there were few situations in which they could meet eligible men without damaging their own reputations by going out unescorted.

In 1875, only 337 respectable women worked outside the home, and all but 20 of them were unmarried at the time. Most were employed as servants in private homes or in restaurants and boarding houses. Other female occupations included sewing, running small businesses, and teaching school. (See Figure I.)

FIGURE I*
Adult Women's Occupations on the Comstock in 1875

General Category		Absolute Frequency	Relative Frequency (Percent)
Dependent	Married Women/Living with Husbands	2,446	68.5
	Adult Daughters Living at Home	109	3.0
	Other Female Relatives of Household Head	41	1.1
	Widows with No Other Occupation Listed	147	4.1
Working Class Employment	Servant	208	5.9
	Laundress	3	0.1
	Seamstress	39	1.1
Petit Bourgeois Employment	Lodging/Boarding House Owner or Manager	44	1.2
	Saloon Owner	3	0.1
	Merchant	2	0.1
	Milliner	5	0.1
	Other Petit Bourgeois (e.g., hairdresser or telegraph operator)	5	0.1
Professional Employment	School Teacher	20	0.6
	Nun	13	0.4
Disreputable Dependent/Living with One Man	No Occupation, Housekeeper or Euphemism for Fallen Woman	180	5.0
Disreputable	Madam	9	0.2
	Prostitutes	298	8.2
Column Total		3,572	99.8 = 100%

*Source: Nevada Legislature; 1875 Census.

Desire for the few available jobs was fierce, and women frequently advertised for dressmaking work or for domestic situations with private families. In the latter case, they not only competed with one another, but also with Chinese men. Domestics could expect to earn from $15 to $50 a month, depending upon the nature of their work and whether or not they received room and board.[16] During the same bonanza periods, miners earned at least $80 a month.[17] Other respectable women's jobs brought similarly low wages, but competition was equally great for them, reaching its peak in the case of school teaching.

Teaching was almost the only women's work on the Comstock considered to be worthy of ladies. There were a number of efforts to exclude married women from teaching positions, because of the vast number of single ladies seeking them. For example, in 1877, 120 married women applied for less than 20 posts, and the clamor for teaching jobs was so loud that it prompted Professor J. N. Flint, the male Superintendent of Schools for Storey County, to assert:

> It is greatly to be regretted that school teaching is, in the estimation of the female sex, the only respectable occupation which a young lady can follow.
> Some women who could be good clerks or waitresses are not good teachers. They must realize any occupation giving them an honest living is respectable.[18]

Despite such pleas, teaching remained the only available occupation outside the home conferring women with relatively high status, and it was a poor second to the vocation of marriage. Most women on the Comstock were married, and a large number of other women were related to a male household head in some other way. Some wives helped their husbands manage their businesses, such as boarding houses or saloons, but according to census data, their primary defining statuses were their marital relationships.

Poor and working class wives labored long hours cleaning, cooking, raising children, and producing goods for home consumption. Upper and middle class women frequently had servants perform household tasks and supervise their offspring, and their work consisted of shopping, caring for their appearances, organizing elaborate luncheons and parties, and participating in church and civic volunteer activities. The leisured class of women performing no physical labor and emulating the social formalities common to the upper crust of established cities embodied the concept of the lady as a delicate, fragile being. Hearty women forced to do essential work within or outside their homes had less individual value and social status than ladies. However, whatever their social class, respectable women shared a common moral and social superiority to prostitutes.

Another group of 180 women behaved as if they were married, but were not legally bound to their mates. Most of the women in permanent liaisons lived with working class men amidst respectable families, and many of them raised children. In some cases women informally adopted their partners' surnames, but revealed their status to census takers. Some women living with men drifted from one partner to another and also worked in the fast life, but others stayed with one man.

These relationships grew out of the custom of substituting desertion for divorce, as some men came to or left the Comstock after deliberately abandoning their families. Other men had no original intention of forsaking their wives, but gradually gave up the possibility of sending for them. While these men were willing to forget their previous bonds, they would not risk charges of bigamy by remarrying. Women probably committed themselves to consensual relationships because living with a man was frequently necessary for their economic survival. The fact that many of them had children indicates that they were either widows or deserted wives who desperately needed financial support. Moreover, they could pretend to be married and enjoy the social benefits of wifedom, and the risks of abandonment were no greater than those faced by legal wives. Such permanent liaisons did not diminish the importance of marriage, but merely underscored the necessity of living in a family unit.

Adultery, Divorce, and Prostitution

No matter how sheltered she was, no Comstock lady could have been unaware of the presence and practice of prostitutes. Local newspapers carried almost daily notes on events in the vice district, the city's most notorious bawdy saloons were but a few steps away from its major stores, and middle class women supported frequent, sporadic crusades to drive fancy women from residential neighborhoods and limit the location of houses of ill fame. These crusades strengthened the moral boundaries between respectable women and prostitutes, as did informal rules ostracizing prostitutes from reputable social events. Although harlots had performed pivotal roles in the community's early civic and social life, by 1869 respectable women could brag that "Ladies of the *demimonde* no longer expect to eat dinners and grace the parties of the haute ton."[19]

Wives not only knew that prostitution existed, but also realized that some husbands visited painted women. However, during the twenty-year boom period only two women publicly confronted their husbands about visits to prostitutes. The absence of general female outrage against such association reflected the widespread belief that bawds did not threaten respectable marriages and the general ideology that men had greater, more violent sexual urges than women. The traditional separation of sexuality from maternity and from married women's other roles also reinforced wives' ostensible tolerance for prostitution. However, many women avenged their husbands' visits to the vice districts through their own adultery.

The large number of single men on the Comstock made discreet extramarital affairs an attractive, viable option for scorned wives. Upper class women developed an intricate set of social rituals allowing them the company of male escorts from their social class without provoking scandal. So long as lovers attended church functions together and avoided any public demonstration of affection, they could go to other, more frivolous events and preserve the illusion of respectable, platonic friendship.[20] Middle class women were involved with men boarding in their homes, and working class wives had relationships with neighboring single men. Amorous adventures among people in these classes did not conform to the stylized rituals for adultery common to elites, and less affluent individuals were primarily concerned with finding enough privacy to remain undiscovered. However, recorded adultery in all classes usually involved married women and unmarried men.

While wives' actual behavior did not conform to the rigid Victorian ideology negating ladies' sexuality and demanding their fidelity to a single man, women were expected to appear to be faithful to their husbands. The burden for concealment of adultery rested almost entirely upon women. If love affairs were discovered, women were usually targets for both their husbands' wrath and community disapproval. Many women were brutally beaten and/or summarily divorced for adultery. While unforgiven adultery was listed as grounds for divorce for either partner, in Nevada from 1867 through 1886, two-thirds of the 100 divorces for simple adultery were granted to irate husbands.[21] Moreover, when a wife's adultery furnished cause for divorce, the woman forfeited all her claims to community property, while no such penalties applied to adulterous husbands. Both law and social custom punished women's indiscretions far more than men's. Usually, men's relationships with prostitutes did not even constitute adultery, since they were based on impersonal sexual exchange which did not threaten the emotional bonds of marriage.

Formal severing of marital ties still stigmatized women and also frequently thrust them out into an unwelcoming labor market. In 1880, the first year such information was recorded in the manuscript census for Nevada, a disproportionate number of Comstock prostitutes were listed as divorced. Local newspapers sometimes published cautionary tales of formerly prominent women who had drifted into drunken, debased prostitution. These stories, along with more explicit editorials against divorce, were implicitly directed toward women contemplating dissolving their marriages. A few women simply skipped divorce and left their mates to enter the sporting life. One Virginia City prostitute left her husband while she was pregnant and took up residence in a Salt Lake City brothel, while another wife waited until her husband was away and removed herself and all of their furniture to a nearby bordello.[22]

In spite of the presence of permanent liaisons, the common practice of adultery, and much public knowledge of the lures of the fast life, a rigid boundary still separated respectable women from prostitutes. The essence of feminine respectability was shelter by one man within the nuclear family, while the essence of prostitution was indiscriminate sexual exchange with many partners. The lady was a private woman, while the harlot was a public one. Once a Comstock woman crossed the line separating respectability and prostitution she was seldom welcome in the respectable community. The ideology separating ladies from harlots was so strong that a jury returned a verdict of justifiable homicide when a Comstock woman shot a man who had publicly called her "a damned whore."[23]

The high ratio of men to women, alienated labor, women's marginal inclusion in the labor force, and the ideology permitting men sexual independence but denying it to respectable women all encouraged prostitution on the Comstock. However, the Comstock bonanza did not last long enough to create a class of prostitutes born within the city, and social conditions on the mining frontier sustained rather than generated prostitution. In 1875, the 307 active prostitutes on the Lode represented the single largest category of female labor outside the home, and that category came close to being larger than all other female occupations combined. While the respectable occupational structure was nearly closed to women, the irregular marketplace welcomed them as part of its own working class.

Prostitution and the Irregular Economy

The term "irregular economy" does not imply any unusual market relations, but merely designates the often illegal and immoral status of various exchange patterns found in the vice districts of the Comstock and every other large nineteenth century city. The traffic in irregular goods and services reflected regular market patterns, and the irregular economy could only prosper because it supplemented the regular economy and served the interests of the mine and ore mill owners. Capitalists benefited indirectly from the irregular trade in drugs, drink, gambling, and women, because those diversions served as panaceas for their workers. Moreover, some of the city's leading citizens owned land and buildings in the bawdy

These two buildings were the last remains of the once glittering main bawdy district of Virginia City. This picture, which faces north on D Street, was taken in the late nineteen-fifties.

districts, which they leased at very high rates of profit. In 1877, John Piper, owner of the local opera house and an active local legislator opposed to limiting the location of brothels, rented Piper's Row to prostitutes.[24] Many other holdings in the bawdy district were untraceable. However, a search through 1875 assessment records and the 1875 manuscript census revealed that D Street vice district land ownership was unequally divided between respectable and disreputable owners.[25]

In 1875, only eight of forty-one registered owners of land occupied by prostitutes on D Street actually resided on the premises. Two such owners were madams who each held several lots and tenements, and two others were madams who only owned the land and buildings which they occupied. Four men listed in the census respectively as a speculator, saloon owner, a gunsmith and unemployed also resided on their own D Street land.

Nine other people owned brothel district land, but lived in high status residential districts. They were two reputable saloon owners, three merchants, and the wives of an assayer, an independent professional, and a speculator. A respectable widow who lived with her child and a servant also owned brothel land. However, the largest single lot in the main vice district belonged to the obscure estate of a Mrs. Ford.

It was not feasible to trace the direct beneficiaries of that estate, nor was it feasible to locate definitely the other twenty-one individuals holding the titles on D Street land. The difficulties in tracing those land owners, as well as the available information on others, suggests that most D Street land was probably held by members of the reputable upper and middle classes. This inference is supported by modern studies of New York City which uncovered elusive ownership patterns, eventually revealing local elites.[24]

The high rate of return from irregular enterprise induced respectable individuals to invest in them. This return rate reflected both the risks inherent in illegal operations and the relatively small amount of fixed capital indigenous to the criminal community. Capital did not remain within the irregular marketplace, but instead filtered back to less lucrative but less risky investments.

The irregular occupational structure generally resembled its larger legal counterpart. However, there was more room for individual entrepreneurs in the criminal community than in respectable occupations. Although most land in the vice district was secretly owned by respectable elites, most of its major businesses were run by a different set of disreputable elites, including saloon owners, madams of large brothels, and theatrical entrepreneurs. Below the elites was a small middle stratum of doctors and lawyers catering primarily to the disreputable community, managers, shopkeepers, small scale madams, and high status prostitutes who worked on their own. The status of the professional criminal, however, was somewhat blurred. For example, some professional gamblers carried their own faro layouts and spent many years perfecting their skills, while others were relative amateurs, resorting to sleights of hand at three-card monte. Similarly, some prostitutes working alone earned high fees from a small select clientele, while others lived in shacks, taking any customers they could attract.

Most people in the criminal community were part of its vast working class. Some men were employed by saloons and gambling dens, while others worked at menial jobs ranging from running errands to cleaning livery stables. Still others robbed stagecoaches, picked pockets, engaged in petty confidence games, or lived off prostitutes. Many of these men, along with others on the fringes of the irregular marketplace, were casual laborers who were unemployed much of the time.

Just as women were denied access to high status legal occupations because of pervasive sex-role stereotyping and discrimination, they were also kept at the lower echelons of the criminal community. With the exception of a few high status madams and whores, confidence artists, and some wives of owners of irregular businesses, almost all of the women in the criminal community were common prostitutes. Even those practicing small scale larceny, shoplifting, and bad check passing also turned tricks. However, while prostitutes theoretically belonged to the criminal working class, seldom holding major investments or amassing great profit from their labor, there were enormous status gradations among them.

Stratification Within Prostitution

Individual fancy women plied their trade everywhere on the Comstock, from elite residential neighborhoods to working class slums, but most organized prostitution was found in Virginia City's three differentiated vice districts.[27] Badly built, cheaply run houses in Chinatown offered customers gambling, liquor, opium, and prostitutes. These haunts were known for the dangers of robbery and sudden violence. However, for lawlessness and sheer vileness, nothing on the Comstock could compare to the tiny, predominantly white Barbary Coast on C Street. This district was located on Virginia City's main thoroughfare close to its major businesses and only consisted of five or six small saloons, yet it was the scene of gross profanity, lewd exhibitions, beatings, and murders.[28]

The better sporting resorts were clustered together on C and D Streets. These included bawdy theaters, dance houses, saloons, gambling rooms, and brothels, with picturesque names, such as Bow Windows and Brick House. A contemporary description of the Alhambra Theater caught the flavor of the whole district:

> . . . [the theater] is famous for neither the chasteness of its performance nor the moral tone which it seeks to exert upon its frequenters . . . Good people go there sometimes, and very bad ofttimes. This is a free country, and the grown men and women who go there might find a worse place if it were closed.[29]

Every form of prostitution practiced in nineteenth century America flourished in the bawdy districts and the neighborhoods surrounding them. However, even though various kinds of painted women worked in close proximity to one another, residential patterns within the districts reflected status differences. Prostitutes could live in large or small brothels, in well kept or rundown boarding houses, in their own cottages, in rooms behind saloons, or in cribs. The large variety of workplaces available to prostitutes and the subtle, but definite differences among ostensibly similar living and working situations make it difficult to discover where each individual prostitute fit in the stratification system, but a general outline of the status structure within prostitution can be drawn.

Madams were entrepreneurs at the top of the stratification pyramid, but in many ways they were *outside* actual prostitution. Although they occasionally took customers, they did not earn their livings from selling their own bodies, but instead managed the sexual commerce of other women. There were nine madams listed in the 1875 census, and two of them had large holdings in the D Street district. No single description can capture the many sides of Comstock madams, but notes on three of the Lode's most famous brothelkeepers illuminate some of their many facets.

Nellie Sayers ran a "ginshop of the lowest class" on the Barbary Coast.[30] Her small, one-story house had a barroom, kitchen, and two bedrooms in which four prostitutes lived and slept. Allegations of adultery, accessory to murder, and kidnapping a minor finally forced Nellie to close her establishment.[31]

Rose Benjamin, an Englishwoman in her thirties, was not so villainous as Nellie Sayers, but she was equally notorious. In 1875, her brothel on D Street housed seven prostitutes over whom she presided from a residence in another part of town. She was involved in several legal actions, including a suit against a prostitute in her debt and a battle to retain custody of an infant deeded her by another employee.[32]

Finally, Cad Thompson owned a brothel on the Comstock from 1866 through at least 1880. Her house was the scene of pranks and piano-playing. Cad's nickname, "the Brick," indicates her reputation as a good sport.[33]

Information about high status prostitutes who managed nothing other than their own sexual commerce is difficult to find. Unlike madams, those women had little need for public recognition of their sale of sex and many of them only remained on the Comstock for a short time. Misstresses of the upper class were usually hidden by their patrons and attempted to live behind a veil of respectability. Visiting actresses, who appeared in light plays and "shape shows" such as *The Black Crook* were often available for a price. The most famous members of this group were high-ranking prostitutes available only to selected clients.[34] To be sure, not all actresses were prostitutes, and some, such as Lotta Crabtree, capitalized on their virtue. However, others gave private exhibitions as "modele artistes," or even joined Rose Benjamin's house after their engagements were over.[35]

Another group of high status prostitutes was most important during the Comstock's first decade. They lived alone in cottages and could be selective of their clientele.[36] Most of them saw only one customer a night. A neighboring cottage prostitute described Julia Bulette's plans on the night of her murder:

> . . . she did not tell me the name of the man who was to sleep with her; said he was a friend; a friend is generally spoken of among us in that way.[37]

After these prostitutes came women working in the largest parlor houses, the finest saloons, and the best dance halls. The next rank of women worked in small brothels and bars. Chinese prostitutes were close to the bottom of the status structure, although there was status differentiation among the Chinese houses. At the nadir of the status structure were bawds living in ill kept rooms in the red light districts or in shacks at the outskirts of the community.

The stratification system of prostitutes reflected a number of nuances within the profession. Usually, the more flagrant a prostitute was, the less status she held.[38] Thus, women who sat at the windows of cribs or solicited customers outside saloons ranked considerably lower than those who were kept as clandestine mistresses or remained within comfortable brothels.

The status of a form of prostitution also depended upon the extent to which attributes other than pure sex entered into bargains with customers. The higher a harlot's occupational rank, the more other attributes were involved in the exchange. High status mistresses sold companionship and temporary fidelity along with sex. Visiting actresses and women dancing in major saloons could command high prices because their talent and celebrity increased the value of their sexual services. Even women in the major brothels sold more than sex, since conversations and conviviality in the public rooms were part of the attraction of the important parlor houses.

High status prostitutes had more control over their daily lives than their lower ranking sisters, and could turn away visibly diseased or violent customers. Moreover, better class whores usually saw only one man each night, since they could command high fees from each customer. The social class of the patrons was an extremely important, albeit somewhat tautological influence on a prostitute's rank. Rich men usually sought out high status whores. When regular patrons of a form of prostitution were wealthy, it had high status within the profession.

What form of prostitution a woman engaged in depended upon her race, ethnicity, initial social class, education, appearance, specific talents, and experience within the profession. Many of these attributes are difficult to measure for Comstock prostitutes, since it is impossible to trace their careers prior to their arrival on the mining frontier. Nevertheless a general profile of women who were prostitutes casts some light on their backgrounds and professional experience.

Prostitutes' Ethnicity

Most prostitutes came to the mining frontier already established in the *demimonde*. Many of the American born drifted to Nevada from other cities where they had been unable to support themselves in any other occupation.[19] Others were immigrants who became prostitutes shortly after they arrived in this country or actually journeyed to the United States in order to earn a living in the sporting life. Despite the fact that so many people on the Comstock were immigrants, a much larger proportion of prostitutes than respectable women were foreign born. (See Figure II.)

FIGURE II*
PLACE OF BIRTH AND RESPECTABILITY
OF COMSTOCK WOMEN IN 1875

Birthplace	Respectable Women	Prostitutes	Women in Permanent Liaisons	Total
U.S.A. (White)	87.5%	7.1%	5.4%	1,252 (35.0%)
U.S.A. (Black and Indian)	77.3%	13.6%	9.1%	22 (0.6%)
Canada	90.3%	4.6%	5.1%	175 (4.9%)
Central and South America	48.9%	46.7%	4.4%	45 (1.3%)
China and Japan	12.0%	81.5%	6.5%	92 (2.6%)
Ireland	90.6%	4.9%	4.5%	1,136 (31.8%)
England, Wales, Scotland	92.9%	4.0%	3.1%	450 (12.6%)
France and Switzerland	74.2%	19.7%	6.1%	66 (1.8%)
Germany and Austria	77.0%	5.2%	7.8%	231 (6.5%)
Scandinavia and the Low Countries	87.5%	6.3%	6.3%	32 (0.9%)
Balkans and Southern Europe (e.g., Italy, Greece, Spain)	89.5%	5.3%	5.3%	38 (1.1%)
Other (e.g., East Indies, Australia, aboard ship)	66.7%	16.7%	16.7%	12 (0.3%)
None Listed	57.1%	38.1%	4.8%	21 (0.6%)
	86.4% (3,085)	8.6% (307)	5.0% (180)	3,572 (100%)
U.S.A. (White) and Canada)	87.8%	6.9%	5.4%	1,427
Foreign Countries or non-White American	85.4%	9.8%	4.8%	2,145

*Source: 1875 Nevada Census

American born, British, French, and German women were members of the highest status ethnic groups within prostitution. When a native born hurdy girl attempted suicide, the newspaper story about her noted her comparative advantages, commenting that she was an "American girl and good looking."[40] German harlots were similarly valued, and an enterprising saloon owner in Carson City specifically imported a group of

Teutonic whores to raise the tone of his establishment.[41] In 1852 and 1853 hundreds of French prostitutes arrived on the Pacific Coast with free passage gained from giant national lotteries conducted by Louis Napoleon who sought to rid France of some of its criminal and potentially revolutionary elements.[42] Many of these skilled women soon rose to the top level of San Francisco's disreputable community, and their alluring reputations and the general glamor associated with Second Empire France contributed to the high status ascribed to French harlots on the Comstock.

While foreign birth sometimes added to a prostitute's status, non-white skin color always detracted from it. Black and Chinese prostitutes lived in segregated areas and never lived in an establishment also containing white women. South and Central American prostitutes could ply their trade in the main red light district, but they were often isolated in "Spanish houses" and bars hiring only brown harlots. While white customers patronized women of color, Black and Asian men seldom sought out white prostitutes.

Chinese prostitutes were located at the low end of the continuum within prostitution. They were prostitute-slaves whose earnings were kept by male brothel keepers associated with the great Chinese secret societies headquartered in San Francisco.[43] These women had been sold once in China and again when they reached the Pacific Coast. This slavery was common knowledge on the Comstock, and the kidnapping of a Chinese whore merely evoked a comparison of American horse-stealing with Chinese woman-stealing.[44]

With the exception of Chinese and Black women who clearly ranked below all other prostitutes, ethnicity did not directly determine a woman's status within the profession. Harlots of every other national origin could be found among rich men's mistresses and also among the slatterns occupying shanties on the city's fringes. However, ethnicity frequently determined how women were grouped within categories of prostitution, as illustrated by the distinctions among brothel prostitutes. For example, Bow Windows was among the city's highest status bordellos, and customers often went there for parties and musical entertainment, as well as sex. In 1880, it contained five women, from Europe and the United States. (See Figure III.)

FIGURE III

ROSTER OF BOW WINDOWS BROTHEL AT 15 SO. D ST.*

Name	Occupation	Marital Status	Age	Birthplace
Caroline W. Thompson (also known as Cad the Brick)	Madam	Widowed	53	Ireland
Annie Burnett	Prostitute	Single	28	U.S.A.
Kitty Caymont	Prostitute	Single	29	U.S.A.
Emma Hall	Prostitute	Single	27	U.S.A.
Annie Miller	Prostitute	Married	32	France

*Source: U.S. Manuscript Census, 1880

A lower status brothel specialized in Mexican women, and it was the important "Spanish house" in the city. Other houses with five or more women included French and American born prostitutes, and also Irish women. Irish prostitutes had lower ethnic status than those from other western European countries, and they were generally excluded from the best houses. However, Irish women were important in the smaller brothels serving working men, and were also active in saloons and hurdy houses catering primarily to the large Irish working class.

Ranking below the larger brothels were a number of smaller establishments scattered through the vice districts and fanning out into working class residential neighborhoods. While these houses of from two to four women were often internally homogeneous, prostitutes of every nationality lived in them, and it is impossible to order the small brothels simply from information about the ages and ethnicities of the women working in them.

By and large, the status of an ethnic group within prostitution reflected its status in the larger occupational structure. However, French and German harlots were particularly valued because of a mystique of sophistication surrounding their sexuality. Ethnicity was related to women's initial class position and education, both of which were also important in determining their status within the profession. Of all of the background characteristics listed in the 1875 census, ethnicity was most strongly related to a bawd's status; and age, traditionally regarded as critical in determining a woman's rank, was not particularly relevant to Comstock prostitutes' position in the fast life.

Prostitutes' Age

Most Comstock prostitutes were less than thirty years old, and many were under eighteen. (See Figure IV.) However, respectable people never protested against prostitutes in their early teens, unless girls from the local community were in danger of being recruited into the sporting life.[45]

FIGURE IV
AGE STRUCTURE OF THE ADULT FEMALE POPULATION IN 1875

Age	Respectable Women	Prostitutes	Women in Permanent Liaisons	Row Total
18 or below*	118	35	15	168
19-24	550	101	51	701
25-29	634	75	33	742
30-34	639	42	36	718
35-39	489	29	28	546
40-44	336	19	10	365
45-49	158	5	6	169
50-54	70	0	1	71
55-59	33	0	0	33
60-98	58	1	0	59
Column Total	3,085	307	180	3,572
	86.4%	8.6%	5.0%	100%

*Women under eighteen were not counted as adult unless they were married or employed outside the home.

Source: 1875 Nevada Census

Except in the case of madams, there was no clear association between a prostitute's age and her status within the profession. Of nine madams active in 1875, only one was under thirty, and this is not surprising, since both capital and experience were necessary to run a successful bawdy bar or brothel. The necessary characteristics for other job categories within prostitution were more ephemeral and not so strongly associated with age. For example, Julia Bulette, the Comstock's most famous courtesan, was approaching middle age (thirty-five). This fact flies in the face of much popular and scholarly writing about the fast life.

Moralists often traced prositutes' downward progress from opulent parlor houses to the gutters, and sociologists have emphasized youth as a desirable attribute in women's sexual exchange, asserting that the younger the prostitute, the higher her potential status within the profession.[46] However, age is not always directly related to attractive appearance, one of the key determinants of a harlot's status. Sexual specialization experience, conversational ability, and vivid interactional style are other important assets which may develop with age. It is probable that fancy women's age did not negatively affect their status until they began to look old, and women could remain in the type of prostitution they entered for well over a decade.

How Prostitutes Lived

Many prostitutes lived and worked alone, but their situations differed greatly depending upon their status within the profession. Both the Comstock's highest status courtesans and its outcast slatterns plied their trade by themselves. However, rich men's mistresses generally lived secluded lives, while low status women of the town often solicited openly in the streets.

Rich men's mistresses occupied their own cottages in residential neighborhoods or lived in well kept boarding houses or hotels. Little else is known about these women, because their prostitution was so clandestine. The only public notes about this group of harlots discuss a few tragedies occurring when their patrons left them or when they were discovered by their lovers' wives.

One Cornish woman left her husband because she had fallen in love with another married man. After that affair, she became a mine owner's mistress and eventually poisoned herself after he left her alone in a small room she had rented in a respectable neighborhood.[47] Another hapless mistress suffered injuries when her lover's wife discovered them in a comfortable room in the International Hotel. The affronted spouse did nothing to her husband, but shattered a handy bottle of champagne over his companion's head.[48]

More information is available about visiting actresses who stayed at the city's best hotels. Not all actresses who visited the Comstock were whores, and some women who appeared in legitimate dramas or were major musical stars vigorously defended their virtue. However, women cast in light plays and song and dance productions were frequently available to men. The Swiss Bell Ringers, a troop of Lancashire women, performed on the stage, and after their engagement was over they moved into one of the city's better brothels.[49] Other actresses were more discreet, yet they often added to their incomes and obtained favorable publicity by dispensing their sexual favors.

Most high status actresses traveled from city to city, and their transience explains the fact that only one prostitute was classified as an actress in the 1875 census. Moreover, other women appearing on the stage were simply listed as prostitutes or gave no occupational listing. Most of these women worked in bawdy theaters, the largest of which was the Alhambra Melodeon at the corner of Union and D Streets in the heart of the city's main red light district. The prostitutes singing and dancing in melodeons ranked well below actresses employed in respectable theaters, and their status corresponded with that of women working large saloons.

Although the bawdy theaters had small private rooms in which prostitutes could entertain customers, some disreputable actresses took men home to their boarding houses.[50] Women working large saloons and dance halls also lived in rooms on the edges of the D Street district. The "pretty waiter girls," "beer jerkers," "hurdy girls," and "slingers," were paid low wages for waiting on tables and entertaining and were generally expected to supplement their incomes by taking patrons. During working hours they merely flirted with men, and they usually had only one customer a night.

A large number of women working alone were not attached to any disreputable institutions, and they lived in cribs or shanties, soliciting customers in front of saloons or in the crowded streets. They occasionally had lower class men live with them for several weeks or months, but they usually returned to their lonely occupations. Many of these bawds were drunks, habitually arrested for disorderly conduct, and others were so impoverished and/or diseased that they eventually came to depend upon charity for survival.

Women working in brothels traded independence and control of their earnings for other advantages. They gave at least half of their income to madams in exchange for bed and board, a place to work, an established clientele, and a modicum of organized protection against violence. Employment at a better bordello also offered prostitutes entrance into the parlor house circuit, and they sometimes spent part of the year in San Francisco brothels. However, the women employed in the houses not only had to give up a large part of their wages, but also had to submit to supervision of their dress, manners, and recreational activities.

While no Comstock bordello was as lavish as the great houses in San Francisco, which abounded in antiques and crystal chandeliers and served only fine champagne, the best Nevada brothels had large comfortable salons with pianos. Liquor and conversation were provided in these public areas, and customers stopped by to drink and to listen to music, as well as to engage prostitutes. The major *maisons des joies* were relaxing meeting places, and sexual commerce was conducted beneath a veil of conviviality. Prostitutes had their own private rooms which servants cleaned, and the madams sent their washing to Chinatown laundries.

Little is known about the private barter between brothel prostitutes and customers, except that men had a choice of a short visit or of remaining all night. Prostitutes in the best houses probably received from a $10 to a $20 gold piece from each customer, since that was the price for short visits to top San Francisco parlor houses during the same period.[51] Fees for uncommon sexual practices were higher, and there are indications that these services were available in the best houses. One harlot at Bow Windows, known as the German Muscle Woman, was noted for having a ready supply of whips, and the availability of young girls and several sets of sisters at the best houses also suggest some willingness to accommodate sexual perversions.[52]

Most brothel prostitutes lived in houses of two to four women, charging substantially lower prices than harlots working in major bordellos. A few of these small houses were run by madams, but in most cases the prostitutes working in them either gave most of their earnings to a male landlord or split the cost of running their establishment among themselves. A description of one such house noted that it had a small reception parlor with a badly worn horsehair sofa, a spotted carpet, and three chairs. The madam was an old woman, and according to the account, it was as elegant as three-fourths of the Comstock's houses.[53]

A small number of bawds worked in Barbary Coast dives, where they occasionally helped set up drinks, but neither waited on tables nor danced nor sang. These small saloons were comparable to the lowest ranking brothels and each housed only one or two harlots. The Barbary Coast was notorious for fights, shootings, card cheating, and drugged drinks. Prostitutes working in saloons along the Coast were frequently ill-treated and were occasionally locked up for "safekeeping." Two women sometimes shared the same bed in cramped backrooms where they both slept and brought customers.[34]

Although life on the Barbary Coast was sometimes horrible, the women working in those saloons could usually leave, while Asian harlots were trapped as slaves in the Chinatown houses. They were often beaten by their owners and kidnapped by men from rival secret societies. Most Asian prostitutes wore Chinese-style clothes, either dressing simply in black pajamas and red-checked aprons or wearing more elaborate silk costumes.[35] There is no information about Chinese prostitutes' prices on the Comstock, but the usual fee for a short visit to an Asian brothel in San Francisco was $1.[36]

The Myth of Mobility

The conditions under which most harlots lived and worked did not allow them to accumulate enough money to leave the fast life and establish small, respectable businesses or simply live off their savings. Historical fiction about frontier prostitutes often contains allusions to the use of prostitution as a path to respectable financial autonomy, as well as references to harlots who married rich patrons and became pillars of elite society.[37] Neither of these themes can be verified empirically, since prostitutes who move from sin to respectability would have changed their names and hidden their pasts. However, evidence from the Comstock suggests that comparatively few prostitutes left the criminal community before they died.[38]

Many prostitutes died young, killed by the routine misfortunes that were an integral part of the skin trade. Such problems included violence from customers, faulty abortions, and addiction to alcohol and narcotics. One common "solution" to these related difficulties was suicide — the greatest hazard of all.

Prostitutes were routine targets for indiscriminate male hostility. Sometimes men's anger took the form of pranks, insults, and ridicule, which shady ladies were expected to bear with tolerance. Other incidents could not be dismissed so easily, since physical brutality frequently left lasting reminders. Nevertheless, patrons smashed furniture in brothels and bars, threw rocks at harlots, and beat them with impunity. Some D Street prostitutes wore whistles with which they could summon police, but they seldom called upon lawmen to help them to deal with routine violence, because the brutality of customers was an individual risk inherent in prostitution.

At least eight Comstock prostitutes were killed by men during the twenty-year boom, and there were many other near misses. However, with the exception Julia Bulette's assassin, no man was ever convicted of murdering or attempting to murder a prostitute. They ranked so low in the scheme of human types that there were few serious efforts to find their killers.

Other hazards of the fast life were more elusive than brutal customers. Imperfect birth control methods made contraception a constant problem. Although condoms, diaphragms, and douches were available from mail order houses and pharmacies, none of these devices was entirely effective. Moreover, some contraceptives, such as carbolic acid douches, were very dangerous.[39]

Pharmacies also sold abortifacients ranging from oil of tansy to strychnine. While both the sale of abortive substances and the performance of abortions were illegal in Nevada, the law prohibiting them was seldom enforced on the Comstock.[40] Abortion was never noted in the newspapers, unless harm to a woman forced public mention of the subject. Two prostitutes were known to have died from faulty abortions, and probably others were killed by similar operations, but had their deaths attributed to other causes.[41]

Some prostitutes endured pregnancy under harsh conditions and were later faced with finding homes for their children. Foster homes, orphanages, and boarding schools were alternatives usually available only to high status prostitutes. Sometimes a woman's parents might take a child, or, if she had her child prior to entering the fast life, the father might claim it. Despite these choices many women without resources were faced with the choice of killing their children or raising them in the disreputable community.

Infanticide was enough of a problem that Nevada passed a law defining concealment of the death of a bastard as a criminal offense, and adding that the criminal involved could also be indicted for murder.[42] While only one of six murdered infants on the Comstock was linked with a prostitute, the existence of a law against infanticide indicated that it may have been more widespread than the records suggest, and many bodies could have remained undiscovered.[43]

In 1875, according to the census, twenty-five prostitutes had children with them, and infants were living in six different Comstock brothels. There are no histories of what became of the children raised in these circumstances. The strains of pregnancy under extremely difficult circumstances and the decisions to be made once children were born undoubtedly wore down prostitutes' physical and emotional stamina.

Venereal diseases also debilitated prostitutes and contributed to their early deaths. While there is no specific information about disease rates on the Comstock, a number of studies indicate that syphilis and gonorrhea were highly prevalent in nineteenth-century America. In 1874, it was estimated that one out of 18.5 people in New York City was syphilitic, and a later treatise claimed that one out of every 22 people throughout the United States was infected with syphilis.[44] On the Comstock, surviving hospital records and newspapers do not explicitly mention venereal diseases, but mention of "cancer of the brain" and "internal disease of unknown origin." However, common newspaper advertisements for various cures indicate that syphilis and gonorrhea were widespread problems. One such ad read:

> Surest and quickest known [cure] for private diseases of both sexes, young and old. The worst cases of stricture and chronic venereal disease quickly retrieved. No mercury used.[65]

If Comstock prostitutes contracted venereal diseases, they would have spread to customers, some of whom were married. However, there was never any public recognition of that danger, although it is probable that fears of it contributed to respectable women's intimate motives to curtail prostitution. During the same period, New York feminists did speak out against prostitution on the grounds that it endangered wives and their unborn children with disease.[66] However, on the Comstock feminism was considered to be nearly as dangerous as syphilis, and venereal disease remained a hidden, private problem.

The routine hazards of ill treatment, contraception, and venereal disease contributed to another problem — alcohol and narcotic abuse. It is doubtful if women became prostitutes in order to obtain these drugs, since they were cheap and readily available on the free market. Instead, drugs made prostitution possible for many women, because liquor and narcotics allowed them to function in situations fraught with physical and emotional degradation.

Many low status harlots were chronic alcoholics who became involved in street brawls when they were drunk. The negative impact of alcohol on prostitutes' careers caused some to turn to other drugs, and the results were equally disastrous. Pharmacists sold laudanum, morphine, and raw opium over the counter, and opium derivatives were also components of patent medicines. Narcotic addiction was never considered a public issue on the Comstock except in the case of the Chinese, and growing anti-Asian sentiment was responsible for an ordinance declaring opium dens a public nuisance. However, the city fathers quickly made it clear that they were not concerned if Chinese people or disreputable whites smoked the demon poppy, but were merely worried about protecting respectable citizens from the Asian menace.[67]

Prostitutes not only took drugs to make their lives more bearable, but also used them to die when their lives grew unendurable. Morphine and laudanum were the two poisons most commonly taken by the fifteen harlots who killed themselves and the eighteen others who attempted suicide between 1863 and 1880. The actual number of suicides and attempts is probably far larger, since suicides among all classes often went unreported, attempts were frequently ignored, and some fancy women took their lives in other communities on the parlor house circuit. There was no clear pattern of suicides among harlots; those of every age, nationality, and status within the profession killed themselves.

The profits from prostitution seldom rested in the harlots' hands, but were instead amassed by madams, other disreputable entrepreneurs, and respectable elites with investments in the irregular economy. Julia Bulette was a member of a small group of upper middle status prostitutes who occupied individual cottages. She was among the most successful Comstock harlots, and her popularity allowed her to adopt a petit bourgeois lifestyle. However, when Julia Bulette died, she left behind large debts for professional expenses of rent, clothing, liquor to serve her patrons, and medical services. Her final estate was valued at $1,200, and the claims against it had to be met at one-third of their value.[68]

If these were the complete assets of one of the Comstock's highest status, best loved prostitutes, others of lower rank must have accumulated far less. On the other hand, madams of all kinds became wealthy. For example, Mit Raymond, the fifty-six-year-old owner of a prostitute bawdy saloon, left a substantial estate, including $40,000 worth of real estate in Sacramento, Oakland, and Marysville, California.[69]

Friends and Enemies

The quality of the relationships prostitutes had with men made it difficult, if not impossible, for them to achieve social mobility through marriage. In one case, a former Comstock prostitute did become rich after she married a pimp and moved to a mining community in eastern Nevada, where they owned several brothels and also invested in some legitimate businesses. However, after three generations, her heirs are still stigmatized by association with prostitution.[70] Many prostitutes never became seriously involved with men, and those who did often entered into liaisons or marriage with individuals who were also part of the criminal community, and the women either kept on working in the skin trade or assumed other roles in the irregular marketplace.

Five key masculine roles were salient to prostitution: customer, lover, pimp, employer, and lawman. None of these roles was mutually exclusive, since police received painted women's favors and special customers could eventually turn into lovers. However, at a given time, only one masculine role was critical in defining the relationship between a harlot and a man.

While men often sought them out for companionship as well as sex, that interaction was merely an additional service supplied by fancy women, and their friendships with customers were superficial. The underlying foundation of economic exchange, and the overwhelming difference in social power between prostitutes and customers, mitigated the possibility of deep, lasting mutual esteem. Thus, a former patron wrote this entry in his diary when a bawd he had known killed herself:

> Little Ida that I used to ---- some two years ago was found dead in her bed at Bow Windows (Jenny Tyler's) this morning. She had been rather dissipated for some time past and lately had taken to opium. —Ida Vernon was her name — a man was sleeping with her and found her cold in the morning. Rest in Peace Ida — she was her worst enemy.[71]

Some prostitutes wisely separated business from pleasure and seldom became entangled with respectable patrons. However, a number of sporting women did take male lovers from the criminal community. Marriage or long term affairs were more feasible for madams than for other fast women, since madams' jobs did not require that they barter their own sexuality, and they could separate love and sex from business. Some Comstock madams had consorts who owned their own disreputable businesses or pursued professional criminal careers, and their relationships had a measure of equality. However, the men in romantic relationships with common prostitutes invariably exploited them to a greater degree than men involved with madams. Either prostitutes' lovers were economically independent and used their greater social and economic power to dominate the relationship, or, more commonly, they lived off a harlot's earnings.

Despite informal prohibitions against discussing pimps, and a formal city ordinance banning "all lewd and dissolute persons who live in and about houses of ill fame," pimps thrived on the Comstock.[12] The 1875 census listed thirty-eight obvious parasites residing in brothels or with individual prostitutes and calling themselves "sports," "speculators," or "gentlemen of leisure." More such men may have lived on the Comstock, but they did not dwell with painted women and could not be definitely identified.

Eleven of the pimps were born in southern or border states recently disrupted by the Civil War, seventeen came from the eastern United States, one was from the midwest, and two did not list their birthplaces. Only seven pimps were foreign born. One was from Germany and six were Irish. Most of these fancy men were between thirty-five and forty-four years old. The successful ones usually came to the Comstock from other American cities, and their ethnicities indicate that their ability to live by their wits and manipulate women was enhanced by their familiarity with American culture.

Unlike their modern counterparts who exercise power over an average of two or three harlots at a time, Comstock pimps usually had only one woman.[13] However, in other respects the relationships between painted women and fancy men have changed little over the past century. The liaisons were based primarily on prostitutes' emotional commitment, rather than on fear or coercion. Pimps rarely solicited customers for their women or assisted with business in other ways, except to protect harlots sporadically from unusually rowdy or violent customers. Their principal function was to provide prostitutes with an illusion of romance that could not be found with anyone outside the fast life. Since higher status men in the disreputable community probably preferred liaisons with women who could promise them temporary sexual fidelity, prostitutes had to find lovers among parasites.

There is little information about the few fancy men who may have been honest, loyal, and true to their women. However, there are numerous reports of Comstock sports who mistreated prostitutes and gambled away their women's earnings. By and large, pimps took painted women's money, abused them, and eventually left. Some fancy men were forced out of the community when they became involved in murders and other major misdeeds, but most simply moved on to the fast life in other boom towns.

The men who ran bawdy saloons and theaters, owned buildings in the red light districts, or bought and sold Asian prostitutes did not belong in the same social category as gentlemen of leisure. Although these men earned money through prostitutes, they did not necessarily have love affairs with them. The financial arrangements between prostitutes and male entrepreneurs and managers of disreputable enterprises were relatively impersonal; while pimps encouraged tumultuous, one-sided romances.

Like pimps and disreputable entrepreneurs, police frequently took money from prostitutes, but lawmen often gave even less than other men in return for sexual favors. It was common for prostitutes to bribe police with money and/or sex in order to avoid arrest for discretionary offenses, such as disorderly conduct. Sometimes officers brutally arrested harlots who wouldn't pay them, and occasionally they were called to account for misusing their power.[74] However, the commerce between prostitutes and police usually continued unhindered by the city ordinance forbidding on-duty police to enter bawdy establishments except to discharge their professional duties.[75]

Police pay was low, and some lawmen were recruited from the fringe of the criminal community. However, while police were close to prostitutes, their relationships were characterized by unequal power. Sexual intimacy and other favors, such as providing alibis, were exchanged for protection from arrest; and most interactions between bawds and lawmen were comparable to impersonal prostitute-customer transactions. As agents of the respectable community, lawmen always had the power to betray fast women, and the sheriff was no more the prostitute's comrade than the vice cop is the modern streetwalker's confidant.

The only close, long standing friends prostitutes had were other women of ill repute. They lived together, drank together, fought and reconciled, protected one another from violent customers and petty madams, and sometimes attempted joint suicides. While lesbianism was never documented among Comstock prostitutes, it was common among harlots in other communities and probably occurred on the Comstock as well.[76]

Intimacy between prostitutes was facilitated by the bonds they shared through a common argot, set of customs, and pattern of career experiences. They were also bound together by their separation from the respectable community and by their social distance from customers. The trade talk of prostitution and the sharing of anecdotes and philosophy among women cemented their bonds, and even fancy men could not fully participate in such discussions, since they had not sold their bodies.

Even if love between harlots went unconsummated, other, non-sexual aspects of it were clearly evident. Prostitutes in small brothels sometimes shared the same beds after customers had departed. Women of higher rank traveled in pairs on the parlor house circuit and paid visits down the mountain to other fancy women in Carson City. Harlots gave one another small keepsakes, traded clothes, and recommended their friends to customers. When courtesans died, other women in the fast life buried them, and if they left any property, it was usually to their female friends.

Conclusion

Comstock prostitutes' daily lives resembled those of other women of ill repute dwelling in cities throughout the United States during the same period. Drawn to the mining frontier by prospects of wealth, those who came of their own choice usually remained poor, caught in a cycle of sexual and economic exploitation. Chinese bawds worked and died as slaves, and their situation was an extreme extension of the degradation experienced by other women in the fast life.

The traffic in women was legally tolerated and secretly encouraged because of the immense profits it brought respectable elites and because it was considered necessary to sustain the large labor force of lone men. Moreover, much popular ideology supported St. Augustine's assertion that prostitution was as essential to marriage as cesspools were to a palace, and many people believed that harlots provided a necessary outlet for the overwhelming sexual urges that good men could not inflict upon their innocent, fragile wives.

Although married women's frequent adultery contradicted the belief system negating ladies' sexuality, that ideology was strong enough to force the burden of punishment for adultery and/or divorce on women. Both respectable women and prostitutes depended upon men for their economic and social survival. While one group remained isolated within their parlors, the other was confined behind the veil separating the bawdy districts from the respectable community. However, both ladies and harlots alike shared a common fate of having their sexual behavior critical in defining their social identities. Ostensible fidelity and sexual reserve were key characteristics of respectability, while promiscuity and apparent sexual abandon were major aspects of disreputability.

The centrality of sexual conduct in defining women's social identities reflected the pervasive belief that moral women could control their instincts, while men could not be held accountable for their strong sexual drives. Women's sexual behavior was also critical to their social identities because few females could attain social position by earning a living outside the home. Men derived a sense of who they were by means of their occupation, while women seldom did.

In 1870 only 14.7 per cent of all women over sixteen years old in the United States were breadwinners."[7] This marginal inclusion of women in the productive and service spheres of the economy blurred the absolute boundaries separating prostitutes and wives in traditional societies, because respectability was no longer an ascribed characteristic. Working women had to both earn their livings and protect their moral reputations, and prostitution became a matter of "choice," rather than a role into which one was born. However, that choice was often illusory, since few jobs were available to women, and those that were usually had poor pay, seasonal layoffs, and grueling working conditions. Moreover, the ideological dichotomy between ladies and most working women was grounded in the reality that many women worked under the control of male supervisors or employers who took sexual advantage of them."[8]

Women's precarious economic position in the larger society was mirrored in the irregular marketplace. While the criminal community welcomed prostitutes, most women were excluded from other, more lucrative occupations. Moreover, many men employed in irregular capacities could cross over into reputable jobs, while prostitutes were damned as part of the *demimonde*. The whole stratification system within prostitution was a distorted reflection of sex stratification in the larger society. High ranking courtesans were valued for ladylike manners and attractive appearance, and prostitutes' race critically influenced their professional rank. Racism forced women of color into the most menial respectable jobs and also doomed them to the lowest echelons of prostitution.

The economic organization of industrial capitalism not only contributed to the supply of prostitutes, but also to the demand for them. Famines and political upheavals sweeping nineteenth-century Asia, South America, and Europe impelled women and men to seek their fortunes in the United States. Both immigrant and native born men worked long hours under dehumanizing conditions. Many workers sought emotional release and fleeting power through relationships with women of ill repute. As male workers were transformed into interchangeable objects in the factories, mills and mines, they in turn objectified women and traded part of their wages for sexual contact.

Prostitution was an integral part of the social and economic structure of all large American cities during the mid-nineteenth century. Although the traffic in women was labeled deviant, it was an essential part of social life. While prostitution's internal social organization has changed dramatically over the past century, it is still embedded in social structure. Sexism, racism, and capitalism continue to shape the skin trade. The common emphasis on the lures of the fast life obscures the social roots of prostitution. Myths about prostitutes' mobility and glorious careers were attempts to turn dirt into gold, but like other forms of alchemy they failed, and dirt remains dirt.

Notes

1. *Virginia City Territorial Enterprise*, June 27, 1867, p. 3, col. 1.

2. A large number of popular books on prostitution describe famous courtesans, wealthy madams, and call girls. Among these works are: Lesley Blanch, ed., *The Game of Hearts: Harriet Wilson's Memoirs* (New York: Simon and Schuster, 1955), Joanna Richardson, *The Courtesans: The Demimonde in Nineteenth Century France* (Cleveland: World Publishing Company, 1967), Curt Gentry, *The Madams of San Francisco* (New York: Ballantine Books, 1971), and, of course, Xaviera Hollander, *The Happy Hooker* (New York: Dell Publishing Company, 1972).

3. Several classic works on prostitution spend a disproportionate amount of time discussing life among high status harlots. For example, *see* Simone De Beauvoir, *The Second Sex* (New York, Alfred A. Knopf, Inc., 1952) ch. xix. Many scholars implicitly assume that all prostitution resembles elite sexual commerce. Thus, the quote about prostitution coming close to getting something for nothing appeared in one of the landmark articles in the sociology of deviance, Kinsley Davis, "The Sociology of Prostitution," *American Sociological Review*, II (October, 1937), p. 750.

4. Some of the best recent scholarship debunking the myths about prostitution includes Stephen Marcus, *The Other Victorians: A Study of Sexuality and Pornography in Mid-Nineteenth Century England* (New York: Basic Books, Inc. Publishers, 1964), Kate Millett, *The Prostitution Papers* (New York: Avon Books, 1973), and Gail Sheehy, *Hustling: Prostitution in Our Wide Open Society* (New York: Delacorte Press, 1973). Another important contribution to the emerging scholarship on sexual barter is the revitalization of Emma Goldman, *The Traffic in Women and Other Essays on Feminism* (New York: Times Change Press, 1970).

5. This study used almost every important primary and secondary source of data for the Comstock boom years from 1860 through 1880. Sources included territorial manuscript

censuses for 1860 and 1861 and the manuscript United States Census for 1870 and 1880. Special emphasis was placed upon the manuscript state census of 1875, since it provided the only detailed data on the community during a bonanza period, when there was a maximum number of prostitutes, a large general population, and an established, albeit flexible class structure. Newspapers carrying frequent small items about prostitution were another central source. Every surviving issue of the *Territorial Enterprise* was used, because it was the largest, best written, and most influential paper on the Comstock. Information from the *Enterprise* was supplemented with data from the *Gold Hill Evening News*, the *Virginia Daily Union*, and the *Virginia Evening Chronicle*. National publications, such as the *New York Times* and the *Overland Monthly*, also carried news about the mining frontier. Other printed materials included journals of the Nevada legislature, business and mining directories, and contemporary histories. These sources were supplemented by three available prostitutes' probates, diaries of respectable citizens, and a scattered collection of ephemera and photographs housed in the Nevada Historial Society, Reno. Comparative data were gathered from published histories of nineteenth-century prostitution in San Francisco and New York City. Finally, valuable insights about the similarities and differences between past and present prostitution were gained from brief fieldwork in Ely, a modern Nevada mining town, and extensive contact with members of COYOTE, the San Francisco loose women's organization.

6. Nevada Legislature (1875 Census), *Appendix to the Journals of the Senate and Assembly of the Eighth Session of the Legislature of the State of Nevada*, Vol. III (Carson City: John J. Hill, State printer, 187), p. 615.

7. Louis Wirth, "Urbanism as a Way of Life," in *Louis Wirth On Cities and Social Life*, ed. by Albert Reiss, Jr. (Chicago: The University of Chicago Press, 1964), pp. 62-66.

8. Russell R. Elliott, *History of Nevada* (Lincoln: University Nebraska Press, 1973), pp. 123-144.

9. Wilbur S. Shepperson, *Restless Strangers: Nevada's Immigrants and Their Interpreters* (Reno: University of Nevada Press, 1970), pp. 13-14.

10. See for example, *San Francisco Chronicle*, May 8, 1883, p. 3, col. 7-8 on the divorce action filed by Theresa Fair against James Fair in District Court of Storey County. See also, Kenneth Church Lamott, *Who Killed Mr. Crettenden?: Being A True Account of the Notorious Murder That Stunned San Francisco, the Laura D. Fair Case*, (New York: D. McKay Co.: 1963).

11. See for example, *Gold Hill News*, Feb. 24, 1864, p. 3, col. 1, and *Territorial Enterprise*, July 7, 1868, p. 3, col. 2.

12. Robert B. Merrifield, "Nevada, 1859-1881: The Impact of an Advanced Technological Society Upon a Frontier Area" (unpublished Ph.D. dissertation, University of Chicago, 1957), p. 33.

13. See for example, Mrs. C. M. Churchill, *Little Sheaves: Gathered While Gleaning After Reapers* (San Francisco, 1874), pp. 77-78 and *Territorial Enterprise* March 11, 1872, p. 2., col. 1 and June 15, 1872, p. 3, col. 3.

14. Robert B. Merrifield, "Nevada, 1859-1881," p. 163, and *Territorial Enterprise*, September 11, 1877, p. 3, col. 2.

15. Barbara Welter, "The Cult of True Womanhood: 1820-1860," in *The American Family in Social-Historial Perspective*, ed. by Michael Gordon (New York: St. Martin's Press, Inc.), pp. 227-250 and Eli Zaretsky, "Capitalism, the Family, and Personal Life: Part I," *Socialist Revolution*, III (January-April, 1973), pp. 102-115.

16. *Territorial Enterprise*, March 9, 1879, p. 27, col. 3-4 and Louise M. Palmer, "How We Live in Nevada," *Overland Monthly*, 11 (May, 1869), p. 461. See also Alfred Doten Diaries, Special Collections, University of Nevada at Reno, October 12, 1874. (While these diaries have been published by the University of Nevada Press, the manuscripts were used because they were more accurate and had not been abridged in editing.)

17. The average wage was $4 per day for an eight- to ten-hour day. See Elliott, *History of Nevada*, pp. 142-143.

18. *Territorial Enterprise*, July 28, 1877, p. 3, col. 2.

19. Palmer, "How We Live in Nevada," p. 462.

20. *Ibid.*, pp. 461-462.

21. Carroll D. Wright, Commissioner of Labor, *Marriage and Divorce in the United States* (Washington: Government Printing Office, 1897), p. 103 and pp. 708-711.

22. *Virginia Evening Bulletin*, April 16, 1863, p. 3, col. 1, and *Territorial Enterprise*, August 4, 1875, p. 3, col. 3.

23. *Gold Hill Evening News*, December 12, 1863, p. 3, col. 2.

24. *Virginia City Evening Chronicle*, February 21, 1877, p. 3, col. 3; February 22, 1877, p. 2, col. 2 and p. 3, col. 2; and *Territorial Enterprise*, Feb. 15, 1877, p. 2, col. 2 and p. 3, col. 3.

25. This search was quite difficult because prostitutes could be located by address, but not necessarily by lot parameters. In order to be accurate, the blocks known to have been almost entirely devoted to commercial vice were examined. First, land ownership was studied. Then lists of the owners were compared with listings in the 1875 manuscript census and with lists of prostitutes and madams in the 1880 manuscript census. Ownership was established only when there was definite correspondence between last names and first names or initials.

26. Sheehy, *Hustling*, pp. 116-154.

27. Two of those districts loosely conformed to ordinances relegating the traffic in women to Chinatown and an area on North D Street. The third, the Barbary Coast, was always illegal. The exact location of prostitution was established through the United States Census manuscripts for 1880, which listed clear street addresses.

28. *See*, for example, *Territorial Enterprise*, March 11, 1873, p. 3, col. 2; June 3, 1874, p. 3, col. 2; and January 20, 1877, p. 3, cols. 2-4.

29. *Territorial Enterprise*, November 7, 1878, p. 2, col. 3.

30. *Territorial Enterprise*, August 5, 1875, p. 3, col. 2.

31. *Ibid.*, August 6, 1875, p. 3, col. 2 and June 7, 1877, p. 3, cols. 2-4.

32. *Ibid.*, June 28, 1875, p. 3, col. 3; August 4, 1875, p. 3, col. 3; July 10, 1877, p. 3, col. 2.

33. *Ibid.*,November 20, 1866, p. 3, col. 1.

34. Although Lola Montez never visited the Comstock, and Adah Isaacs Menken is not known to have formed any liaisons there, each of these women exemplifies the actress-courtesan of the American frontier.

35. *Territorial Enterprise*, April 18, 1871, p. 3, col. 1 and August 17, 1872, p. 3, col. 1.

36. *Ibid.*, June 27, 1867, p. 3, cols. 1-3.

37. Testimony of Gertrude Holmes quoted in *Territorial Enterprise*, June 27, 1867, p. 3, cols. 1-3.

38. *See* Sheehy, *Hustling*, pp. 35-36, for an excellent typology differentiating high and low status prostitutes.

39. The harsh urban economic conditions forcing women into prostitution are documented in the cases of 2,000 New York harlots interviewed by William Sanger in 1858 for his classic work on the subject. See William W. Sanger, M.D., *The History of Prostitution: Its Extent, Causes and Effects Throughout the World* (New York: The Medical Publishing Company, 1897), chs. xxxii and xxxiii.

40. *Territorial Enterprise*, October 6, 1867, p. 3, col. 2.

41. Shepperson, *Restless Strangers*, p. 103.

42. Gentry, *The Madams of San Francisco*, pp. 72-75, and Karl Marx, *The Eighteenth Brumaire of Louis Bonaparte*, trans. by Daniel De Leon (New York: New York Labor News Company, 1957), pp. 107-108.

43. Stanford M. Lyman, *The Asian in the West* (Reno: University of Nevada Press, 1971), pp. 18-19.

44. *Territorial Enterprise*, June 9, 1878, p. 3, col. 5.

45. *Ibid.*, June 7, 1877, p. 3, col. 4.

46. Travis Hirschi, "The Professional Prostitute," *Berkeley Journal of Sociology*, VII (Spring, 1962), p. 42, and Sanger, *The History of Prostitution*, p. 557. Both of these works discuss the negative relationship between age and status within the profession, yet modern

call girls in COYOTE have frequently been in the business for more than ten years, and they assert that the key variable defining a woman's status within the profession is the level at which she entered. Young streetwalkers grow to be older streetwalkers, and young call girls simply mature at their high professional rank.

47. *Territorial Enterprise*, September 24, 1871, p. 3, col. 2.

48. *Elko Independent* (Elko, Nevada), July 14, 1879, p. 2, col. 1.

49. Shepperson, *Restless Strangers*, p. 103.

50. Some hurdy houses and bawdy theaters emphasized the availability of "private and dressing rooms," such as those noted in the Villa de Belvilier's opening announcement in the *Territorial Enterprise*, June 13, 1867, p. 2, col. 6. However, most did not, and customers sometimes fought over who would accompany hurdy girls home after hours. *See*, for example, *Territorial Enterprise*, January 14, 1872, p. 3, col. 2.

51. Gentry, *The Madams of San Francisco*, p. 153.

52. Shepperson, *Restless Strangers*, pp. 102-103.

53. *Gold Hill Evening News*, December 20, 1873, p. 3, col. 2.

54. *Territorial Enterprise*, August 6, 1875, p. 3, col. 3.

55. *Ibid.*, June 22,1867, p. 3, col. 1, and Doten Diaries, Feb. 13, 1866.

56. Gentry, *The Madams of San Francisco*, p. 57.

57. Dee Brown, *The Gentle Tamers: Women of the Old Wild West* (New York: Bantam Books, 1974). This popular history presents many legends about frontier prostitutes as if they were fact and also contains copious references to other sources which glorify western harlots.

58. Various causes of prostitutes' early deaths have been noted elsewhere in this article. Few of them left behind enough property to go through probate, and even those who did had comparatively little material security. *See* the probates of Susan Ballard, Jessie Lester, and Julia Bulette, Storey County Courthouse.

59. John S. Haller and Robin M. Haller, *The Physician and Sexuality in Victorian America*, (Urbaña: University of Illinois Press, 1974), pp. 113-124.

60. Nevada, *Statutes of the State of Nevada Passed at the Twelfth Session of the Legislature* (Carson City: State Printing Office, 1885), p. 1020. This law was first passed in 1869.

61. *Territorial Enterprise*, January 3, 1877, p. 3, col. 4 and October 12, 1880, p. 3, col. 3. These are the only two recorded prostitutes' abortions.

62. Nevada, *Statutes of the State of Nevada Passed at the Twelfth Session of the Legislature, loc. cit.*

63. For a discussion of the ways in which legislation reflects problematic areas of social life see Kai T. Erikson, *Wayward Puritans: A Study in the Sociology of Deviance* (New York: John Wiley and Sons, 1966).

64. Haller and Haller, *The Physician and Sexuality*, p. 258.

65. *Territorial Enterprise*, April 17, 1872, p. 2, col. 3.

66. Pamela Roby, *Politics and Prostitution: A Case of Formulation, Enforcement, and Judicial Administration of New York State Penal Laws* (Cambridge: Harvard University Press, forthcoming).

67. *Territorial Enterprise*, August 30, 1876, p. 3, col. 3, September 13, 1876, p. 3, col. 2, and September 15, 1876, p. 2, col. 1.

68. Debts Against the Estate of Julia Bulette, Storey County Court House, Virginia City, Nevada.

69. *Territorial Enterprise*, June 3, 1874, p. 3, col. 2, and June 6, 1874, p. 3, col. 4.

70. Personal interview with a member of the family.

71. Doten Diaries, February 6, 1868.

72. William R. Gillis, ed., *The Nevada Directory for 1868-1869* (San Francisco: M. D. Carr and Co. Book and Job Printers, 1868), p. 263. Business and mining directories frequently compiled city ordinances, and this reference is to the law against pimping on the Comstock.

73. For material on modern pimps see Christina Milner and Richard Milner, *Black Players: The Secret Life of Black Pimps* (Boston: Little Brown and Co., 1972), p. 12.

74. *Territorial Enterprise*, May 5, 1875, p. 3, col. 2, September 9, 1876, p. 3, col. 3, and October 18, 1876, p. 3, col. 1.

75. Gillis, *The Nevada Directory for 1868-9*, pp. 256-257.

76. Haller and Haller, *The Physician and Sexuality*, pp. 106-107. This is a general discussion about prohibitions against lesbianism in the nineteenth century. One of the most famous frontier tales about lesbians describes the day that Calamity Jane was finally dismissed from a brothel in Bozeman, Montana, for corrupting the other inmates. See Lucius Beebe and Charles Clegg, *The American West* (New York City: Bonanza Books, 1955), p. 349.

77. U.S. Congress, Senate, *Report on the Condition of Women and Child Wage-Earners in the United States*, by Helen L. Sumner under the direction of Charles P. Neill, Commissioner of Labor (Washington, D.C.: Government Printing Office, 1910), p. 11.

78. Sanger, *The History of Prostitution*, pp. 532-534.

Ameyuki-san: Japanese Prostitutes in Nineteenth-Century America

YUJI ICHIOKA

In her recent work, Yamazaki Tomoko studies the Japanese prostitutes who went to China and especially to Southeast Asia in the late nineteenth and early twentieth centuries.[1] Ruthlessly exploited by both capital and men, they were the most downtrodden of their sex, being worse off than their contemporary counterparts in Japan because of the alien environment in which they were forced to live and work. Believing that past studies of Japanese women generally have been limited to members of the "elite," Yamazaki devotes her work to these prostitutes and interprets them as her "starting point" for a larger study of Japanese women in the modern era. Japanese prostitutes also appeared in America in the last two decades of the nineteenth century. Though numerically less than the prostitutes in China and Southeast Asia, they were the first significant number of Japanese women here. They too were equally downtrodden and constitute the point of departure of any study of women in Japanese immigrant society.

A Ford Foundation grant administered by the Institute of American Cultures, in cooperation with the Asian American Studies Center, both of the University of California at Los Angeles, made possible the research for this essay. The author gratefully acknowledges the grant and those who made it possible.

YUJI ICHIOKA, editor of *A Buried Past: An Annotated Bibliography of the Japanese American Research Project* (Berkeley, 1974), is currently doing primary research on the history of Japanese immigrant society in America before World War II using Japanese-language sources.

Few Japanese women immigrated to America in the nineteenth century. The first phase of Japanese immigration consisted predominantly of males. Indigent students began to arrive in fair numbers from the mid-1880s, and many laborers followed closely on their heels from 1890. American immigration statistics record 2,637 Japanese arrivals from 1861 to 1890, of whom only 279 were females, and 27,440 arrivals between 1891 and 1900, of whom 916 were females.[2] Japanese government passport statistics corroborate this predominance of men; out of 36,806 passports issued from 1868 to 1900 to persons destined for the continental United States, only 2,036 were issued to women, 800 to females classified as laborers.[3] According to U.S. census data, in 1900, there were only 985 females out of 24,326 Japanese on the continental United States.[4] Japanese government population statistics are higher for the same year, but reflect an almost identical sex-ratio imbalance—1,130 females out of 32,493 Japanese.[5] Despite the discrepancies in the statistics of the two governments, both sets attest to the fact that few women came to America in the initial phase of Japanese immigration.

The small female population in 1900, numbering in the neighborhood of a thousand, included many prostitutes who, in all likelihood, comprised the majority. No documented evidence on the first appearance of the prostitutes nor precise figures on their numbers and geographical distribution exist. Oral tradition has it that they appeared in Denver, Colorado as early as the 1860s.[6] If historically true, this is extraordinary, for up until the mid-1860s the Tokugawa prohibition against foreign travel remained in force. In 1866 the Bakufu partially lifted the ban and permitted merchants and students to go abroad. Laborers were not allowed to leave legally until 1869, and only those who had been hired by westerners in accordance with treaty provisions. Thus, assuming the veracity of the oral tradition, it means that these women had to have departed surreptitiously from Japan before the beginning of the Meiji era in 1868. San Francisco more than likely had Japanese prostitutes prior to the 1880s, but again there is no extant evidence.[7]

As an historical fact they appeared in the late 1880s. Japanese consular reports bear out their arrival. In January 1890 the San Francisco consul reported that the prostitutes had begun to arrive in the preceding years and estimated that thirty worked in the city.[8] By March 1891 the estimate rose to fifty prostitutes who worked in ten brothels described as "almost openly operated."[9] By 1898, at the very least, there were 161 throughout California who were to be found in virtually every Japanese settlement.[10] Prostitutes turned up in other states as well. After the opening of a regular shipping lane between Japan and Victoria, B.C. in 1887, they started to appear in the Pacific Northwest. In May 1890 the Vancouver consul reported fifty prostitutes in Seattle.[11] The San Francisco consulate, in an extensive report, recorded seventy-one known prostitutes in that town by 1891.[12] Seattle was by no means the only town. The same report noted that Spokane had had fifty to sixty prostitutes in 1889 and had seventeen in 1891. Portland had nineteen in 1891. The earliest known prostitutes in Montana were in 1884 in Butte.[13] In 1897 the Tacoma consul reported sixty-nine in Washington, seventy-five in Oregon, twenty-three in Idaho, sixteen in Montana, and twelve in Utah.[14]

None of the foregoing consular figures can be interpreted literally and accepted as completely reliable. Because of geographical distances, local consulates were unable to check every female within their jurisdiction to ascertain whether or not they were prostitutes. Moreover, the prostitutes constantly moved from one locale to another, making the figures for any place at any time subject to sudden change. But the statistics do provide evidence that they began to appear in the late 1880s and increased in the 1890s. They were dispersed widely on the Pacific Coast and in the western states and, likely as not, were much more numerous than the statistics indicate.[15]

From the 1870s China and Southeast Asia were the major overseas destinations of Japanese prostitutes.[16] As an organized traffic, women were taken normally to the port of Nagasaki, and then smuggled out to Hong Kong and Shanghai, and later to Singapore, there to be sold and forced into prostitution Many of them originated from Amakusa, a small group of islands off the western coast of Kyushu near Nagasaki, where impoverished rural families, unable to survive economically, sold their daughters. Other young women were abducted or lured under false pretenses. This illicit traffic was so heavy that upwards of 5,000 Japanese prostitutes were in Singapore alone by 1909.[17] Some of these women may have been sent to America by the Chinese, in particular those who had been sold to Hong Kong merchants before the late 1880s. For how else can the presence of Japanese prostitutes in Butte, Montana in 1884, a booming mining town with Chinese laborers, be explained? The women in Butte, and perhaps others, having been sold to Chinese merchants in Hong Kong, were probably rerouted to America to work as prostitutes in Chinese labor camps.

The majority of prostitutes in America were brought over by Japanese men. As agents of procurers or as procurers themselves, they obtained women in Japan and transported them across the Pacific. As soon as they landed in a port, they sold the women or engaged them in prostitution. In many instances the procurers were former seamen who had jumped ship and settled down in a port city. An early history of the Japanese in the Pacific Northwest states that many prostitutes "stowed away on sailing vessels . . . and became the prey of wicked seamen who, in collusion with others who had already arrived in America, abetted their illegal passage."[18] Recalling his experience shortly after the turn of the century, an Issei remembers an old seaman who told a story of an unscrupulous agent in Nagasaki who

> told young girls from the countryside "if they went abroad, white families would employ them at high wages." Once he had groups of three to five girls, he sent them to Hong Kong or Singapore and most of them further on to the Pacific Coast. . . .
>
> Ship officers took a set commission from boatswains for each girl and delivered the girls to the procuring bosses. . . .
>
> Except for passenger-freighters, merchant ships were sailing vessels at the time and comprised from 70 to 80 percent of all cargo-bearing ships. Every sawmill company in the Pacific Northwest owned from ten to as many as fifty sailing vessels to transport lumber to various parts of the world. Most of the cooks on these ships were Japanese; four or five were aboard each vessel. When the ships sailed for Southeast Asia, they always stopped at Nagasaki and took on Japanese women.[19]

Some accounts indicate that the women were placed into boxes and loaded as cargo to avoid detection by immigration officials. Aware of conditions on the west coast, Japanese seamen played a prominent role in the arrival of the prostitutes.

Other men personally travelled back and forth from Japan to America bringing women with them on each occasion.

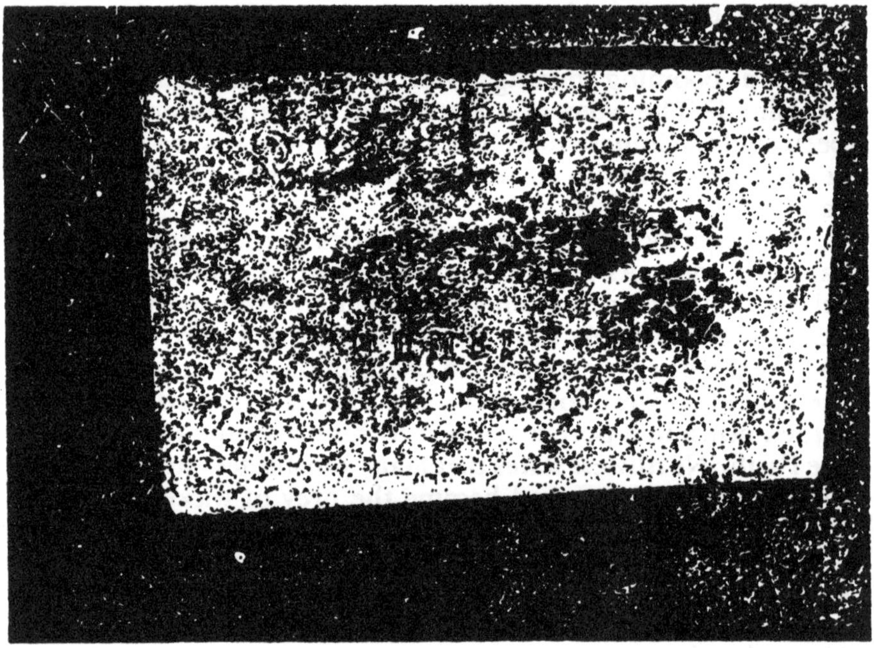

Gravestone marked *mumei* (unknown), San Francisco. Photo by Jere Takahashi.

According to the San Francisco consul, for example, Watanabe Masanobu, an operator of a brothel in Salt Lake City, left San Francisco in November 1891 to procure additional women in Japan.[20] Similarly, Arai Seikichi, who ran a brothel in San Francisco, sailed for Japan in February 1892 with the same objective in mind.[21] Hagiwara Shin was another individual who returned to Japan to procure women. In August 1891 he came back to San Francisco, where he had two brothels, with a woman who, he claimed, was his cousin.[22] He would have returned with three more women had he not been stopped by Japanese officials in Yokohama.

The most notorious procurer in San Francisco was Hasegawa Genji. Instead of going to Japan himself, he had women shipped regularly to him. In May 1890 he was sufficiently well-heeled to be able to hire counsel when two women he had sent for were denied landing and detained by immigration officials.

Securing writs of habeas corpus, he successfully landed them and proceeded to work them as prostitutes in his brothels.[23] In the next year, four other women were likewise denied landing and detained. Hasegawa again sought their release through petitions for writs of habeas corpus, contesting the administrative decision of the immigration officials up to the U.S. Supreme Court.[24]

A few specific accounts of how individual prostitutes actually came are available. One is that of a woman who originated from Amakusa itself. As related to an Issei writer, hers is a personal account.

I'm a daughter of a farming household in Amakusa. Around 1889-1890 a smooth-talking man appeared on my island. This man came to sell sea products processed in Nagasaki, and in the town he often told interesting tales. His stories were about foreign lands. Salmon was plentiful near Vladivostok; as children played in boats, the salmon jumped into them. Children used pearls and coral as toys on the beaches of Southeast Asia. Gold nuggets were waiting to be picked up on the riverbanks of America.

I got close to him at my grandmother's house. He tried to persuade me to go on a trip to Nagasaki. The distance between my home and Nagasaki was no more than the space between the nose and eyes. Since it took less than an hour by small boat to go there, I got on a boat with him one moonlit night. He took me to a seamen's inn in Nagasaki and fed me a nice meal.

On the next day I went with him to look at a foreign ship. It was a large steamship called the *Oceanic* bound for America. Boarding such a huge ship for the first time, I walked the decks enjoying the new experience. Then the man introduced me to a seaman on the ship. The seaman was about thirty-seven or thirty-eight-years-old, probably from Kyushu, and very good humored. He jokingly said, "Why don't you go to America on the ship?" When I replied, "I'd like to go and see America, but since I don't know anyone there, I can't," he answered, "Nonsense, many Japanese are in America, and they're all rich. If you stick it out for two or three years, you can become rich to the tune of several thousand yen." When I said, "But my mother will worry about me," he answered, "If you write letters afterwards, she need not worry."

Just as I was half thinking about wanting to go and half worrying, the passengers quickened their pace as a noise like the clanging of a bell sounded. The ship had hoisted anchor and had left port. The man with whom I had come was nowhere to be seen. "Since the ship is on its way," the seaman said, "I'll take you to America. Don't worry at all."

The ship bobbed on the Pacific Ocean. The waves gradually grew higher. The seaman put me in a room to sleep. "I'll bring you meals so don't leave it," he said. "If by chance you're discovered, you'll be thrown into the sea."

"If discovered, you'll be thrown into the sea"—that was frightening. True enough, thinking back on it now, I was a female stowaway, which was not a trifling matter.

The ship reached San Francisco after twenty days at sea. One evening the seaman dressed me in western clothes and took me off the ship. Pulled by his hand in the pitch darkness of the night, I just trailed behind him.

I arrived at an unknown house and was introduced to other women. I'll end my story here, for I'll tread upon people's reputations the more I go into details.[25]

The Nagasaki merchant and the seaman were in cahoots in the case of this woman. The merchant enticed her to go to Nagasaki and board the ship, and the seaman had her at his mercy once it sailed. Shanghaied in this manner, the woman arrived in San Francisco where she was delivered to a procurer by the seaman.

Another example recounts the story of an Oteru-san who was deceived under different circumstances.

Oteru-san was a person from Ejiri in Shizuoka Prefecture. A wealthy returnee from America was doing business in Ejiri at the time. Young people always clustered about him because he had lots of money and told unusual stories. When they did, he said, "If one went to America, even children could earn four to five dollars per day, and with a little more work one could make up to ten to fifteen dollars in a day." He also told them about the wonders of city life.

For young people already given to idle dreams, they naturally wanted to go to America where things were so beautiful and earn such money. Upon asking him how to get there, he said that he could help them since he had acquaintances on ships and any number of friends in America. Then he started to play his hidden cards. This well-to-do man had actually made his money in prostitution in America. On the surface he was engaged in a legitimate business, but in reality he was the boss of a kidnapping ring. Sometimes Oteru-san visited him with two or three other girls. In the end they were taken in by his words. On a village festival night, they sneaked out of their homes and went to Yokohama with his assistance. From there they sailed for Seattle.

As soon as they landed in Seattle, their room was watched closely so that they could not meet other people. They thought it peculiar, but believed this was an American custom and didn't pay much attention. They came to Oakland from Seattle and were sequestered somewhere. The man who was attached to them locked the door whenever he went out. They felt suspicious, but they couldn't do anything. Then two women came one day. Consoled in many ways, they were told that they would be going to San Francisco to work with other girls. They went somewhat elated only to discover the house there was also strange with many women. They sensed it was not a respectable house. That evening the middle-aged women who had come to get them informed Oteru-san, "You must work as a prostitute." "I was shocked," she remembered, "and said I couldn't do it. Please forgive me, but let me do some other work." The more she pleaded, they castigated her and ordered her to stop trembling. Her life of shame commenced from that point. As she recalled the past while crying, she said, "I made an error which determined my whole life."[26]

In contrast to the first woman, Oteru-san's arrival was connected with a man who had been in America. Operating as the boss of an abducting ring, this man coaxed young women to leave their villages. With the aid of seamen, he sent her and others here, where, unknown to them at the outset, they were to be handed over to a procurer. In both cases verbal subterfuge rather than physical force was employed to induce them to leave Japan, and seamen were the crucial intermediary.

A third and last example is that of Yamada Waka, a noted writer in Japan before World War II. A native of Kurigahama, a small fishing village near Yokohama, she too was beckoned to come to America by a man who had been here. Believing his exaggerated tales of riches in this country, she accompanied him to Seattle in 1902. Upon landing, he compelled her to become a prostitute in a Seattle brothel under the nickname, Oyae of Arabia. In 1903, befriended by the Seattle correspondent of the *Shin Sekai*, an immigrant newspaper of San Francisco, she fled with him to San Francisco, only to be forced into prostitution again in a Chinatown brothel. Fortunately for her, she managed to escape and gained refuge in the Chinese Mission Home, a Presbyterian rescue mission in Chinatown, and through eventual self-education became a writer-critic upon her return to Japan. Although Yamada Waka arrived after the turn of the century, her initial fate illustrates the case of women brought by men who personally returned to Japan to secure them.[27]

Other prostitutes probably left Japan under different circumstances. In the three examples, the women were innocent country "bumpkins" who were ignorant of American conditions. Believing the alluring tales of America men told them, they were lured to America and ended up as prostitutes after they arrived. The exact geographical origins and the economic backgrounds of all the prostitutes are unknown. Thus, one can only speculate that there were other women, unlike the three, who were sold into prostitution before they left Japan, as were the young daughters of impoverished rural families in Amakusa who went to China and Southeast Asia.

Lacking personal memoirs, it is impossible to depict accurately the life of the prostitutes in America. Fragmentary bits-and-pieces written by outsiders, however, do offer a partial glimpse. No matter where the prostitutes were, pimp-gamblers who preyed upon them invariably were present. In 1891 approximately 250 to 260 Japanese resided in Seattle, but only ten persons were employed legitimately. Apart from the known seventy-one prostitutes, the remaining individuals, in the judgement of a consular staff, were either vagrant types or pimp-gamblers who parasitically lived off the earnings of the prostitutes.[28] The same held true of other towns in the Pacific Northwest; thirty pimps in Spokane and forty to fifty in Portland were attached to the prostitutes there in 1891. Colloquially referred to as *amegoro*, meaning American thugs, the pimps held the women as chattels in some cases. A representative of the Ministers' Association of Seattle wrote to the San Francisco consul in January 1892 and informed him of the "condition of the Japanese fallen women" in his city:

> We are informed that of the 70-80 [prostitutes] quite a number are . . . in virtual slavery, brought over . . . under false pretenses and kept . . . by bosses who hold them in bondage. . . . We are informed that certain individuals visit Japan, induce these unfortunates to come here, pay their passage under a contract that such amount shall be paid back out of the earning of the women, that these men then compel them to enter a life of shame, keep them under a system of terrorism, take all their earning and keep them month after month in this condition of bondage; and that these women being ignorant of the value of our money thus pay many times the amount of their passage money though desiring to get out of the life of shame.[29]

Okina Kyūin, a well-known early Issei writer, describes the *amegoro* in the following way:

> *Amegoro* were behind the women, men who had been in abject poverty in Japan or who had come to America with ambitions, but abhorred honest work and had gone the wayward path. To carouse and gamble, they duped women and forced them into prostitution. The worse ones fraudulently married several women and sold them off to the Chinese.[30]

These *amegoro* were not averse to violence in the least. Holding women in bondage by coercion, they instilled fear in even the Japanese in legitimate occupations. Fearful of physical retaliation, the handful of "respectable" individuals in Seattle in 1891 refused to take action against them when asked to do so by a consular staff member.[31] The San Francisco *Daily Report* disclosed the presence of about 125 in San Francisco in 1892 with Hasegawa Genji as one of their leaders. They too intimidated other Japanese in the city by threats of violence.[32] Such persons were culpable of unforgivable deeds. Two of them kidnapped a thirteen-year-old daughter of a fellow immigrant in Portland in 1891, took the child to Salem, and forced her into prostitution.[33] In 1900 another individual sold his four-month-pregnant paramour to a Chinatown brothel in San Jose.[34]

Depending upon their clientele, the prostitutes were divided into three categories. The *hakujin-tori* catered exclusively to white men, the *Shinajin-tori* had Chinese customers, and the *Nihonjin-tori* dealt with Japanese. This division of prostitutes no doubt mirrored not only white American prejudices but Japanese ones as well. White men did not frequent brothels patronized by Asian men, nor did Japanese men associate with Japanese prostitutes who cavorted with Chinese men. In Seattle the houses of prostitution, known by names like Tokyo House, were located on or around King Street in the heart of the Japanese settlement, while those in San Francisco were all situated in or near Chinatown off of Dupont Street (present-day Grant Avenue) and, ironically, on St. Mary's Street. Not all prostitutes worked in brothels. Innumerable small bar-restaurants, which hired *shakufu* or barmaids, proliferated in the inchoate immigrant communities in the 1890s. Not every *shakufu* was a prostitute, but some were, and they worked in these bar-restaurants rather than in brothels.

Hardly any detailed descriptions of the houses or of the prostitutes in them are available. Of the few, there is this depiction of the prostitutes in San Francisco on Brooklyn Place in Chinatown:

> The girls were exhibited in a kind of cage. Each was dressed in a gaudy red garment. Each had painted cheeks, and a peculiar wreath-like ornament upon the head, which instead of being the crown of a pure and noble womanhood was the emblem of shame.[35]

The prostitutes in Fresno are described in this language:

> There are close to fifty to sixty Japanese prostitutes in this place.... They construct crude hovels of two nine-by-nine-foot rooms in several filthy three to four feet wide alleys wedged in a slum area and accessible by side and rear entrances. When evening sets in, they show off their "wares" by leaving the doors open and wearing grotesque, bright Japanese or Chinese garments with beds by their sides.[36]

All of the houses may or may not have been so wretched, but one can imagine the adverse conditions under which the prostitutes labored in other locales.

Besides being forced into prostitution, the prostitutes were exploited in other ways. Take the example of Tanaka Chūshichi. Described as totally illiterate but shrewd, he was an erstwhile seaman. In Seattle he linked up with a prostitute and took her to Ogden, Utah, where he had her work while he lived the life of a pimp. In 1891 a Chinese labor contractor from Rock Springs, Wyoming took a fancy to the woman upon visiting Ogden, and Tanaka agreed to let him take her as his mistress back to Rock Springs. Then Tanaka had the woman prevail upon the Chinese contractor, who had contracting rights with the Oregon Short Line, to permit him to become his sub-contractor. Once he obtained the right, he journeyed to Portland to recruit Japanese laborers. Successfully rounding up forty laborers, he headquartered himself in Nampa, Idaho in October 1891, earning the dubious honor of becoming the first Japanese railroad contractor. This historic first was inseparable from a prostitute whose name is even unrecorded.[37] The first railroad labor contractor in California and Nevada was none other than Hasegawa Genji. In his case, his profits from his brothels probably enabled him to accumulate capital with which he entered the railroad labor contracting business in May 1892 with the Southern Pacific. The presence of former pimps in the business of railroad labor contracting in the 1890s has led an Issei historian to go so far as to assert that "pimps monopolized it."[38] While no doubt an overstatement, his assertion alludes to the fact that certain individuals had been associated with prostitution in one way or another before they became contractors.

The initial success of Furuya Masajirō was also linked closely to the prostitutes. A merchant, labor contractor, and banker, he was the wealthiest Japanese immigrant in Washington in his heyday. Alongside Ban Shinzaburō, another labor contractor-merchant based in Portland, and Ushijima Kinji in California (commonly known as George Shima, the Potato King), he was counted as one of the three most financially successful persons in America among the Issei. Possessed of little formal education, Furuya landed in Seattle in April 1890, his arrival coinciding with the growing number of Japanese prostitutes in the town. Having been apprenticed as a tailor-seamster, he opened a small tailor shop and specialized in dressmaking to secure the business of the prostitutes. As he made his rounds soliciting their orders, he slowly gained their confidence so that they began to deposit money with him for safekeeping. This practice gave Furuya access to capital with which he opened up his first retail store in December 1892, a brief two years and eight months after his arrival.[39] From that time he parlayed his business into labor contracting, import-export, and even banking. Furuya may have become a successful businessman without the savings of the prostitutes. Yet the fact remains that his initial enterprise, the foundation of his later prosperity as it were, depended upon the prostitutes and their deposits placed in his hands.

Many derogatory terms in Japanese were applied to the prostitutes. A descriptive noun often employed by Japanese government officials was *senpu*, which means base women. Infused with negative meaning, it reflected the moral and bureaucratic biases of the officials who viewed the women as "undesirables." A prostitute who catered to white men was a *hakujinchō*, a white man's bird, birds being a common metaphor symbolizing prostitutes. A prostitute who slept with anyone was called a *mokugyo-kō*. A *mokugyo* is a portable wooden drum commonly found in Buddhist temples. Oval in shape with two carved fishes at each end, it has a slit at the top which, to lascivious males, resembles the female organ. A fastidious prostitute was tagged a *nembutsu-kō*, *nembutsu* being to Buddhists what "Hail Mary" is to Catholics, a ritual invocation to the Amida Buddha. Compared to the *mokugyo-kō*, the *nembutsu-kō* was better, at least from the sarcastic male point of view. Another term, *iden*, designated a prostitute who moved from one house to another. This word originated from *iten*, which means to change one's domicile. The character *ten* of *iten* was replaced by *den*, meaning the buttocks, so that the original meaning was altered to mean to move one's buttocks, or, more coarsely, to move one's ass!

The prostitutes drew the attention of the American press very early. The *Post-Intelligencer* of Seattle carried articles in February and April 1891 reporting the arrest of Japanese prostitutes, and sarcastically noted, in the latter month, that "the Japs all gave half English, half Japanese names, such as 'Jap Mary' and 'Jap Lizzie,' etc.," at the time they were booked.[40] In San Francisco the *Bulletin* assumed the lead in January 1890 in printing a story about them. Under the caption "Japanese Women—Their Importation For Immoral Purposes," the story quoted a police official as saying that "the majority . . . are in houses of ill-fame, having been imported for that purpose," and that "their colony is growing" with "every steamer from Japan bringing reinforcements."[41] During the remainder of 1890 the San Francisco press published a few more items on Japanese women suspected of prostitution, but it was not until the following years that they became notably newsworthy.[42]

In 1891 and 1892 the *Bulletin, Daily Report, Call,* and *Examiner* all printed sensational stories. In February 1891 the *Examiner* reported the arrest of two young Japanese prostitutes in a police raid which, it claimed, had caused "consternation and alarm in the Japanese quarter."[43] A few months later, in May, the *Bulletin* took up where it had left off in 1890. Reviewing the past arrival of Japanese women, it said:

> The first of them to arrive were imported for immoral purposes, and since that time scarcely a steamer arrived . . . that did not carry one or two recruits for the army of abandoned women in this city. This colony increased slowly but surely until . . . one whole block was occupied exclusively by them. . . .[44]

Shortly after, using its favorite headline "The Slave Trade," the *Daily Report* compared the Japanese to the Chinese:

> The Chinese are not the only people in San Francisco engaged in the slave trade. For some years the Japanese have also been busily engaged in the traffic. . . . Nearly all the Japanese women who come to San Francisco are . . . destined for houses of ill-fame.[45]

The press coverage in the spring of 1892 had the same content and tenor. The *Examiner* emphatically stated that "Japanese women are imported for vicious purposes."[46] Continuing its self-proclaimed crusade against Japanese prostitution, the *Bulletin* declared that:

> the women here are of the lowest class, and, like the Chinese women, are imported only to lead a life of shame. Of course this is not true of all of them, but it is of far the greater number. Like the Chinese women, they are held in bondage and are obliged to turn over their wages of sin to their masters and importers.[47]

The *Call* parroted the *Bulletin*:

> Six years ago there was hardly a Japanese woman to be found in this city. Now they are to be seen in great numbers.
>
> They have taken exclusive possession of St. Mary's street, where they hold forth without restraint by the police and hail every passer-by with the familiar cry of the siren.
>
> Perhaps Japan has sent us her very worst, but the samples seen here have given our people anything but a good opinion of Japanese morals.[48]

And the *Daily Report* warned of the danger ahead: "The importation of Japanese women for immoral purposes promises to become as notorious as the Chinese slave trade."[49] Likening Japanese prostitution to that of the Chinese, this adverse publicity was a part of the first agitation simultaneously raised against Japanese laborers by the San Francisco press.

Japanese government officials were appalled at the arrival and presence of the prostitutes. The San Francisco and Vancouver consuls forwarded frequent dispatches on them to the Foreign Ministry in which they consistently advised Tokyo to take steps to stop their departure from Japan. Highly sensitive to the American image of Japan and the Japanese, the negative press coverage heightened the consuls' sense of consternation.

In February 1891 certain eastern newspapers carried an article on an alleged incident involving the "auction" of Japanese girls in San Francisco which alarmed Tateno Gōzō, the Japanese minister in Washington, D.C., prompting him to order Chinda Sutemi, the San Francisco consul, to undertake an immediate inquiry.[50] Chinda discovered that the story was fabricated, but stated in a March dispatch that "the rumor could not have spread if the vice of the Japanese prostitutes had not already become a public scandal." Continuing, he predicted that:

> If matters are left as they are today, illicit Japanese houses inevitably will be established soon all over the country as in Hong Kong, Shanghai, and Singapore. . . . At present the Japanese are prone to incur the enmity of Americans like the Chinese. If we allow the prostitutes to carry on unhindered, what will be unavoidable is that prostitution will become a basic pretext in the hands of Japanese exclusionists.[51]

Chinda here expressed the greatest apprehension of Japanese government officials. The prostitutes were not mere stains on Japan's national honor, although that was admittedly scandalous enough. Fully aware of what had happened to the Chinese, he feared their presence would become, as he called it, a "pretext" for a campaign, similar to the Chinese exclusion movement, to exclude the Japanese. The San Francisco newspapers would confirm his fear less than two months later when they explicitly linked Japanese prostitution to that of the Chinese. To forestall the possibility, Chinda therefore concluded that "the most urgent task is to close up the avenues by which new prostitutes arrive in the city."[52]

The measures adopted by the Japanese government to curb the departure of prostitutes from Japan coincided with new immigration legislation in America. Congress amended previous enactments regulating immigration on 3 March 1891, creating the office of Superintendent of Immigration within the Treasury Department to oversee the operation of immigration stations. Along with earlier enactments, the new legislation prohibited the entry of certain classes of aliens, among them prostitutes, contract laborers, and paupers. In the spring of 1891, two German tramp steamers sailed into San Francisco carrying 120 Japanese laborers, including a number of women—the *Remus* on April 21 with fifty-three and the *Pemptos* on April 22 with sixty-seven.[53] Many of them were denied landing permission because they were considered contract laborers or paupers apt to become public charges. In response to the consular dispatches on the prostitutes and the new legislation, Okabe Nagatsune, the Vice Foreign Minister, had instructed Chinda on April 8 to assign a consular staff to the immigration station as an interpreter.[54] The idea was to cooperate with immigration officials to spot potential or actual prostitutes and prevent their disembarkation whenever ships arrived with Japanese passengers. With Chinda's intervention and assistance, the majority of the laborers aboard the *Remus* and *Pemptos* were allowed to land eventually, but nine females were deported. Suspecting that they were prostitutes, Chinda did not intervene on their behalf. Thereafter Tokyo instructed passport-issuing offices in Japan to screen carefully all applicants in order to make certain that they did not fall into the classes of aliens excluded by the new legislation. Though this measure did not completely halt the flow of prostitutes to America, it did have the effect of reducing the number of new arrivals.

Immigrant leaders in San Francisco were equally dismayed at the prostitutes. As early as 1889, the Gospel Society, the first immigrant organization in North America, had appealed to the Japanese government to stop the passage of indigent persons.[55] In May 1891 the Greater Japanese Association, the earliest precursor of later Japanese associations, specifically petitioned the Foreign Ministry to curtail the departure of prostitutes from Japan. The petition in part read:

> Lately in the cities of California, Washington, and Oregon in America, Japanese women who ply the infamous trade, namely, prostitution, are increasing in number by the months. Among the cities, San Francisco is the most notorious with many women forming a block in a row of adjacent houses. Engaged in their illicit business, they sense no shame at all at the scandalous sight they present. Because they do not, a public outcry has been aroused among the American people, so that recent female arrivals are continually denied landing permission. . . . These women are a blot on our national image and national morality. . . . The reasons for the ban on Chinese immigration and the call for the expulsion of the Chinese were many and varied, but *the main one was that Chinese women were prostitutes*. . . . It is evident that, if this notorious vice spreads, America will adopt measures against us in the same manner as she did formerly against the Chinese. (emphasis added)[56]

Signed by eighteen members of the executive board, the petition echoed Chinda's opinions. Asserting that the prostitutes dishonored Japan as a nation, it attributed the main reason for Chinese exclusion to Chinese prostitutes. By analogy, if Japanese prostitutes increased in number, Japanese exclusion was a distinct possibility. Neither Japanese government officials nor immigrant leaders alluded sympathetically to the plight of the prostitutes. They simply condemned them out of hand. Deeming the "face" of the Japanese nation and of the "respectable" Japanese residents of primary importance, they feared that Japan and they would be judged by Americans in the same light as they themselves judged the prostitutes.

Within the small Japanese female population in the 1890s, prostitutes were numerous, probably composing the majority of Japanese women. Brought over by Japanese men, they were forced into prostitution, sometimes being held in a virtual state of bondage by thugs who preyed upon them. The Japanese exclusion movement, which fully surfaced in 1900, did not start out of an historical vacuum. Anti-Japanese agitation, linking the newly arriving Japanese to the Chinese, occurred in the 1890s, auguring what was to erupt with full force at the turn of the century, when all Japanese were to be declared undesirable. Knowing the Chinese had been excluded in 1882, both Japanese government officials and immigrant leaders looked askance at the prostitutes. Afraid the prostitutes would become the measuring rod by which white Americans would judge all Japanese in America, they self-righteously decried their presence and took measures to limit their numbers in the vain hope of avoiding the same fate as the Chinese.

What eventually happened to these women is unknown. Some no doubt managed to return to Japan, others perhaps married here. Most probably died nameless. The majority of Issei women immigrated to America after 1900. Their forerunners were these unjustly maligned prostitutes in the nineteenth century, the *Ameyuki-san.*[57] Exploited in so many ways and despised by all quarters, like their contemporaries in China and Southeast Asia, they occupied the lowest level of society. One expressed her view of the world from that lowly position:

> How do you see people today? From the way I see them, they're all whores. Whores without human feelings (ninjō). . . . And people at large, in apparent glee, respect male whores who have power.[58]

NOTES

1. Yamazaki Tomoko, *Sandakan Hachiban Shōkan* (Tokyo, 1972). A partial translation of this work can be found in Tomoko Moore and Steffen Richards (trans.), "Sandakan No. 8 Brothel," *Bulletin of Concerned Asian Scholars* (Oct./Dec. 1975), 52-60. The prostitutes who went to China and Southeast Asia are known as *Karayuki-san* because they were first transported to China. *Kara* means China, *yuki* stems from the verb to go. I have labelled the prostitutes who came to America *Ameyuki-san*, taking the first two syllables, *Ame*, from the Japanese romanization of America.

2. Compiled from Superintendent of Immigration, *Annual Reports* (Washington, D.C., 1892-1900). Since these reports do not have statistical breakdowns by sex for Japanese arrivals from 1891 to 1895, the number of females should be higher.

3. Compiled from Naikaku Tōkeikyoku, *Nihon Teikoku Tōkei Nenkan* (Tokyo, 1882-1901).

4. U.S. Census Office, *Twelfth Census of the United States*, 1900, *Population*, I (Washington, 1901), cxxiii and 492.

5. Naikaku Tōkeikyoku, *Nihon Teikoku Tōkei Nenkan* (1901), 69-70.

6. Itō Kazuo, *Hoku-Bei Hyakunen Sakura* (Seattle, 1969), 887. This work has been translated as Shinichiro Nakamura and Jean S. Gerard (trans.), *Issei* (Seattle, 1973).

7. Shakuma, "Rekishi Inmetsu no Tan," (ca. 1922), Oka Papers, box 134, folder 6, Japanese American Research Project Collection. This source consists of ninety-seven articles published in the *Nichibei Shimbun* on the early history of Japanese immigrants. A pioneer immigrant himself, the author is Washizu Bunzō. Shakuma is his pen name.

8. Kawakita Shunsuke to Asada [Tokunori], 21 January 1890, reel 1, Japanese Foreign Ministry Archival Documents, Japanese American Research Project Collection (hereafter cited as JFMAD, JARP).

9. Chinda Sutemi to Aoki Shūzō, 10 March 1891, Nihon Gaimushō, *Nihon Gaikō Bunsho*, XXIV (Tokyo, 1952), 462.

10. Mutsu Hirokichi to Komura Jutarō, 11 August 1898, reel 6, Japanese Foreign Ministry Archival Documents, Asian American Studies Center, UCLA (hereafter cited as JFMAD, AASC). The geographical distribution was as follows: San Francisco, thirty-eight; Fresno, thirty; Sacramento, fifteen; Vacaville, seven; Watsonville, three; Hanford, seven; Bakersfield, seven; Los Angeles, eight; Stockton, ten; Santa Barbara, six; Chico, five; San Jose, two; Marysville, three; and other locales, twenty. Consul Mutsu stressed in his dispatch that these figures were the very minimum.

11. Sugimura Shun to Aoki, 8 May 1890, reel 1, JFMAD, JARP.

12. Chinda to Hayashi Kaoru, 30 July 1891, enclosure; Fujita Yoshirō to Chinda, 22 July 1891, Nihon Gaimushō, *Nihon Gaikō Bunsho*, 500.

13. Shakuma, "Rekishi Inmetsu no Tan." See also Rokki Jihōsha, *Sanchūbu to Nihonjin* (Salt Lake City, 1925), 75.

14. Saitō Miki to Komura, 2 April 1897, reel 6, JFMAD, AASC.

15. Takeuchi Kōjirō, *Beikoku Seihokubu Nihon Iminshi* (Seattle, 1929), 33, estimates as high as 600 prostitutes were in Seattle in 1895.

16. Yamazaki, *Sandakan Hachiban Shōkan*; Irie Toraji, *Hōjin Kaigai Hatten-*

shi, I (Tokyo, 1938), 231-236; and Mori Katsumi, *Jinshin Baibai—Kaigai Dekasegijo* (Tokyo, 1959). Even though white slavery in Japan was outlawed in 1872, it was never fully stamped out.

17. Mori, *Jinshin Baibai*, 150.

18. Takeuchi, *Beikoku Seihokubu Nihon Iminshi*, 33.

19. Itō, *Hoku-Bei Hyakunen Sakura*, 893-894. The translation is mine.

20. Chinda to Hayashi, 16 January 1892, Nihon Gaimushō, *Nihon Gaikō Bunsho*, XXV (Tokyo, 1952), 683-684.

21. Chinda to Hayashi, 4 February 1892, *ibid*., 684-685.

22. Chinda to Enomoto Takeaki, 3 September 1891, reel 1, JFMAD, JARP.

23. Chinda to Aoki, 20 May 1891, *ibid*.

24. *Ibid*., and Chinda to Enomoto, 30 July 1891, reel 1, JFMAD, JARP. The four women arrived aboard the *Belgic* on 7 May 1891. Hasegawa's efforts to obtain their release were publicized by the San Francisco press. See the *Bulletin*, 14, 19, 23 May 1891; *Daily Report*, 19 May 1891; and *Call*, 14 May 1891. He contested the administrative decision in the Nishimura case, the first Japanese-related litigation to reach the U.S. Supreme Court. For the legal details, see *Nishimura Ekiu [sic] v. U.S.*, 142 U.S. 651 (1892). The proper romanization of her first name is Iku.

25. Shakuma, "Rekishi Inmetsu no Tan."

26. Heigan, "Nijūhachinenkan no Yo ga Kaikō," *Shin Sekai*, 8 September 1931. Like the series by Washizu Bunzō, this source also consists of newspaper articles—100 in all—on the early history of Japanese immigrants. The author is Ninomiya Risaku. Heigan is his pen name.

27. Oka Shigeki, "Arabya Oyae Shusse Monogatari," *Amerika Shimbun*, 12, 26 February and 5 March 1938. A slightly different version of what happened to Yamada Waka can be found in Takeuchi, *Beikoku Seihokubu Nihon Iminshi*, 486-489. For a brief description of her life in the Chinese Mission Home, see Woman's Occidental Board of Foreign Missions, *31st Annual Report* (San Francisco, 1904), 57.

28. Chinda to Hayashi, 30 July 1891, enclosure, Fujita to Chinda, 22 July 1891, Nihon Gaimushō, *Nihon Gaikō Bunsho*, 491.

29. A. Inwood to Chinda, 25 January 1892, reel 1, JFMAD, JARP.

30. Okina Kyūin Zenshū Kankōkai, *Okina Kyūin Zenshū*, II (Toyama, 1972), 374.

31. Chinda to Hayashi, 30 July 1891, enclosure, Fujita to Chinda, 22 July 1891, Nihon Gaimushō, *Nihon Gaikō Bunsho*, 491-492. In June 1891 the Foreign Ministry instructed Chinda Sutemi, the San Francisco consul, to dispatch a consular staff member to the Pacific Northwest to investigate the condition of Japanese residents. Fujita Yoshirō, who was sent by Chinda in July, urged the "respectable" Japanese in Seattle to band together and take action when he met with them.

32. *Daily Report*, 4 May 1892.

33. Chinda to Hayashi, 30 July 1891, enclosure, Fujita to Chinda, 22 July 1891, Nihon Gaimushō, *Nihon Gaikō Bunsho*, 499.

34. *Shin Sekai*, 26 February-1, 5 March 1900. For a later example of a woman passed from one pimp to another, see the affidavit of a Japanese prostitute in U.S. Congress, Senate, *Reports of the Immigration Commission*, 61 Cong., 3 sess., doc. 753 (Washington, 1911), 109-110.

35. Woman's Occidental Board of Foreign Missions, *26th Annual Report* (San Francisco, 1899), 85.

36. Nihon Gaimushō, *Nihon Gaikō Bunsho: Tai-Bei Imin Mondai Keika Gaiyō* (Tokyo, 1972), 213. Although this observation was made by Hanihara Masanao in 1908, its value in depicting the general environment in which the prostitutes labored is no less diminished. The second secretary of the Japanese Embassy, Hanihara travelled throughout the western states and the Pacific Coast and observed the Japanese immigrant communities at first hand.

37. Shakuma, "Rekishi Inmetsu no Tan." Zaibei Nihonjinkai, *Zaibei Nihonjinshi* (San Francisco, 1940), 62, records the same story.

38. Shakuma, "Rekishi Inmetsu no Tan."

39. Takeuchi, *Beikoku Seihokubu Nihon Iminshi*, 38-39. The early Seattle Japanese community was divided into two opposing factions, one representing the economic interests of Furuya Masajirō and the other the Oriental Trading Company headed by Takahashi Tetsuo and Yamaoka Ototaka. The *Taihoku Nippō*, under whose auspices this work was published, was hostile to Furuya. Okina Kyūin Zenshū Kankōkai, *Okina Kyūin Zenshū*, 374-375, repeats the same story, however. Okina was employed by Furuya at one time and did not belong to the opposing faction. The savings placed in Furuya's hands are generally referred to as *hesokurikin*, that is, money which had been saved secretly by the prostitutes unbeknown to their pimps.

40. *Post-Intelligencer*, 15 February and 19 April 1891.

41. *Bulletin*, 11 January 1890.

42. *Ibid.*, 24 February 1890; *Call*, 16 April 1890.

43. *Examiner*, 18 February 1891.

44. *Bulletin*, 4 May 1891.

45. *Daily Report*, 19 May 1891.

46. *Examiner*, 28 April 1892.

47. *Bulletin*, 4 May 1892.

48. *Call*, 4 May 1892.

49. *Daily Report*, 4 May 1892.

50. Tateno Gōzō to Aoki, 3 March 1891; Chinda to Aoki, 10 March 1891, enclosure, Washington *Evening Star*, 11 February 1891, reel 1, JFMAD, JARP.

51. Chinda to Aoki, 10 March 1891, Nihon Gaimushō, *Nihon Gaikō Bunsho*, XXIV, 461. The *Chronicle*, 19 February 1891, published a story that the rumor was not true.

52. Chinda to Aoki, *ibid.*

53. Chinda to Aoki, 25 April and 7 May 1891, Nihon Gaimushō, *Nihon Gaikō Bunsho*, XXIV, 463-466, 480-487.

54. Okabe Nagatsune to Chinda, 8 April 1891, Nihon Gaimushō, *Nihon Gaikō Bunsho*, XXIV, 463. Okabe also instructed Chinda to cooperate with the local police and the Society for the Suppression of Vice to stamp out Japanese prostitution in the city. Similar instructions were sent to the Vancouver consul.

55. Kawakita to Aoki, 11 June 1889, enclosure, Ōzawa Eizō to Kawakita, 6 June 1889, reel 1, JFMAD, JARP. A Christian organization, the Gospel Society was founded in 1877. Ōzawa was the secretary of the organization in 1889.

56. Chinda to Okabe, 13 June 1891, enclosure, "Fuseigyō Fujoshi Torai Kinshi Seigan," 16 May 1891, reel 1, JFMAD, JARP.

57. In addition to the much celebrated Okei, a member of the 1869 Wakamatsu Tea Colony, female students have been singled out as pioneers of Japanese women in America, especially Tsuda Umeko, Nagai Shigeko, Ueda Teiko, Yoshimasu Ryūko, and Yamakawa Sutematsu who arrived with the Iwakura Mission in 1871. Sent by the Hokkaido Colonization Commission, they were members of the elite who all returned to Japan. In this sense they cannot be interpreted as the forerunners of Issei women.

58. Shakuma, "Rekishi Inmetsu no Tan." This particular woman relates that she became a prostitute in order to help a man out of financial straits.

Capitalists with Rooms

Prostitution in Helena Montana, 1865-1900

by Paula Petrik

Above all else, Helena, Montana, in the nineteenth century was a city of commerce, banking and enterprise. Its leaders were the plucky entrepreneurs who had pursued the main chance beginning in the gold rush of the 1860s, on through the halcyon 1880s and into the troubled 1890s. Samuel T. Hauser, W. A. Chessman, Lewis Hershfield, A. M. Holter, T. C. Power and other lesser-known businessmen dominated Helena's banking, transportation, wholesale and retail trade, and contributed significantly to the overall development of the city. They were recognized as important by contemporaries, then, and by historians, now. Josephine Airey, Lillie McGraw, Mollie Byrnes, Henrietta Bischoff, and Louise Courselle, however, are not listed with the great entrepreneurs nor are they recognized as significant in the economic life of nineteenth-century Helena. Yet, they might have been listed among the capitalist elite, save for the nature of their business. Joe, Lillie, Mollie, and a good many like-minded women were Helena's prostitutes and madams, and while they were not included in Helena's Board of Trade or commercial clubs, they, too, built an "empire" in Helena, a business of considerable proportion that was an important component of the local economy. Between 1865 and 1886, Helena's residents of the demimonde constituted the largest single women's employment outside the home. Keeping a house was second, although a distant second, only to keeping house as the largest female occupation.[1] But, as with other business empires, Helena's demimonde lost its stability and internal strength. At century's end, it was a shadow of what it once was. How that empire was built, who built it, and why it faded is an integral part of the history of Helena and a surprising chapter of the history of women in the American West.

BETWEEN ITS FOUNDING in 1864 and the arrival of the railroad in 1883, Helena's demographic character changed very little. It was like many western towns having their economic base in mining — an urban village. Urban in that within months, Helena had its own theater, school, library, churches, and newspapers. Helena's residents had barely left their tents for log cabins when a dozen social and civic clubs sprang up. Yet, in terms of size it remained a village or at the most a small town. In 1870, Helena numbered a little over 3,000 inhabitants; by 1880, it had increased its population by 17 per cent to a little over 3,600. After 1883, Helena grew. By 1890, its population had tripled and numbered nearly 13,000, an impressive figure for a relatively isolated community, but after 1893, a demographic disaster overtook the community. By the federal census in 1900, Helena had lost nearly a quarter of its population. During this thirty-five year period, the most salient characteristic of Helena's population was the preponderance of young, single men.[2] In some age groups they outnumbered the women by as much as five to one, and though the ratio of men to women gradually evened, this feature of Helena's population affected the development of the community.[3] One result was to intensify the community's orientation toward a predominately service economy.

Young, unmarried men needed a multitude of services — housing, food, clothing, and recreation — services that under normal nineteenth-century circumstances were provided by women within the home and family circle. In Helena during the period, families were at a premium. Consequently, these domestic services were transferred onto Main Street. Women operated boarding houses, restaurants, laundries, and manufactured clothing. In addition, they furnished much of the entertainment, ranging from managing saloons to acting as dancing partners in the "hurdy gurdy houses." Part of this entertainment industry included sexual favors, and to provide such services, Helena had its own flock of "soiled doves." Like women's legitimate business enterprises, prostitution in Helena was an entrepreneurial activity characterized by property ownership, a high degree of business acumen and skill, and, in its "empire" days, by an increasingly complex social organization.

From 1865 until 1883, Helena's tenderloin was dominated by proprietor prostitutes, women who operated alone primarily, owned their own dwelling on the "line," or had sufficient capital to do so.[4] Women like Louisiana Martinea, Eleanor Alphonsine Dumont, Henrietta Bischoff, Kate Silvers, and Louise Coursella arrived in Helena with capital, paying between $300 and $1000 for their property in cash or in "good clean bankable gulch gold dust."[5] Between 1865 and 1870 over $50,000 changed hands as these proprietor prostitutes made their initial investments or exchanged holdings.[6] Like their male counterparts, the merchants who supplied the miners, Helena's fancy ladies migrated from other mining camps or bonanza towns whose best days had passed.[7] Similarly, after the fashion of Last Chance Gulch merchants, they were inclined toward dealing with one another. In this respect, they constituted a kind of businesswomen's network.

Between 1865 and 1870, for example, women made 265 separate property transactions. Thirty-seven "soiled doves" were responsible for 119 or 44 per cent of these. Likewise, when the women of the demimonde found it necessary to mortgage their property, they preferred, whether by choice or the circumstances of their business, to deal with women. All twenty mortgages made to women in the period were made to women of the demimonde, and nearly a third of the mortgages were made by one fancy lady to another. When the women could not borrow from each other, they turned to neighboring businessmen. Both respectable and not so respectable city merchants loaned money in the tenderloin — sometimes to these entrepreneurs' financial dismay.[8] These financial transactions, moreover, were neighborhood affairs. Both the fancy ladies and legitimate business occupied the same area of the community. Prostitution was not only geographically integrated into the community, but it was also an important element in the social structure of the town and operated with the tacit consent of Helena's citizens, male and

1. The female workforce in 1870, defined as all those women eighteen or older, totalled 485 women of whom 22 per cent were employed in an occupation other than keeping house: Actress—1, Boarding-house keeper—4, Cook—4, Dressmaker—3, Gambler—2, Prostitute—56, Saloon-keeper—1, Seamstress—2, Servant—19, Teacher—3, Waitress—8, Washerwoman—4, Keeping house—338, No occupation—39. In 1880 the female workforce numbered 741 of whom 22 per cent were employed outside the home: Actress—1, Boarding-house keeper—6, Chambermaid—1, Clerk—1, Cook—1, Dressmaker—9, Hairworker—1, Hotel worker—1, Housekeeper—4, Laborer—1, Librarian—1, Midwife—1, Milliner—3, Nurse—9, Nurse administrator—1, Photographer—1, School principal—1, Prostitute—53, Real estate owner—1, Seamstress—8, Servant—31, Teacher—19, Washerwoman—4, Keeping house—449, No occupation—127. Information taken from the Manuscript U. S. Census for 1870 and 1880.

2. Statistical analysis derived from the *U.S. Manuscript Census, 1870, 1880, 1900.*

3. *Ibid.*

4. See Table, p. 33.

5. *Record of Deeds, Book C*, p. 200; *Book D*, p. 324; *Book I*, p. 98, Lewis & Clark County Courthouse, Helena.

6. Statistics derived from analysis of 116 property transactions of prostitutes between 1865 and 1870.

7. *Helena City Directory, 1867*, (Helena: Fisk Brothers, 1867); *U.S. Manuscript Census, 1870.* Comparison of the two sources suggests that the city directory asked for place of last residence rather than place of birth or origin.

8. Thirteen mortgages went unpaid. Nine of these were made by men to prostitutes. The greatest losses were incurred by Edward Zimmerman and Louise Coursalle. Mortgage cancellation does not seem to have been a task that either the contracting parties or the county clerk were especially meticulous about. Oftentimes a mortgage went uncancelled, and yet, the same parties did business again.

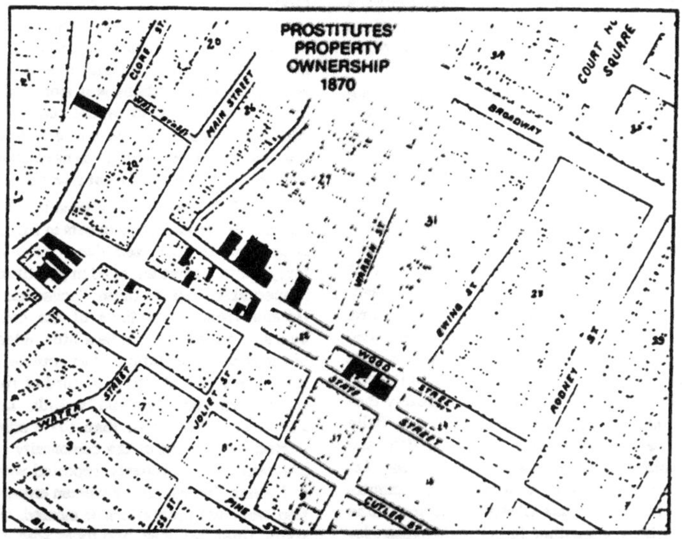

Helena's upper Main Street area, where today the Lewis & Clark County Library, Federal Building and Last Chance Gulch Mall are now located, was the center of the prostitutes' land holdings from 1870 to 1900. The modern map, below, will orient readers familiar with contemporary Helena to the location of the prostitutes' houses in the 1870 map, above, and other maps in this article that show property holdings in 1880 and 1890. The small mark on Broadway, between Davis and Park Ave. (below) indicates the location of the Lewis & Clark County Courthouse, which is noted in the upper right-hand corner of each detail map.

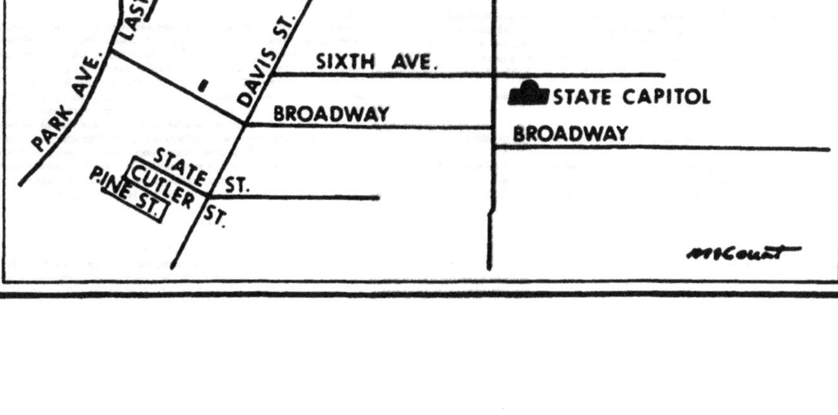

female alike.[9] This is evident in the legal system's response to the demimonde and in middle-class women's attitudes toward the goings-on on Wood Street.

With respect to the courts, there was a notable lack of legal and judicial concern with sexual commerce. No woman before 1886 was arrested for prostitution or for keeping a bawdy house.[10] This is particularly striking since the police court itself was located within the "red light" district.[11] The courts essentially arbitrated squabbles in the demimonde that could not be resolved by the conflicting parties, and, in addition, maintained a minimum level of peace and order there for the benefit of its respectable citizens.[12] C. L. Vawter, a prosperous merchant, ran afoul of Belle Crafton on April 6, 1881. She pulled a revolver from her reticule and threatened to send Vawter to his heavenly reward. The outraged hardware store owner complained immediately that Belle had "exhibited a deadly weapon," and Belle was arrested a few hours later. Just as swiftly, she swept into court, pled guilty, and paid her fine. On another occasion, the court intervened in a month-long quarrel between Annie Glessner and Josephine Airey, at one time or another fining both women for disturbing the peace or assault.[13]

Like the judges, middling women took a tolerant view of the tenderloin. In a face-to-face community such as Helena, it was difficult to keep prostitution hidden. Other women in the town could scarcely avoid coming into contact with the fancy ladies, and while they may not have liked the situation, their disapproval in those few instances when they made reference to prostitution was reserved more for the men who visited Wood Street than for the women who worked there. Writing to her sister in 1871, Elizabeth Chester Fisk, the wife of the *Helena Herald*'s editor, noted when a "young man who used to sing and dance in a hurdy house and was an especial favorite with Daisey Dean (a low, bad woman who keeps a saloon) preached at the Methodist Church." Later, in 1873, she related an incident that had preceded the wedding of "Mr. B.," whom Elizabeth described as an aging roue who was often seen drunk on the streets. "I have heard," wrote Elizabeth, "of a charming little tableau down at the green house when Mr. B.'s old Wood Street mistress drew a revolver on his future bride and threatened to kill her."[14] For Elizabeth, a man's or woman's association with drink and gambling was more damning than his or her involvement in sexual commerce. And since Elizabeth lived nearly on top of Helena's tenderloin, she had ample opportunity to have knowledge, if only superficial, of Wood Street's workers.

In 1870, there were a good number of ladies of negotiable virtue on the streets to further Elizabeth's education. In that year there were approximately forty white women engaged in prostitution. Like their respectable sisters, these "soiled doves" came to Helena from all sections of the country. On the average, they tended to be a little older than the rest of the female population. Most notable, however, was their economic situation. A third of the white fancy ladies reported personal wealth, an average of $2500 or $1000 more than the median wealth reported by the men of the community, and nearly 60 per cent owned property, reported wealth, or both.[15] In Helena, though all the women engaged in prostitution were not proprietors or monied, over half had a sound financial base, and those who were not entrepreneurs in their own right worked under the purview of other women.

Prostitution on Last Chance Gulch was women's business anchored in women's property and capital. A micro-economic system, prostitution reflected the vicissitudes of the regular business community. A local depression in 1871 thinned the ranks of the proprietor prostitutes as earlier fires had. Only a few of the original female entrepreneurs remained. They were joined by another woman, Josephine Airey, who had left Helena in 1869 to try her luck in White Pine, Nevada.[16] When she returned in 1871, she sensed economic possibility in the midst of depression and set about reorganizing the demimonde. And although Joe's story is marked with success, her biography is illustrative of other prostitutes who operated on a smaller scale.

9. In the early part of the period under consideration, the business district was concentrated along Wood and Bridge (State) Streets. As Helena moved toward the twentieth century, the commercial area shifted onto Main Street. At one time, for example, the Hershfields operated a branch of their banking operation on Bridge Street. See maps pages 31, 35, 37.

10. Derived from analysis of forty-four court cases involving known prostitutes between 1873 and 1883.

11. The police court was eventually located on the north side of Block 13.

12. Nearly half of the complaints between 1873 and 1883 involved one whore complaining against another. The other half of the court cases concerned men, usually law officers, who brought assault or disturbance charges against the fancy ladies.

13. *Record of Criminal Actions*, Case No. 975, Case No. 198.

14. Elizabeth Chester Fisk to her sister Fannie, January 22, 1871; Elizabeth Chester Fisk to her Mother, March 30, 1873, Fisk Family Papers, Montana Historical Society (MHS), Helena.

15. Statistics derived from analysis of *U.S. Manuscript Census, 1870*. See Table, p. 33.

16. Josephine Airey "Chicago Joe" Hensley has been the subject of what little research has been done on prostitution in Helena. See Rex C. Myers, "An Inning for Sin: Chicago Joe and Her Hurdy Gurdy Girls," *Montana The Magazine of Western History*, Vol. XXVII, (Spring 1977), pp. 25-33. Herbert M. Peet, "Joe Found Dictionary Better Defense Than Statutes in 'Hurdy Gurdy' House Trial," *Great Falls Tribune*, July 10, 1955, pp. 2, 17. Chicago Joe was illiterate and could not write her name. Her name in various sources is spelled at least seven different ways. I have chosen the one used with the greatest frequency. Numerous notorized documents attest to the fact that at one time Josephine Hensley was known as Josephine Airey. The only times she reverted to her given name were on the occasions of her two marriages: the first to Albert Haskins in 1869 (for which there is no extant divorce record) and the second in 1878 to James T. Hensley.

17. *Record of Deeds*, *Book F*, p. 194.

18. The record of Chicago Joe's property transactions is a long and detailed one. For examples see *Record of Deeds*, *Book L*, p. 230; *Book F*, pp. 377, 379, 432; *Book M*, p. 438; *Book H*, p. 70. The inventory of Chicago Joe's property included: Lots 9, 10, 11, 4, 7, 12, 16, 17, 18, 19, 20, 22, 23, 24, 28, 29, 30, 31,

FACTS ON HELENA'S PROSTITUTES

GEOGRAPHIC ORIGIN	1870 PROSTITUTES	1870 GENERAL POPULATION
Immigrant	27%	23%
Northeast	19%	18%
Midwest	31%	18%
West	4%	8%
South	23%	12%

GEOGRAPHIC ORIGIN	1880 PROSTITUTES	1880 GENERAL POPULATION
Immigrant	24%	23%
Northeast	28%	22%
Midwest	31%	13%
West	4%	20%
South	14%	13%

GEOGRAPHIC ORIGIN	1900 PROSTITUTES	1900 GENERAL POPULATION
Immigrant	38%	25%
Northeast	6%	13%
Midwest	26%	21%
West	8%	34%
South	11%	7%

HOUSEHOLD TYPE	1870	1880	1886	1900
Nuclear Family	4%	16%		1%
Exclusively Female	38%	10%		58%
Sexually Mixed	4%	50%		3%
Single Female	54%	23%		38%

WEALTH	1870	1880	1886	1900
Prostitutes Reporting or Having Wealth	45%	30%	22%	0%
PROPERTY OWNERSHIP	1870	1880	1886	1900
Prostitutes Owning Property	45%	13%	12%	0%

COMBINED FINANCIAL RESOURCES	1870	1880	1886	1900
Prostitutes Reporting Wealth or Property or Both	57%	36%	22%	0%

SOMETIME IN 1858 a fourteen-year-old girl with the unprepossessing name of Mary Welch arrived in New York harbor. Mary quickly made her way to Chicago and there learned the ways of the city's night life. As was customary in the demimonde, she changed her name to one with more elegance. Thereafter she styled herself "Josephine Airey" and was known by that name when she arrived in Montana Territory sometime in 1867. Like the "soiled doves" before her, Josephine arrived in Helena with capital and shortly purchased property in the Wood Street area.[17] Beginning in 1871, Joe entered into a series of business deals that eventually made her the queen of the city's "red light" district.[18]

Like any successful nineteenth-century entrepreneur, Josephine needed greater capital to invest in order to expand and profit. To that end she raised money on what real and personal property she possessed by mortgage. In 1871 Joe mortgaged her property to Harriet Truett, wife of the probate judge. Although Mrs. Truett's interest rate bordered on usury and her terms were unyielding, Joe fulfilled the contract.[19] She approached Selig Lavenberg, a Bridge Street dry goods merchant, for her second mortgage. He and his brother, Alex, had extended mortgages to the fancy ladies on other occasions.[20]

Alex Lavenberg emulated the informal relationships found in the demimonde. The R. G. Dun agent described Alex as "Very hard pay. 'L' lives here with a woman not his wife. He is a very hard case."[21] Undeterred by the Lavenberg character, Joe mortgaged all her property and personalty. Lavenberg's terms were not as strict as Harriet Truett's, but Joe literally stood to lose the camisole off her back. Josephine Airey had mortgaged everything, including

and 32 in Block 21; Lots 1, 2 in Block 15; Lot 27 in Block 2; Lots 7, 6 in Block 27; Lot 2 in Block 28; and Lot 27 in Block 2 Capitol Hill Addition. See map p. 37.

19. *Record of Mortgages*, Book F, p. 149.

20. *Record of Mortgages*, Book F, p. 432; Book G, p. 392.

21. R. G. Dun Reports, Vol. I, Montana and Nevada Territories, p. 240.

her underwear — "three dozen pair underclothes." Despite a fire on January 9, 1874, that nearly brought Joe's financial plans to naught, she was able to pay the unsavory Lavenberg six months before the note was due.[22] Joe's gambles had paid off; her position on Wood Street was assured. But the other proprietor prostitutes were not so lucky. Those who had remained in Helena after the initial placer boom could not recoup their losses, and, in consequence, left Helena for greener pastures or more fire-resistant communities.[23] Josephine spent the succeeding years acquiring these departed doves' property as well as that of others who had left the territory. By 1883, Joe was the largest land owner on Wood Street.

IN 1880, the census taker found Helena's "red light" district in transition. The demographic character of the white prostitutes had changed very little. They were, on the average, a little younger and mirrored the regional origins of the city's legitimate settlers. And the wealth was still there; nearly a third had some kind of working capital. But in the 1870s property ownership by prostitutes had decreased by a third, while Helena's total financial base (property ownership or wealth) had decreased by 20 per cent.[24] In one sense, prostitutes lost their autonomy because they had become primarily renters.

Yet, even as the economic base of Helena's tenderloin narrowed, there was money to be made. Some prostitutes, the "summer women," only worked in the city from June to September when the mines were open and building trades busy. Winter in Helena for the prostitutes meant an economic drain on their resources. Working men who remained in town restrained their spending, and the prostitutes' best customers, the miners, either left for jobs in a warmer climate or economized until the mines reopened in the spring. In the early period, prostitution was seasonal employment and contributed to the already high transiency rate of the demimonde population as a whole. In 1880, several prostitutes maintained bank accounts. Their earnings ranged from Belle Crafton's monthly earnings of $179 to Rosa Diamond's $337 per month. A fancy lady plying her trade along Wood Street could expect an average monthly income of $233. When skilled male artisans could command between $90 and $100 a month and when bank clerks earned $125 per month, fancy ladies' earnings were impressive. Compared with the $65 monthly wage the highest paid saleswoman could receive, their compensation was royal.[25] Even

Montana Historical Society

Mary Welch, also known as Josephine Airey "Chicago Joe" Hensley.

though a "soiled dove" had expenses, she could expect to make a profit of $500 during a summer on Wood Street, or not so typically she could, like Rosa Diamond, leave with $1000 in her portmanteau.

Money in the tenderloin opened up the possibility for both upward mobility in the demimonde's hierarchy and outward mobility into marriage and respectibility. In light of prostitution's high transiency rate, tracing the West's fancy ladies proves virtually impossible. But there are some tantalizing glimpses of women who made these successful transitions. Louise Courselle, for example, left Helena after the fire in 1874 and established herself in Bozeman where she expanded her operation into a bawdy house.[26] Although it is not possible to know exactly what business Mollie Grahm entered into, it is certain that she became Mrs. J. A. Aiken and moved to Portland. Delores Jarra was one of those women

22. *Record of Mortgages, Book H*, p. 70.

23. M. E. Leeson, *History of Montana, 1885* (Chicago: Warner, Beers and Company, 1885), p. 717. Among those listed with losses in the fire are Louise Courselle, Nellie Perkins, and Mollie Grahm. Their losses amounted to nearly $12,000.

24. Statistics derived from analysis of *U.S. Manuscript Census, 1880*. See Table, p. 33.

25. Bank deposit statistics based on analysis of seven bank accounts between June and September, 1880. First National Bank Collection, Individual Ledgers, Vols. 21, 22; Merchants National Bank Collection, Individual Ledgers, Vols. 32, 33, MHS; *Report of the Secretary of the Helena Board of Trade, 1887*, pp. 12, 14.

26. *U.S. Manuscript Census, 1880*.

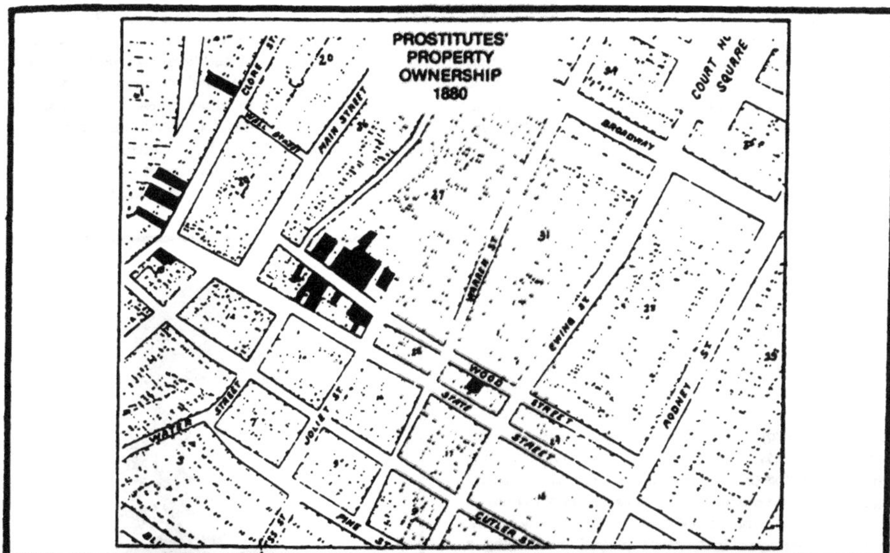

who made the transition from prostitution to marriage and family life. Before she entered into her liaison with John Stanchfield she legally "died" by transferring all her Wood Street property to her minor daughters and making Stanchfield their legal guardian. This effectively protected her investments, provided for her daughters, and supplied the family with rental income from the "Twin Cottages" on Wood Street. To further her daughters' separation from the demimonde and from her own irregular lifestyle, she enrolled them in a girls' boarding school in Helena. She and Stanchfield continued to live on the ranch she had purchased in the Prickly Pear Valley.[27] And finally, Josephine Airey was able to move up out of actual prostitution into a managerial position.

In 1878 Josephine Airey married James T. "Black Hawk" Hensley, a local gambling talent, and by 1886 she had acquired the name that would stay with her for the remainder of her life — "Chicago Joe." The demimonde had expanded once again: Lillie McGraw and Belle Crafton joined Joe. A number of lesser lights owned property on Wood Street, but Joe and her new associates together dominated that area until the end of the nineteenth century. They became the principle architects of the Wood Street "empire."[28]

At this time, Helena's demimonde was experiencing yet another transformation. Although prostitution continued to be carried on in women's social and economic space, that entrepreneurial enclave was, by 1883, becoming separated from the regular business community. Legitimate merchants who had earlier felt free to do business with the fancy ladies no longer dealt on Wood Street.[29] The demimonde was becoming a world unto itself. Part of this segregation resulted from the city's incorporation in 1881 and the battery of civic ordinances concomitant with this reorganization.

A FEW YEARS after its incorporation, Helena entered into an increasing frenzy of moral reform. Along with vagrancy, opium use, drunkenness, and public profanity, prostitution caught the attention of the city fathers. Within a two year period the city council enacted a series of ordinances that were intended to curtail sexual com-

27. *Record of Deeds*, Book 6, p. 303; Probate No. 187, Old Series.

28. Lillie McGraw, also known as Bridget Ryan, was born in St. Louis, Missouri. She arrived in Helena sometime in 1875 from Portland, Oregon, but it was not until 1880 that Lillie established herself on Wood Street. The inventory of her property included lots 11, 12, 13, and part of 91 in Block 27. In the late 1880s she sold part of lots 13 and 91 to James Stranahan, the architect and first owner of the "Bluestone House." After Stranahan's untimely death the property passed to J. S. M. Neill, a local newspaper editor and real estate investor. The "Bluestone House" is often confused with the "Castle," and this is not an unlikely confusion. Lillie McGraw's houses of prostitution were located directly south of Stranahan's house, and the "Castle" was situated across Wood Street facing on Joliet Street. There is no evidence to suggest that the "Bluestone House" was connected with prostitution in the early period. Mollie Byrnes, also known as Belle Crafton, was born in New Orleans, Louisiana. She, too, became a Helena resident in the early 1880s, and purchased property on Wood Street. At one time or another the inventory of her property included: lot 6 in Block 21, the site of the Kiyus Saloon; lot 10 in Block 27; lot 4 in Block 23; and Lot 1 in Block 22. The latter was the site of the "Castle."

29. Helena's commercial area had by this time moved securely onto Main Street leaving the Wood Street district to the "soiled doves." In addition, there are no further instances after 1883 of businessmen loaning money to the demimonde.

merce. The first of these in 1884 prohibited solicitation for the purpose of prostitution. Passed in 1885, the second resolution effectively barred prostitution from the legitimate business area and created a de facto district in much the same way local laws had in other western communities. And finally, in the summer of 1886, the city fathers made a determined effort to remove prostitution from their midst. In bald terms, prostitution and any of allied forms were prohibited from the city. Almost immediately this last ordinance and the state law that had prompted it were put to the test.[30]

In August 1886, authorities charged Chicago Joe with operating a "hurdy gurdy house." The assistant county attorney in his opening argument described "hurdies" as immoral "establishments where men's souls were lured to the shores of sin by the combined seductive influence of wine, women, and dance." Joe's lawyer, armed with a Webster's Dictionary, countered with a technical defense based on the legal definition of "hurdy gurdy." Specious as it was, the counsel for the defense carried the day by pointing out that the music at Joe's saloon was provided by a violin, piano, and cornet and not by a hurdy gurdy, a boxed, stringed instrument played by turning a crank. The jury returned a verdict of "not guilty." Once the state and local statutes were found faulty, neither Joe nor the other Wood Street regulars were threatened with legal action.[31] The community continued to turn a blind eye toward Wood Street.

During the same years Helena put its civic house in order, the city experienced a building boom and a change in its leisure tastes. The Wood Street customers wanted more than a quick rendezvous in a clapboard house. They wanted the kind of sophistication, elegance, and entertainment found in Helena's sister cities, Denver and San Francisco. Entrepreneurs on Wood Street sensed the shift in the market and went about reorganizing services to accommodate their clientele. As a result, the fancy ladies undertook a building program of their own. The three leaders of the demimonde refurbished and expanded their establishments. Chicago Joe built the Coliseum, a vaudevillian variety theater, and Belle Crafton, now known as Mollie Byrnes, constructed a tasteful *maison de joie*, later known as the "Castle." Not to be outdone, Lillie McGraw remodelled and added to her Joliet Street houses.[32] As Helena's demimonde changed externally, it also altered internally. By 1886, prostitution had become big business.

The social organization of prostitution had grown increasingly complex. Fewer women operated alone; the majority now worked in bawdy houses or under the purview of one of the demimonde's leaders. These bawdy houses exhibited a high degree of managerial specialization and organization, having acquired a group of mid-level managers. In addition, the houses maintained communication with "red light" districts in other cities. Lillie McGraw kept her ties with Portland's tenderloin, and Joe continued to import women from Chicago. Prostitutes now numbered the time they spent in a city by the weeks rather than by months or years.[33]

Montana Historical Society

Rosa Diamond, who left Helena richer by $1000.

AS THE DEMIMONDE underwent this transformation, the fast life with its attendant hazards — alcoholism, alienation, drug addiction — began to take its toll. No Wood Street woman before the mid-1880s had died of a drug overdose, nor had any prostitute taken her own life. After the middle of the decade, this changed. Each year saw several Wood or Clore Street regulars succumb to the hazards of their profession. Blanche Mitchell and Kitty Williams, both aged twenty-six, committed suicide by taking an overdose of morphine. Lillie Fillmore died of syphilis at thirty. And Nellie Sommers, a black prostitute on Clore Street, ended her life with whiskey laced with arnica.[34] Whoring no longer held out the illusion of opportunity for the

30. *Ordinances of the City of Helena*, pp. 59, 126-127, 136.

31. *Helena Daily Herald*, August 23, 1886.

32. *Report of the Secretary of the Helena Board of Trade*, 1887, p. 10; *Helena Daily Record*, January 1, 1889; Sanborn-Perris Insurance Map, 1888.

33. Coroner's Inquisition No. 278. From this and other inquests it is possible to glean some idea of the internal organization of Helena's bawdy houses. The inquest cited is concerned with the double suicide attempt of Dora Forrest and Madge Dowd in which Dora Forrest perished.

34. *Register of Deaths in Lewis and Clark County*, 1883-1907.

35. *Record of Marriages*, License No. 194.

36. *Helena City Directory*, 1891; Abstract No. 2482, Helena Abstract and Title Company (hereafter HATC).

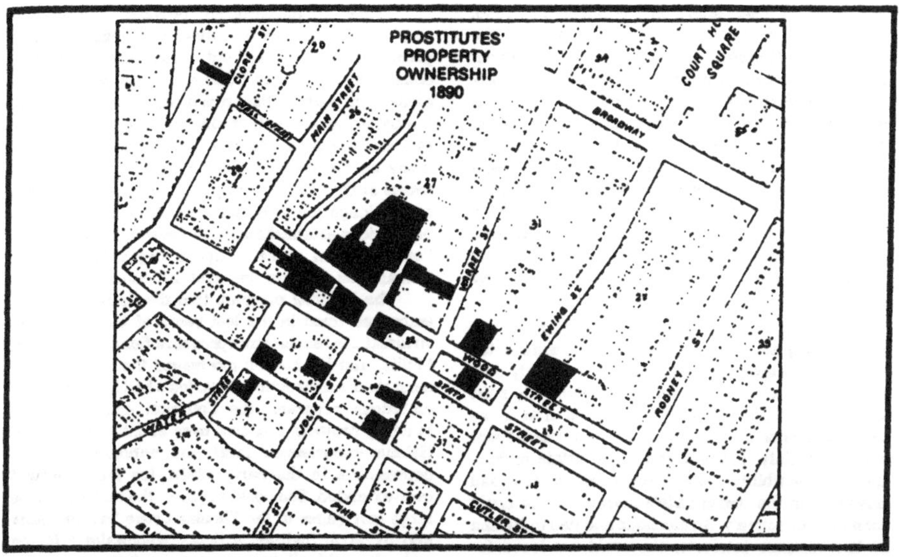

"line workers." And even for those who occupied the few places at the top of the demimonde's hierarchy, the possibility of escape into a better life dimmed. One of those who tried to cross the line into respectibility was Mollie Byrnes.

After completing the "Castle," Mollie made her bid for nineteenth-century middle-class existence. For her consort she chose Thomas Butler Eddingfield, a salesman at Feldberg's clothing store. When they married in 1890, Mollie was thirty-two and Eddingfield was twenty-eight.[38] The next year, Mollie leased the "Castle" to a demimonde parvenu, Lillie Ashton, and she and Thomas moved up to her new residence at 212 State Street.[38] For three years Mollie enjoyed the life she had planned, but Thomas Butler Eddingfield proved to be a poor matrimonial choice.

On July 9, 1898, Mollie petitioned the district court for a divorce, charging that Thomas had repeatedly beaten her over the previous five years and that he had "applied to her vile and opprobrious epithets, calling her 'low shanty Irish' and reflecting upon her chastity as a wife." Mollie further specified that Thomas had secured large sums of money from her on the pretense of going into business. Instead of taking up a trade, Thomas had consumed the money "in dissipation and riotous living." In addition, Mollie charged that her husband drank to such excess "as to be disqualified thereby the greater part of the time from properly attending to business." Although Eddingfield may have rightly reflected on his wife's fidelity, he was perfectly aware of Mollie's past and had anticipated an easy and indulgent life. For the sake of respectibility, Mollie stayed with a man who abused her and humiliated her. But this woman, who had once threatened C. L. Vawter with a revolver, had had enough. The court found Mollie's claims justified, and on August 31, 1898, the Eddingfield marriage was dissolved. Thomas Eddingfield failed to appear.[37]

Mollie, however, did not easily give up her goals of marriage and middle-class life. Less than a month later, on September 24, 1898, she married William "Willie" Weinsheimer, a man who purported to be a wealthy sheep rancher from Marysville.[38] Despite their recent divorce, Mollie and Eddingfield continued to see one another. In February of 1899, for whatever reason, Mollie and Thomas got drunk together. In the course of the evening, Mollie sold Thomas an undivided half interest in the State Street property. A few weeks later Eddingfield filed the bill of sale at the county clerk's office. When Mollie discovered what had happened, she brought suit against Eddingfield to void the deed. She complained that Thomas had induced her "to drink of drugged or intoxicating beverages until she became utterly incapable of doing business. . . ." and that while she was in this condition, Eddingfield had persuaded her to convey the property to him.[39] The court ruled that the "consideration of $1.00 for such deed was grossly inadequate" and ordered Eddingfield to restore the property to Mollie.[40]

37. Civil Case No. 4460.

38. *Record of Marriages*, License No. 2845; Probate No. 348, New Series.

39. Civil Case No. 4646.

40. *Ibid.*; *Record of Deeds*, Book 44, p. 349.

Nearly a year later, on December 11, 1899, Mollie sold the "Castle" to John Steinbrenner, the owner of the Cosmopolitan Hotel, for $7000 subject to her lease to Lillie Ashton.[41] The property had provided a comfortable income for Mollie and her husbands in the preceding years, and Willie Weinsheimer saw it all slipping away from him. On December 9, 1900, Mollie made a will that designated Weinsheimer as her sole heir. Although Mollie was literate, she signed the document with an "X".[42] Three days later she was dead of acute alcoholism, and Willie Weinsheimer became a rich man. Mollie had sold off much of her property earlier, but her estate was still valued at $20,000.[43]

Mollie made two poor matrimonial choices, one of which may have cost her her life. It is, perhaps, too much of a coincidence that Mollie conveniently died so soon after she made Weinsheimer her only heir; perhaps Weinsheimer resorted to poison after all as Mollie's brother hinted in a subsequent contestment trial.[44] Certainly, Mollie's attempt to attain middle-class respectibility failed, since, while she had moved up in the demimonde's hierarchy, she could not move out entirely. An alcoholic and tied to Helena by her business interests, she could not leave for greener pastures. Besides, it was no longer so easy to blend into the West's transient population; cities were settling down. Like most nineteenth-century women, Mollie wanted marriage and the whole panoply of that life. The men who were attracted to Mollie did not want her, they wanted her money. In the 1890s prostitution was no longer even a dubious opportunity. But a decade before her death, Mollie clearly did not feel her fortunes begin to change. The "empire" was at its zenith, and for Mollie and the denizens of the demimonde in 1890, there was much to be optimistic about.

IN THAT YEAR there were eight land-owning demimonde women who held property with an assessed value of $102,560. They contributed nearly $1000 to the city's coffers in personal and property tax. Only a few of Helena's most successful entrepreneurs and the Northern Pacific Railroad paid more tax than the demimonde. These women and other female investors controlled nearly all the property in Helena's Wood Street area. Catherine Richardson, Emma Howard, and others like them, although they kept their distance from Wood and Clore Streets, were content to rent to the fancy ladies and profit accordingly.[45]

These businesswomen provided housing or employment for approximately one hundred white prostitutes who worked out of the nearly thirty-five houses in the district.[46] Some of these women lived alone or in pairs in the cribs along Clore Street or in the better houses on both sides of Wood Street. Lillie McGraw's *maison de joie* could accommodate as many as ten women; Lillie Ashton, Mollie Byrnes' lessee at the "Castle," employed up to seven women; and Chicago Joe provided work for a good many in her various establishments. But even at its height, the "empire" was cracking apart. Beginning in 1890, Chicago Joe ran into financial difficulties.[47]

The building program that the demimonde had embarked upon in the last years of the 1880s had strained the female entrepreneurs financially. Lillie, Mollie, and Joe had all mortgaged their property to meet their construction costs. Joe's had been the most ambitious program (the Coliseum and her other building projects had cost over $30,000) and when Helena experienced local and national financial depressions in the early 1890s, Joe found herself over-extended. She could not meet the terms of three large mortgages to the Thomas Cruse Savings Bank and to Jacob Switzer, a liquor wholesaler.[48] In the end, she sold all her property to Switzer for the amount of his mortgages, a sum far less than the value of the property. More importantly, on a spring afternoon in 1896, two-thirds of the demimonde passed out of women's control.[49] Neither Mollie Byrnes nor Lillie McGraw suffered the financial losses that Joe did, but both Lillie's and Mollie's property ultimately went to businessmen who saw opportunity in the demimonde.

What economic reverses did not do, the years did. On July 17, 1898, Lillie McGraw died of cirrhosis of the liver at the age of sixty-one, at her house on Joliet Street. Her property was leased for a time to Allie Carleton, an enterprising young madam from Butte, but Lillie's heirs, unable to pay the property tax, saw the lots go on the sheriff's block in 1900.[50] A little over a year after Lillie's death, on October 23, 1899, Chicago Joe died of pneumonia in her home on Wood Street: she was fifty-six. Joe left the world as she had come into it — poor, illiterate, and honorable. Three months before her death, she made the last interest payment and satisfied her mortgage to Jacob Switzer. And, finally, Mollie "Belle Crafton" Byrnes died at the age of forty-two on December 12, 1900.[51] All the dowager queens of the demimonde were dead at the opening of the twentieth century. With their passing, prostitution came under men's control and ceased to be women's business.

41. Abstract No. 2482, HATC.

42. Will No. 349, New Series.

43. Probate No. 349, New Series.

44. *Ibid.* Record of the subsequent contestment trial is contained in the probate documents.

45. *Tax Assessment List*, 1890.

46. Sanborn-Perris Insurance Map, 1890.

47. Probate No. 187, New Series; *U.S. Manuscript Census*, 1900.

48. *Record of Mortgages*, Book 5, p. 38; Book 10, p. 434.

When the census enumerator made his rounds in the summer of 1900, his tabulations reflected this. The "soiled doves" were fewer, a little older, and primarily foreign-born. They lived by themselves or in exclusively female households, paying rent to landlords and not landladies. Not one woman owned property in the tenderloin, neither did any have accounts in the banking houses that succeeded the failed banks in the 1890s. Although several of the old houses were still in operation, Helena's demimonde had moved away from Wood Street onto Clore Street.[53] With this shift, male pimps assumed a larger role in the sexual market place. At the turn of the century, Helena's "red light" district had much of the sadness, desperation, and exploitation that were the hallmarks of prostitution of other cities.[53] Not until after World War I would prostitution again become the province of women with the advent of Ida "Jew Ida" Levy, Glenn Parker, and Dorothy "Big Dorothy" Baker.

HISTORIANS, like their counterparts in the arts, have often glorified the harlot's progress and concentrated their efforts on the flamboyant lifestyles of high-class, successful madams: the Comstock's Julia Bulette, Denver's Mattie Silks, and the great madams of San Francisco.[54] More recently, both have taken the opposite tack. Several historians have argued that the majority of fancy ladies died in poverty and degradation, trapped in a profession not of their choosing.[55] Helena's example shows that the answer lies somewhere between these two extremes. Between 1865 and 1883, for every woman who had a definite chance to leave prostitution, having accumulated enough capital, there were two who had less of a chance. Whether any significant number from either group managed to edge safely into middle-class respectibility is purely a speculative matter. Certainly, there is evidence from Helena to suggest gain within the profession. Of those who can be traced, a good number of them were able to move out of actual prostitution and up in the tenderloin's hierarchy. By the same token, there is evidence that indicates this upward mobility within prostitution and possible outward mobility into nineteenth-century society became virtually impossible for Helena's fancy ladies after 1890.

There is no denying that the social and economic conditions of the nineteenth century created an environment conducive to the development of prostitution. Women were refused any but the most menial and lowest-paying work. At the same time society paraded before women all the material wealth available only to a limited number of them. For a young woman alone, over-worked, or poor, prostitution was a means to survive and to acquire the luxuries industrial America produced. Nevertheless, it has been argued that achieving success through prostitution was, at best, a pyrrhic victory. For prosperity in the demimonde, a whore paid equal social costs. Yet, the history of women in the nineteenth century is littered with comparable hollow triumphs. Sexually vulnerable, nineteenth-century women embraced the ideology of "passionlessness"; in doing so, they traded their sexuality for their elevation to moral and intellectual beings.[56] Catherine Beecher sought to enlarge women's influence by turning the home into a female domain and domesticity into a science. Instead, the home became a prison and domesticity, destiny.[57] Similarly, the frontier provided some women with the opportunity to capitalize on a dubious situation. If nineteenth century capitalism depended, in part, upon the exploitation of women's sexuality, at least the fancy ladies of the urban mining frontier could, in some measure, control and profit from their own exploitation. Only so long as the social structure of the frontier remained loose and the West's population continued to be fluid was this possible. Once the social structures tightened and settled, prostitution became another circumscribed role for women. The history of prostitution in Helena is illustrative of this process. Between 1865 and 1883, the fancy ladies did achieve the economic means for upward and outward mobility. They were "capitalists with rooms." The years afterward saw this possibility closed to them. In the same year that the U.S. Census Bureau could no longer draw a frontier line, Helena's Wood Street "empire" began to topple.

The history of prostitution in Helena also suggests something less easily documented. Although the "empire" lasted only a brief time, it left a legacy for other women in the community that made itself felt into the twentieth century. Responding to a social in-

49. *Record of Deeds*, Book 37, p. 396.

50. Probate No. 187, New Series; *Register of Deaths in Lewis and Clark County*.

51. Cancellation of the Switzer mortgages was made July 18, 1899. All of Chicago Joe's property transactions were signed "Josephine 'X' Hensley, her mark." In later years, Nellie Reynolds, one of Joe's managers, accompanied Joe and signed for her. *Register of Deaths in Lewis and Clark County*.

52. Statistics derived from analysis of the *U.S. Manuscript Census, 1900*. See Table, p. 33.

53. For an indication of the changes on Clore Street see William L. Lang, "The Nearly Forgotten Blacks on Last Chance Gulch, 1900-1912," *Pacific Northwest Quarterly*, 70 (April 1979), p. 56; Lang, "Tempest on Clore Street: Race and Politics in Helena, Montana, 1906," *Scratchgravel Hills*, 3 (Summer 1980), pp. 9-14.

54. Dee Brown, *The Gentle Tamers: Women of the Old Wild West* (New York: Bantam Books, 1974); Curt Gentry, *The Madams of San Francisco* (New York: Dell Publishing Company, 1971).

55. Marion Goldman, "Sexual Commerce on the Comstock Lode," *Nevada Historical Quarterly*, XXI (Summer 1978), pp. 99, 118; George M. Blackburn and Sherman L. Richards, "The Prostitutes and Gamblers of Virginia City, Nevada, 1870," *Pacific Historical Review*, XLVIII (May 1979), pp. 239-258.

56. Nancy Cott, "Passionlessness: An Interpretation of Victorian Sexual Ideology, 1790-1850," *Signs*, 4 (Winter 1978), pp. 219-236.

57. Kathryn Kish Sklar, *Catherine Beecher*, (New York: W. W. Norton and Company, 1973).

vestigator's questions, a Helena bartender in 1953 said: "This is Montana . . . Women have a right to sit in bars . . . Nobody thinks anything of it around here . . . They're all good fellows . . . Not a hustler among them . . . We got houses for that."[58] Implicit in the barkeep's answer is an attitude that did not develop overnight. Aside from expressing a nineteenth-century attitude about prostitution's deflecting male sexuality away from respectible women, the bartender hints at two inter-connected ideas related to both regionality and women. There is the sense in his remarks that the West, in this case, Montana, is somehow different, and second, that the women of that region have social rights unavailable to women elsewhere. Women outside the demimonde had acquired the freedom to come and go as they pleased in all manner of public places without fear of censure. From the barkeep's point of view prostitution had something to do with this phenomenon. In this he was probably correct. Since prostitution removed the threat of male sexuality and eroded nineteenth-century ideas of female propriety, respectable women profited over the years from other women's willingness to trade with their bodies.

AUTHOR'S NOTE:

No social historian could piece together a narrative from various local documents without the assistance of those who work with these sources on a daily basis. My appreciation and thanks go to Clara Gilreath, Clerk of Court, and staff: Judy Harris, Mary Root, Mary Harris, Hilda Funk, Darlene Johnson, and Nancy Jones: to Wilma Grant, Deputy Clerk and Recorder; to Diane Ducello, Classification Office, Lewis & Clark County, for aid in securing maps; to Bill Gowan of Helena Abstract and Title who took time from his busy day to initiate me into the mysteries of property transactions; and finally to Judge Gordon R. Bennett who never failed to give me words of encouragement.

ABOUT THE AUTHOR

Paula Petrik is Assistant Professor of History at Montana State University in Bozeman and is completing her Ph.D. dissertation at State University of New York at Binghampton. Her dissertation topic, "The Bonanza Town: Women and Family on the Rocky Mountain Frontier, Helena, Montana, 1865-1900," includes the findings presented here plus much more about the lives of Helena women in the Victorian Era. Raised in Sidney, Montana, Ms. Petrik has published reviews, short stories and poems in addition to being the recipient of numerous academic honors, including a Fulbright-Hays Grant to Great Britain in 1979-1980. Her degrees include a B.A. fron Cornell, M.F.A. from University of Montana, and M.A. from SUNY-Binghampton.

58. Attorney General of the State of Montana, *Confidential Report on Commercial Prostitution*, 1953, p. 2, MHS.

This general scene of Helena, looking north into t Helena Valley and taken about 1915, shows t Wood and State Streets area where prostituti headquartered in the 1880s. Starting at the end the central street (Joliet St.) in this photo where t stone "Bluestone House" stands, the first crossi street is Wood, the next State, and the neare

Montana Historical Society

ler. Mollie Byrnes' "Castle" stands at the corner /ood and Joliet. Across the street, at the corner of le and Joliet stands Chicago Joe's first establish- nt, and at the west end of that block (down the hill ard Last Chance Gulch) the dark-roofed large ding is Joe's Coliseum Theatre with her Red Star oon just to the west of it. Just below the "Bluestone House," on the northwest corner of Wood and Joliet was Lillie McGraw's *maison de joie*. Up Wood Street, behind the "Castle" were small houses that were rented by prostitutes, and in fact many of the houses in this area were used, rented or owned by prostitutes at one time or other in the 1870 to 1900 period.

MEDICAL INSPECTION OF PROSTITUTES IN AMERICA IN THE NINETEENTH CENTURY: THE ST. LOUIS EXPERIMENT AND ITS SEQUEL *

JOHN C. BURNHAM

The story of the official physicians who inspected prostitutes in continental Europe during the nineteenth century does not constitute one of the more inspiring chapters in the history of medicine. Despite the opportunities of the medical examiners, few of them made any contribution to knowledge about any aspect of venereal diseases. Except for some government statistics, the validity and meaning of which were debated for generations among physicians and public health officials, not even epidemiology profited from this great opportunity for research.[1]

Yet the systematic attempts begun in the time of Napoleon to control venereal diseases are of the greatest interest.[2] Syphilis, with which the medical inspection of public women was concerned primarily, had been known since the sixteenth century to be contagious and venereal in nature (giving rise, for example, to the old maxim, " One night with Venus and a lifetime with mercury "). The system of compulsory medical inspection of prostitutes, or reglementation, as it came to be called in English, involved the not unfamiliar practice of segregation and quarantine of the ill. As George Rosen has pointed out, such an arrangement was suitable for countries with a strong cameralist tradition in which the population was accustomed to medical police regulation of everyday life.[3] With the growth of cities and a commensurate increase in numbers of women of the night, the hazard of disease seemed to demand some such control.

* Read at the forty-third annual meeting of the American Association for the History of Medicine, Birmingham, Alabama, April 3, 1970.

[1] This debate can be found most easily by consulting the publications of the international purity movement, in its late stages in the United States in *The Philanthropist* (continued as *Vigilance*). The confusion over statistics is spelled out in detail in *Conférence internationale pour la prophylaxie de la syphilis et des maladies vénériennes* (Brussels: Lamartin, 1900).

[2] A convenient summary of the history of reglementation is to be found in Vern L. Bullough, *The History of Prostitution* (New Hyde Park, N. Y.: University Books, 1964), pp. 166-172. More detailed accounts are in C. J. Lecour, *La prostitution à Paris et à Londres, 1789-1870* (Paris, 1870) ; Yves Guyot, *Prostitution under the Regulation System*, trans. Edgar Beckit Truman (London, 1884).

[3] George Rosen, " The fate of the concept of medical police, 1780-1890," *Centaurus*, 1956, *5*: 97-111.

In England and America, however, systems of medical inspection of prostitutes did not flourish.[4] In the middle and late nineteenth century, when the public health movement was well under way in those countries, there were attempts to institute the continental system as one of a number of public health measures. Ultimately these endeavors were defeated.[5] Reglementation, one might perhaps conclude, did not thrive where liberal traditions against controls over personal life prevailed (the liberal traditions including attitudes of laissez faire and caveat emptor). Or one can conclude that moral standards in the Victorian Anglo-American community impinged directly upon medical questions. Such was certainly the belief of American physicians of that day. In 1899 a New Orleans physician, Sigmund Lustgarten, reviewed the debate on the issue and concluded, "The United States will, I feel, still stand by and watch the experiments made abroad, before adopting measures foreign to the spirit of its people, and its laws."[6]

The history of government-enforced inspection of prostitutes in the United States sheds light particularly upon this latter question, the influence of community standards and values upon the practice of medicine. Owsei Temkin has pointed out that the ancient question of the moral significance of syphilis changed when physicians accumulated additional information about the disease in the nineteenth century.[7] Even the

[4] It should of course be recognized that many enterprising persons engaged in the prostitution business arranged to have the girls and women in their charge inspected regularly by a physician, simply as a matter of public relations and good business. The subject of the present paper is rather the official attempts to impose inspection of all prostitutes and hospitalization of those ill with venereal disease, by law, as a public health measure. There were a number of cases in which the police of a city, with or without the cooperation of the board of health, enforced an unofficial or unrecognized reglementation, usually by threatening to arrest prostitutes who refused to take medical treatment. See, for example, Arthur C. Bauer, "The regulation of prostitution as a hygienic measure," *Cincinnati Lancet-Clin.*, 1894, ns *33*: 411-416. An even more unofficial effort is described by Julius Rosenstirn, *Our Nation's Health Endangered by Poisonous Infection Through the Social Malady; The Protective Work of the Municipal Clinic of San Francisco and Its Fight for Existence* (San Francisco: Town Talk Press, 1913).

[5] A fragmentary account can be found in Aaron M. Powell, *State Regulation of Vice. Regulation Efforts in America. The Geneva Congress* (New York, 1878). A summary history is Howard B. Woolston, *Prostitution in the United States Prior to the Entrance of the United States into the World War* (New York: Century Co., 1921).

[6] S. Lustgarten, "The Question of Legal Control of Prostitution in the United States of America," *Conférence internationale pour la prophylaxie de la syphilis, op. cit.*, vol. II. appendix, p. 42. Two volumes provide general background: Abraham Flexner, *Prostitution in Europe* (New York: Century Co., 1914), and Woolston, *op. cit.*

[7] Owsei Temkin, "Zur Geschichte von 'Moral und Syphilis,'" *Arch. f. Gesch. d. Med.*, 1927, *19*: 331-348, especially pp. 346-347. See also Robert E. Riegel, "Changing American attitudes toward prostitution," *J. Hist. Ideas*, 1968, *29*: 437-452.

new knowledge, however, did not affect appreciably the status of reglementation as a standard public health measure in Europe, where officials continued to believe that the chief source of contagion was prostitutes. Many Americans in the medical fraternity shared these European attitudes. Before 1870, however, few of these men were willing to speak up concerning either prostitution—the social evil, as they called it—or its connection with disease.

Just before the Civil War, in 1858, William Sanger, a prominent New York physician, published a comprehensive study of prostitution in New York City and advocated strongly the adoption of the Parisian system of compulsory medical inspection of prostitutes, under a special medical department of the police. Sanger argued that in Paris "the number of cases of disease and the virulence of its form have materially abated." [8] His monumental volume, however, was almost unique as an American contribution to the medical and social literature on prostitution. Most subsequent advocates of reglementation in the United States cited Sanger but relied primarily on the more extensive English medical literature for evidence and authority. That literature originated in 1857, when an eminent London venereologist and student of Ricord, William J. Acton, published a painstaking review of prostitution and made the same strong recommendation as that of Sanger, for compulsory medical inspection.[9] In the years following, British government and military officials published medical opinions confirming the need for examining public women. The few American advocates of medical inspection who spoke up in the decade after Sanger published drew on this British material. Such, for example, was the editor of the *California Medical Gazette,* who in 1869 expressed the hope that San Francisco would "be the first city in our broad Union to adopt the French police system of examination of prostitutes." [10] He was destined to be disappointed, for it turned out, in fact, to be St. Louis, in 1870.

For some time much of the discussion of reglementation in the United States centered around the so-called St. Louis experiment. From 1870 to 1874 that city set up a system of government inspection of prostitutes

[8] William W. Sanger, *History of Prostitution: Its Extent, Causes, and Effects Throughout the World* (New York, 1858; 2nd. ed. 1898).

[9] William Acton, *Prostitution, Considered in Its Moral, Social, & Sanitary Aspects, in London and Other Large Cities: With Proposals for the Mitigation and Prevention of Its Attendant Evils* (London, 1857; 2nd ed., 1870). A convenient summary of Acton's work is Peter Fryer, "Introduction," in William Acton, *Prostitution* (New York: Praeger, 1969 reprint), pp. 7-19.

[10] "Venereal contagion," *California M. Gaz.,* 1869, *1*: 171.

and quarantine of those women found diseased. After the Civil War, many American cities had created boards of public health, usually following the example of New York, with a physician as health officer. The major concern of such boards was anything that offended the senses: the dirty, the smelly, the foul.[11] St. Louis had such a board, which was trying to clean up food establishments, abate odoriferous tanneries, and run the hospitals (essentially charitable institutions). Somewhat surprisingly, the city health officer, Dr. William L. Barrett, in his third annual report, in 1870, made a strong plea for medical regulation of "the social evil," as he called it. "It is," he wrote, "destroying the health and vigor of a large portion of our inhabitants, and tainting their blood with an ineradicable poison. . . ." [At that time venereal contagion was believed by many to be effected by some self-perpetuating poison operating on and through mucous tissue.] Citing Sanger's work, Barrett asserted that prostitution could not be suppressed and therefore ought to be rendered as harmless to the community as possible.[12]

Taking advantage of a city charter provision (included by state legislators with this end in mind) permitting St. Louis "to regulate or suppress" prostitution, the City Council on July 5, 1870, passed the so-called "Social Evil Ordinance." Under the ordinance, six physicians were appointed by the Board of Health to inspect the registered public women in each of six districts in the city. Those women found afflicted with venereal disease were committed to a special Social Evil Hospital until certified cured. The Social Evil Hospital was to be financed by fees levied on licensed houses and individual prostitutes.[13] Although amended several times, the Social Evil Ordinance remained in effect until 1874, when it was nullified by the Missouri state legistature. For several years after nullification of the law, some medical inspection and the Social Evil Hospital operated on a voluntary basis and then faded away.[14]

[11] Howard D. Kramer, "Early municipal and state boards of health," *Bull. Hist. Med.*, 1950, *24*: 503-529; Wilson G. Smillie, *Public Health, Its Promise for the Future, A Chronicle of the Development of Public Health in the United States, 1607-1914* (New York: Macmillan, 1955), section III; John Duffy, *A History of Public Health in New York City, 1625-1866* (New York: Russell Sage Foundation, 1968), chap. 24; *St. Louis Bd. of Health Ann. Rep.*, 1868-1874. Prostitution was just one among many urban problems with which cities in that period were trying to cope. The distress of San Francisco was typical: "There is occasion for alarm in this city at the spread of the evil. Formerly a few streets contained all of those to whom virtue was a by-word. Now, scarcely a prominent street but is represented by the gilded palaces of sin. . . . Instead of decreasing, the evil is spreading." (*San Francisco Chron.*, July 6, 1871, p. 2.)

[12] William L. Barrett, in *St. Louis Bd. of Health, 3rd Ann. Rep.* (1870), pp. 29-32.

[13] See *Missouri Democrat*, July 6, 1870, p. 4; July 7, 1870, p. 4; *Missouri Republican*, July 7, 1870, pp. 2-3.

[14] Some highlights are reported in *Missouri Democrat*, September 1, 1870, p. 4; Septem-

It is extremely difficult to discover just who in St. Louis, before Health Officer Barrett's report, favored setting up medical inspection. The newspapers referred to a group of public-spirited citizens, led by Colonel Ferdinand Meyer of the Board of Police Commissioners, who obtained the enabling legislation from the state. The Mayor, Joseph Brown,[15] and many city councilmen seemed to believe in the sanitary efficaciousness of the ordinance when the subject came up. Except for Barrett, physicians of the city did not appear to be the major movers behind this important public health legislation.[16]

The members of the St. Louis Medical Society provide a good sample of contemporary medical opinion. In the late 1860's, Missouri physicians had been involved in controversy and agitation to get regular physicians licensed and thus established against their competition. In 1870, therefore, the St. Louis Society was largely preoccupied with the question of professional standards.[17] Nevertheless, in May of that year, S. F. Newman,

ber 3, 1870, p. 4; January 6, 1872, p. 4; *Missouri Republican*, August 26, 1870, p. 2; *St. Louis Republican*, February 20, 1874, p. 5; March 3, 1874, p. 5; March 19, 1874, p. 1; March 28, 1874, p. 5; April 1, 1874, p. 5; April 3, 1874, p. 8; April 17, 1874, p. 8; May 23, 1874, p. 2; June 10, 1874, p. 5; *St. Louis Globe-Democrat*, January 14, 1876, p. 4; January 21, 1876, p. 3; May 20, 1876, p. 3. See J. Thomas Scharf, *History of Saint Louis City and County* (Philadelphia, 1883), vol. II, p. 1551; William Hyde and Howard L. Conard, eds., *Encyclopedia of the History of St. Louis, A Compendium of History and Biography for Ready Reference* (New York, 1899), vol. IV, p. 2093; *Laws of Missouri, General and Local Laws Passed at the Adjourned Session of the XXVIIth General Assembly* (Jefferson City, 1874), pp. 384-385. The St. Louis experiment has often been called the only system of compulsory inspection of prostitutes ever set up in the United States. There were other instances, one noted below, and another just after the turn of the century. The latter was the effort of the mayor of Minneapolis, A. A. Ames, a physician, to establish reglementation by police regulations in 1902. The most effective opposition to this scheme was, interestingly enough, that of other physicians. See, for example, *Minneapolis J.*, March 20, 1902, p. 4; Harold Zink, *City Bosses in the United States, A Study of Twenty Municipal Bosses* (Durham, N. C.,: Duke Univ. Press, 1930), pp. 344-349; Marion D. Shutter, et al., *Report of the Vice Commission of Minneapolis* (Minneapolis: H. M. Hall, 1911), pp. 24-25. As is noted below, by the turn of the twentieth century a larger and larger proportion of influential physicians was being enrolled in the purity movement.

[15] Brown, who provides a good example of the advocates of reglementation, was a Scottish-born railroad executive and businessman. Nothing obvious in his background differentiates him from many opponents of the plan. For details on the non-medical politics and local history of the law, see John C. Burnham, "The social evil ordinance—A social experiment in nineteenth century St. Louis," *Bull. Missouri Hist. Soc.*, 1971, *27*: 203-217.

[16] For example, see *Missouri Democrat*, July 21, 1870, p. 4. Interestingly enough, there is no evidence that the important German population in St. Louis, including well-known German physicians, was in any way involved in bringing the Continental system to that city.

[17] See, for example, *Tr. M. A. State of Missouri*, 1867-1869, *passim*.

one of the leading practitioners of the city, offered a resolution in support of " any wise measures on the part of the Honorable Board of health which look to the proper regulation of houses of prostitution." The reasons spelled out in the proposal were both moral—regulation would reduce temptations to youth by curbing harlotry—and medical, the latter including the observation that " the public welfare demands that means be devised to restrict and regulate this vice, so as to strip it as far as possible of its awful consequences. . . ." A number of the Society members immediately objected to the resolution on moral grounds, and it therefore eventually was laid on the table.[18]

About a year later, after the ordinance had been enacted anyway, the Society did pass a resolution concerning it. Characteristically, the physicians' concern expressed in this 1871 resolution centered upon the specific medical inspectors who had been appointed, at least some of whom Society members did not consider fully qualified. Only incidentally did the resolution endorse the ordinance. According to the wording of the resolution, the working of the ordinance had confirmed " the salutary and beneficial results which have for a long time obtained in Europe," and those results promised to increase if better qualified physicians were appointed.[19]

As in the Medical Society, so in the larger community of St. Louis initial and continuing opposition to reglementation was mounted on moral grounds. The purity leaders were largely Protestant clergymen, and one of them, William Greenleaf Eliot, took credit for agitation that eventually led to nullification.[20] Since proponents, both medical and lay, constantly confused moral and hygienic arguments, opposition on moral grounds was entirely relevant and in order in the dialogue that developed around and following the St. Louis experiment. In 1873, in his plea for a chance to continue the experiment, for example, Health Officer Barrett produced widely quoted figures showing a decrease in not only venereal cases but in the number of prostitutes in the city. While the diminution of the number of public women could have been considered

[18] Minutes of the St. Louis Medical Society, May 21, 1870, p. 705, and June 11, 1870, p. 707. Historical Library, St. Louis Medical Society, St. Louis, Missouri. *Missouri Republican*, June 13, 1870, p. 2.

[19] Minutes of the St. Louis Medical Society, June 17, 1871, pp. 758-765; *Missouri Democrat*, June 18, 1871, p. 4.

[20] See, for example, *Missouri Democrat*, August 29, 1870, p. 4; *Missouri Republican*, February 28, 1873, p. 8; April 6, 1873, p. 6; April 9, 1873, p. 5; August 6, 1873, p. 8. Charlotte C. Eliot, *William Greenleaf Eliot, Minister, Educator, Philanthropist* (Boston: Houghton, Mifflin, 1904), chap. XII. William G. Eliot, *A Practical Discussion of the Great Social Question of the Day* (New York, 1879).

strictly a sanitary matter, neither Barrett nor his colleagues so restricted themselves. Two years before, for instance, Barrett had claimed that the law had already "lessened disease, suffering and death; reclaimed fallen women, and restored them to society, friends and home, and prevented them from becoming abandoned and profligate." Given this argument that reglementation led to moral improvement, it was not inappropriate, then, that the experiment was ended in the name of public morality rather than on the basis of its sanitary efficaciousness or lack thereof.[21]

The St. Louis experiment did nevertheless open the door in 1870 to a national discussion of the hygienic value of government-enforced medical inspection of prostitutes. Within a few days after the ordinance was passed, for instance, the editors of *The Medical Gazette,* of New York, were congratulating St. Louis on taking the first step in an inevitable national movement. The social evil, said the editors, "will always exist, and we can do little toward limiting it; but we can do something towards limiting the spread of syphilis, and it is high time that we should direct our energies to that task."[22] For a number of years various influential American physicians spoke up in a similar vein. Chicago, Cincinnati, and San Francisco, for example, all harbored strong reglementation movements in the early 1870's, inspired explicitly by the St. Louis experiment. As a Cincinnati medical editor explained: "As we advocate quarantine, Boards of Health, the collection of statistical data, and spread of science generally, so we also devote the *Lancet* to the advocacy of social evil laws, to the end that we may have less venereal disease and better facilities for studying the little we may have."[23]

The fact that these movements got started before the results from St. Louis were in—that is, immediately after passage of the Social Evil Ordinance—suggests that there existed already the basis for medical agitation for inspection of prostitutes, and in fact a more comprehensive movement soon overshadowed the St. Louis experiment. This movement had determinants far more profound than mere reaction to the St. Louis ordinance. Even before 1870 similar legislation had been proposed in

[21] See William L. Barrett, in *St. Louis Bd. of Health, 4th Ann. Rep.* (1871), pp. 22-43; *idem, 6th Ann. Rep.* (1873), pp. 29-48, reprinted as William L. Barret[t], *Prostitution in Its Relation to Public Health* [St. Louis, 1873].

[22] *M. Gaz.*, 1870, *5*: 82.

[23] For example, see [D. G. Brinton?], "Why exercise control over prostitution?" *M. & S. Rep.*, 1875, *32*: 495-496; James E. Washington, "A social evil act needed," *Nashville J. Med. and Surg.*, 1877, *10*: 175-183 (citing the St. Louis experiment); *Chicago Times*, October 29, 1870, p. 2; *San Francisco Chron.*, July 6, 1871, p. 2; *Missouri Democrat,* August 29, 1870, p. 4; *St. Louis Republican*, February 1, 1874, p. 8; *Lancet* [Cincinnati], quoted in "The social evil," *Cincinnati M. News,* 1873, *2*: 122-129.

other cities, and Cincinnati, for example, came close to being the experimental city.[24] Prostitutes had been strictly inspected and regulated in some areas during the Civil War, it turned out, and in New York, for years after Sanger's book was published, influential citizens advocated medical inspection of public women. In 1867, for instance, the grand jury there spoke out specifically on the issue.[25]

The political defeat of the St. Louis experiment for some reason tended to discredit it, but the discussion of reglementation nevertheless continued among physicians.[26] A number of eminent practitioners boldly advocated inspection. In the mid-1870's the renowned Philadelphia surgeon, Samuel D. Gross, spoke out in favor of some legal measures similar to the British Contagious Diseases Acts. In addressing the American Medical Association in 1874, he observed:

> We send missionaries among the heathen in foreign lands, but neglect this fearful plague-spot at our own doors and at our own fireside . . . . we permit our own brother to contract a loathsome disease . . . taint and infect his offspring unto the third or even unto the fourth generation. The only remedy for this evil is the licensing of prostitution.[27]

Gross's efforts to initiate national discussion of an inspection program were seconded in 1876 by J. Marion Sims, father of American gynecology, in his presidential address to the American Medical Association. Formerly, said Sims, syphilis had been an exclusively medical matter, a disease to be treated. With the new knowledge at hand, he continued,

> it is no longer a question for the therapeutist, but one for the sanitarian, the philanthropist, the legislator, the statesman. . . . Shall it be said that we, the representatives of the medical profession of a great nation, the custodians of the health of forty millions of people, cognizant of all these facts, will longer let the people remain in ignorance of the dangers that surround them? . . . We must sound the alarm.

Sims shrewdly perceived that the physician as reglementarian had to enter the public arena. The growing public health movement had already

[24] See J. H. Tate, "The Board of Health and prostitution," *Cincinnati M. Repert.*, 1869, *2*: 97; J. J. Quinn, "The social evil," *Cincinnati M. Advance*, 1876, *3*: 579-581.

[25] W. M. Chambers, in *Tr. A. M. A.*, 1875, *26*: 237-238; *Pub. Health Papers and Rep.*, 1880, *6*: 411, also quoted in Sanger, *op. cit.* ftn. 8 above, 2nd ed., p. 697. See, for example, *New York Tribune*, June 3, 1867, p. 5; *Journal of the Assembly of New York*, 1867, vol. I, pp. 561, 677; vol. II, pp. 1029, 1491, etc. See, in general, Powell, *op. cit.* ftn. 5 above.

[26] See, for example, the controversy stirred up by the Cleveland Board of Health in 1882-1883: "The care of prostitutes in Cleveland," *M. Rec.*, 1883, *23*: 97-98; *Cleveland Herald*, January 30, 1883, p. 2.

[27] S. D. Gross, "Syphilis in its relation to the national health," *Tr. A.M.A.*, 1874, *25*: 249-292.

forced the doctors into playing a quasi-political role, and practitioners such as Sims were prepared to take medical knowledge, even about venereal diseases, to the public, or at least to local boards of health, for action.[28]

Characteristically, the Association ordered 10,000 copies of Sims's address distributed but nevertheless did not respond to Gross's eloquent plea to give reglementation official Association endorsement. As in the St. Louis Medical Society, members of the AMA in a heated debate divided between advocates and opponents of compulsory medical inspection of prostitutes, and the issue was never resolved in that organization.[29]

In general, then, members of the medical profession reacted to the suggestion of a system of reglementation in one of three ways: they favored any sensible public health measure to curb venereal diseases, especially syphilis, or they doubted the efficacy of medical inspection of prostitutes although sympathizing with the sanitary aims of the program, or they shared the moral outrage of those who opposed what they characterized as legalizing and licensing vice. Each of these reactions requires a little exploration.

The public health campaign for reglementation, from Sanger's brave effort before the Civil War down to the twentieth century, was essentially constant. Physicians continued to believe that prostitutes were the main carriers of venereal poison and that medical inspection would cut down on disease and, incidentally, provide pressure and opportunity for the women to reform themselves. Two medical advances gave urgency to this public health program. In the mid-nineteenth century, physicians discovered the so-called syphilis of the innocent, for by that time the evidence was clear that wives, children, wet nurses, and others become infected through no fault of their own,[30] and the common view that venereal diseases were punishment for moral transgressions was open to question. Indeed, so well was the epidemiology of venereal illnesses developed that the germ theory of disease had nothing fundamental to add to it.

In the 1890's the campaign for public prophylaxis took on a new stridency after a number of venereologists had worked out the full clinical

[28] J. Marion Sims, "Address of J. Marion Sims, M.D., President of the Association," *Tr. A.M.A.*, 1876, *27*: 100-111, also published in part separately as *Legislation and "Contagious Diseases"* (Philadelphia, 1876). See, for example, J. R. Black, "Preventing the extension of syphilis," *Cincinnati Lancet and Observer*, 1876, *19*: 1057-1063, who cited Sims's address.

[29] See *Tr. A. M. A.*, 1875, *26*: 226-228, 232-244; 1876, *27*: 43.

[30] A good example of the American literature on this subject is L. Duncan Bulkley, *Syphilis in the Innocent (Syphilis Insontium), Clinically and Historically Considered with a Plan for Legal Control of the Disease* (New York, 1894); Bulkley, interestingly enough, believed in the inspection of men as well as women.

effects of syphilis and gonorrhea. By the 1880's, long before the discovery of the spirochete, Fournier and Erb and others had assembled widely accepted evidence showing that many afflictions, including paresis, locomotor ataxia, and some arthritic affections, were of luetic origin. Paresis, or general paralysis, as it was known, was the object of particular fear and loathing among both physicians and laymen. Often euphemistically referred to as "softening of the brain," the disease spread terror among late Victorian Americans, a terror that was compounded by the proof that it grew out of syphilis contracted many years before. Contemporaneously Noeggerath and Neisser and their colleagues were demonstrating that gonorrhea was a serious disease not easily amenable to treatment and responsible for blindness and sterility and other gynecological disorders. Many physicians at the end of the century were frankly horrified by these new findings and urged some kind of action. Eventually there was action, but it did not come in the form of reglementation.[31]

The international medical congresses of the nineteenth century, particularly those dealing with quarantine and contagion, helped to inspire all of the public health movement, including that part of it devoted to venereal diseases, and many Americans cited international meetings as the initial source of their concern rather than, say, the St. Louis experiment. A recommendation made at an international medical congress in Paris in 1867 was particularly important in inspiring agitation for medical inspection.[32] But the international movement for reglementation did not

[31] See below. A general summary of discoveries regarding syphilis is William Allen Pusey, *The History and Epidemiology of Syphilis* (Springfield, Ill.: Thomas, 1933), pp. 59-64; Charles C. Norris, *Gonorrhea in Women, Its Pathology, Symptomatology, Diagnosis, and Treatment; Together with a Review of the Rare Varieties of the Disease which Occur in Men, Women and Children* (Philadelphia: Saunders, 1913), chap. I, provides an excellent annotated account of discoveries about gonorrhea. For early examples, see E. L. Keyes, *Venereal Diseases, Including Stricture of the Male Urethra* (New York, 1880), and the reglementationist plea of Frederic Russell Sturgis, "The Hygiene of Syphilis," in A. H. Buck, ed., *A Treatise on Hygiene and Public Health* (New York, 1879), vol. II, pp. 537-544. A later summary was offered by James J. Walsh, reported in *Tr. Am. Soc. San. and Moral Prophylax.*, 1907-1908, *2*: 54: "We now knew that one out of every five persons who died in our insane asylums went there because of these social diseases. We knew that three fourths of all women operated on gave a history of one of these diseases. It was only within the past two decades that certain grave nervous affections, including locomotor ataxia, had been traced to these social evils." The new knowledge was popularized surprisingly quickly; see, for example, Henry M. Hurd, "The relation of general paresis and syphilitic insanity," *Am. J. Insan.*, 1886, *43*: 1.

[32] See, for example, Arne Barkhuus, "The sanitary conferences," *Ciba Symposium*, 1943, *1-2*: 1563-1579, 1584; M. H. Henry, "The discussion on the prevention of

find a broad enough basis of support to work effectively through the public health movement in America.

A dramatic confrontation at the Indianapolis meetings of the American Public Health Association in 1882 summarizes succinctly what happened in the movement in general. Albert L. Gihon, Medical Director of the U. S. Navy, presented a report from the committee on venereal diseases urging each state to enact a law that would make venereal diseases and other contagious illnesses subject to compulsory reporting and treatment. One clause was understood, perhaps incorrectly, perhaps not, as opening the door for local governmental medical inspection and quarantine of prostitutes. John Shaw Billings, the famous medical administrator and librarian, moved to lay the entire subject upon the table, arguing that even discussing the topic had already brought the religious pressure groups upon the Association. Public health advocates, he declared, would damage their own political effectiveness by endorsing the measure. It would, he said, embarrass them " in obtaining power to deal with things which lie next to our hand,—getting sewerage in the villages, doing away with polluted well-water, etc. . . ." The members present, by a vote of thirty-eight to twenty, followed Billings's advice. Afterwards Gihon said that he regretted Billings's remarks and thought that had he been in practice and seen more cases he would not have made them, but Gihon promised not to trouble the Association again with the subject. Then he added:

> I have for seven years worked on this matter, and I do not intend to give it up. As long as I remember the one good woman who is now in my mind,—a woman pure and good and virtuous beyond expression; a wife who died a miserable, wretched agonizing death, through contact with her husband, who diseased her,— as long as I remember that woman I pledge myself to work on in this field.[33]

The contentions of well-meaning advocates of medical inspection of prostitutes were often rejected because many physicians doubted that

syphilis, with reference to the regulation of prostitution, at the Third International Medical Congress, held at Vienna, August, 1873.—With additional remarks," *Am. J. Syphilog. and Dermat.*, 1874, *5*: 17-28; Louis Chéry, *Syphilis, maladies vénériennes et prostitution, esquisse d'hygiène sociale, documents récents sur la législation des filles publiques et des maladies sexuelles* (Toulouse: Diron, [1911]), p. 72.

[33] *Pub. Health Papers and Rep.*, 1882, *8*: 281-287, 329-336. Gihon had introduced the subject to the Association three years before, and in 1880 the Association had passed two resolutions calling the attention of public health authorities and legislators to the need for some kind of action; see Albert L. Gihon, " On the protection of the innocent and helpless members of the community from venereal diseases and their consequences," *Pub. Health Papers and Rep.*, 1879, *5*: 55-65, and discussion, pp. 177-185; *Pub. Health Papers and Rep.*, 1880, *6*: 402-415, 426-431, 437-444; 1881, *7*: 411-417, 423-428.

such measures were really effective. The skeptics believed that venereal diseases were spread largely by women who, for one reason or another, were not registered and probably could not be, and who were therefore not going to be inspected. Such doubts eventually discredited, for example, even the Parisian inspection system.[84]

The other basis for skepticism was that the inspection process itself was not efficient enough to be justified. Health Officer Barrett of St. Louis, for example, in 1871 took pains to explain that the number of syphilitics who did not manifest a discoverable lesion was statistically very small, not enough to impair the efficacy of the inspection system.[85] But other physicians did not agree with assessments such as Barrett's, and their arguments were at the very least disquieting to advocates of reglementation. In 1871 the editors of the *Medical Record* reprinted from the prestigious British *Medical Times and Gazette* a comprehensive survey of the world literature on the subject, casting serious doubts upon the ability of the most skilled physician to detect syphilis in women by

[84] See, for example, *IIe Conférence internationale pour la prophylaxie de la syphilis et des maladies vénériennes* (Brussels: Lamartin, 1903).

[85] William L. Barrett, *op. cit.* ftn. 21 above, *4th Ann. Rep.*, p. 41. In the case of gonorrhea, technical difficulties inhibited the use of bacteriological techniques for detection and diagnosis. From the first reports of Neisser's discovery of the gonococcus, medical writers took much interest in the pathological and bacteriological issues raised. It was several decades, however, before bacteriological means were considered an essential part of diagnostic procedure. See, for instance, J. L. Milton, *On the Pathology and Treatment of Gonorrhoea and Spermatorrhoea* (New York, 1887), in which Neisser's work is recognized, but the discussion of the use of the microscope in diagnosis is limited (p. 19) to its failure as an extension of the usual visual methods of diagnosis. Later even skilled workers found it difficult to stain satisfactorily and to identify the gonococci for certain, and in particular stages of the disease, of course, these pathogens are very scarce. See, for example, Abraham L. Wolbarst, "Observations in the diagnosis and treatment of acute gonorrhea, with special reference to the value of protargol as a therapeutic agent," *J. Cutan. and Genito-Urin. Dis.*, 1901, *19*: 556-558, and the complete review of the technique and literature in David Thomson, *Gonorrhoea* (London: Frowde *et al.*, 1923), chaps. III, XII. By the 1910's, however, it was customary to demand "microscopic demonstration of the gonococcus . . . in every case." (Ernst Portner, *Genitourinary Diagnosis and Therapy for Urologists and General Practitioners*, trans. Bransford Lewis [St. Louis: Mosby, 1913], p. 160). In the late nineteenth century the difficulties of diagnosing gonorrhea in women by bacteriological examination seemed especially forbidding to physicians in the field. See, for example, the discussion in *J. Cutan. and Genito-Urin. Dis.*, 1891, *9*: 219-221; George Parker Holden and F. E. Doughty, *A Practical Working Handbook in the Diagnosis and Treatment of Diseases of the Genito-Urinary System, and Syphilis* (Philadelphia, 1897), pp. 236-240. In 1895 W. R. Pryor of New York was led to assert that although inspection of public women might limit the spread of syphilis, the difficulties of detecting gonorrhea in prostitutes were so great as to render the procedure profitless; "Latent gonorrhea in women," *J. Cutan. and Genito-Urin. Dis.*, 1895, *13*: 94-95.

inspection. Until well after 1900 the method of inspection was essentially visual. The Wassermann test for syphilis was announced only in 1906, and not until several years after that were it and other laboratory methods of diagnosis in general use in American medicine. Although Neisser had identified the gonococcus in 1879, use of the microscope in the diagnosis of gonorrhea was not common before the 1900's except for purposes of confirmation and differential diagnosis, in cases in which pus or other symptoms had already been found by visual methods. Even very late in the nineteenth century, then, skeptics could show in detail how faulty the inspection process was because of technical inadequacies alone.[36]

An excellent example of the late nineteenth-century skeptic was Edmund Andrews, professor of principles and practice of surgery in the Chicago Medical College, who in 1875 spoke effectively at the American Medical Association meetings in opposition to Gross's advocacy of a public health program against venereal diseases.[37] In 1867, after a trip to Europe, Andrews had reported and documented his skepticism of reglementation.[38] When news of the St. Louis experiment caused some prominent citizens to initiate a move to bring the system to Chicago in 1871, Andrews in a widely quoted article and pamphlet denounced the measure as ineffectual. After reciting the evidence that reglementation was not preventing the spread of syphilis, Andrews remarked that

> it is a matter of utter astonishment, that any surgeon, or even any man of uneducated common sense, should suppose that a medical examination can give the least security to cohabitation with prostitutes. . . . There would be no possibility of checking the disease by such methods, unless the men as well as the women were examined, and all prostitution prevented, except where both parties were proved to be healthy. Now, I submit the question, whether it is advisable for the community to adopt a costly system, which, while it affects no diminution of general disease, acts as a delusive advertisement to lead men to suppose that the chambers of prostitution have at last become almost safe resorts.

All that Andrews could advocate instead, however, was voluntary treatment and toleration of prostitution as it existed.[39]

[36] "Syphilis in the female," *M. Rec.*, 1871, *5*: 538-539.

[37] Edmund Andrews, in *Tr. A.M.A.*, 1875, *26*: 233-236.

[38] Edmund Andrews, "Venereal diseases and prostitution under the license system of Europe.—The laws, statistics, and results of the system," *Chicago M. Exam.*, 1867, *7*: 603-616.

[39] Edmund Andrews, "Prostitution and its sanitary management," *Chicago M. Exam.*, 1871, *12*: 65-97, especially p. 90, also published in part separately (Chicago, 1871). For an example of the impact of Andrews's work, see "Should prostitution be licensed?" *Pacific M. and S. J.*, 1867, *9*: 294-299. Another example is R. A. Thomas, "A few observations on state regulation of prostitution," *Maryland M. J.*, 1882, *8*: 469-472, 1882, *9*: 31-37.

It is amazing that in the face of the problems raised by skeptics such as Andrews, the medical advocates of inspection did not back down in the late nineteenth century. But the newly discovered extreme dangers of the diseases led many conscientious physicians to advocate any action whatsoever on the chance that it might lead to at least a little amelioration. Typically, such physicians were those who continued to believe that prostitution was an ineradicable human phenomenon and who, at the same time, were deeply alarmed by the new clinical and pathological evidence of the ravages of the diseases.[40] Ironically, such counsels of desperation eventually carried a large number of physicians into the camp of the moralists. The converts found it more bearable to believe that prostitution could be eliminated than to believe that the diseases would have to be tolerated as an essential of the human condition.

Those who opposed compulsory medical inspection of prostitutes on the moral grounds that it constituted recognizing or legalizing sin were at first not necessarily optimistic about eliminating prostitution, but they at least hoped to hold it in check. Unwittingly they got themselves involved in a number of social changes that around the turn of the twentieth century metamorphosed the essentially medical public health campaign to control venereal diseases.

The new moralists of the late nineteenth century were already far removed in attitude from those who held venereal disease to be a punishment for sin. The initial systematic opposition to governmental licensing and inspection of public women arose among laymen. The chief organizer of an international movement to that end was an Englishwoman, Mrs. Josephine Butler, who was inspired to action by her uplift work among women affected by the notorious British Contagious Diseases Acts that created a limited system of reglementation. A number of British clergymen and public-spirited Victorians joined Mrs. Butler and her female collaborators in reform, and by 1869, before the St. Louis experiment was initiated, the British purity forces had organized—indeed, in time for involvement of their propaganda and personal aid in the successful fight to nullify the St. Louis Social Evil Ordinance.[41]

[40] See, for example, W. L. Mussey, "Syphilis as a menace to public health," *Cincinnati Lancet-Clin.*, 1894, ns *33*: 133-137; Denslow Lewis, "What should be the policy of the state toward prostitution?" *M. Rec.*, 1895, *48*: 651-653; Salathiel Ewing, reported in *M. News*, 1899, *75*: 346-347.

[41] The most convenient source is Josephine Butler, *Personal Reminiscences of a Great Crusade* (London, 1896), in which many letters and documents are reprinted. See especially p. 72, where a letter from Eliot is cited. See Charlotte C. Eliot, *op. cit.* ftn. 20 above, p. 300; William G. Eliot, *op. cit.* ftn. 20 above, pp. 22-23.

Following old lines of trans-Atlantic communication among reformers, especially Quakers, the British group quickly established formal American outposts on the East Coast.[42] As David Pivar has shown, the same personnel and channels were involved as in the pre-Civil War abolitionist crusade, and the reformers of the 1870's came to be known as the new abolitionists, this time working for the abolition of prostitution rather than of slavery. The new abolitionists early included in their ranks a number of physicians, who, as in St. Louis in 1870, reacted spontaneously to the call of morality. Unlike many of their colleagues, they believed that the social evil might actually be destroyed. In America the movement to abolish prostitution gradually grew into a movement to purify all of society, not only by abolishing various evil institutions such as the brothel and saloon, but by bringing children up to live clean lives. This upper middle class movement for purity of mind and body attracted an increasingly large number of physicians. They argued, among other things, that venereal diseases could best be controlled by destroying prostitution and immorality. Some British physicians were abolitionists from the beginning, and they and other opponents of medical inspection tried hard to recruit American medical men into the anti-prostitution movement. By 1900, as Pivar points out, both of the leading purity organizations were headed by M. D.'s.[43]

Many, perhaps most, physicians, however, continued to believe that prostitution and immorality were ineradicable and beyond the proper province of medicine anyway. Then, in the early years of the twentieth century, a group of basically conservative American venereal specialists, led by the formidable Prince A. Morrow of New York, decided that the consequences of syphilis and gonorrhea were so horrible that many traditional attitudes and institutions, not just the red light district, had to be changed. These physicians entered into public life and launched the social hygiene movement. They united with the purity forces and, by the

[42] Butler, *op. cit.*, pp. 73, 217.

[43] David Pivar, "The New Abolitionism, The Quest for Social Purity, 1876-1900" (Doctoral diss., Univ. of Pennsylvania, 1965). See, for example, J. Birkbeck Nevins, ed., *An Adress to Members of the American Legislature and of the Medical Profession, from the British, Continental, and General Federation for the Abolition of State Regulation of Prostitution, and the National Medical Association (Great Britain and Ireland) for the Abolition of State Regulation of Prostitution, on Recent Proposals to Introduce the System of Regulating or Licensing Prostitution into the United States, with the History and Results of Such Legislation on the Continent of Europe and in England* (London, 1877). Often the opposition of physicians on moral grounds was spontaneous, as in the St. Louis Medical Society; see, for example, the report in *Philadelphia Inquirer*, April 18, 1874, p. 1; *M. News*, 1882, *40*: 310.

time of World War I, had achieved new standards of sexual behavior, for the middle classes at least, and the destruction of prostitution in its traditional form in America.[44]

By the twentieth century, then, the medical inspection of prostitutes, whatever its actual sanitary effectiveness, was no longer a socially viable alternative for controlling venereal diseases in the United States. Ironically, the modern method of control, improved morality plus individual treatment, grew out of the efforts of the abolitionists who had opposed public health advocates of an earlier day on moral grounds. Some physicians had tried to remove moral considerations from their advocacy of medical preventive measures, but Americans in St. Louis and elsewhere seemed unable to keep moral arguments out of their public health campaigns. Then, in the twentieth century, prophylaxis improved greatly, in large part because physicians followed to a logical conclusion the bringing of moral considerations into the area of professional responsibility.

[44] This movement is summarized in John C. Burnham, "Medical Specialists and Movements Toward Social Control in the Progressive Era: Three Examples," in Jerry Israel, ed., *Building the Organizational Society* (New York: Free Press, 1971). See also Joseph Mayer, *The Regulation of Commercialized Vice, An Analysis of the Transition From Segregation to Repression in the United States* (New York: Klebold Press, 1922). Already in the nineteenth century American physicians had shown far greater affinity than Europeans for such ideas as inspection of men and outlawing the act of infecting another person with venereal disease; see, for example, "Zenith, M.D.," in *M. Rec.*, 1871, *6*: 93. See, in general, Charles Walter Clarke, *Taboo, The Story of the Pioneers of Social Hygiene* (Washington: Public Affairs Press, 1961).

CHANGING AMERICAN ATTITUDES TOWARD PROSTITUTION (1800–1920)

By Robert E. Riegel

Prostitution, as old as history, has been as differently regarded as human nature has from time to time been differently conceived. Early XIXth-century Americans stressed personal choice and responsibility, both for the prostitute and for her patron. Late in the century increasing emphasis was placed on social factors, and by the early XXth century the Progressives were viewing prostitution as one item in a complex pattern of social maladjustments, with individual responsibility less stressed.[1]

The attitude of XIXth-century America toward prostitution was rather self-contradictory. One side of the picture was a generally resigned acceptance of the institution as inevitable. Everyone knew of its existence, even though Victorian manners excluded it from polite conversation. People might disagree about its extent,[2] and be unaware of its considerable variety, from the luxurious house of assignation where a businessman might spend a night of illicit romance with someone else's wife to the low dive patronized by streetwalkers and their pickups, but even the most naive knew of the local red light district and of the street soliciting.[3]

The literate American was further informed of violations of the prescribed moral code by his newspaper, which was often peppered liberally with items on prostitution, on sexual abnormalities, on cures for venereal disease, on refuges for expectant but unmarried mothers, on suits for seduction or for the support of illegitimate children, on prosecutions of abortion-

[1] This account deals with white prostitution. Minority groups, particularly Negro and Indian, had special problems, but affected very little the general thinking on the subject.

[2] Some guesses as to the amount of prostitution appear in W. W. Sanger, *The History of Prostitution* (New York, 1858), 575–6, 608–618; Matthew Smith, *Sunshine and Shadow in New York* (Hartford, 1869), 371–389; Rev. Ralph Wardlaw, *Lectures on Magdalenism* (New York, 1843), 47; J. D. McCabe, *New York by Sunlight and Gaslight* (New York, 1882), 474–495; Mrs. D. L. Child, *The History of the Condition of Women* (2 vols., Boston, 1843), 2: 261; Frank Marryat, *Second Series of a Diary in America* (Philadelphia, 1840), 113–4; G. W. Pierson, *Tocqueville and Beaumont in America* (New York, 1938), 375.

[3] Descriptions of the various houses, mostly in New York, appear in Sanger, *Prostitution*, 549–574; Smith, *Sunshine and Shadow*, 371–389; George Ellington, *The Women of New York, or the Underworld of the Great City* (New York, 1869), 163–328; John H. Warren Jr., *Thirty Years' Battle with Crime* (Poughkeepsie, 1874), 100–132; descriptions of small town and rural prostitution are generally unavailable.

ists, and on cases of deserted children.[4] Such phenomena apparently were accepted by Americans as normal, with only infrequent and generally ineffective protests.

The other side of the story was that all statements made publicly opposed prostitution strenuously and advocated chastity as an attainable ideal. This point of view was stated with ever increasing vigor because while Americans felt deeply that they could look forward in the near future to an approximately perfect world under the beneficent influences of Christianity and democracy they realized sadly that no improvement was apparent in the area of sex; in fact, the growing cities with their blaring vice areas and their highly visible streetwalkers gave the impression that conditions were getting worse.

The basic argument against prostitution was personal and moral—that irregular sex relations were a breaking of God's law; the classic argument that the "bad" woman protected the "good" was never advanced. The moral argument was backed by many others. Illegitimacy was possible, with its attendant social problems. Physical and mental deterioration might include "the terrible disease with which God punishes this crime."[5] Regret was expressed for "the public show of extravagance, audacity and licentiousness of the women of the town,"[6] who gave bad examples to youth. Newer western communities in particular found prostitutes flaunting their attractions abroad, to the distress of the conservative and moral.[7]

Parents everywhere were worried about the effects on their children of seeing women soliciting in the streets; of hearing boisterous mirth, cursing, and obscenities issuing from houses of ill-fame; of seeing in the windows partly or entirely naked women seeking to attract patrons. The law-abiding citizen was also worried by the declining value of his property as a red light district approached him.

Prostitution acted as a magnet for other evils. Drinking and the use of drugs were commonplace. Patrons of the brothels frequently were robbed and sometimes beaten; well known was the sliding panel which gave easy access to the man's wallet. The old "badger game" continued, the partly or entirely unclothed couple confronted by a fake brother or husband. Blackmail was a distinct possibility, and particularly when the woman was colored. Houses of prostitution attracted petty criminals, sex perverts, and other undesirables. And the evil spread as tobacco stores, saloons, dance

[4] F. L. Olmsted, *A Journey in the Seaboard Slave States* (New York, 1856), 507–8, cites a doctor as saying that in 1853 there were more illegitimate than legitimate babies in South Carolina.

[5] *The New Englander* (New Haven) May 1859, 17: 473.

[6] *Niles Weekly Register* (Baltimore) Oct. 14, 1820, 18:99.

[7] Elizabeth Margo, *Taming the Forty-Niner* (New York, 1955); William Taylor, *California Life* (1961), 176–9. One man wrote in 1851 that "the price of virtue is too dear to be resisted by most of the frail sex."—Anthony and Allison Sirna (eds.), *The Wanderings of Edward Ely* (New York, 1954), 86–87. For a short time in the days of the gold rush, San Francisco had a society dominated by prostitutes, to the shocked horror of every visitor.

halls and theaters became places to recruit customers, and as touts scoured the towns to collect girls and patrons.[8]

Violence was connected frequently with prostitution. Brawls brought serious injury and even death; murder was far from unknown. Most notorious was the axe slaying of the prostitute Helen Jewett in New York in 1836. Accounts of the trial of R. L. Robinson for the murder filled the papers. The circumstantial evidence was very strong, but probably carried little weight with the jury because it was presented mainly by prostitutes; possibly there was tampering with the jury, but in any event the sympathy of the city went to the handsome, nineteen-year old socialite, who did not himself testify. The judge's charge favored the defendant, and when the jury brought in its verdict of "Not guilty" the crowded court room cheered. This case not only involved the violence to which opponents of prostitution objected, but also expressed the tolerance with which the general public viewed a young man sowing his wild oats, and the lack of sympathy for a prostitute.[9]

Prostitution involved patrons as well as prostitutes, and among these patrons must have been men who approved prostitution, at least for themselves, even though they could not state such approval publicly. Apparently a good many men were not much disturbed by moralistic admonitions, nor even by the warning that prostitution "palsies the limbs, shatters the frame, and makes every bone, muscle and nerve, an avenue of pain. It weakens the reason, the judgment, and the mental faculties. It prostrates the affections of the heart, and every noble feeling and aspiration of the soul."[10]

The moralist always lauded chastity as the proper goal for a young, unmarried man, but he also recognized that such a man had strong sex urges and hence advised a spartan life that would check the passionate male nature.[11] The young man was told to avoid highly seasoned foods, strong drinks, feather beds, erotic music, and the drama; the theaters were "but richly decorated and splendid gateways to the haunts of prostitution, to the chambers of death."[12] He should avoid inflammatory books and

[8] Turning the pages of any metropolitan newspaper unveils dozens of accounts of the practices at houses of prostitution. Many of the cases involved men who appealed to the police, and in fact robbery was so frequent that the *New York Times* (Oct. 18, 1858) headed a particular item as "The Old Story."

[9] *New York Morning Courier* June 3, 4, 6, 7, 8, 10, 1836; *Advocate of Moral Reform* (New York) Apr. 15, 1836, 2: 57; Allan Nevins (ed.), *The Diary of Philip Hone 1828–1851* (New York, 1927), 210–1, 213–4.

[10] Rev. Rufus W. Clark, *Lectures on the Formation of Character, Temptations and Mission of Young Men* (Boston, 1853), 191. Somewhat inconsistent with the laudation of chastity was the general opinion that a group such as the Shakers, which accepted chastity as a way of life, was composed of sapless, dried-up curiosities.

[11] *New Englander* May 1859, 17: 469–488; Sylvester Graham, *A Lecture to Young Men on Chastity* (Providence, 1834) makes the interesting point that intercourse outside of marriage is more exciting than that inside marriage; Clark, *Lectures*.

[12] Clark, *Lectures*, 120.

pictures.[13] He should work hard and sublimate his passions. Above all he should listen to his conscience and cultivate the God-given instinct of purity so that he might attain the moral standards of pure women.[14] Such advice often sounded as though the author himself doubted its effectiveness. The usual belief was that men were naturally gross creatures with deplorable appetites, and that one had to expect that they would find illicit outlets for their passions.

The attraction of the prostitute for the unmarried man is understandable, but less obvious is the attitude of the married man, and there is considerable evidence that married men patronized houses of prostitution frequently.[15] Such action by a married man was the product of the sex ideas of the time. Sex even within marriage was approved by the great majority of writers only if designed to carry out God's injunction to be fruitful and replenish the earth; it was considered wicked if only for personal enjoyment. In addition there was the presumption that while man was normally sensual a "good" woman felt no sexual urges.[16] The considerate husband could then assume that his importunities would be accepted by his wife only out of love for him, and would in fact be distasteful.[17] Furthermore, the chances of pregnancy were considerable, and numerous children threatened the health of the wife and the finances of the family. Abortion was by current standards illegal, immoral, and physically dangerous. Contraceptives were but little known, and most Americans were probably unaware of any effective means of prevention.[18] Under these circumstances many married men

[13] *Boston Recorder* Apr. 14, 1830 tells of ladies' reform groups founding seamen's homes that are to be free of "pollution."

[14] Typical statements are by "C. P. N." in *Woman's Journal* (Boston) July 5, 1873, 4: 216 and by "Christian Common Sense" in *Nation* Mar. 14, 1867, 4: 220.

[15] *Advocate of Moral Reform* Oct. 1, 1836, 2: 139 tells of an observer at a particular house in New York who watched fifty men enter, and was able to identify over a third as married.

[16] One unusual solution was presented in Christian Philanthropist, *The History and Philosophy of Marriage, or Monogamy and Polygamy Compared* (Boston, 1869), 169; the author favored polygamy even though he himself was not a Mormon.

[17] The usual statement was much like that of Isabella Beecher Hooker in her *Womanhood* (Boston, 1874), 13 when she spoke of "the unreasoning and inordinate indulgence of animal passion on the part of the man, and affectionate submission on the part of the woman." A few iconoclasts braved public sentiment by holding sex expression desirable in itself, and that women as well as men enjoyed it. Among these were Dr. S. Pancoast, *The Ladies' Medical Guide* (6th ed., Philadelphia, 1859), 231–3; T. L. and M. S. G. Nichols, *Marriage* (New York, 1854); T. C. Claflin, *The Ethics of Sexual Equality* (New York, 1873) and *Essays on Social Topics* (London, 1898), 16; O. S. Fowler, *Sexual Science* (Philadelphia, 1870), 743–803—by a phrenologist; Charles Knowlton, *Fruits of Philosophy* (Boston, 1833), Introduction; Elizabeth Blackwell, *The Human Element in Sex* (London, 1894), 42–57; Rev. A. C. Tompkins in *Arena*, July 1895, 13: 22 asserted that "sexual desire belongs equally to the male and female human beings."

[18] Peter Fryer, *The Birth Controllers* (New York, 1965); Norman E. Himes,

went to houses of prostitution rather than adopt the self-control urged so generally.

XIXth-century thinking easily explained male patronage of the prostitute, but had more difficulty with the motives of the prostitute. It was presumed every woman was instinctively "pure," feeling no base physical urges; "chastity is the natural inheritance of woman."[19] In fact, a woman was supposed to resist instinctively any approach by a man, and to prefer death to dishonor. As the *Advocate of Moral Reform* put the matter: "no woman ever voluntarily surrendered the blessings of a fair name. The sensitive plant shrinks not more instinctively from the touch, than the nature of woman from defilement."[20] Obviously she would never take the lead in sexual adventure; "bad women are made so by worse men, who deceive, betray, and desert them, after trifling with and playing upon their warmest feelings and richest affections."[21] The current picture, then, was of women who were instinctively pure, but at the same time innocent, credulous, affectionate, anxious to please—easy prey to men who "go prowling about, seeking to seduce and ruin girls."[22] A girl entered a life of shame not from preference but because she had been seduced, raped, or tricked into a fraudulent marriage.[23]

The obvious advice to a girl was that she should avoid such seductive activities as attending plays, reading romantic novels, listening to sensual music, dancing when clasped in a man's arms, and attending parties that might inspire romantic thoughts. She was advised to be carefully objective in picking an upright and religious man upon whom to bestow her affections. She should not arouse male passions by permitting any physical demonstrations before marriage; the careful girl avoided being alone with a man, and particularly at night after the family had gone to bed.[24] Whether because women were in fact what they were held to be or because they tried desperately to live up to current ideals, chastity among unmarried women was normal—which possibly improved the business of the prostitute.

Medical History of Contraception (Baltimore, 1936); S. H. Ditzion, *Marriage, Morals, and Sex in America* (New York, 1953), 317–353; Victor Robinson, *Pioneers of Birth Control* (New York, 1919).

[19] *The Revolution* (New York) June 25, 1868, 1: 389.

[20] *Advocate of Moral Reform* Jan. 1835, 1: 31.

[21] J. R. Creecy, *Scenes in the South* (Washington, 1860), 142.

[22] Dio Lewis, *Our Girls* (New York, 1871), 181–2.

[23] J. R. McDowall, *Magdalen Facts* (New York, 1832), *passim; Advocate of Moral Reform, passim; Friend of Virtue* (Boston), *passim;* A. A. Parker, *Trip to the West* (Concord, N. H., 1835), 82–85.

[24] *Advocate of Moral Reform* is filled with such advice, but note particularly its series "Temptations and Perils of Young Females," in issues of Feb. 1, 1849, 15: 21–22, Mar. 1 1849, 15: 37–38, Apr. 2, 1849, 15: 53; *Friend of Virtue* is likewise filled with good advice; L. P. Brockett, *Woman, her rights, wrongs, privileges, and responsibilities* (Cincinnati, 1870), 210–224; Anon., *Woman, As She Was, Is, and Should Be* (New York, 1849) 197 advances the idea that women's waste and extravagance scare men from marriage and into the arms of prostitutes.

The view that women were instinctively pure, while men were generally passionate, was held not only by the conservatively-minded but also by reformers who were working for equality for women. Their idea of achieving sexual equality was to raise men to the "higher" standards of women. Prostitution, they argued, "is the direct result of the exclusion of women from public affairs." [25] They were sure that voting women would eliminate houses of prostitution, for "how long would any city government that is responsible for imprisoning honest girls in brothels hold its power, if its reelection depended in any degree on the votes of women?" [26] As women began to attain the vote, feminists insisted that women always voted to eliminate vice.

A more complex argument of even older vintage was that women with the vote would find more jobs open to them, and hence would not be forced to make their living from sex, either inside or outside of marriage. Inside marriage they would be sufficiently independent to resist the demands of their husbands, and some feminists held that sexual expression would ultimately be limited to a small part of the year, as with lower animals. Outside marriage, the natural revulsion of women against defilement, together with their ability to obtain well-paying jobs, would bring the practical elimination of prostitution.[27]

The current attitude toward the prostitute was slightly confused. Any woman who had sinned, either through prostitution or by having a child outside of marriage, was ostracized but at the same time viewed sympathetically as a victim of man's passion and trickery: "A ruined female is like a beautiful star, turned aside from the glorious path in which she rolled in music around the sun." [28]

The Dying Prostitute—An Elegy
Weep o'er the mis'ries of a wretched maid,
Who sacrific'd to man her health and fame:
Whose love and truth, and trust were all repaid
By want and woe, disease and shame.[29]

This attitude continued through the XIXth century, although after about 1830 the word "prostitute" would have been replaced by some such euphemism as "soiled dove." In any case the only acceptable solution for a novelist was to have the erring woman die.[30]

[25] H. B. Blackwell in *Woman's Journal* Dec. 14, 1895, 26: 393, 396–7 and Dec. 21, 1895, 26: 401–4; the quotation is on p. 402.

[26] *Woman's Journal* Dec. 6, 1902, 33: 385.

[27] E. C. Stanton and others, *History of Woman Suffrage* (3 vols., n. p., 1889), 1: 224; *Woman's Journal* Aug. 7, 1875, 6: 252 and Sept. 21, 1872, 3: 30.

[28] *The Ladies' Garland* (Philadelphia) Apr. 18, 1837, 1: 3.

[29] *The American Museum* (Philadelphia) Aug. 1787, 2: 206.

[30] Margaret Wyman, "The Rise of the Fallen Woman." in *American Quarterly* Summer 1951, 3: 167–177. By the end of the century words like prostitute and prostitution were again in common use in print.

In addition to the Niagara of advice designed to save a girl from sin, various institutional homes, both Catholic and Protestant, were established as refuges for girls who otherwise might be headed for destruction; the girls were usually placed in such institutions by the courts when home conditions were intolerable. Best known was the American Female Guardian Society.[31] A similar idea was involved in the development of city missions, of which the most notable was the Five Points Mission, established in one of the worst parts of New York in the 1850's, partly to replace the uplifting influences of the Protestant churches that had moved uptown.[32]

Various groups with names such as Magdalen Society or Female Reform Society appeared from early in the century to warn girls against ways of life that might lead to moral degradation, and to help those who had slipped. Sometimes they exhibited a tinge of salacious titillation, as when the Galesburg, Illinois, society reported in 1845: "Although we have not been called upon to mourn the fall of any members of our society, yet some circumstances lead us to apprehend that there have been recent outrages upon the cause of moral purity within the bounds of our congregation."[33] Some of the societies established homes for prostitutes. The women were usually given training, probably in housework, and then placed in jobs—preferably at some distance so they would not be haunted by the past.[34]

While efforts were made at economic rehabilitation, the main stress in work with prostitutes was on appeals by prayer and exhortation to women's basically good nature. The American Society for Promoting the Observance of the Seventh Commandment stated that its object was "to convert these abandoned people to God by preaching."[35] Philanthropically minded citizens, including ministers, made emotional appeals to the consciences of prostitutes, with frequent references to Mary Magdalen.[36] Periodically the inmates of homes were subjected to more or less maudlin sentiments

[31] *Advocate of Moral Reform* Aug. 15, 1860, 26: 248 and June 1, 1869, 35: 123–8; *Frank Leslie's Illustrated Newspaper* (New York) Aug. 21, 1869, 28: 353, 360–3; such homes did not admit prostitutes.

[32] *The Una* (Providence, R. I.) Nov. 1853. 1: 69; *Times* Nov. 12, 1852 and June 18, 1853; *Gleason's Pictorial Drawing-Room Companion* (Boston) Jan. 15, 1853, 4: 40, 48; *Ladies' Repository* (Cincinnati) Apr. 1858, 18: 200–2.

[33] E. C. Calkins, *They Broke the Prairie* (New York, 1937), 167.

[34] N. K. Teeters, *They Were in Prison* (Philadelphia, 1937), 266–9; Bernard Duke of Saxe-Weimar Eisenach, *Travels Through North America* (2 vols., Philadelphia, 1828), 2: 10; McDowall, *Magdalen Facts*, 54–62; Bertha-Monica Stearns, "Reform Periodicals and Female Reformers 1830–1860," in *American Historical Review* July 1932, 37: 678–699, 684–5; *Boston Recorder* Jan. 20, 1830; *Leslie's* Aug. 21, 1869, 38: 353, 360–2; Ellington, *Women of New York*, 623–8, 643–5; *Putnam's Monthly Magazine* (New York) June 1853, 1: 685.

[35] G. H. Barnes (ed.), *Letters of Theodore Dwight Weld, Angelina Grimké Weld and Sarah Grimké, 1822–1844* (2 vols., New York, 1934), 1: 131.

[36] A typical case is in *Advocate of Moral Reform* May 15, 1869, 35: 112–3; Fredrika Bremer, *The Homes of the New World* (New York, 1854), 1: 69 speaks of the efforts of the novelist Catherine Sedgwick to "call forth their better natures."

designed to buttress their intentions to reform. One wonders at the effect of little children singing:

Were not the sinful Mary's tears
Acceptable to Heaven
When o'er the faults of former years
She wept and was forgiven? [37]

Efforts to reform prostitutes received great publicity in New York during the 1830's. Charitable ladies holding Sunday Schools for the prostitutes at Bellevue decided they needed more time than was afforded by the usual sixty-day sentence, and so in 1830 formed the New York Magdalen Society to work in the Five Points area, where poverty and prostitution went hand in hand. The financial agent was Arthur Tappan, the omnipresent reformer. The society issued in 1831 its first and only report, detailing vice conditions in New York; it apparently was too much for New York sensibilities. Some called it "a disgraceful document," [38] while others worried about the possibility of its getting into the hands of women and children, and feared mob action if the report were reprinted.[39] The one clear result was the demise of the society, with the work transferred to other hands.

The leading new worker in the Magdalen Society was a young and highly devoted Presbyterian divine, John Robert McDowall, who had come to New York to labor in the slums, and had become associated with Arthur Tappan. With the abandonment of the Society, McDowall inspired two new societies, one male and the other female, to continue the work. Even though practically destitute himself, he issued his *Magdalen Facts* (1832) describing vice conditions in New York, and then his *McDowall's Journal*, which was something of a confession magazine. McDowall's troubles were vastly increased when an audit indicated that he had been careless at least with the funds of the two societies; the Presbyterian Church ejected him.

McDowall's troubles led to the collapse of his organizations. The men's group was transformed into the Society for Promoting the Observance of the Seventh Commandment (1834), and *McDowall's Journal* was replaced by *The Advocate of Moral Reform*. The women's group became the New York Female Moral Reform Society; it provided homes for repentant females, but its greater efforts were devoted to work that might lessen the chances of women becoming prostitutes.[40]

[37] *Times* May 10, 1859, 5.

[38] Hone, *Diary*, 1: 45.

[39] *Morning Courier* July 1, 1831, July 12, 1831, and Aug. 22, 1831.

[40] Concerning the McDowall affair see J. R. McDowall, *Magdalen Facts* (1832), particularly 66–78, 92–98; *Reports of the New York Female Benevolent Society;* John Wheelwright, *Charges Preferred Against the New York Female Benevolent Society* (New York, 1836); Bertha-Monica Stearns, "Reform Periodicals," 681–4; *Advocate of Moral Reform, passim;* G. H. Barnes, *The Anti-Slavery Impulse 1830–1844* (New York, 1957), 24–26; Grace Adams and Edward Hutter, "Sex in Old New York," in *American Mercury* (New York) May 1941, 52: 550–7; R. A. Parker, *A Yankee Saint* (New York, 1935), 69–72.

Reforming prostitutes by moral exhortation was presumably reinforced by legal punishment which would be a deterrent and at the same time put the women in a proper frame of mind for reform.[41] The actions of the police were in fact quite ineffective. Even though the police had the necessary legislation at their command, knew the locations of the houses, and could recognize many of the prostitutes, they generally did nothing. Their assumption seems to have been that prostitution was ineradicable, and that the best they could do would be to keep it from getting completely out of hand. The result was segregated vice areas, with street soliciting permitted as long as it did not become too blatant.

From time to time throughout the XIXth and early XXth centuries the police picked up girls from the streets or raided various houses; now and then male visitors were also taken into custody. Normally the madames and girls were taken to court and fined, but jail sentences in some cases might be suspended. The usual charge was keeping a disorderly house, vagrancy, or indecent exposure.[42] The accusation was made that sometimes the arrested girls were not prostitutes until after they had been incarcerated at the "college of vice at Bellevue."[43] Periodically came the charge that the police were only harassing the business to make sure it paid for protection. In any event, those engaged in prostitution appeared to accept fines and even jail sentences philosophically as part of the costs of the trade.

At times the general public became exasperated and took more direct action. Some of the police raids were inspired by strongly expressed public sentiment.[44] And when the police failed to act a mob might take matters into its own hands, attacking and burning some of the more notorious houses.[45] All the moral indignation, the preaching, the houses of reformation, and the pressure of the police may have limited the growth of prostitution, but had little result either in lessening prostitution or in reforming the prostitutes. As one commentator stated: "But few philanthropic and Christian efforts have met such general and signal failure as attempts to rescue fallen women."[46] Both the reformation of the prostitute and the elimination of prostitution seemed very remote through the XIXth century.

Basic to a more successful attack on prostitution was a more realistic

[41] *Advocate of Moral Reform* Apr. 1, 1853, 19: 62–63.

[42] Examples of notices of such raids are in *Times* Jan. 1, 1852, Sept. 5, 1854, Mar. 9, 1855, May 24, 1855, Aug. 7, 1855, Aug. 3, 1858, Aug. 9, 1858, Sept. 13, 1858, June 14, 1859, June 15, 1859, June 17, 1859, June 21, 1859, June 29, 1859, Nov. 15, 1860, June 17, 1859; *New York Transcript* June 27, 1830; *Morning Courier* June 15, 1830, June 29, 1830, July 26, 1830; *Niles' Register* Oct. 14, 1820, 19: 99; *The Home Guardian* (Boston) Sept. 1871, 33: 277–280.

[43] McDowall, *Magdalen Facts*, cover; *Times* May 25, 1855.

[44] *Times* May 21, 1855, 3; May 22, 1855, 4; June 19, 1855, 3.

[45] *Niles' Register* Dec. 17, 1825, 29: 256; *Thomas Longworth American Almanac* (1839), Appendix A, 6, 10; *Detroit Tribune* quoted in *Times* June 25, 1857, 2.

[46] Anon., "Fallen Women," in *Ladies' Repository* (Cincinnati) Sept. 1869, 29: 219–222.

appraisal of the prostitute. Little hope was possible as long as people accepted the dogma that every woman was innately not sensual, that she would rather starve than enter a life of shame, that she fell from grace only because of trickery, seduction, or rape, and that reform depended primarily upon appeals to her instincts and emotions.

A change of attitude toward the prostitute began to appear about mid-century, notably with the work of Dr. William Sanger, the resident physician at the women's prison on Blackwell's Island. Under his direction two thousand prostitutes were asked to answer questionnaires given them by the police.[47] The women interviewed were generally young and badly educated; a high proportion were foreign-born. Those gainfully employed before becoming prostitutes had generally been paid low wages. Dr. Sanger estimated that because of physical mistreatment, liquor, and disease, the average professional life of a prostitute was four years.[48]

The Sanger survey cast considerable doubt on the classical analysis of motivation. Only 309 of the 2000 blamed their lapses from virtue on seduction or rape, and in view of the temptation of the girls to advance such commonly accepted explanations, the number is more apt to be too high than too low. Eight hundred and thirty-four gave explanations which implied that the type of life attracted them—as "inclination," "easy life," "bad companions," "persuaded," and "too idle to work"; particularly interesting were the 513 who answered "inclination" and thereby raised doubts as to the inevitable lack of sex interest in women. One hundred and eighty-one gave drink as the main cause, and if these are added to the 834, then a good half entered prostitution because they were attracted by that way of life, even though some of them had their judgments clouded by alcohol.

The economic motive, which was to be emphasized by later reformers, was not highly visible. Dr. Sanger himself stressed the monotony of mill life, together with close working contacts with the opposite sex; but since his own table gives only thirty-seven former factory girls, he is far from convincing. Less than a third of the girls (525) claimed "destitution" as the prime motivating factor, although of course economic motives may have weighed heavily in the search for an easier, more pleasant, or more exciting life. Generally one feels that the economic motive was important but not overwhelming.

The one factor certainly underestimated by all contemporary comments, including those of Dr. Sanger, was emotional maladjustment. The high proportion coming from broken homes plus those who blamed "ill treatment by family" produce an impressive total. Certain other explanations, such as the desire for an easier, more pleasant, more exciting life, while possibly

[47] W. W. Sanger, *The History of Prostitution* (New York, 1858); further analysis is based on this book. See also *Times* Jan. 28, 1856, 3.

[48] "J. H. B." in *Advocate of Moral Reform* Aug. 1, 1846, 12: 114 estimated five years.

classifiable as economic, might just as plausibly be interpreted as suggesting psychological troubles. Certainly emotional maladjustments were important, even though they can not be measured precisely.

Explanations of why women became prostitutes changed gradually during the years after the Civil War. Increased emphasis was given to social pressures of all sorts, which was in accord with the thinking that produced the Social Gospel. While people earlier in the century had worried about such matters as lascivious books and plays, late parties, and other environmental influences, the dominant feeling was that prostitutes ordinarily were women, once pure and lovely, who had been seduced by sensual men. This analysis continued to find acceptance, but increasingly the stress was on a girl's being attracted herself to prostitution rather than being tricked.

Among the factors producing prostitution, emphasis was placed more and more on the economic, which again was in accordance with the attitude of the late XIXth century. On this line of reasoning, women still remained innately pure and men still remained aggressive villains; but now men were less the unprincipled lotharios who seduced the ladies and more the conscienceless employers who by low wages, long hours, and bad working conditions practically forced women into prostitution, which of course was made economically profitable by other men.[49]

The emphasis on the idea of economic motivation was accepted enthusiastically by many feminists, who had long stressed the lack of proper job openings and pay as prime reasons for women remaining in subjection. They argued that men had limited the opportunities of women so that women would become easy sexual prey, either with or without marriage. One of the results was prostitution, which was entirely male-inspired. As Caroline Dall put the matter: "lust is a better paymaster than the mill owner or the tailor,"[50] or even more simply, prostitution was caused by "the want of bread."[51]

[49] Theodore Schroeder, "Prostitution as a Social Problem," in *The Arena* (Boston) Feb. 1909, 41: 196–201; *Woman's Journal* Mar. 9, 1872, 3: 74, Feb. 15, 1873, 4: 50, Dec. 14, 1895, 26: 393, 396–7, Jan. 18, 1879, 10: 22; Helen Campbell, "The Working-Woman of Today," in *Arena* Aug. 1891, 4: 329–339; J. W. Walton, "A Study of the Social Evil," in *The American Journal of Politics* (New York) Dec. 1893, 3: 605–617; E. R. Groves, *The American Woman* (rev. ed. New York, 1944), 267; *Home Guardian* Nov. 1871, 33: 333–4; S. D. Smallhausen and V. F. Calverton (eds.), *Woman's Coming of Age* (New York, 1931), 339; Ellen B. Dietrich in *Woman's Journal* May 27, 1893, 24: 162; Chester Giraud, *Embattled Maiden: The Life of Anna Dickinson* (New York, 1951), 155; Carl N. Degler, "Charlotte Perkins Gilman on the Theory and Practice of Feminism," in *American Quarterly* Spring 1956, 8: 21–39, 28; Charlotte Gilman, *The Man-Made World* (New York, 1911), 244–260.

[50] Caroline H. Dall, *The College, The Market, and the Court* (Boston, 1867), 135.

[51] Caroline H. Dall, *Woman's Right to Labor* (Boston, 1860), 15.

Considerable attention was given during the post-Civil War years to the possibility of confining prostitution to recognized parts of the cities, registering the prostitutes, and providing regular physical examinations. Those favoring such action viewed prostitution as inevitable. They maintained that controls such as existed in Europe would be better than the effort at complete elimination, which would only spread the problem. Several cities tried isolation and control, and others talked of it; most widely known was the St. Louis control law which was in operation during the early 1870's.[52]

The opposition, who were exceedingly vocal and in the majority, expressed deep religious and moral indignation at what they considered implied governmental sanction of prostitution through licensing, whereby "men may sin with impunity, and unchastity escape its natural and God-ordained punishment."[53] Opponents contended that such systems, both in Europe and in America, had involved an increase of vice and of venereal disease. Many insisted that registration should include male patrons. Feminists tended to sympathize with prostitutes because they were women, and to hold that control would violate their personal liberties, making them practically slaves. Some fear was expressed that physical examinations given by rather coarse male doctors might violate the modesty of the women.[54]

The argument over segregated vice districts was to some extent unreal. Most cities had such segregation in fact, although by action of the police rather than by law. The only differences made by a regular licensing system would have been further restrictions (as on music and liquor), regular medical inspections, and possibly the use of the license fees for such purposes as the support of Magdalen homes. The real argument was between tolerating prostitution, whether by registration or by extra-legal police action, and attempting to eliminate it completely.

The attitude toward prostitution steadily changed during the 1890's and

[52] Among the favorable statements are *Nation* Feb. 21, 1867, 4: 153–4; *Times* Feb. 10, 1867, 5: 1; *New York Tribune* June 3, 1876; Sanger, *Prostitution* (1898 ed.), 677–699; Anon., "Municipalities and Vice," in *Municipal Affairs* (New York) Dec. 1900, 4: 698–707; *The Survey* (New York) Jan. 15, 1916, 35: 447–8, which comments on the furore when Billy Sunday the evangelist favored segregation.

[53] Hooker, *Womanhood*, 95.

[54] Adverse comments appear in *Scribner's Monthly* (New York) Aug. 1876, 12: 591–2; J. W. Walton, "A Study of the Social Evil," in *American Journal of Politics* Dec. 1893, 3: 605–617; Dr. E. O. Buxton, "The Social Evil and Its Remedy," in *American Journal of Politics* July 1883, 3: 39–50; *The Philanthropist* quoted in *The Woman's Column* (Boston) vol. 7, Jan. 6, 1894; *Woman's Column* vol. 8, Feb. 16, 1895; *The Outlook* (New York) Feb. 23, 1895, 51: 303, Mar. 16, 1895, 51: 420, Dec. 8, 1900, 66: 874–6; Anon., "Another View of Municipalities and Vice," in *Municipal Affairs* June 1901, 5: 376–387; *The Social Evil* (1902), *passim*—report of the New York committee of fifteen; *Woman's Journal*—dozens of references for the years after 1870.

1900's. The stress on individual responsibility in both causation and reform lost ground, though the change was one of emphasis rather than of replacement. A good many commentators continued to insist that the basic problem was that of lustful men preying on pure and innocent women, and that the only proper solution was greater self-control by men; as one of them wrote: "I am profoundly convinced that the future of civilization hangs upon this pivot point." [55] Emily Blackwell deplored "the full indulgence of unbridled instincts" by men while they expected chastity from women, and held that "the enforced chastity of women has modified the sex instinct so that it now exists in a more spiritual form"; she concluded that as women advanced they would reform men, and that "licentiousness will inevitably shrink and disappear." [56] Mrs. Charlotte Gilman agreed in general, feeling that men had been overdeveloped sexually—like stallions—and would in time return to normal.[57] The proper route to reform, according to such people, was to increase the freedom of women, and particularly to give them the vote. Presumably a woman receiving an adequate salary would not become a prostitute, and women with the vote would not tolerate prostitution.

The newer point of view was that prostitution was the product of a multitude of factors, connected particularly with the growing cities, and that it could be handled only by a whole battery of reforms. The discussion of prostitution became involved with such matters as better pay and working conditions, slum clearance, prohibition, elimination of pornographic literature, better sex education, improved sports programs, and enlarged facilities for wholesome recreation. The influential Jane Addams in her various writings, including particularly *A New Conscience and An Ancient Evil* (1913), stressed economic causation, but at the same time mentioned such other factors as education, recreation, and liquor. Much more radical —and less influential—was Emma Goldman, who also stressed economic causation, but was looking forward to the currently unacceptable ideal of a completely free world in which every woman, single or married, could experience "the rapture of love, the ecstasy of passion, which reaches its culminating expression in the sex embrace." [58] The more usual reform attitude was that women in general preferred "purity," and that prostitution might at least be lessened greatly with a whole battery of "progressive" reforms, involving particulary economic adjustments.[59] The most stressed

[55] B. O. Flower, "Wellsprings and Fountains of Immorality," in *Arena* Dec. 1894, 11: 56–70, Jan. 1895, 11: 167–175, Feb. 1895, 11: 399–412, May 1895, 12: 337–352—the quotation is 11: 62. See also *Woman's Journal* June 17, 1893, 24: 186–7 on the World's Congress on Social Purity, held in Chicago.

[56] *Woman's Journal* Feb. 5, 1910, 41: 23.

[57] "The Oldest Profession in the World," in *The Forerunner* (New York) Mar. 1913, 4: 65.

[58] *Mother Earth* (New York), March 1913, 8: 211.

[59] Roy Lubove, "The Progressive and the Prostitute," in *The Historian* May 1962, 24: 308–330 is a good survey. For examples of the newer point of view see Rev. F. M. Goodchild, "The Social Evil in New York," in *Arena* Nov. 1896, 15:

factor was the economic, and by the 1900's many people saw prostitution itself as a big business—something like a Standard Oil Company of vice—with national and even international ramifications. According to this analysis, agents of the organization scoured the world for girls, whom they obtained by trickery, drugs, and force, and then made practically slaves.[60] One result of this point of view was the Mann Act of 1910, to prevent women from being transported across state lines for immoral purposes. The belief in a widespread organization to enslave unwilling prostitutes was at least a gross exaggeration. Prostitution was, of course, a business, frequently involving organization at the local level, but there was no national or international organization.

The prostitute herself was frequently explained as the slave of a conscienceless, profit-making organization or as the victim of economic necessity, and it was argued that the novelists and dramatists tended to romanticize her.[61] There was, however, evidence that ran against that explanation. One New York survey was a detailed analysis of the Macy department store. It concluded that while a good many of the clerks were quite sophisticated and may have given wrong ideas to young and innocent girls, their moral standards were generally high and their great goals in life were not excitement and frothy pleasure but home and children. To the surprise of many, it concluded that the few girls who entered prostitution were more apt to come from the well paid than the poorly paid employees.[62]

574–586; Jane Addams, "Jane Addams Page," in *Ladies' Home Journal* (Philadelphia) Nov. 1913, 30: 25; *Idem*, "Why Girls Go Wrong," in *Ladies Home Journal* Sept. 1907, 24: 13–14; *Idem*, "A New Conscience and an Ancient Evil," in *McClure's Magazine* (New York) Nov. 1911, 38: 232–240, Dec. 1911, 38: 232–240, Jan. 1912, 38: 338–344, Feb. 1912, 38: 471–8, Mar. 1912, 38: 592–8; *Ibid., A New Conscience and an Ancient Evil* (1913)—mostly the *McClure* articles; *Survey* Dec. 11, 1909, 23: 349–350 which includes a statement of Maude E. Minor, probation officer of the New York night court; *Survey* May 6, 1911, 26: 215, 239–249; *Idem*, Mar. 8, 1913, 29: 811–6; Ben B. Lindsay, "Why Girls Go Wrong," in *Ladies' Home Journal* Jan. 1907, 24: 13.

[60] E. A. Bell, *Fighting the Traffic in Young Girls or War on the White Slave Trade* (n. p. 1910) typifies this attitude. A series of articles in *McClure's* stressed police corruption—S. S. McClure, "The Tammanyizing of a Civilization," in *McClure's* Nov. 1909, 34: 117–8; G. K. Turner, "The City of Chicago: A Study of the Great Immoralities," *Ibid.*, June 1909, 33: 117–134; G. K. Turner, "The Daughters of the Poor . . . ," *Ibid.*, Nov. 1909, 34: 45–61. Brand Whitlock, *Forty Years Of It* (New York, 1920), 268–296 emphasizes economic causation but sees prostitution as much more complex than did most Progressives, and is scathing about the existence of force, trickery, and "white slavery."

[61] Best known of the novels were Stephen Crane, *Maggie A Girl of the Streets* (New York, 1893) and Theodore Dreiser, *Sister Carrie* (New York, 1900). For a spate of plays that appeared just before World War I see *Literary Digest* Oct. 4, 1913, 47: 577–8.

[62] *The Committee of Fourteen in New York—Department Store Investigation Report of the Sub-Committee* (15 pp., 1915). See also *Report on Condition of Women and Child Wage-Earners in the United States*, Senate Doc. 645, 61st

A simple economic explanation of prostitution appealed to many reformers and to the general public, but was not in fact adequate, as many experts realized.

Surveys of prostitution frequently mentioned the high proportion of immigrants. That the proportion was high had been recognized as early as the Dr. Sanger report, and presumably can be explained partly by the fact that most investigations were in the large cities of the East. Attention was also given the feeble-minded, but the evidence was poor and conclusions varied; some reports contended that a good half of the prostitutes were feeble-minded, others that the number of the mentally inferior was very small.

Much discussion concerned the age of consent, which for most of the century was in the region of ten to thirteen. The argument for raising the age was that a man would be much less likely to seduce a young girl if he realized that the law would classify the act as rape. Proponents of change wept over the "animal lust and moral degradation of man, and the destruction of womanhood." [63] More conservative observations agreed that the age should be raised, but pointed out that if it were made too high no jury would convict, and that mature looking girls, including prostitutes, would be able to blackmail men whom they had in fact seduced.[64] Starting in the 1880's most states raised the age—usually to sixteen or seventeen, but sometimes to eighteen.[65]

Another related reform movement was the drive for better sex education, both at home and in the schools. Home instruction had long been approved in theory, although such instruction often meant little more, apparently, than general moral advice, with possibly a few flowery references to physical processes.[66] Many parents presented nothing of practical utility, perhaps because of embarrassment. In consequence there was increased agitation for improved sex education,[67] with a growing feeling that it should be presented by the schools.

Various national groups were concerned with the problem of prostitution.

Congress, 2nd Session (19 vols., Washington 1910–1912), 5: 28–36; *Literary Digest* Aug. 9, 1913, 47: 199–200.

[63] *Arena* Feb. 1891, 3: 382.

[64] *Woman's Journal* Aug. 13, 1887, 16: 26 and Jan. 3, 1889, 20: 70; *Arena* July 1895, 14: 209–225 and Sept. 1895, 14: 1–32.

[65] G. E. Howard, *History of Matrimonial Institutions* (3 vols., Chicago, 1904), 3: 198–200; *Arena* Oct. 1895, 14: 205–220; *Ibid.*, Jan. 1895, 11: 192–215; Charles Edholm, *Traffic in Girls and the Florence Crittenden Mission* (Chicago, 1883), 67.

[66] Hooker, *Womanhood*, 7–27; *Public Ledger* Mar. 9, 1837; Graham, *Chastity*, 8; Elizabeth Blackwell, *The Laws of Life* (New York, 1852); *Scribner's* Mar. 1881, 21: 793.

[67] *Woman's Column* vol. 5, July 2, 1892; *Literary Digest* Oct. 7, 1899, 19: 444; *Ladies' Home Journal* Oct. 1906, 23: 5 and Mar. 1908, 25: 22; P. G. Kammerer, *The Unmarried Mother* (Boston, 1918), 77–101; Dr. Prince A. Morrow, *Social Diseases and Marriage* (New York, 1904); *Idem, The Teaching of Sex Hygiene* (New York, 1913); William T. Foster, *The Social Emergency* (Cambridge, 1914).

Most influential was the American Vigilance Association, formed in 1912 as a combination of earlier groups. David Starr Jordan was the president, and Jane Addams was on the executive board. The director of investigation was George J. Kneeland, who was responsible for one of the better books dealing with causation; the story he told was quite complicated, and did not give priority to any one factor.[68] The American Vigilance Association joined with two other groups in 1916 to become the American Federation for Social Hygiene.

Even more provocative of public discussion were the reports of numerous state and city investigating commissions, which became practically an avalanche in the years just prior to World War I.[69] Their statements of causes and possible cures varied widely, but they were unanimous in holding that red light districts should be eliminated. Probably they reflected general public opinion; at least there were few objectors who had the temerity to put their views into print. Most outstanding of the skeptics was Brand Whitlock, reform mayor of Cleveland, who said about suppression: "all that has been done about it has been much worse in its effect than if we had never done anything."[70] Whitlock insisted that real improvements could come only from long run reforms, including better living conditions, more independence for women, and improved sex education. He felt that direct police action did little more than spread the evil. But regardless of a few such misgivings, many efforts were made to stamp out prostitution by police action. City after city announced the elimination of its red light district. The results were approved by most Americans, although there were periodic hints that things were far from perfect, with the prostitutes plying their trade more widely and surreptitiously, and with the development of "call houses" and other methods of evading the law.[71] During World War I the army used segregation and control to some extent, but after the war there was no tendency to revert to XIXth-century conditions. Prostitution, of course, remained and certain houses were well known, but the blatant vice districts of the past were no longer in evidence. Whether or not the total amount of illicit sex experience had declined is another matter.

University of Texas, El Paso.

[68] George J. Kneeland, *Commercialized Prostitution in New York* (New York, 1913).

[69] See Lubove article, cited earlier. The reports of these investigations were almost always printed, and in addition there were dozens of articles in such magazines as the *Outlook*, *Annals of the American Academy*, *McClure's*, *Survey*, *Woman's Journal*, *Literary Digest*. A general statement appears in George Creel, "Where Is the Vice Flight?" in *Harper's Weekly* Oct. 10, 1914, 59: 340–2.

[70] *Literary Digest* Mar. 7, 1914, 48: 494; see also Brand Whitlock, "The White Slave," in *Forum* Feb. 1914, 15: 193–216.

[71] For some comments on the difficulties involved in suppression see Rev. John P. Peters, "The Story of the Committee of Fourteen in New York," in *Social Hygiene* (New York) July 1918, 14: 347–388; *Idem*, "Suppression of the 'Raines Law Hotels'" in *Annals* (1908), 32: 556–566; *The Social Evil* (1902)—report of the New York committee of fifteen; *Literary Digest* Nov. 9, 1912, 45: 846; *Survey* Feb. 27, 1915, 33: 572.

The Progressives and the Prostitute

Roy Lubove *

In the decade following 1907 urban America engaged in a spectacular vice crusade. Prostitution in general and "white slavery" in particular became the objects of a nationwide campaign of exposé and repression. Hysterical Americans feared that no woman was safe from the human "fiends" who used drugs, alcohol, and physical violence to force or deceive unsuspecting females into a life of immorality and bondage. Clifford G. Roe, counsel for the American Vigilance Association, protested that "most large cities are in fact market places where girls are sold and bought":

> An America commercialized has commercialized its daughters. Who would have ever prophesied a century ago that today like hardware and groceries the daughters of the people would be bought and sold? But to such a day as this our greed for money has brought us. How low have we sunk when now we make commerce of virtue and market the sanctity of the home?

Even school children were not inviolate: General Theodore A. Bingham, onetime Police Commissioner of New York City, complained that emissaries of vice hunted for victims in the vicinity of public schools. They hoped to debauch young girls, to corrupt their minds and bodies in order to season them for the human flesh market. The white-slave hysteria was not the mere figment of alarmists' imagination. Even Jane Addams insisted that the "organized traffic in

* The author is Research Fellow at the Center for the Study of the History of Liberty in America and Instructor in History at Harvard University. He was granted his Ph.D. (1960) by Cornell University. He has published articles on social reform in the Progressive Era in *New York History*, *Mid-America*, the *Mississippi Valley Historical Review*, *Social Research*, and *Social Studies*. The University of Pittsburgh Press has announced that it will publish his full-length manuscript, The Progressive and the Slums, this spring.

what has come to be called white slaves must be suppressed."[1]

Two features distinguished the vice crusade in the years before World War I. Its scope and intensity were unprecedented. Never before had so many Americans written so much about prostitution and its consequences nor organized so many committees and associations to repress the evil. The campaign against prostitution was indeed a tribute to the capacity of Progressive America for moral indignation; it troubled countless persons that thousands of women—frequently against their will it was alleged—led lives of shame and degradation. Not only the prostitutes but their customers suffered from the ravages of venereal disease. Worst of all, married men transmitted their infections to unsuspecting wives. Guilty and innocent, present and future generations alike, suffered from the thoughtlessness of promiscuous males:

> Upon humanitarian principles, in the interest of virtuous wives, who should no longer be poisoned with foul infections; in the interest of children, who should no longer be deprived of their rightful heritage of vitality and vigor; in the interest of the race, which should no longer be decimated and deteriorated, the dreadful curse of venereal disease should be lifted from the marriage relation.[2]

The real tragedy of prostitution, then, was the immense human waste involved. The reformers drew their intense indignation from their conviction that where prostitution went, there also went disease and moral degradation, race-suicide and physical enervation.

In broadest terms, the vice crusade can be interpreted as part of the more general struggle after 1900 to preserve the nation's human resources. Like those reforms which sought to improve working and housing conditions for men,

[1] Clifford G. Roe, *The Prodigal Daughter: The White Slave Evil and the Remedy* (Chicago, 1911), 169, 182; Theodore A. Bingham, *The Girl That Disappears: The Real Facts About the White Slave Traffic* (Boston, 1911), 57; Jane Addams, *A New Conscience and an Ancient Evil* (New York, 1913), 17.

[2] Prince A. Morrow, *Social Diseases and Marriage* (New York, 1904), 385.

women, and children, the drive to repress prostitution represented an effort to liberate the human personality from one particular form of demoralizing exploitation. Thus, the influential Committee of Fourteen in New York (organized in 1905 to suppress disorderly saloons) referred to "the economic and political and industrial changes . . . resulting in a new body of law which expresses a growing social conscience with reference to wealth, power and official responsibility." The Committee believed that the time had come "when courageous, fair-minded citizens are willing to preserve moral integrity and conserve human resources in the same spirit that they are striving for political and business integrity and the conservation of material resources." Similarly, the Minneapolis Vice Commission explained that a city must be "judged by its human product as well as by its bank clearings." [8]

The assumption of vice crusaders that their task involved the protection of the nation's human resources — the liberation of personality from the physical and moral bondage of prostitution — resulted in a constructive as well as a repressive program. Arguing that low wages, harsh working conditions, squalid housing, lack of wholesome recreational facilities, and antiquated court and correctional procedures encouraged prostitution, the vice crusader tended to support a wide variety of liberal reforms.

Besides a characteristic emphasis upon the conservation of America's human resources, the Progressive vice campaign was distinguished by a vision of the prostitute as victim both of her environment and sinister "interests" who manipulated her as a tool for their own profits. The Progressive vice reformer invariably interpreted prostitution as a commercialized system, organized and managed by men who worked incessantly to augment both the demand for prosti-

[8] The Research Committee of the Committee of Fourteen, *The Social Evil in New York City: A Study of Law Enforcement* (New York, 1910), xiv, xv; The Vice Commission of Minneapolis, *Report* (1911), 99.

tues and the supply. The venom of the reformer was directed not against the prostitute, but against those third parties — procurers, pimps, madams, proprietors of saloons, hotels, dance halls — who "artificially" stimulated the supply-demand relationship. As the Philadelphia Vice Commission succinctly explained:

> We find that we are dealing with a problem more of men than of women. Commercialized vice is a business conducted largely by men, and the profits go mainly to men. Women are merely the instruments, and rarely receive more than a fraction of their wage. Eliminate the disorderly saloon, the procurer, the cadet, and the abnormal profits of the landlord, and a long stride is taken toward the solution of the vice problem — you have checked the supply and reduced the profits of the business.[4]

In his efforts to reduce the volume of prostitution by strangling the artificially stimulated supply-demand relationship, the vice crusader encountered both indifference and skepticism. To those who argued that prostitution had always existed in the past, successfully evading efforts aimed at suppression, the reformer answered that past failure was no excuse for present apathy. More importantly, the reformer rejected the doctrine of "sexual necessity" or "wild oats" as scientifically unsound. Beneath the façade of Victorian respectability had existed the assumption that male virility and health depended upon at least a minimum indulgence in sexual intercourse. The prostitute existed as the instrument through whom the unmarried male sowed his "wild oats" (while holding the vessel of his sexual satisfaction in contempt). Hence the double standard of morality which protected the promiscuous male but damned the sinning female. The Progressive vice reformer asserted that the doctrine of male sexual necessity was a lie, that incontinence rather than continence resulted in the greater menace to

[4] The Vice Commission of Philadelphia, *Report* (1913), 4-5. Cf. Morals Efficiency Commission of Pittsburgh, *Report and Recommendations* (1913), 6.

health. The historian William E. H. Lecky's famous tribute to the prostitute was presumably invalidated by twentieth-century sex hygiene:

> Herself the supreme type of vice, she is ultimately the most efficient guardian of virtue. But for her, the unchallenged purity of countless happy homes would be polluted, and not a few who, in the pride of their untempted chastity, think of her with an indignant shudder, would have known the agony of remorse and of despair. On that one degraded and ignoble form are concentrated the passions that might have filled the world with shame. She remains, while creeds and civilisations rise and fall, the eternal priestess of humanity, blasted for the sins of the people.[5]

Although a few individuals and organizations had campaigned against the social evil before 1907, the following years witnessed for the first time the rise of a well-organized national vice crusade. The widespread and open prostitution in major American cities, combined with the muckraking and reform temper of the time, was enough in itself to sweep prostitution into the limelight. The so-called white-slave revelations, however, added a unique and explosive dimension to the problem.

The white-slave hysteria erupted in Chicago in 1907. Whereas Lincoln Steffens had concentrated earlier upon the corrupt alliance between politics and business in American cities, George Kibbe Turner in an article for *McClure's* blasted the "tremendous and elaborate organization — financial and political — for creating and attracting and protecting the criminal in Chicago." Like the liquor and gambling traffic, Chicago had organized prostitution "from the supplying of young girls to the drugging of the older and less salable women out of existence — with all the nicety of modern industry. As in the stock-yards, not one shred of

[5] W. E. H. Lecky, *History of European Morals from Augustus to Charlemagne* (New York, 1955), II, 283.

flesh is wasted."[6] A series of white-slave prosecutions inaugurated the same year by Clifford G. Roe, assistant state's attorney, confirmed Turner's serious allegations. In the following year the Federal government acted against the white slavers. Aided by immigration authorities, the United States District Attorney in Illinois opened a series of sensational white-slave trials. Theodore Roosevelt proclaimed America's adherence to the international white-slave treaty formulated in Paris six years earlier, while the immigration laws were tightened to facilitate the prosecution of panders who imported prostitutes from abroad.

By 1910 few doubted that a commercialized network of white slavery existed in America, involving the importation of prostitutes from abroad and the seduction of American girls for immoral purposes. No less an authority than the United States Immigration Commission confirmed the fact in reports delivered in 1909 and 1910. Describing the procurer as a participant in "the most accursed business ever devised by man," the Commission explained how he used his "cunning" understanding of human nature to manipulate the pride, vanity, loyalty, and ambition of girls in the hope of ensnaring them.[7] The Commission's work resulted in the passage of the Mann Act of 1910, which prohibited the transportation of women across state lines for immoral purposes. Between June 1910 and January 1915 more than a thousand white slavers were convicted under this Act.

In 1909 George Kibbe Turner once again directed his muckraking talents to the exposure of commercialized vice, focusing the attention of the nation upon New York. In another *McClure's* article, he lashed out against the Jewish and Italian slavers whose "exploitation of young women as

[6] George Kibbe Turner, "The City of Chicago: A Study of the Great Immoralities," *McClure's Magazine*, XXVIII (1906-1907), 575, 582.

[7] Senate, *Reports of the Immigration Commission: Importation and Harboring of Women for Immoral Purposes*, Document No. 753, 61st. Cong., 3rd. sess., 65.

money-earning machines has reached a development on the East Side of New York probably not equaled anywhere else in the world." [8] A special grand jury investigated the white-slave issue in New York shortly after Turner's indictment. This jury, whose foreman was John D. Rockefeller, Jr., substantiated the existence of a "trafficking in the bodies of women." [9] Shortly afterwards, Rockefeller organized the Bureau of Social Hygiene, a scientific fact-finding body designed to investigate the causes and remedies for prostitution.

Even a superficial sampling of contemporary evidence leaves no doubt that a white-slave traffic existed in the United States. By the nature of the business, however, it is impossible to tell how many procurers actually operated or to ascertain the number of women forced into prostitution by force or fraud. Moreover, Progressive vice crusaders differed in their understanding of the term white slavery. For many, white slavery implied the existence of a national vice syndicate with international connections, whose agents frequently employed force or deception — alcohol, drugs, fake marriages — to trap their victims. [10] At the other extreme, white slavery was interpreted as simply the system

[8] George Kibbe Turner, "The Daughters of the Poor: A Plain Story of the Development of New York City as a Leading Center of the White Slave Trade of the World, under Tammany Hall," *McClure's Magazine*, XXXIV (1909-1910), 54. Also by Turner see "Tammany's Control of New York by Professional Criminals," *McClure's Magazine*, XXXIII (1909), 117-134. The fact that many of the procurers were of foreign birth or parentage, notably Jewish and Italian, resulted frequently in hysterical denunciations. Ernest A. Bell, a Chicago missionary and a leader in the struggle against Chicago's white slavery traffic thus asked whether we shall "defend our American civilization, or lower our flag to the most despicable foreigners — French, Irish, Italians, Jews and Mongolians [on the West coast]? [Ernest A. Bell, ed., *War on the White Slave Trade: A Book Designed to Awaken the Sleeping and to Protect the Innocent* (Chicago, 1909), 260. Bell added that we do not "speak against them for their nationality, but for their crimes."]

[9] *Presentment* of the Additional Grand Jury for the January Term of the Court of General Sessions in the County of New York, in the matter of the investigation as to the alleged existence in the County of New York of an organized traffic in women for immoral purposes (Filed June 29, 1910), 6.

[10] Edwin W. Sims, "The White Slave Trade of To-Day" in Bell, *War on the White Slave Trade*, 56, is a good example of this extreme position.

of commercialized vice involving the saloon, disorderly hotel, dance hall, and similar agencies which found it profitable to stimulate the supply-demand relationship. Finally, some reformers minimized the role of violence or fraud in the white-slave system, arguing that the real enslavement was moral. In the opinion of Maude E. Miner, secretary of the New York Probation Association, the girls were not "except in rare instances, physically enslaved; but through loss of freedom of will and of action, they have been bound to prostitution. Their demoralization of character has constituted moral enslavement." [11]

Judging from the most reliable contemporary evidence, it can be assumed that an indeterminate number of men were engaged in the business of professional seduction and procurement but that no nationally organized white-slave syndicate existed. This was the conclusion reached by both the United States Immigration Commission and the Rockefeller grand jury. However, the latter did find that associations and clubs had existed, composed mainly of procurers, while one was still in operation. This was the New York Independent Benevolent Association, organized in 1894, averaging a membership of 100. The Association aided the member panders in case of illness and assured proper burial rites in case of death. [12]

The disclaimers by official bodies of an organized white-slave traffic did not necessarily influence the large number of Americans who found the concept of a white-slave con-

[11] Maude E. Miner, *The Slavery of Prostitution: A Plea for Emancipation* (New York, 1916), ix.

[12] The United States Immigration Commission reported that it found no evidence "of a great monopolistic [vice] corporation" and did not "believe in its existence." [Senate, *Reports of the Immigration Commission*, 76.] Likewise, the Rockefeller grand jury found "no evidence of an organized traffic in women, but of a traffic carried on by individuals." [*Presentment*, 9.] The Vice Commission of Chicago agreed that while white slavers might work together informally, "it has been demonstrated" that they were "not organized." [*The Social Evil in Chicago. A Study of Existing Conditions with Recommendations by the Vice Commission of Chicago* (1911), 41.]

spiracy more satisfying, particularly where the girls involved were innocents whose only crime had been a misguided love of their seducers. Americans liked their white slavery spiced with drugs, alcohol, and the melodrama of forcible abduction. Thus, in 1914 the New York Committee of Fourteen complained of an unfounded hysteria growing out of newspaper charges that women were being pricked with a poison needle "in the semi-light of a moving picture hall or some such similar place." [13] With exasperation Brand Whitlock complained that "it was always the same: some poor girl had been abducted, borne off to a brothel, ruined by men employed for that purpose, turned over to aged satyrs, and never heard of more." [14] Surely it was easier to wax compassionate over the young innocent forced into hell than to be concerned over the tough, hardened prostitute who wished reformers and uplifters would go there.

A flood of white-slave literature of which Reginald W. Kauffman's *The House of Bondage* is a representative example poured off the presses. This best seller neatly capsuled the popular image of white slavery. Mary Denbigh, a small-town girl, bored at home, overworked, and fearful of the harsh discipline of her parents, is captivated by Max Crossman, a thick-accented German-Jewish procurer. He is her first encounter with what is ostensibly New York sophistication, glamour, and affluence. On the pretence of marriage, Max persuades her to leave for New York with him; and he lures the thoughtless but trusting girl to the receiving room of a bordello, where he quickly renders her senseless with champagne. She awakens the next morning in a locked room without her clothes. Rose Légère, the madam, threat-

[13] Committee of Fourteen, *Annual Report* (1914), 50.

[14] Brand Whitlock, *Forty Years of It* (New York, 1920), 273. Frederic C. Howe was another who believed that the amount of white slavery was disproportionate to the hysteria which the issue generated. He complained that "the press played up every arrest that suggested organized vice, and soon the country was convinced that it harbored an army of white-slavers, mostly recruited from south and central Europe." [*The Confessions of a Reformer* (New York, 1925), 268.]

ens to beat her if she causes trouble. Gradually, Mary (whose name has been changed to the more alluring Violet) learns the nature of the "system" which had ruined her. Rose, it seems, must pay protection money to the cop on the beat, who will turn most of it over to his superior and ultimately to the district boss. She discovers that like Max "there were hundreds of young chaps all over the country who make their living by selling girls to places like this — and worse than this; and there are more who make better livings by making one, or two, or even three girls walk the street for them." Violet learns that she can never hope to buy her way out of the bordello. Although she theoretically earned half the fee for each customer served, "rent and board and *lingerie* demanded, and must needs secure, prices that left each woman hopelessly in debt to the mistress of the house."

With the assistance of a customer Violet manages to escape after a period of weeks — only to learn there was no escape. The "life" had already destroyed her:

> Lacking rouge, her cheeks, once so pink and firm, were pasty and pendant; her lips hung loose; her blue eyes were dull and blurred; even her hair appeared colorless and brittle. Little lines had formed at the corners of her eyes; her skin seemed rough and cracked, other lines were already faintly showing from her nostrils to the corners of her mouth.

The ultimate irony is that not even Rose will accept Violet back into the bordello once the latter realizes she cannot return to normal society. She is doomed to walk the streets until either the river or Potter's field claims her.

Given the reformer's conception of vice as a man's business in which the prostitute was merely a victim of his greed and deception, combined with the shanghaied innocent image which emerges from the white-slave hysteria, it was not surprising that Progressive indignation was directed against the commercial exploiters rather than the prostitute. If nothing else, the Progressive vice crusade humanized the prostitute. Instead of the wicked symbol of disease and lust, she became a somewhat romantic object of charity, compassion, and sympathetic understanding. To the degree that this revised image was combined with a rebellion against the double standard of morality, progress had been made in the long struggle for the equality of the sexes. As Lavinia Dock of the Nurses' Settlement astutely perceived: "If unregulated sexual practice were really necessary for men, there could be no element of shame or wrong in it, and there could therefore, obviously, be none for the women, for no act that is physically necessary is wrong, no matter how primal it may be." [15] In short, if the prostitute sinned, so also did her customer; his lust, after all, created her profession. Men, truly, could not cast the first stone.

In 1900 a Committee of Fifteen was organized to investigate the vice problem in New York City and to assist the state Tenement House Commission of that year in enacting repressive legislation. [16] This Committee was the ancestor of the extraordinary parade of official and unofficial vice commissions which spread from city to city after 1910. Believing that accurate knowledge of existing conditions was the necessary foundation for action, the vice commissions investigated such cities as Chicago, Minneapolis, Syracuse, Cleveland, Baltimore, Philadelphia, Pittsburgh, Little Rock, and Louisville — among others — and the states of Massachusetts, Wisconsin, and Illinois. [17] Their reports not only provide a vivid factual picture of contemporary urban vice but a convenient source for understanding the specific program of repression and reform developed by Progressive vice crusaders. Above all, the vice commissions were striking testi-

[15] Lavinia L. Dock, *Hygiene and Morality* (New York, 1910), 62.

[16] The Committee of Fifteen, *The Social Evil, with Special Reference to Conditions Existing in the City of New York* (New York, 1902).

[17] Other cities included Atlanta; Bridgeport; Denver; Elmira; Grand Rapids; Hartford; Kansas City, Mo.; Lancaster; Lexington; Newark; New York; Portland, Maine; Portland, Ore.; Richmond; St. Louis; Shreveport; and Honolulu.

mony to the fears of Progressive Americans that prostitution had become one of the most serious problems of urban social control.

Since the vice reports were very similar in terms of the conditions discovered and the recommendations for reform, it is necessary to focus attention on only one. Chicago's Commission was not only the first officially appointed by municipal authorities but also its report was among the most influential and comprehensive. Like Chicago's, subsequent reports contained a general description of conditions, a repressive program designed to squelch existing prostitution, and a constructive or preventive program aimed at improving urban living and working conditions.

Uppermost in the Commission's judgment was the conservation of the community's physical and moral resources. Physically, of course, this meant protection from the scourge of venereal disease:

> Prostitution is pregnant with disease, a disease infecting not only the guilty, but contaminating the innocent wife and child in the home with sickening certainty almost inconceivable; a disease to be feared with as great horror as a leprous plague; a disease scattering misery broadcast, and leaving in its wake sterility, insanity, paralysis, the blinded eyes of little babes, the twisted limbs of deformed children, degradation, physical rot and mental decay.

Observing that the social evil was "more degenerating to the morals and ideals of the nation than all other agencies against decency combined," [18] the Commission carefully emphasized the point that vice implied not a simple, casual relationship between a prostitute and her customer, but a carefully manipulated commercialized racket:

> The first truth that the Commission desires to impress upon its citizens of Chicago is the fact that prostitution in this city is a *Commercialized Business* of large propor-

[18] Vice Commission, *The Social Evil in Chicago*, 25, 26.

> tions with tremendous profits of more than Fifteen Million Dollars per year, controlled largely by men, not women. Separate the male exploiter from the problem, and we minimize its extent and abate its flagrant outward expression. In addition we check an artificial stimulus which has been given the *business* so that larger profits may be made by the men exploiters.[19]

The Commission accepted the fact that "so long as there is lust in the hearts of men, [the social evil] will seek out some method of expression."[20] The theory, as Abraham Flexner explained, was that "certain forms of vice represent not the human weakness of the participants but the commercial interest of the exploiter." A repressive program was designed to suppress whatever volume of vice represented "sheer artificial manipulation." The remnant, Flexner continued, was "due to more deep-seated conditions – to individual weakness, depravity, or misfortune and to social and industrial conditions."[21] Unless these were changed, any further attempt at suppression would probably change the form of prostitution rather than reduce its volume. Consequently, the vice reformers leveled their attack primarily upon those individuals and institutions which, for personal profit, advertised vice, stimulated men's demand, and labored to maintain the supply of prostitutes.

As far as the demand factor was concerned, it was the bordello and segregated vice district, the pimp, saloon, disorderly hotel or lodging-house, and dance hall that were most frequently condemned by the Chicago Commission and its successors. In the early twentieth century most large and many smaller American cities contained officially tolerated vice districts.[22] With the connivance of police and politicians, street soliciting was permitted as well as the

[19] *Ibid.*, 32.

[20] *Ibid.*, 27.

[21] Abraham Flexner, "Next Steps in Dealing with Prostitution," *Social Hygiene*, I (1914-1915), 533, 535.

[22] These are described in almost any of the vice commission reports.

operation of parlor houses. Far more important than corruption or graft in explaining the continued existence of these districts were certain popular assumptions which the vice reformers knew they had to discredit in order to succeed. One was the doctrine of male sexual necessity. This was related to the fear that if the districts were closed, respectable women would be attacked. Many erroneously believed that gonorrhea was no more lethal than a "bad cold," harmless and easily cured. In addition, many Americans assumed that the interests of public order and health could best be served if prostitution were segregated — in the face of evidence that segregation and regulation were not succeeding even in Europe.[23] The vice crusaders argued that these assumptions which had historically justified tolerance of vice districts were not only false but that the flagrantly open display of vice in these places artificially stimulated the supply-demand relationship. The bordello, for example, represented a permanent, insatiable market for the procurer and simultaneously increased the demand for prostitutes by providing a convenient, easily accessible rendezvous for promiscuous males. It is important to note that Progressive reformers regarded clandestine or secretive prostitution as a positive gain. To the argument that repression simply scattered prostitution, driving it "underground," they replied that whatever measures reduced the convenience of contact between prostitute and customer represented progress.

The pimp — protector and lover of the prostitute — was another key figure in the system of commercialized vice. His task was to develop trade for his girls. Though he was often a brutal tyrant, the prositute rarely betrayed her pimp. As the United States Immigration Commission explained, he bound her to him "in part by her real affection for him

[23] The most comprehensive and influential criticism of the segregation, licensing, and regulation program was Abraham Flexner, *Prostitution in Europe* (New York, 1914). This was one of the research projects sponsored by Rockefeller's Bureau of Social Hygiene.

(in many cases he is her first lover), by the care which he gives her, by the threats which he makes against her, by even his brutality." [24]

Progressive reformers frequently condemned the disorderly hotels and lodging houses which catered to the vice trade. Their relationship to the demand factor is obvious. In return for the payment of profitable rentals, the proprietors of these places were glad to accommodate streetwalkers and other prostitutes. Particularly objectionable to reformers were the tenement landlords and agents who rented apartments to prostitutes in poor residential districts, thus exposing the children of workers and immigrants to the social evil at a tender age. An investigator for the Chicago Commission discovered that forty-four out of sixty-five real estate agents and owners he questioned were willing to rent their property for a "sporting house." [25]

The vice commissions uniformly stressed the close relationship between the saloon and commercialized prostitution. Indeed, the saloon had no equal as an instigator of demand. Saloonkeepers, reformers complained, encouraged prostitutes to solicit in their establishments. In a private room to the rear, the prostitute and her customer might have a few drinks before retiring to a nearby disorderly hotel or flat. Under a kickback arrangement, the prostitute would be served colored water instead of liquor. If the saloon owned rooms and apartments in the same building, the prostitute led her customer to one of these. In this case, the saloonkeepers profited from both rental of the rooms and from drinks carried upstairs. Finally, the saloonkeeper had a vested interest in the system of segregated vice districts. He

[24] Senate, *Reports of the Immigration Commission*, 76. For a modern statement on the relationship between prostitute and pimp see John M. Murtaugh and Sara Harris, *Cast the First Stone* (New York, 1958), 109-124.

[25] Vice Commission, *The Social Evil in Chicago*, 89. In an investigation of New York vice sponsored by the Bureau of Social Hygiene, it was discovered that only seventeen out of 122 real estate agents refused to rent property for immoral purposes. [George J. Kneeland, *Commercialized Prostitution in New York City* (New York, 1913), 115-116.]

supplied bordellos which relied heavily upon liquor sales as a source of prosperity.

The combination of saloon and nearby dance hall was particularly vicious in the eyes of reformers. An evening at the dance hall was a common form of recreation for the urban poor. Admission was cheap. Young girls came to dance, meet men, and generally enjoy the excitement and gaiety. The Commission counted 275 dance halls in Chicago in 1910. Proprietors made no effort to guard against the presence of disreputable persons. Prostitutes and procurers "continually on the lookout for new victims" frequented the halls. Conditions in one of these dance halls were described by a commission investigator:

> A number of young girls were in the balcony drinking with fellows between dances. Investigator met girl who said she was 17 years of age this month. He danced with three different girls, two of whom proposed going to a hotel if he had the money, the third girl said they could get a room on West Madison street.[26]

The Citizens' Committee of Portland, Maine, complained that there was "no public resort for the youth in the city more likely to lead to habits of vice than the public dance halls, when improperly conducted and allowed to go unregulated and uncontrolled."[27] George J. Kneeland, one of the most experienced vice investigators of the period, argued that "no places of amusement are so filled with moral dangers to boys and girls as certain public dance halls in New York City":

> Wine, whisky, and beer, freely sold in connection with certain public dances, are responsible for much vulgarity and obscenity. Young girls have been seen to yield themselves in wild abandon to their influence, and have been carried half fainting to dark corners of the hall and there,

[26] Vice Commission, *The Social Evil in Chicago*, 185, 186.

[27] Citizens' Committee of Portland (Maine), *First Report*, 17.

almost helpless, have been subjected to the most indecent advances.[28]

In order to reduce the volume of prostitution by restricting the sources of supply and demand, the Chicago Vice Commission recommended a series of repressive measures. The most important of these included the closing of the segregated district; a relentless pursuit of procurers and pimps; regulation and supervision of hotels, rooming houses, saloons, dance halls, and any other agencies which profited from prostitution. A survey of twenty-five vice investigations between 1910 and 1915 disclosed that all supported a policy of repression involving the elimination of segregated vice districts. Forty-four percent of them demanded the licensing and control of rooming or lodging-houses, while forty-eight percent favored the licensing and control of hotels. Almost half the commissions recommended the prohibition of private booths, screens, and connecting rooms in saloons; thirty-two percent demanded the licensing and supervision of dance halls, including personal patrol by a woman police officer.[29]

The vice commissions offered a constructive as well as a repressive policy. They realized that a lasting reduction in the volume of prostitution depended, in part, upon improving urban living and working conditions. Similarly, the successful rehabilitation of prostitutes could not be accomplished by fines or sentences to the workhouse and prison. Court and correctional procedures had to be reformed.

Most Progressive vice reformers thought that poverty and low wages, if not a direct cause of the moral breakdown of women, were at least contributing factors. "Is it any

[28] Kneeland, *Commercialized Prostitution in New York City*, 70. Kneeland added (p. 72) that "some of the girls who frequent these public dance halls reveal their loose morals by their manners and action, but many are innocent working girls who seek legitimate recreation." The sinister element was the "usually well-dressed, well-mannered" pimp who attended "with the cold-blooded purpose of finding new subjects of debauchery and of subsequent exploitation for gain."

[29] Joseph Mayer, "The Passing of the Red Light District — Vice Investigations and Results," *Social Hygiene*, IV (1918), 197-209.

wonder," asked the Chicago Commission, "that a tempted girl who receives only six dollars per week working with her hands sells her body for twenty-five dollars per week when she learns there is a demand for it and men are willing to pay the price?" In the blunt words of the Senate Vice Committee of Illinois, poverty was "the principal cause, direct and indirect, of prostitution." The pivotal recommendation of the Illinois Commission was the enactment of a minimum wage law pertaining to women and minors.[30] Frequently coupled with the demand for higher wages was the suggestion that employers in stores and factories provide adequate social and sanitary facilities for female employees. Thus, the large army of Progressive vice reformers lent their support to the drive for increased wages and improved working conditions.

No constructive measure was more emphasized by vice reformers than the need for wholesome urban recreational facilities. Maude E. Miner explained that "the instinct to play and to associate with companions is natural and normal." Unfortunately, because our cities had failed to satisfy this instinct, "private commercial interests have exploited for great financial gain this love of pleasure."[31] Thus the vice commissions and others frequently recommended the establishment of social centers in schools and churches and the expansion of the city's playground and athletic facilities.

Vice reformers often supported the nationwide Progressive campaign to improve urban housing conditions. Like the "housers," they assumed that overcrowded and squalid housing deteriorated individual moral standards and loosened the controlling bonds of family life, thereby making the individual more susceptible to the temptations of vice than if he lived in sanitary, comfortable surroundings.

[30] Vice Commission, *The Social Evil in Chicago*, 43; Senate Vice Committee, State of Illinois, *Report* (1916), 23.

[31] Miner, *Slavery of Prostitution*, 79.

According to the Chicago Commission, it was time that "better housing conditions should be studied and applied. The population in certain quarters of the city is becoming more and more congested. Aside from the dangers resulting from insanitary conditions, bad housing breeds vice and crime." [32]

A problem to which vice reformers devoted considerable thought was that of devising satisfactory court and correctional procedures. The occasional roundups and fines of prostitutes or madams were worse than useless; they amounted to a *de facto* licensing system. Similarly, short prison terms did not aid the prostitute, if she so desired, in returning to normal life. The Chicago Commission recommended an end to the fine system. It hoped that municipal authorities instead would establish a detention home for women controlled by probation officers and an industrial home with hospital accommodations. The Commission also advised the segregation of hardened delinquents from novices combined with "more enlightened methods of care and education" for the latter. Subsequent commissions endorsed these same reforms as well as closer supervision of the mentally sub-average girls and women often lured into prostitution. If the attitude of Progressive reformers was harshly punitive toward procurers, pimps, and other agents of commercialized vice, their attitude toward the prostitute was sympathetic and correctional.

As part of their constructive program, vice reformers joined with the vigorous sex or social hygiene movement of the period in an effort to break down the barriers of ignorance, prudery, and false modesty. "The policy of silence," they argued, had failed. [33] Complaining that ignor-

[32] Vice Commission, *The Social Evil in Chicago*, 245; Cf. Wisconsin Legislative Committee to Investigate the White Slave Traffic and Kindred Subjects, *Report and Recommendations* (1914), 122.

[33] William T. Foster, *The Social Emergency: Studies in Sex Hygiene and Morals* (Cambridge, Mass., 1914), 6. In a sense, the vice crusade was part of a broader social hygiene movement which originated in 1901 when a Com-

ance of sexual realities menaced the welfare of young girls (and boys), they pushed a program of sex education in public and normal schools and stressed the importance of parental responsibility in enlightening their children. A key plank in their program of sex education was the abandonment of the doctrine of male sex necessity which had justified "wild oats" and the double moral standard. Above all, they sought to impress upon the American people the serious physical consequences of venereal disease. In this connection, they fought for legislation to curb the quack doctors and distributors of ineffective remedies. Still another folk superstition was described by the Indiana State Board of Health as the "Emission Lie": "It is used as a bogy man to scare a young man into fits and make him believe that an automatic function of nature for the relief of overcharged seminal vesicles, is an indication he is suffering from sexual weakness and is on the road to the mad house." [34] Like the doctrine of sexual necessity, the Emission Lie too easily resulted in a tolerance of commercialized vice.

In the opinion of some, the efforts of the vice reformers and the sex hygiene movement succeeded too well. One critic complained that "a wave of sex hysteria and sex discussion seems to have invaded this country. Our former reticence of matters of sex is giving way to a frankness that would even startle Paris." As to the idea of white slavery, it was "not only strongly established in the popular mind, but is one in which the public veritably revels." [35] A flood

mittee of Seven of the New York Medical Society delivered an important report on the subject of venereal disease. The chairman of this Committee, Dr. Prince A. Morrow, published his influential book *Social Diseases and Marriage* in 1904 and was active in forming the American Society of Social and Moral Prophylaxis the following year. By 1912 eighteen social hygiene associations had been formed in American cities and states. This organizational activity was supplemented by a voluminous literature on sex hygiene.

[34] Indiana State Board of Health, *Social Hygiene vs. The Sexual Plagues, with their Rapid Invasion of the American Home* (1910), 22.

[35] "Sex O'Clock in America," *Current Opinion*, LV (1913), 113; "Popular Gullibility as Exhibited in the New White Slavery Hysteria," *Current Opinion*, LVI (1914), 129.

of white-slave plays, novels, and movies caused some to fear that the whole campaign for sexual enlightenment was being degraded by commercial-minded hucksters.

At least one definite conclusion can be reached concerning the vice crusade of the Progressive era, which culminated in the zealous repressive campaign of the Commissions on Training Camp Activities during World War I. It produced an impressive amount of legislation. In 1910 twenty-two states and territories had legislation pertaining to pandering; the comparable figure for 1921 was forty-eight. During those same years most states enacted injunction and abatement laws — by which private citizens could restrain the operation of bordellos by means of a court order — and included venereal disease among those legally reportable to health boards. Many states established reformatories for women, prohibited venereal disease advertisements to eliminate the fake nostrum peddlers, and required medical examinations for venereal disease prior to marriage. At the same time the reformers succeeded in closing up the vice districts of many American cities — a significant accomplishment which frequently followed the investigation and report of a vice commission.[36]

It is difficult to say, however, whether the pandering laws, the closing of the segregated districts, and the sex hygiene legislation reduced the total volume of prostitution. It frequently happened that the closing of a city's vice district simply scattered the prostitutes elsewhere in the city or drove them to surrounding communities. Although St. Louis closed its district in 1914, it was reported that "street solicitation and private houses have largely increased." Similarly, although San Francisco closed more than 200 houses in 1917, it seemed that prostitution still flourished "apparently

[36] Joseph Mayer, *The Regulation of Commercialized Vice: An Analysis of the Transition from Segregation to Repression in the United States* (New York, 1922), 31.

with the connivance of the police in scattered hotels and apartment houses." The repression of the red-light district in Kansas City, Missouri, resulted in an immediate increase in street-walking; and repression in Little Rock, Arkansas, forced a migration of prostitutes across the river where they continued to operate.[37] After an analysis of the repressive campaign in New York City between 1900 and 1931, W. C. Waterman could reach no definite conclusion concerning the effect upon the total volume of prostitution. Very definitely, however, repression did force commercialized vice to change its form of expression. Waterman found that the red-light house and street-walking had virtually disappeared. On the other hand, the amount of tenement "call flat" prostitution had increased; the private "dance studio" had replaced the "massage parlor" of the past; and the closed dance hall replaced the saloon and "public" dance halls of the past.[38]

In summary, the Progressive vice reformer's view of prostitution as a commercialized system of exploitation inspired a policy of repression directed against the promoters who stimulated the supply-demand relationship and thus contributed to the decline of the red-light district in American cities. This transition from open and flagrant street-walking and segregated red-light districts to more clandestine operations was viewed by vice reformers as a distinct gain:

> It had become patent that segregation did nothing that was claimed for it. On the contrary, conditions flagrant and intolerable had come in its wake. Segregation had really never segregated. Regulation and medical inspection proved to be failures, and the district the most virulent source of venereal infection. The district enabled vice to organize on a vast scale and greatly augment its

[37] "How St. Louis Treats Prostitutes," *Survey*, XXXVI (1916), 497; "Church Crusade on the Barbary Coast," *Survey*, XXXVII (1916-1917), 695; Karl L. Schreiber, "The Closing of Houses of Prostitution in Kansas City," National Conference of Charities and Correction, *Proceedings* (1914), 243; Louis Witt, "Reform in Little Rock," *Ibid.*, 245.

[38] Willoughby C. Waterman, *Prostitution and Its Repression in New York City, 1900-1931* (New York, 1932), 149-150.

> traffic. The resultant advertisement made vice more easy of access and provided a source of sexual brutalization and degeneracy. Segregation corrupted the police force, stimulated illegal sale of liquor, increased crime and debauchery and fostered sexual perversion.[39]

The crusade against commercialized prostitution which erupted in the decade after 1907 represented, in broader perspective, one of the most significant efforts of Progressive America to conserve the nation's human resources. It was an experiment in social control, closely related to the attempts of other reformers to improve urban living and working conditions and to the struggle to dispel ignorance and misconceptions surrounding the subject of sex. Unlike the prohibitionists who labored to abolish the evils connected with alcohol by abolishing alcohol, the Progressive vice reformers focused their wrath instead upon the interests which they claimed corrupted and exploited for personal gain the natural sexual instincts of others; and they shifted attention from prostitution as an expression of individual moral perversity to prostitution as a business enterprise which flourished on ignorance and socio-economic deprivation.

[39] Mayer, "The Passing of the Red Light District," 198.

Prostitution, the Alien Woman and the Progressive Imagination, 1910-1915

EGAL FELDMAN
Wisconsin State University, Superior

IN NO PERIOD OF AMERICAN HISTORY DID THE CUSTODIANS OF AMERICAN morality direct more serious attention to the eradication of prostitution than they did in the few years preceding World War I.[1] With the passage of the Mann Act in 1910 their efforts also embraced the interests of the national government. Ministers, social workers, men and women of medicine, science and letters all joined in the unusually massive assault. Their united determination to eradicate white slavery reminds one of the previous crusade against black servitude. In both cases its participants first pressed for international and interstate regulation of the traffic. Rescue homes in bleak urban areas suggest memories of the underground railroad; while an abundant literature designed to expose the intricate, sinister workings of the institution leave the impression of another chapter in the writings of abolitionism.[2]

The energetic outburst against sexual immorality, however, grew out of a relatively new presumption; it was predicated upon the conviction that society's and man's behavior can be controlled and regulated; that man and his environment are both perfectible. Edward A. Ross' *Social Control* (1901), or Ellen H. Richards' *Euthenics: the Science of Con-*

1 Between 1890 and 1909 the *Readers' Guide to Periodical Literature* lists 36 entries under the subject of "Prostitution"; between the years 1910 and 1914 entries climb sharply to 156 and drop to 41 from 1915 to 1924.

2 The analogy was first presented in Jane Addams, *A New Conscience and an Ancient Evil* (New York, 1912), pp. 4-5; for a review of the literature see Louis Filler, *Crusaders for American Liberalism* (Yellow Springs, Ohio, 1950), pp. 285-95.

trollable Environment (1910), are examples of books which periodically re-enforced such hopes, infusing progressive uplifters with the confidence that success would be theirs.[3] "Whatever one may hold as to ultimate dealings with the subject," remarked the prominent physician Abraham Flexner, in 1914, "it is clear that prostitution is at any rate a modifiable phenomenon." Commissioned in 1912 by the New York Bureau of Social Hygiene to investigate European prostitution, Flexner grew confident that within man's reach was the power, if not to eradicate totally, certainly to minimize the age-old custom of commercialized sexual pleasure. "Civilization," wrote Flexner with a militant optimism so characteristic of his generation,

> has stripped for a life-and-death wrestle with tuberculosis, alcohol and other plagues. It is on the verge of a similar struggle with the crasser forms of commercialized vice. Sooner or later, it must fling down the gauntlet to the whole horrible thing. This will be the real contest—a contest that will tax the courage, the self-denial, the faith, the resources of humanity to their utmost.[4]

The Flexner report on vice, published in 1914, drove forward another point, that prostitution was an urban problem whose precise character was largely dependent upon the size of the town.[5] The belief that temptations of modern urban living could easily overwhelm the virtuous was, in fact, a somewhat old but typical notion of the age. "Thrilled by the mere propinquity of city excitements and eager to share" in them, observed the Head Worker, Jane Addams, the young and innocent found it enormously difficult to "keep to the gray and monotonous path of regular work." This particular observation was meant for the benefit of rustic maidens who found themselves in the big metropolis, alone and unattended by family or friends for the first time. "From the point of view of the traffickers in white slaves," Miss Addams noticed, "it is much cheaper and safer to procure country girls . . . because they are much more easily secreted than girls from the city. A country girl entering a vicious life quickly feels the disgrace and soon becomes too broken-spirited and discouraged to make any effort to escape." [6]

Yet it was the condition of the unemployed, friendless immigrant girl that seemed to worry her most. "Loneliness and detachment which the city tends to breed in its inhabitants is easily intensified in such a girl

[3] For an interesting discussion of the influence of Edward A. Ross see Christopher Lasch, *The New Radicalism in America, 1889-1963* (New York, 1965), p. 170; Ellen A. Richards, *Euthenics: the Science of Controllable Environment* (Boston, 1910).

[4] Abraham Flexner, *Prostitution in Europe* (New York, 1914), pp. vii, 395-402.

[5] *Ibid.*, p. 5.

[6] Addams, *New Conscience*, pp. 145, 147, 216.

into isolation and a desolating feeling of belonging nowhere," warned Miss Addams. "At such moments a black oppression, the instinctive fear of solitude, will send a lonely girl restlessly to walk the streets even when she is 'too tired to stand,' and where her desire for companionship in itself constitutes a grave danger." [7]

To many Americans, less sensitive, less insightful than Jane Addams, the discovery of a thriving existence of commercialized prostitution in the midst of American cities became the basis for a blanket indictment of urban living. "What forces are there, hidden in American cities, which are dragging them . . . into a state of semibarbarism?" queried a leading popularizer of urban mismanagement and vice in 1907.[8] To many the city emerged as a monster, a veritable house of ill repute. "If I lived in the country and had a young daughter I would go to any length of hardship and privation myself rather than allow her to go into the city to work or to study" was a typical reaction. "The best and the surest way for parents of girls in the country to protect them from the clutches of the 'white slaver' is to keep them in the country." [9] That the city was an illusive trap set carefully for country virgins was a notion strongly endorsed in these years by numerous respected educators, clerics and lawyers.[10] But what is of greater consequence here was the prevalent notion that behind the scenes of urban vice were found the nation's newcomers. Surely it was the foreigner, a good many upright Americans were convinced, who was organizing, supporting and thriving upon the lucrative traffic of prostitution.[11] One might say that there was a nativist assault on prostitution which envisioned well-organized networks of vice connecting European and American cities; export-import syndicates thriving on the trade of loose women, diabolical agencies forever searching for new opportunities in the American metropolis.

Southern Italians and Russian Jews came under special attack by those who dreamed of a purer America. Behind men like Paul Kelly and Jimmie Kelly "and other Italians masquerading under Irish names" were detected the networks of international vice.[12] Serious discussions of procuring and pimping inevitably led to an anti-Semitic rhetoric. "It is an absolute fact that corrupt Jews are now the backbone of the loathsome

[7] *Ibid.*, p. 89.

[8] George Kibbe Turner, "The City of Chicago, A Study of the Great Immoralities," *McClure's Magazine*, XXVIII (Apr. 1907), 575; S. S. McClure, "The Tammanyizing of a Civilization," *McClure's Magazine*, XXXIV (Nov. 1909), 127.

[9] Ernest A. Bell, ed., *Fighting the Traffic in Young Girls, or War on the White Slave Trade* (Chicago, 1910), pp. 70-71.

[10] See, for example, the long list of contributors to this volume (Bell, *Fighting the Traffic . . .*) on the Title Page.

[11] *Ibid.*, pp. 181-82.

[12] McClure, *McClure's Magazine*, XXVIII, 117, 124-25, 126-27; Bell, pp. 71-72, 187-88.

traffic in New York and Chicago," wrote one irate puritan with dogmatic certainty.[13] It was "the Jewish dealer in women, a product of New York politics, who has vitiated, more than any other single agency, the moral life of the great cities of America in the past ten years," wrote George Kibbe Turner in the respectable and widely read *McClure's Magazine* in 1909. Turner's influential articles, appearing regularly in this popular organ of muckrakers, had for years contained a sharp nativist ring, and his animosity was aimed most directly at New York's Jewry. The traffic in women, wrote Turner, was lodged solidly in the hands of "a large number of criminals," most of whom were "Austrian, Russian, and Hungarian Jews." Well guarded by corrupt Tammany politicians, the lewd enterprise had centered its headquarters in New York City, under the guise of a "Jewish society that goes under the name of the New York Independent Benevolent Association." This organization, explained Turner,

> was started in 1896 by a party of dealers who were returning from attendance at the funeral of Sam Engel, a brother of Martin Engel, the Tammany leader of the red-light assembly district. In the usual post-funeral discussion of the frailty of human life, the fact was brought out that the sentiment of the Jews of the East Side against men of their profession barred them generally from societies giving death benefits, and even caused discrimination against them in the purchase of burial-places in the cemetery. A society was quickly incorporated under the laws of New York, and a burial-plot secured and enclosed in Washington cemetery in Brooklyn.[14]

Through the good offices of the Benevolent Association, houses of prostitution in numerous American cities were amply supplied. Focusing less upon any one particular nationality or ethnic group one commentator accused all aliens at once, and warned that

> unless we make energetic and successful war upon the red light districts . . . we shall have Oriental brothel slavery thrust upon us . . . with all its unnatural and abnormal practices, established among us by the French traders. Jew traders, too, will people our "levees" with Polish Jewesses and any others who will make money for them. Shall we defend our American civilization, or lower our flag to the most despicable foreigners—French, Irish, Italians, Jews and Mongolians? . . . On both coasts and throughout all our cities, only an awakening of the whole Christian conscience and intelligence can save us from the importation of Parisian and Polish pollution, which is already corrupting the manhood and youth of every large city in the nation.[15]

13 Turner, "The Daughters of the Poor," *McClure's Magazine*, XXXIV, 57-58.
14 Turner, *McClure's Magazine*, XXXIV, 57-58.
15 Bell, pp. 260-62.

The link between prostitution and the alien was solidified in the public imagination when confirmed by government investigators. The subject of prostitution served as fodder for the more nativistic passages of the United States Immigration report of 1911 and left the impression, at times, that vice followed immigration as night does day. "A very large proportion of the pimps living in the United States are foreigners," reported the federal investigators, making special note of the fact that "Egyptian, French, Chinese, Belgian, Spanish, Japanese, Greek, Slavic, Hungarian, Italian, and Russian" were the nationalities involved most frequently in the traffic of women. Failing to uncover any evidence of an international "monopolistic corporation whose business it is to import and exploit these unfortunate women," the commissioners were, nevertheless, convinced that there were gentlemen's agreements among foreign procurers, singling out the French and Jews for special attention. "There are large numbers of Jews scattered throughout the United States," they wrote, "who seduce and keep girls. Some of them are engaged in importation, but apparently they prey rather upon young girls whom they find on the street, in the dance halls, and similar places, and whom, by the methods already indicated — love-making and pretenses of marriage — they deceive and ruin." The Italian panderer, they noted, was "vicious and criminal," and was more "feared by their women than are the pimps of other nationalities." [16]

The nativist assault on prostitution proved awkward and somewhat embarrassing to the liberal friends of aliens who were equally swept up by the desire to eradicate commercialized vice. American Jews, for example, were stunned by Turner's revelations, resenting especially his blanket indictment of an entire immigrant group, the Eastern European Jew. Yet subsequent investigations proved that a considerable number of Jews were involved in the business of commercialized vice. The prominent rabbinical figure, Dr. Emil G. Hirsch, preached a special sermon at the Sinai Temple in Chicago on September 25, 1909, when he learned that the President of a neighboring congregation was deeply implicated. "Over on the West Side," thundered Rabbi Hirsch, "the worst thing has occurred that has ever happened to our race. The name of God and Jew has been profaned as never before." In the wake of this revelation, Jews of Chicago, led by Adolf Kraus, President of the local B'nai B'rith Chapter, and Clifford G. Roe, a distinguished attorney, laid plans to combat the scourge of white slavery in their midst.[17]

[16] United States Immigration Commission, *Abstracts of Reports of the Immigration Commission*, II, 61st Congress 3d Sess. (Washington, D.C., 1911), pp. 342-43.

[17] McClure, *McClure's Magazine*, XXVIII, 122-23.

There were, in fact, two separate campaigns during these years, a nativistic attack on prostitution with all its ugly xenophobic overtones paralleled by an anti-nativist outburst. Whereas the former crusade was irrational, evangelical, uncompromising and completely divorced from the humanitarianism of the early twentieth century, the latter was closely associated with the temper of the social gospel, the social settlement and the more rational humanitarian ambitions of progressivism. The latter's task was more complex, for not only did the anti-nativist assume the responsibility of scientifically searching for the true causes of the disease, but hoped also to clear the fog of prejudice which engulfed the entire issue. In short, he hoped to explain the causes and discover solutions for the problem of prostitution and at the same time to disassociate the reputation of the immigrant from commercialized vice.

Obviously the attack on prostitution was not always polarized between the friends and enemies of aliens. Many of its participants fell somewhere between the two extremes. Nevertheless, in order to appreciate fully the precise nature of the crusade, one should be aware of its emotional extremities.

That the immigrant was a victim as well as a cause was conceded by many. If the tentacles of the "syndicate" stretched across the ocean, the first victim, it was noticed, was usually an innocent unprotected young immigrant. "In other words," explained one investigator, the "watchers for human prey scan the immigrants as they come down the gang plank of a vessel which has just arrived and 'spot' the girls who are unaccompanied by fathers, mothers, brothers or relatives to protect them." Once detected, the victim was approached "by a man who speaks her language." Tempting "promises of an easy time, plenty of money, fine clothes and the usual stock of allurements—or a fake marriage" follow. "In some instances the hunters really marry the victims." If this cultivated approach proved ineffective "intoxication and drugging" were applied to reduce the victim to a state of helplessness and total servitude.

> Once a white slave is sold and landed in a house or dive she becomes a prisoner . . . [in]a room having but one door, to which the keeper holds the key. . . . What mockery it is to have in our harbor in New York the Statue of Liberty with outstretched arms welcoming the foreign girl to the land of the free! How she must sneer at it and rebuke the country with such an emblematic monument at its very gate when she finds here a slavery whose chains bind the captive more securely than those in the country from which she has come! [18]

This tendency to bewail the innocence of the alien female threatened by

18 Bell, pp. 58-59, 153; Turner, *McClure's Magazine*, XXXIV, 46, 54.

the predatory desire of her male counterpart revealed an ambivalent strain in the American attack upon vice. It was also echoed by the United States Immigration Commission's investigations and reports, so frequently referred to by contemporary journalists writing on the subject of white slavery. Attributing the cause of prostitution to the coming of the New Immigration, federal investigators, nevertheless, oozed compassion and concern over the fate of the immigrant female. "The alien woman is ignorant of the language of the country, knows nothing beyond a few blocks of the city where she lives, has usually no money, and no knowledge of the rescue homes and institutions which might help her," they reported in 1910. Even then nativist Turner waxed "melancholy" over the discovery of "little Italian peasant girls, taken from various dens, where they lay, shivering and afraid, under the lighted candles and crucifixes in their bedrooms." [19]

That the immigrant girl was the major casualty of commercialized vice was, in fact, underscored by a number of investigations conducted independently by private agencies during these years. One, launched in Chicago in 1910 by a Church Federation meeting "composed of clergy representing six hundred congregations," requested the Mayor of Chicago to "appoint a commission made up of men and women who command the respect and confidence of the public at large." The Mayor complied, and in March 1910 appointed a Vice Commission consisting of medical and legal experts, Protestant, Catholic and Jewish clergy, leading businessmen and sociologists.[20] The final draft of the Commission's report conceded that "the immigrant woman furnishes a large supply to the demand," but it placed the blame on the lack of protection offered to her by government and private agencies. "Generally virtuous when she comes to this country," it explained, "she is ruined and exploited because there is no adequate protection and assistance given her after she reaches the United States." [21] It was for this reason that Jane Addams and her Hull House staff insisted so strongly upon the need for governmental protective machinery to guard the "foreign girl who speaks no English, who has not the remotest idea in what part of the city her fellow-countrymen live, who does not know the police station or any agency to which she may apply" during the first days following her arrival. It was at this vulnerable juncture, Chicago's social workers warned, that the young immigrant was "as valuable to a white trafficker as a girl imported directly for the trade." [22]

19 Turner, *McClure's Magazine*, XXXIV, 58; *Abstracts of Reports of the Immigration Commission*, II, 342.

20 The Vice Commission of Chicago, *The Social Evil in Chicago* (Chicago, 1911), pp. 1-5.

21 *Ibid.*, p. 40.

22 Addams, *A New Conscience*, pp. 26, 40.

Indeed, a New York City investigation in 1913 indicated some surprise that, given the deplorable conditions of immigrant life, the involvement of the alien woman in prostitution was not larger. Conducted by Katharine Bement Davis, Superintendent of the State Reformatory for Women at Bedford Hills, New York, the study was based upon the records of a few thousand prostitutes committed to state reformatories. It was mostly concerned with the relationship of prostitution to the city's heterogeneous population, and concluded that American-born women contributed overwhelmingly more than their proportion to New York prostitution.[23] But even here the immigrant was not handed a total clearance, for the sins of his children devolved upon him. If the foreign-born contributed less than their expected quota, the group that contributed "out of proportion to its percentage in the population" was their American-born daughters. Miss Davis admitted, of course, that there was a reasonable explanation for this.

> When we remember that here we have a group in which the fathers and mothers belong to a civilization with speech, tradition and habits different from those of the country in which they are living, the children, native-born Americans with American companions and American schooling, adopt ideals often not of the highest and are very apt, even when quite young, to feel that they know more than their parents.[24]

America's discovery of prostitution and its growing conviction that its roots were European gave rise to a demand, advocated especially by nativists, that immigrant ladies of doubtful behavior be immediately deported; but a number of reformers, friends of aliens, counseled differently. "Certainly the immigration laws might do better than to send a girl back to her parents, diseased and disgraced, because America had failed to safeguard her virtue from the machinations of well-known but unrestrained criminals," warned one of the nation's leading social workers. "Certainly no one will doubt that it is the business of the city itself to extend much more protection to young girls who so thoughtlessly walk upon its streets."[25] Kate Waller Barrett, an authority on the deportation of prostitutes, and a special adviser to the government on matters of immigration, objected also to rash and heartless solutions. In her reports she stressed the social injustice, the misunderstanding that immigrant women were constantly subjected to. "Nothing is more in keeping with the wishes of a man when he has gotten a woman in trouble than to have her

23 George J. Kneeland, *Commercialized Prostitution in New York City* (New York, 1913). pp. 163-67, 198-99.

24 *Ibid.*, pp. 167-68, 200-4.

25 Addams, *A New Conscience*, pp. 34-35.

deported, and thus put the ocean between them," she argued on one occasion, as only a woman of determined militancy could.[26] A holder of doctoral degrees in medicine and science, President of the National Council of Women, Mrs. Barrett was appointed as Special Agent of the United States Immigration Service in 1914. Her task was to join with European officials in discussions concerning the relationship of the growing European immigration to the United States and the white slave traffic. Her final report of this experience, insisting that the roots of prostitution must be sought in the trans-Atlantic voyage, stressed the necessity for preventive and precautionary measures on board the immigrant steamers. Steamship companies should provide free transportation to woman supervisors, she felt, and urged the separation of sexes in both living and recreation and the prohibition of crew members from visiting the steerage quarters "except as their duties require."[27] Focusing specially upon the case of the deportee, she urged that an international committee be formed to grapple with the problem. "The question of the unattached immigrant woman is comparatively new," she pointed out, quite different from that of the male immigrant with whom America has had years of experience. A woman accused of prostitution must not be flung out of the country upon flimsy evidence, without due process of law.[28]

To remove the conditions responsible for the "fall" of alien woman was a task pre-World War I reformers undertook, and they began the moment the unaccompanied female arrived. Chicago's Immigrants' Protective League was founded in part for that reason. Its first Annual Report in 1910 talked ominously of immigrant girls who failed to arrive at their expected destination, whose "ultimate fate . . . could never be discovered." Its agents kept in constant communication with Ellis Island authorities, in part to request lists of names of alien women traveling alone to Chicago and other interior cities. Officials of the League awaited their arrival, and ordered an immediate search for those who did not appear at the time expected.[29] Each year the League published its list of "Girls We Have Been Unable to Locate," and the names of the missing continued to multiply. According to Grace Abbott, Director of the League, a 10 per cent annual rate of disappearance was not unusual during the years of the

[26] Frank B. Lenz, ed., *Immigration—Some New Phases of the Problem* (San Francisco, 1915), p. 10.

[27] United States Department of Labor, Bureau of Immigration, *Annual Report of the Commissioner General of Immigration to the Secretary of Labor, 1914* (Washington, D. C., 1915), pp. 14, 363, 380-82.

[28] *Ibid.*, pp. 384-86.

[29] Edith Abbott, *Immigration: Select Documents and Case Records* (Chicago, 1924), pp. 608-12; Immigrants' Protective League, *Fourth Annual Report of the Immigrants' Protective League for the Year Ending January 1st, 1913* (Chicago, 1913), p. 13.

great migration.[30] Worried kin turned frequently to the League for information, which occasionally confirmed their worst fears. "We learned that she had been called for by a notoriously disreputable man and taken to a rooming house on Washington near Halsted," reported League officials after an investigation of the whereabouts of a young Lithuanian girl in 1913. "Everything pointed to the conclusion that the girl either voluntarily or by deception was leading an immoral life, but neither we nor the agencies to which the case was reported could locate the girl." [31]

Immigrant lodging houses and hotels were for this reason frequently attacked by reformers and scrutinized periodically by government and private agents. The insufficient care exercised by such institutions "in discharging young immigrant women and girls who have been placed in their charge by immigration authorities" was a frequent cause of complaint. That a number of such homes served as recruiting centers for houses of prostitution was established by a number of investigations.[32] The founding of the Clara de Hirsch Home for Immigrant Girls in March 1904 was motivated by such discoveries. Its aim, as expressed by its founders, was "to protect the girl at her very entrance to this country, to afford her temporary shelter, to see to it that she reaches her prospective destination in safety." Immediate priority was extended to those without friends or relatives "or such who are called for by single men or married men without their wives." Once housed, declared a spokesman for the Home in 1912, "we do not permit any girls to leave our premises without making a thorough personal investigation of the prospective living quarters . . . surroundings, the number of lodgers, and rooming facilities," and "are constantly studying new measures and means for the safeguarding of our girls." [33]

For similar reasons private employment agencies, especially those serving newcomers, were eyed suspiciously. That a number were supplying personnel to houses of ill repute was established by Frances Kellor's investigation of employment agencies early in the century. The link between the alien and commercialized vice, explained Kellor, was the "runner," a "suave, attractive young man who can win the confidence of the immigrant girls." He was expected to have an acquaintance with alien tongues

[30] *Ibid., Annual Report, 1909-1910*, pp. 4, 13-15, 18; Grace Abbott, *The Immigrant and the Community* (New York, 1917), p. 13.

[31] Immigrants' Protective League, *Fourth Annual Report, 1913*, p. 13.

[32] *Abstracts of Reports of the Immigration Commission*, II, 319-21; United States Immigration Commission, *Reports of the Immigration Commission*, "Immigrant Homes and Aid Societies," 61st Congress, 3rd Sess. (Washington, D. C., 1911), pp. 140-42; Bell, pp. 176, 186.

[33] Rose Sommerfeld, "The Clara de Hirsch Home for Working Girls," *American Citizen*, I (Nov. 1912), 253-54.

and customs, for "his business is to bring them to the office by any means." His character "defies description. There seems to be no meanness to which he will not stoop. . . . If a girl refuses to enter a questionable place it is part of the work of the runner to ruin her and make her more amenable to suggestions."[34] Other investigations during the following years confirmed such findings. One conducted by the Immigrants' Protective League in 1908 revealed considerable collusion, but the "commonest offense," according to Grace Abbott, was ignorance of the character of the places to which the immigrant girl was sent "rather than an active connivance in her ruin."[35] Two years later New York City's Lillian Wald made a respectable audience squirm in their pews by informing them that numerous metropolitan employment agencies "were used as markets for selling girls for prices varying from $3.00 to $50.00 or as procuring places where immoral women and men came and selected their victims."[36] New Jersey's Commission of Immigration reported also at this time that 65 per cent of the agencies investigated "were willing to procure girls to work as servants in alleged disorderly houses and for immoral purposes."[37] The United States Immigration Commission confirmed these findings in 1910 and stamped upon them a national concurrence based upon its own investigations.[38] The link between employment agencies and immigrant prostitution helps explain why progressives urged their total abolition and the creation of free publicly-supported institutions in their stead.

In large part the assault on commercialized vice was led by women themselves, either speaking through their organizations or as isolated individuals. The work of the International Institute for Young Women, launched by the National Young Women's Christian Association in 1910, is an example of a moderate but concerted attack. To guard "those who have sailed their immigrating journey alone" and who have gone "through the hazards of arrival with no protection" was its avowed objective. The majority of newcomers, observed one of its officials, were young, "below thirty years of age and the largest group of all between sixteen and twenty-one!" The International Institute was impressed with the importance of getting "a girl *started right!*" and keeping "her from doing

[34] Frances A. Kellor, *Out of Work: A Study of Employment Agencies: Their Treatment of the Unemployed, and Their Influence Upon Homes and Business* (New York, 1904), pp. 80-82.

[35] Grace Abbott, "The Chicago Employment Agency and the Immigrant Worker," *American Journal of Sociology*, XIV (Nov. 1908), 289, 291-92.

[36] Speech made by Lillian Wald on Dec. 4, 1910, Lillian Wald Papers, New York Public Library, New York City.

[37] "Report and Recommendations of the New Jersey Immigration Commission," *Survey*, XXXI (Mar. 14, 1914), 738.

[38] *Reports of the Immigration Commission*, "Immigrant Homes and Aid Societies," pp. 142-43.

all sorts of things she wouldn't think of doing back home."[39] The work of Chicago's Immigrants' Protective League and numerous settlement houses pursued the same objectives with considerably less condescension. Especially effective, however, was the program launched by the National Council of Jewish Women. Founded by ninety-five women during the Chicago World's Fair in 1893, the organization dedicated itself "to the service of faith and humanity through education and philanthropy," and elected a scion of a pioneer settler in Chicago, a philanthropist and educator in her own right, Hannah Greenbaum Solomon, as its first president.[40] Within a few years, at the request of the United States Government, the Council became active in immigration affairs and the prevention of the exploitation of alien women became its major concern. Its delegates participated in international white slavery conferences and its workers, whose preventive work at the docks set an example that other organizations would later follow, became permanent fixtures at Ellis Island and other immigration centers.[41] Easily identifiable by their conspicuous badges, able to speak a number of languages, these workers were on a constant lookout for girls traveling alone. Their leaflets and placards, distributed and posted, were also conspicuous at the various ports of entry. "Beware of those who give you addresses, offer you easy, well-paid work, or even marriage," warned one such broadside in three languages. "There are many evil men and women who have in this way led girls to destruction. Always inquire in regard to these persons of the Council of Jewish Women, which will find out the truth for you and advise you."[42] "Bitter experience" had made such warnings necessary, Marion L. Misch, President of the Council, explained in 1912, especially for the benefit of "decent people" who were unable "to comprehend the moral bias of the white slaver," the fiend in human guise who finds "the steamship piers a prolific hunting-ground."[43] Once admitted, young immigrant girls were not easily released from the anxious, watchful eye of the Coun-

39 Elizabeth Wilson, *Fifty Years of Association Work Among Young Women, 1866-1916* (New York, National Board of the YWCA, 1916), p. 301; William P. Shriver, *Immigrant Forces: Factors in the New Democracy* (New York, Missionary Education Movement of the U. S. & Canada, 1913), p. 139; Edith Terry Bremer, "Foreign Community and Immigration Work of the National Young Women's Christian Association," *Immigrants in America Review*, I (Jan. 1916), 76-78.

40 Mildred G. Welt, "The National Council of Jewish Women," *American Jewish Year Book*, XXXVI (1944-45), 56, 63-64.

41 *American Jewish Year Book*, XXXVI, 65-66.

42 United States Immigration Commission, *Reports of the Immigration Commission*, "Statements and Recommendations Submitted by Societies and Organizations Interested in the Subject of Immigration," 61st Congress, 3d Sess. (Washington, D. C., 1911), pp. 33-34, 36, 47.

43 Marion L. Misch, "The Americanization of the Immigrant Girl," *American Citizen*, I (July 1912), 31.

cil. For weeks their movements were observed, the nature of their adjustment studied. If prostitution proved a trap, as it did on rare occasions, legal machinery was put in gear to defend the hapless female from the deportation horror. To the National Council of Jewish Women immigration and prostitution were not causal in their relationship. It "is not a question of immigration," explained the Council, "if an immigrant girl is so unfortunate as to become the victim of some evil man who has traded on her credulity to put her to shame" but "a purely local and American and social question, and we must be careful not to confuse the two."[44]

In the double task of impressing Americans with the need for public protection for the young newcomer, on the one hand, and dispelling the notion that there was a connection between the rise of prostitution and the increase of immigration, on the other, social workers such as Frances A. Kellor, Jane Addams, Grace Abbott and Lillian Wald stand out prominently. Kellor was one of the first to demand that government protection be offered to the female traveler from the moment she commenced her journey to America. "Has our government any matrons or inspectors who make it impossible for the procurer, who wishes to travel steerage or second cabin for the purpose of meeting her, to accomplish his purpose?" she queried. "Is she safeguarded so carefully that members of the ship's crew cannot mislead her?"[45] Jane Addams cautioned immigrant girls against offers of a quick marriage by pleasant-looking strangers, who might well be agents of disreputable houses.[46] Reasons that led to the involvement of immigrant women with vice were many, declared her coworker, Grace Abbott. Their ignorance of English was in part responsible for their vulnerability. "The more dangerous environment in which they live" was an additional factor. "For it is near an immigrant or colored neighborhood that disreputable dance halls and hotels are usually tolerated." The alien woman also suffers from a hunger for recreation little understood or appreciated by the native-born.[47] In New York City, Lillian Wald, founder of America's first nurses' (Henry Street) settlement in the mid-1890s, met the ugliness head-on. Growing up in a comfortable middle-class environment in Rochester, New York, Miss Wald, like so many other women of her generation, chose a lifetime of service in surroundings of poverty and the struggle of immigrant life. A nurse by training, she preferred to apply her knowledge to the problems of lower Man-

[44] *American Citizen*, I, 45-46.

[45] Frances A. Kellor, "The Protection of Immigrant Women," *Atlantic Monthly*, CI (Feb. 1908), 249-50.

[46] Addams, *A New Conscience*, pp. 38-40.

[47] Grace Abbott, *The Immigrant and the Community*, pp. 71-75.

hattan. "From the very start its poor became her people. She took them to her heart and they gave her quickly their unstinted confidence and trust," Jacob A. Riis, who knew her and the East Side well, wrote in 1913.[48] Like other social and settlement-house workers, she too displayed puritanic zealousness in her desire to protect the alien woman against sexual pitfalls as well as against unsubstantiated charges of prostitution. The vast influx of single women from Eastern Europe did not alarm her, as it did so many others of her generation, for Lillian Wald was certain that the positive value of the European inrush would surely outweigh all sinister nativist forebodings. Nevertheless, she too espoused as necessary a special program of protection and guidance.[49] "The alien is in more danger of moral contamination than the rest of the community," she explained to a convention of social workers in 1908. And, "in the case of the alien girl . . . the danger is increased," especially where she must immediately assume the role of breadwinner. Like Addams, Abbott and Kellor, Lillian Wald sensed the potential danger that grew out of the limited social outlets offered by the American urban environment. The lack of available publicly-supported facilities for amusement and recreation, she cautioned, invariably led to a "pitiful dependence . . . upon the casual pick-up." "A definite and inclusive program is demanded by all ethical standards of a moral society. Existing provisions for meeting such needs," she felt, were "too casual and too haphazard." [50]

In part, the conspicuous evidence of women involved in the attack on vice was due to their relative absence from most movements of social reconstruction in the decades before. America had, after all, never before seen a group of women so well educated, so enlightened, yet with nothing to do. The college-bred women of the late nineteenth century were possessed with an overwhelming desire to act, not just aimlessly, but to participate in some meaningful social and moral venture. They believed, as a perceptive student of the career of Jane Addams wrote, that they had "a special position in history and a special duty to posterity." That they were willing to crash head-on with the most sordid aspects of modern America was also in perfect accord with the utilitarian and activist notions of a blustering, masculine society which credited activity above thought, visible accomplishments above ideas. That the preoccupation of long-sleeved spinsters with the reform of sexual perversions did not totally stun the Victorian mentality was in part due to notions which

48 R. L. Duffus, *Lillian Wald: Neighbor and Crusader* (New York, 1938), pp. 4-5; Jacob A. Riis, "Personals," *Survey*, XXX (July 26, 1913), 551-52.

49 Lillian D. Wald, "The Immigrant Girl," *Proceedings of the National Conference of Charities and Corrections*, June 1909, pp. 261, 264.

50 *Ibid.*, p. 264.

grew out of the same mythology, a mythology that lifted the native-born American woman above the baser animal passions of her male counterpart, attributing to her the custodianship of sexual purity.[51] In another sense, an attack on prostitution was also a means of warning modern industrial and urban America to make way for the New Woman. It was a sharp exhortation that the exploitation exercised by men in factory, lodgings and on the city streets must cease. Surely if modern urban America could be made safe and comfortable for a defenseless immigrant girl, all women and, for that matter, all men too could dwell there in greater comfort and security.

[51] Jill Conway, "Jane Addams: an American Heroine," *Daedalus*, XCIII (Spring 1964), 761-62, 773; for a somewhat different, but provocative, explanation see Christopher Lasch, *The New Radicalism*, pp. 56-57, 64-67.

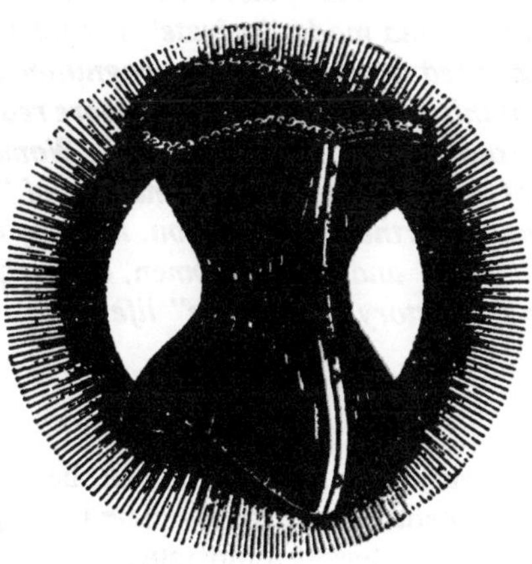

The Private Lives of Public Women: Prostitution in Butte, Montana, 1878–1917

MARY MURPHY

The Cult of True Womanhood excluded one important group of western women—prostitutes. They had left the "private sphere" to become the most public of women and left it for sexual commerce, while "true women" were supposed to be asexual. This belief was reflected in the Butte, Montana, statute Mary Murphy cites in this article, which differentiated "women" from "lewd and dissolute female persons." Western mythology softened this distinction by creating the "whore with the heart of gold," who had all the gentle virtues of proper women. Murphy's study of prostitution in Butte takes us beyond these stereotypes to look at why women became prostitutes, what their private lives were like, and the people who helped or hurt them. Murphy finds no whores with hearts of gold, but she does find women whose lives were as much affected by economic circumstances and emotional needs as other women's.

Because mining towns had many more men than women, they supported large red-light districts and made "private" life fairly public. These circumstances may have led to a more open recognition of the reality of sex. We don't know yet if this recognition included more realistic acknowledgements of female sexuality than the Cult of True Womanhood would suggest. The impact of public sexuality on standards of "normal" male and female behavior merits further investigation. Murphy takes us beyond polarized images of "good" and "bad" women, and helps us rethink an important chapter in the history of "private" life.

The prostitutes who worked in Butte, Montana, before 1917 were daughters of the nineteenth century, yet they violated every tenet of Victorian "womanliness." They were hardly temperate with regard to social or sexual intercourse, they were impious and impure, they lived without true homes or families, and they were anything but submissive. They aggressively sought customers, fought publicly, and cursed not only among themselves but with patrons and the police.[1] Between 1878, when its first hurdy-gurdy house opened, and 1917, when its red-light district closed down, Butte was the temporary home of hundreds, perhaps thousands, of prostitutes. They lived and worked in a one-block area where most of the vices of the nineteenth century were available for a price. The red-light district was

Crapper Jack's Dance Hall and Saloon, Myers Avenue, Cripple Creek, Colorado. Courtesy Glenn Kinnamon.

their home, the demimonde their family. In the world of prostitution the division between public and private, which was so central to nineteenth-century women's lives, was virtually nonexistent. Sexuality, a most private and intimate concern for most people, became blatantly public for prostitutes. Their husbands or lovers were often pimps, and family or lovers' squabbles were regularly reported in the paper as battles among the "denizens" of the district. Prostitutes' clothing and language, even their shopping places, became issues of public policy and regulation.

Prostitution was a highly stratified occupation. Each woman's status was determined by a combination of race, ethnicity, education, sociability, and sexual skill and was reflected in the place in which she worked. Parlor houses, such as Butte's elaborately furnished Windsor and the Irish World, were the top of the line; they functioned as social centers as well as brothels. Madams hired attractive women, usually white, who dressed well, acted like ladies, and played the parts of companions as well as sexual partners. These houses were few, however, and many more prostitutes worked in shabby brothels decorated with brewery calendars and whiskey-stained chairs rather than gilt-framed mirrors and brocade couches. A few prostitutes acquired the resources to work on their own in small cottages on the fringes of the red-light district. But the vast majority of prostitutes in Butte, women of all ages and races, were "everynight workingman's whores" who lived and worked in the cribs lining the streets and alleys of Butte's tenderloin.

Only those women who were private mistresses, served clients in the large parlor houses, or worked out of their own cottages managed to retain a degree of privacy. They catered to a middle-class clientele for whom publicity was undesirable. In return for discretion these women received protection from the police, public censure, and the violence of street life. However, for prostitutes who worked on the street or in cribs, public display was part of the trade. They could not afford both a public and private life.

Prostitutes had no place within the ranks of true womanhood. They were "public women," belonging to all men, not one man, and therefore not quite women at all. The Butte city council expressed this position in its ordinance concerning vagrancy, which drew a distinction between "women" and "lewd and dissolute female persons." These "female persons" were subject to arrest if they conducted themselves in an "improper, profane or obscene manner" within the sight or hearing of women.[2]

The consequences of occupying this position outside "womanhood" were mixed. On the one hand prostitutes were freed from maintaining the facade of middle-class respectability. They were expected to curse, drink, and smoke in public; they frequented saloons and gambling halls where even the most curious of respectable women dared not enter. But the costs of flouting the image of true womanhood far outweighed the pleasures of drinking and smoking in public. The arrival of "true" or "good" women on the frontier brought into sharp relief the bad women of town and exaggerated their outlaw character. Persons who lived through the early days of mining towns recalled prostitutes as "real women beneath their coldly-warm exterior . . . not . . . the hard-shelled harlots they have all been pictured."[3] Such a sympathetic view changed when respectable "real" women established themselves in the West. Prostitutes then forfeited the public courtesies due women, though not all Butte residents were able to recognize a lady when they saw one. In 1909 a man was fined ten dollars for insulting a woman on West Park Street, and the court delivered a lecture on the evils of men loitering on the sidewalks and street corners making "improper remarks to ladies."[4] Prostitutes complied with the new code of manners and used it to their advantage when they were outside the district. One miner observed: "They knew how to act like ladies when away from the district—and did it too. I seen one of them up and give a poke in the face to a masher on Park Street one afternoon, when he . . . tried to flirt with her."[5] Prostitutes tended to exact retribution more directly than did ladies. Operating outside the boundaries of "womanhood" had graver consequences than the loss of courtesy. Because of their status prostitutes enjoyed little protection from insult or violence. In 1881 a man was fined ten dollars for disfiguring a prostitute, the same fine a woman paid when convicted of vagrancy.[6]

The public nature of their lives often denied prostitutes the private comforts of home and family. Though each woman cherished the few possessions which distinguished her crib from every other, nothing could disguise the fact that her bedroom, often her only quarters, was a place of business. A few prostitutes managed to keep a room apart from their cribs, sometimes sharing it with a husband or "secretary," a euphemism for "pimp" apparently used only in Butte. Although a few prostitutes formed long-term relationships with men who had nothing to do with their business, most of their liaisons were with "secretaries" and were rarely formalized by marriage.[7] The lack of legal bonds in their partnerships again denied prostitutes legitimacy in the eyes of respectable society.

The relationship between prostitutes and pimps was the most complex in the demimonde. Some prostitutes considered pimps parasites and would have nothing to do with them. One independent Frenchwoman commenting on the district in 1902, declared, "There are at least twenty-five secretaries on this street who live on the fat of the land because foolish girls will give them their money."[8] Pimps unquestionably exploited prostitutes, living off their earnings and often treating them viciously. But some women willingly allied with pimps. Whatever emotional support, physical protection, sexual satisfaction, or illusion of romance these men "of fancy dress and patent leather shoes" provided seemed to offset the abuse with which they treated their lovers.[9] John Day was arrested for stealing fifty dollars from a woman whose crib he had shared for some time. However, once his lover had him arrested she never came forward to testify against him. May Raymond was "beaten almost into insensibility" by William Beierman, her paramour of eight months, but she did not press charges. In one of the most tragic stories of Butte's tenderloin, Mollie Scott, a young woman employed in a dance hall, was murdered by her husband, "the man whom she had cheerfully supported from the gains of her arduous calling," in a trivial argument about whether she could visit another dancing saloon.[10]

Many prosititutes demanded faithfulness from their paramours, and when they suspected infidelity, they took action. One night at a party Laura Evans decided that her "beau," Arthur, was dancing too frequently with another woman and knocked him through a plate-glass window, nearly cutting his throat. Dolly Arthur lived with one man for twenty-six years. After witnessing his repeated affairs, she told him they could continue living together "but you must never put your hands on me again."[11]

In many respects prostitutes' relationships with pimps were similar to those with madams. Both pimps and madams procured customers, protected prostitutes from violence inflicted by others, and established an emotional bond of some permanence. Yet in the popular culture madams became romanticized, often admired figures, while pimps were always despised. By some criteria madams fit the nineteenth-century ideology of womanliness. They kept a house; they played the role of mother to their "girls"; they wielded influence and used their sexuality behind the scenes, rarely making overt use of what power they may have had. Pimps, however, violated every tenet of nineteenth-century manliness. Men of all classes derived their identity from their work, and pimps did neither "honest" nor "manly" work. They were supported by women; worse, they exploited women's virtue. In an age when men fought for wages that would keep their families "from the soup house and the brothel," pimps, who pushed women into vice, could only be despised.[12]

Middle-class Victorian ideas of manliness and women's lack of passion fated pimps to condemnation and again made prostitutes' lives subject to public scrutiny. While repulsed by prostitution, many Victorians were sympathetic to prostitutes, imagining them to have been trapped by white slavers, driven to sexual commerce by dire economic need, or seduced, abandoned, and then "honor-bound" to take the only course left open to a ruined woman. That women had some choice or might enjoy their work was beyond their understanding, or perhaps threatening to their own sexuality. The possibility that a woman could voluntarily associate with a pimp was unthinkable, and thus women's own needs and motives were ignored in the public campaigns to rid western towns of pimps. During one of the repeated attempts to cleanse Butte of secretaries, Judge Donlan settled the maximum fine of three hundred dollars on one man arrested for vagrancy and censured him for carrying on "the lowest and vilest business that could possibly be imagined for a human being."[13]

Just as prostitutes' relationships with lovers were jeopardized by their work and by public policy, so were their attempts at motherhood. Few prostitutes were wives in the traditional sense, and children had little place in a brothel. In several frontier communities, when children were discovered living in the red-light district they were taken from their mothers and placed in the county poor farm. Prostitutes' appeals to place them in private homes went unheeded.[14] For this reason prostitutes frequently left their children with relatives or paid families to take them in. Many mothers desired to protect their children from the environment of the red-light district and recognized that the transience of their occupation often precluded good care. Many Butte prostitutes had borne children, but only a few lived with them.[15]

Prostitutes could hardly practice the most common forms of nineteenth-century birth control, abstinence and withdrawal, although women undoubtedly made use of pessaries, vaginal sponges, suppositories, and douches. They also resorted to abortion, a decision often painfully calculated.[16] Madeleine Blair, who started working as a prostitute at seventeen had borne two children by the time she was twenty-one. Her daughter died at birth, and she was determined to rear her second child, a son. Intending to save enough money to start a legitimate business, she left him with a nurse and went to Winnipeg to work for the summer. She returned and reclaimed her son, but, not having made enough to start her business, she continued to work as an occasional prostitute. Madeleine soon found herself pregnant again. While she was debating whether to have an abortion, her son died of pneumonia. In grief and anger at the thought of bearing another fatherless child she performed a self-induced abortion in her fifth month. She nearly died from peritonitis but recovered to mourn "with strange perversity and inconsistency" for the child she had "deliberately destroyed."[17]

In Butte between 1900 and 1917, twenty-three women died as a result of abortions. They ranged in age from seventeen to thirty-nine; they were married, single, divorced; black and white. It is unclear how many were prostitutes. These deaths only hint at the number of abortions performed in the city in the late nineteenth and early twentieth centuries. In Montana prostitution was considered a misdemeanor, but having an abortion carried a one-year jail sentence. Because of its illegality only unsuccessful procedures, revealed by sickness or death, were reported, and hundreds of successful abortions went unrecorded.[18]

Creating a home or family was only one of the problems faced by prostitutes. Prostitution was a competitive business in both the parlor houses and the cribs. Although in parlor houses madams often tried to distribute customers equally among the workers, the women vied for men. Since prostitutes split each fee with the madam, it was in their own interest to have as many "callers" as possible, and they tried to build up a regular clientele. Down on the street there was no mediating factor like a madam. Prostitutes posed in the doors and windows of their cribs "as if [they] were a part of a live-stock exhibition."[19] The term "lost sisterhood" which has been applied to prostitutes is apt, for the fierce competition for customers gnawed at any bonds of solidarity. One pimp wrote of the competition among prostitutes, "In rivalry they eat the flesh skin off one another alive."[20]

Rivalry often led to the violence endemic in the district. Women fought with each other verbally and physically, sometimes quarreling over a customer, more often over pimps. They frequently joined in the general brawls that erupted in the saloons and dance halls. Sometimes they fought out of sheer spite. When one prostitute placed the skins of some plums on her neighbor's doorstep rather than in the garbage can, her neighbor attacked her with scissors and inflicted a severe scalp wound.[21]

Although prostitutes occasionally availed themselves of the courts to redress a wrong, more often they acted immediately and personally—and often ended up in court as the accused. When a peddler somehow provoked two "Park Street women," they assaulted him with cayenne pepper and beer bottles. Laura Evans, who bore the scars to prove it, testified that when she and her lover were angry at each other they fought with knives. When a drunken man in the Royal parlor house struck Emma Robinson in the face, she stabbed him.[22]

Prostitutes were much more often on the receiving end of violence, frequently from unpredictable customers. On May 21, 1907, under the headline "Woman of Lower World Is Stabbed by Italian Tamale Vendor," the *Butte Miner* reported in unusual detail an assault in the red-light district. Teodosio Campanelli had given Gussie Clark a dollar, stood outside her crib talking for some time, and then asked for the dollar back. Clark, who had come from Seattle only two days before, called to her neighbor Mollie Quinn, who told her not to return the money. Campanelli pulled a knife; Quinn seized him, permitting Clark to escape while Campanelli stabbed Quinn in the abdomen. Quinn's husband arrived on the scene as she was being placed on a stretcher. As he stood by her side, an elderly woman emerged from the crowd, shook her fist, and cursed him: "You have disgraced your dead father in the boneyard. You told me years ago that you had quit her. Yet here you are . . . May you die the death that woman is dying. And she deserves it, for you were a good boy till you took up with Mollie Quinn." Another prostitute who had witnessed the scene muttered to a reporter, "That's your Christianity."[23]

Denied protection enjoyed by "true women," prostitutes often had only each other to rely upon in times of danger or crises; at such moments some tenuous bonds of sisterhood emerged. The common hazards prostitutes faced sometimes brought them together; abortion, the death of a child, assault by a customer, or attempted suicide suspended the daily competition. There were many incidents like Campanelli's attack on Gussie Clark, and women like Mollie Quinn were often the only defenders other prostitutes had. When a prostitute was killed or committed suicide, it was fellow members of the lost sisterhood who buried her.[24]

Amid the atmosphere of spite and rivalry, and hidden in the dismal quarters of the district, was a corner of the nineteenth-century "female world of love and ritual." Not all prostitutes were like Dolly Arthur, who claimed she "never had a good girlfriend in [her] life."[25] Prostitutes frequently traveled in pairs and sought jobs together. There are many allusions to lesbianism in brothels, and it is likely that women often turned to each other for the love and comfort lacking in their relationships with men.[26]

Sometimes, however, women's pride kept them apart. Laura Evans's friend Spud Murphy left her to set up her own business, which prospered for many years. But as she grew older, she became an alcoholic, lost her house, and ended up as a washerwoman in another red-light district. Evans went to offer her a home with her for the rest of her life, but Spuddy refused to see her, ashamed of the way her life had turned out. She continued to reject any help from Evans and died alone.[27]

Women joined the fast life for a number of reasons, but it did not always lead to what they expected. Investigators from the mid-nineteenth century through the Progressive Era sought to explain why a woman turned to commercialized sex. They posited as causes abuse as a child or wife, poverty, early sexual experience, alcoholism, emotional deprivation, "keeping bad company," or abandonment by a man. All these factors were undoubtedly contributing influences in particular cases. But there were other reasons, too. Some women decided that prostitution would provide them with fancy clothing, a desirable social life, sexual freedom, or simply a better standard of living.[28] Other women joined the sisterhood out of despair, expecting nothing better than the life they had been leading, and probably worse. Some women found the luxury and excitement they desired; others experienced a brief period of financial success, enjoying a standard of living beyond the means of most working-class women. But the constant travel, the threat of arrest, violence, betrayal, and immersion in a world of alcohol, drugs, and disease debilitated women emotionally and physically. Contrary to white-slave tracts, which portrayed women following the path to ruin after visiting an opium den or becoming an alcoholic, it is far more likely that prostitutes turned to opiates and alcohol to numb themselves once they discovered that the fast life was not all they had hoped or was even worse than they had expected.[29]

Alcohol and drugs were a part of the tenderloin culture and addiction only sucked prostitutes more deeply into the life. Alcoholism and drug abuse united members of the demimonde and drew yet another line between them and Butte's respectable citizenry. A Butte bard wrote an epic poem describing a dance attended by Butte's demimonde in 1898. Several verses illustrate the community involved and suggest the widespread use of a variety of drugs.

> All the junkies were invited,
> Yes, every gink and muff,
> Not a single one was slighted
> If they were on the stuff.
> Invitations were presented
> To every hustler and her man.
> They even sent up invites
> To the hopheads in the can.
> "But, before they play the grand march
> Let each dancer have a shot;
> It will act as stimulation,
> And should make the dancin' hot."
> So from scores of hiding places
> Guests brought forth their hypo gats;
> From sleeves, brassieres and bustles,
> Some even hid them in their rats.
>
> Not all the cokies used the needle,
> Some from their opium pipes did whiff;
> Others drained their paregoric,
> A few of "happy dust" did sniff.
> Opium pills or hasheesh
> Came forth from many a sock,
> And some twist from China Alley
> Brought out her old yen hok.[30]

Prostitutes used anodynes other than alcohol and drugs. Some women became addicted to gambling, viewing it as their only chance to create a new life, but more often they only dug themselves more deeply into debt.[31] Others married. In 1882 the *Butte Miner* reported a "matrimonial epidemic" on Park Street when several prostitutes married.[32] Perhaps they hoped for stability if not a total escape from the life. It is impossible to know how many achieved that stability, although western folklore says that many prostitutes wed and vanished happily into the ranks of respectability. Many women, however, could not shed their pasts and either returned to prostitution or chose another alternative.[33]

Suicide was a drastic solution to the despair of prostitutes' lives, but it was often attempted. Some women shot themselves or used arsenic or chloral; more commonly they took overdoses of opiates, which were easily obtained in drugstores.[34] The coy prose with which newspapers usually reported prostitutes' attempted suicides masked the desperation that led to such acts. Lottie Ables had come to Helena in the 1870s. She was nicknamed "Sorrel Mike" after a racehorse that arrived in the territory about the same time. While she was in Helena, she attempted suicide several times. Around 1879 she moved to Butte, where she married a saloonkeeper named Pickett, and apparently continued to work as a prostitute while dancing in Pickett's saloon. But married life was no balm, and two weeks after her wedding she again attempted suicide by drinking a phial of laudanum. Once more she was revived. Ables's life got no easier; a few months later a man was convicted of assault and battery on her. She continued to live and work in Butte, attempting suicide again in July 1880. At some time that year her husband vanished, and her sister moved into the small house she occupied just south of Park Street. In December 1881, Lottie Ables finally died, but not by her own hand. After quarreling with her lover, she went out and found another man. When he left the house without paying for the wine he had drunk, she reputedly drew a pistol. In the ensuing struggle Ables was shot in the abdomen and died the next day. The newspaper reported her age to be around thirty, but she was only twenty-two.[35]

The undeniable tragedy of many prostitutes' lives has led some historians and feminists to cast them in the role of hapless victims of society and male exploitation. In this respect we are as short-sighted as the Victorians who reduced them to one-dimensional caricatures of "bad" women. Butte's prostitutes were victims—victims of a tangled sexual ideology that advocated "passionlessness" in women but recognized the need for prostitution to absorb the "excess lust" of men; victims of a city government that exploited their vulnerable legal position to fill the city treasury; victims of madams and pimps who exploited their emotional vulnerability and need for physical protection and security; and victims of men who denied them any personal dignity, treating them only as sexual objects. Yet, just as women exercised some choice in the process of becoming prostitutes, they sometimes exercised power in their trade and had some pride in their accomplishments. Prostitutes like Dolly Arthur were proud of their popularity, of running a "clean" house where men had a good time and did not have to worry about being robbed. They enjoyed men, they enjoyed their work, and they considered the money they were paid a flattering reflection of their worth. While they disbursed their share of bribes and fines, they also used skill and charm to play upon men's vanities and to protect themselves from the courts, the police, and difficult customers.

In a parlor house a man paid for companionship, entertainment, and a semblance of romance, as well as for intercourse, but in poorer brothels and cribs, no such illusion existed. Prostitutes often had several customers each night, and they reduced sexual intercourse to a mechanical process. One worker described his experience:

She'd lay on her back and get you on top of her so fast, you wouldn't even know you'd come up there on your own power. She'd grind so that you almost felt like you had nothing to do with it. Well, after that, she had you. She could make it get off as quickly as she wanted to, . . . and she didn't waste any time, I'll tell you, . . . I'd say the whole thing, from the time you got in the room until the time you came didn't take three minutes.[36]

Women in the cribs were not selling romance, and unless a man lingered to drink there was no profit in prolonging the engagement. Prostitutes like Madeleine could not reconcile themselves to the fact that some men wanted more than their bodies:

I could not make a demonstration of affection over men nor any pretense or response to their caresses. For the life of me, I could not understand why they should expect it. They had only bought my body. I could not see why they should want more. My love was not for sale, piecemeal, to every man who had the price to pay for my body.[37]

The relationship between prostitute and client was a marketplace transaction, and, as in any other commercial exchange, the customer sought to get as much as he could for his money. Much of the violence directed against prostitutes occurred when a man thought he had purchased more than a woman was willing to give. Because of crib women's low status they were especially fair game for cheating and abuse. Several bloody altercations in the district occurred when women tried to get payment from parsimonious customers. For the most part, however, women controlled what happened in their cribs and in their beds, "turning a trick" on men who thought they had bought "the right to handle [them] at will."[38]

When a man became a nuisance or blind drunk, prostitutes often "made a touch." Some whores felt that it was "against their religion" to let a man get away with a penny in his pocket, and they were not choosy about the means they used to get it. Men who were robbed were frequently reluctant to make a legal complaint for fear of publicity. Dozens of men, including a sheriff from another part of Montana, claimed that they were robbed in Beryl Hasting's house on Mercury Street, but none would swear out a complaint, much to the chagrin of the police.[39]

Although Butte prostitutes exerted some personal power in their individual lives, there is little evidence that they, or any other member of the tenderloin, ever acted collectively to improve their lot. Madams may have used their influence on important men in the city, and individual prostitutes may have had some sway over a policeman or official. But the examples of Denver, where prostitutes formed an organized voting block, or Cripple Creek, Colorado, where dance hall girls founded the Dance Hall Girls Protective Association and called a strike to protest a reduction in their percentage of liquor sales, are absent, or still hidden, in Butte's history.[40]

Perhaps prostitutes' greatest source of power was society's need for them. The prostitutes of the demimonde were indeed residents of a half-world with little legal and no moral standing since they had, in effect, been read out of the ranks of "true women." But prostitutes and their madams, pimps, and liquor and drug suppliers weathered many storms of reform, for they knew there was an enduring demand for their services. Power is exercised in subtle ways by oppressed groups or members of an underclass, many times by giving those in power the illusion of submission. The members of Butte's demimonde, for all their flamboyance, knew how to play a subtle game. They were able to protect themselves by giving something to everyone, even reformers.

In May 1905, Christian reformers invaded the red-light district of Butte. The Reverend C. L. Bovard and the Salvation Army band, accompanied by a thousand men, women, and children, held a revival meeting and then marched through the district singing, "Where Is My Wandering Boy Tonight?" Later that evening the evangelist William Biederwolf addressed the crowd, calling Butte "the lowest sinkhole of vice in the west." The week-long revival culminated in a meeting in the district. The manager of the Casino Theater opened his doors to the evangelist. The orchestra pit was jammed with "gamblers, rounders and male habitues" of the district; the boxes were filled with "women in flimsy garments" accompanied by their secretaries and paramours. For thirty-five minutes Biederwolf addressed the crowd; when he asked those who desired to do better to raise their hands, everyone did. After Biederwolf departed, the bar reopened, the orchestra struck up a tune, and the women went back to work. Someone asked the manager of the Casino whether he intended to give up the liquor trade. He looked up in amazement and said, "Me? I guess not."[41]

Business returned to normal in the district. Prostitutes continued to ply their trade, to be picked up for vagrancy, fined, and released to be arrested the following month. In 1915 the *Miner* reported that the district had a larger population than ever and business was booming. But prosperity was short-lived. The wave of reform that swept through America during World War I touched Butte as well. In 1917 the city attorney declared war on houses of ill repute. The Copper King saloon and hotel, the financial heart of the district, was described as "a haunt for some of the most disreputable characters in the city," and it was closed in the first battle of the campaign against vice. Butte joined two hundred other American cities that shut down their red-light districts by 1920.[42]

The closing of Butte's red-light district did not end prostitution, just as Prohibition which came in 1918, did not end the sale and consumption of liquor. But the two events changed the structure of vice. Earlier in the century when Butte attempted to shut down its district, one prostitute responded by saying that she would merely go into the lodging houses or "rustle" in the streets.[43] That is what happened in 1917. Vice moved underground as prostitutes dispersed through the city and speakeasies replaced corner saloons. Prostitution was a firmly established business in Butte, and prostitutes continued to demonstrate persistence and flexibility in pursuit of their trade. The closing of the red-light district ended a particular form of commercialized vice, affecting both the public and private lives of prostitutes, but it certainly did not extinguish Butte's demimonde.

Notes

1. *Butte Miner*, 11 Sept. 1880, 16 March 1881, 22 Sept. 1881.
2. William E. Carroll, comp., *The Revised Ordinances of the City of Butte* (1914), pp. 460–61.
3. Frank A. Crampton, *Deep Enough: A Working Stiff in the Western Mine Camps* (Denver: Sage Books, 1956), p. 50; reprint (Norman: University of Oklahoma Press, 1982).
4. *Butte Miner*, 20 Aug. 1909.
5. Federal Writers' Project, *Copper Camp* (New York: Hastings House, 1943), p. 181.
6. *Butte Miner*, 6 March 1881; Butte City Ordinance no. 824, 1914.
7. Madeleine Blair maintained a relationship with one man for several years. He was a protector and lover but never acted as a pimp. Other women continued working as prostitutes while they were married to men who had nothing to do with their business. Pearl Heflin for instance, who worked as a prostitute in Butte in 1900, was married to a day laborer.
8. *Butte Miner*, 19 Jan. 1902.
9. Martha Louise Black, *My Ninety Years* (Anchorage: Alaska Northwest Publishing Co., 1976), p. 48.
10. *Butte Miner*, 27 May 1907, 19 Aug. 1909, 5 Aug. 1880.
11. Forbes Parkhill, *The Wildest of the West* (Denver: Sage Books, 1951), p. xiii; June Allen, *Dolly's House* (Ketchikan, Alaska: Tongass Publishing Co., 1976), pp. 20–21.
12. Peter G. Filene, *Him Her Self; Sex Roles in Modern America* (New York: Harcourt Brace Jovanovich, 1974), see chapter 3, "Men & Manliness"; Elizabeth Jameson, "Imperfect Unions: Class and Gender in Cripple Creek, 1894–1904," *Frontiers* 1 (Spring, 1976): 101.
13. *Butte Miner*, 23 July 1910. In 1905 a "crusade" was begun to rid the city of men known as "red-light vagrants." One of the tactics was to arrest and fine prostitutes, presumably with the hope that if deprived of their income, the men would move on. *Butte Miner*, 26 July 1905.
14. Margaret H. Davis, "Harlots and Hymnals: A Historic Confrontation of Vice and Virtue in Waco, Texas," *Mid-South Folklore* 4 (Winter, 1976): 92.
15. "Tenth Census," 1880, vol. 1, "Montana" (manuscript); "Twelfth Census of the Population," 1900, vol. 9, "Silver Bow County" (manuscript). Two children were living with prostitutes in 1880; in 1900 no children were recorded in the red-light district, but the census revealed that prostitutes had borne twenty-six children, twelve of whom were living.
16. Marion S. Goldman, *Gold Diggers and Silver Miners: Prostitution and Social Life on the Comstock Lode* (Ann Arbor: University of Michigan Press, 1981), p. 126.
17. *Madeleine: An Autobiography* (New York: Harper and Brothers, 1910), pp. 196–202.
18. Butte Mortuary Records, 1900–17; *Revised Codes of Montana*, 1907.
19. *Madeleine*, p. 216.
20. U.S. Cong., Senate, *Importing Women for Immoral Purposes: A Partial Report from the Immigration Commission on the Importation and Harboring of Women for Immoral Purposes*, 61st Cong., 2d sess., doc. 196 (Washington, D.C.: Government Printing Office, 1909), p. 59.
21. *Butte Miner*, 4 March 1880, 17 March 1880, 26 May 1880, 5 Oct. 1881, 21 Aug. 1909.
22. *Butte Miner*, 20 Feb. 1881, 26 May 1880; Parkhill, *The Wildest of the West*, p. xiii; *Butte Miner*, 16 Oct. 1903.
23. *Butte Miner*, 21 May 1907.

24. *Butte Miner*, 5 Aug. 1880, 11 Nov. 1881.

25. Dolly Arthur, interview by John Grainger, Ketchikan, Alaska, n.d.

26. Ruth Rosen, *The Lost Sisterhood: Prostitution in America, 1900–1918* (Baltimore: Johns Hopkins University Press, 1982), pp. 104, 163; Paula Petrik, "The Bonanza Town: Women and Family on the Rocky Mountain Frontier, Helena, Montana, 1865–1900" (Ph.D. diss. SUNY-Binghampton, 1982), p. 194; Goldman, *Gold Diggers and Silver Miners*, pp. 116–21.

27. Parkhill, *The Wildest of the West*, p. xv.

28. For a discussion of why women turned to prostitution and an analysis of the many vice commissions, see Rosen, *The Lost Sisterhood*, chap. 8.

29. Parkhill, *The Wildest of the West*, p. xv; *Madeleine*, pp. 228–312. Regular use of opiates also caused disruption or cessation of menstruation; thus it is possible that prostitutes used opiates as a form of birth control. David T. Courtwright, "Opiate Addiction in America, 1880–1940" (Ph.D. diss. Rice University, 1979), p. 93.

30. Federal Writers' Project, pp. 272–73. *Gink* means a fellow or "guy"; *muff*, prostitute; *gat*, pistol or revolver; *rat*, pad with tapering ends over which a woman's hair is arranged; *cokie*, drug addict, cocaine user; *happy dust*, cocaine; *twist*, woman with loose or "twisted" morals.

31. Lucie Cheng Hirata, "Chinese Immigrant Women in Nineteenth Century California," in Carol Berkin and Mary Beth Norton, eds., *Women of America, A History* (Boston: Houghton Mifflin, 1979), p. 232; *Madeleine*, pp. 233–38.

32. *Butte Miner*, 8 Feb. 1882.

33. Crampton, *Deep Enough*, p. 50; Petrik, "The Bonanza Town," pp. 194–99; Anne Ellis, *The Life of an Ordinary Woman* (1929; reprint, Lincoln: University of Nebraska Press, 1980), pp. 222–23; James Gray, *Red Lights on the Prairie* (Toronto: Macmillan, 1971), pp. 179–80.

34. Alfred R. Lindesmith, *Addiction and Opiates* (Chicago: Aldine Publishing Co., 1968), p. 210; Goldman, *Gold Diggers and Silver Miners*, pp. 134–35; *Butte Miner*, 20 Feb. 1880, 26 May 1880, 6 Oct. 1881, 11 Nov. 1881, 7 Aug. 1883, 6 Apr. 1884.

35. *Butte Miner*, 28 Aug. 1879, 7 Oct. 1879, 31 July 1880, 16 Dec. 1881; *Tenth Census*, 1880.

36. Rosen, *The Lost Sisterhood*, p. 96.

37. *Madeleine*, p. 71.

38. *Madeleine*, p. 82.

39. Parkhill, *The Wildest of the West*, p. xii; Anne K. Butler, "The Tarnished Frontier: Prostitution in the Trans-Mississippi West, 1865–1890," (Ph.D. diss., University of Maryland, 1979), p. 119; *Butte Miner*, 5 Oct. 1881, 7 May 1905, 27 May 1907, 20 Feb. 1909, 20 Aug. 1909.

40. Parkhill, *The Wildest of the West*, pp. 23–24; Ruth Rosen, "The Lost Sisterhood: Prostitution During the Progressive Era," (Ph.D. diss., University of California, Berkeley, 1976), p. 132; Jameson, "Imperfect Unions," p. 101.

41. *Butte Miner*, 5 May 1905, 11 May 1905.

42. *Butte Miner*, 16 July 1915, 11 May 1917; Mark Connelly, *The Response to Prostitution in the Progressive Era* (Chapel Hill: University of North Carolina Press, 1980), p. 26.

43. *Butte Miner*, 19 Jan. 1902.

SEDUCED AND ABANDONED IN AN AMERICAN CITY
Cleveland and Its Fallen Women, 1869-1936

MARIAN J. MORTON
John Carroll University

The spectre of the seduced and abandoned woman haunted Cleveland's reformers in the late nineteenth century.[1] The Cleveland Woman's Christian Association, for example, envisioned such a woman, imperiled by urban life:

> In the hustle and activity of the age, the women are following hard after the men. Not satisfied with their quiet country homes, many of them press their way to the cities. What shall be done to care for these women? Be they never so pure, they are liable to fall into disgrace and sin. . . . They do not realize the snare and pitfalls that lie so thickly about them. They do not know that many men go about "like roaring lions seeking whom they devour."[2]

However exaggerated by Victorian sensibilities and rhetoric, these fears for the fallen women were grounded in the very real economic and sexual vulnerability of thousands of women in the growing city. Most of these women have been lost forever to the historian, living and dying in anonymity. Some, however—what

JOURNAL OF URBAN HISTORY, Vol. 11 No. 4, August 1985 443-469 small proportion it is impossible to guess—came to the attention of benevolent and reform-minded citizens. Although these women too remain anonymous, their true identities expunged from the registers of institutions and social work agencies, existing records suggest that despite the great economic and social changes that took place in the city from 1869 to 1936, Cleveland's fallen women remained sexually exploited, cast adrift from family, and so poor that they became the objects of a moralistic charity that sought to reform and reclaim them.

Other Americans shared the anxieties of the Cleveland WCA. The long-standing identification of the city with vice and sin was heightened by decades of explosive urban growth following the Civil War and especially by the waves of European immigrants who swelled the urban populations. To many reformers, "the city was an illusive trap set carefully for country virgins."[3] In this setting the fallen woman came to symbolize much that was wrong with urbanizing America: the greater independence of women and the more permissive sexual behavior already perceptible in the postwar years, the economic exploitation and poverty more visible in the city slums, the collapse of familial and small-town morality, and the decay of orthodox religion in the face of urban anonymity and secularization.[4]

Efforts to rescue these fallen women took many forms in Cleveland and elsewhere. Social purity forces, emulating the antebellum moral reform societies, sought to save prostitutes by stamping out prostitution. Organizations such as the Young Women's Christian Association (YWCA) and the Woman's Christian Temperance Union established residences for young working women where they might be sheltered from vice. For those who already had fallen, the Salvation Army, the National Florence Crittenton Mission, the YWCA, and the local Catholic dioceses opened refuges and maternity homes across the country which, in the evangelical style of nineteenth-century benevolence, tried to rescue both bodies and souls. As part of progressive efforts to systematize and professionalize philanthropy, several cities formed the Inter-City Conference on Illegitimacy; the Cleveland Conference on Illegitimacy shared its goal of preventing unwed motherhood. These attempts, because they were made mostly by middle-class women, have been well documented.[5]

We know less, however, about the fallen women themselves. Historians have been most interested in prostitutes, but although Cleveland reformers certainly worried about prostitution, the seduced and abandoned women described here were for the most part not "painted ladies" or purveyors of the "social evil," but women whose sexual activities were extramarital although not professional. The few existing studies of sexually delinquent women elsewhere suggest that those in Cleveland were not atypical. For example, they resemble the "waifs and the wanton" inmates of the State Industrial School at Lancaster, Massachusetts, the "wayward" women of the Magdalen Asylum of Philadelphia at the turn of the century, and, most closely, the unwed mothers of Boston in 1918.[6] Most important, these women shared poverty, family disruption, and victimization, and offer us another perspective on life in the American city.

The Civil War hastened Cleveland's transformation from a commercial village to an urban metropolis; its population doubled between 1860 and 1870. A war-time boom attracted thousands to the city, many of them immigrants from Western Europe, especially Germany and Ireland, but most from the near-by countryside.[7] The charitable and benevolent associations that served this population were almost entirely church-related and evangelical, predominantly Protestant but with a scattering of Catholic institutions as well. For example, Cleveland's most active relief society, the Bethel House, was originally the Western Seamen's Friends Society, a city mission. In 1884, Bethel House became the organizational basis for Cleveland Associated Charities, the most important dispenser of outdoor relief.

Women flocked to the city too, especially during the war when departing soldiers created job opportunities. The *Cleveland Leader* worried about "the difficulties experienced by young women in employment" and suggested optimistically that "selling jewelry, books, shoes, sewing machines, and dry-goods, and bookkeeping" were jobs that women could manage. Police court records, however, indicate that some women found prostitution more remunerative even though officials frequently arrested keepers and residents of "disorderly houses" and even an occasional patron.[8]

Cleveland's middle-class women, made alert to the dangers of city life by their own missionary and relief activities, were particularly concerned about these urban newcomers. Most active was the Cleveland WCA, an adjunct of the Young Men's Christian Association that shared its evangelical zeal but labored particularly for "women in our midst."[9] The WCA (which became the YWCA in 1893) established, first, a home for "self-dependent"[10] young women and, second, in 1869, the Retreat, the city's first refuge for "women who had lost the glory of their womanhood."[11] In 1873, the Cleveland Catholic Diocese, challenged by the vigorous Protestant proselytising of the Retreat, countered with St. Ann's Maternity Home and Infant Asylum, adminstered by the Sisters of Charity of St. Augustine. The Salvation Army opened its Rescue Home in 1892, as part of its attempt to minister to and convert Cleveland's poor, and the next year the Cleveland homeopathic medical community established the Maternity Home, which shortly afterward became the Maternity Hospital.

It is to the records of these institutions that we must turn first for information about Cleveland's fallen women. The records are not perfect sources. Kept separately by each institution, they most often took the form of annual reports published to encourage generous gifts from their readers, hence stressing their most pitiable cases. Often interpretations of the data were clouded by the class- and ethnic-bound perceptions of the middle-class authors, one generation, for example, stressing "intemperance" as the cause of "down-fall," the next emphasing "feeble-mindedness," Finally, even when the records have survived and the compilers have done careful computations of the number of inmates, the figures do not represent accurately the number of Cleveland women who "fell," only those who "fell" and came to the attention of the refuges and maternity homes. Almost certainly, women at the top and at the very bottom of the socioeconomic scale escaped notice.

These records do provide us with the era's definition of "fallen," a term almost meaningless in today's sexually permissive climate. To Cleveland women reared within Victorian conventions, however, "fallen" referred to women suspected or guilty of sexual delinquency, especially prostitutes. In actual practice, however, the definition often was expanded to include other kinds of deviance from middle-class norms, including poverty, dependence, transience, illness, and out-of-wedlock pregnancy.

The fallen woman whose portrait emerges from these records was seduced and abandoned by men, loosed from familial restraints, and without economic resources. The refuges and maternity homes sought not only to shelter her body but to save her soul. Prostitutes "willing to leave a house of sin" and be reclaimed were the targets of the missionaries of the Retreat and the Salvation Army Rescue, who visited the city's "vilest slums" and "red-light districts."[12] The Retreat claimed to have rescued two prostitutes in 1875.[13] Such missionary work had its antecedents in the Magdalen and Female Moral Reform societies of the antebellum period, which had in fact made few converts in the brothels.[14] Neither did the Retreat or the Salvation Army Rescue.

It was not those who got paid for their sexual favors who needed refuge and shelter, but those who had given them freely, "ruined" by their indiscretions and then deserted. These were women, as eloquently described by the Retreat, who "from want, or sorrow, or deception, had lost the glory of their womanhood ... somebody's daughter, perchance more sinned against than sinning."[15] Just such a woman, for example, arrived at the Retreat in 1872 with a baby in her arms; shortly afterward, however, she was married to a doctor, presumably the infant's father, probably as the result of some discreet pressure applied to the indiscreet doctor by the Retreat's board of managers.[16] Accumulated experiences with cases like this one, most of which did not end so happily, led the Retreat board to comment angrily about women "imposed upon—O, the crime of it! by married men, deceived by the sophistry of libidinous lovers.... Society excuses the sin in men; in the women never."[17] The same sad story is told in the Salvation Army records, as of the woman who was "deceived; told to come to Cleveland to meet her affianced who had preceded her, presumably to rent rooms, when he promised to marry her. She came; the young man heartlessly deserted her... [she] was handed over to us."[18]

The promiscuous behavior of these women was viewed as a moral lapse, fall from God's grace. They would be restored to virtue, therefore, by religious conversion. In the Retreat fallen women were to be converted through Bible classes, daily prayers, and the Christian atmosphere and example of the matron and her pious volunteer helpers. The 1879 "Minutes" noted proudly, "It is believed by the Matron that many of the inmates have really become humble Christians and though rejoicing with trembling, they still hope greatly and give fervent thanks."[19]

Sometimes a woman found her redemption in the Salvation Army's open-handed promises of salvation from sin, as did this girl who had been "Betrayed":

> Susie came in deep trouble, expecting to become a mother. The father of the child had deserted her—her pocketbook was empty—her relatives had closed their doors to her. She had been brought up a Catholic, but determined the Army people would be her best friends in trouble.... One day she came and asked if her baby could be dedicated to God in the Army way as she would like to see him brought up to God's glory and to be of some service in His Kingdom. ... She herself has proven so faithful, that she numbers among our soldiers.[20]

Even the seducer himself might be saved, as in this case of "Romance, Ruin, and Rescue," in which a woman had been "betrayed by her sweetheart, a blacksmith in her home town.... We learned the name of her betrayer and wrote to the officers of the [Army] corps where he lived. The officer visited him and dealt faithfully with him." The betrayer saw the light and married the mother of his child.[21]

Often, especially if they were pregnant out of wedlock, the inmates of the refuges and maternity homes had been deserted by their own families, as was "Betrayed" Susie. The mother Superior of St. Ann's Hospital in 1904 reported that "the majority [of patients] come to us not only to be fed and cared for, but even to be clothed as well. Often, if the family of the unfortunate girl be in a position to provide for her, it, as frequently in a time of trouble and disgrace, abandons her, and thus she becomes an outcast." Some women had even been deserted by their lawful husbands, she continued.[22] The Maternity Hospital also took in "women who have been deserted by worthless husbands in the hour when some protection was needed."[23] Many of the Retreat and the Rescue inmates, however, stayed only briefly because they were temporarily homeless and needed shelter until they could summon the strength and courage to go elsewhere.

Other women had themselves cast aside the restraints of family life in pursuit of sordid and destructive companions and habits. The Retreat, for example, sheltered scores like the 18-year-old runaway who had been "for several months in scenes of sin and vice" before her mother reclaimed her.[24] Young women also were referred to the Retreat by their own parents who could no longer discipline or safeguard their daughters in an unwholesome urban setting that weakened parental control. Alcohol and drugs were a constant temptation. The Salvation Army Rescue proclaimed that "An Opium Fiend has been delivered from the appetite and is now free, having been saved from many vicious habits."[25]

Maternity homes and refuges, therefore, deliberately sought to create a home and family, for they believed that women out of their familial sphere were easily victimized and that domesticity and maternity had redemptive powers.[26] The matron of the home played the maternal role; the inmates were her children, and together they constituted a family. Even after the women's dismissal from the Rescue, "'Mother' ... [kept] track of them and [encouraged] them in their new lives."[27] The Retreat managers described "our Home [as] the 'House Beautiful' of which we read in Bunyan's *Pilgrim's Progress*, a haven between the Hill of Difficulty and the Valley of Temptation. When the girls leave the home, they are better armed for life's difficulties than when they came to us, having been taught, advised, and shown the pathway to right living."[28] Founders and administrators of these homes believed, as did many women reformers and activists of their generation, that a woman's maternal instincts could save both herself and others. Hence, although bearing a child out of wedlock was a sin, it could also be the means to salvation. The Retreat's annual report in 1901 described this process:

> One member of the Retreat family who from being a year ago rebellious, untruthful, quarrelsome, and altogether unsatisfactory, is today transformed through the gentle influence of a well-ordered home (her first opportunity to know of such and of the mightier power of mother-love) into a wholesome, reliable woman efficient in the family and hopeful for the future.

However hopeful this young woman may have been, the report also noted that she had to "depend entirely upon her bread-winning powers" unfortunately were not great in Cleveland at the turn of the century, where the largest number of employed women were domestic servants, as they were elsewhere.[30] It is not surprising, therefore, that a disproportionate number of inmates of the refuges and maternity homes appear to have been domestic servants, both before and after their stays.

It is not surprising also that these women were poor, as servants did not earn much money or come from families with financial resources.[31] The evidence of their poverty is both direct and indirect. They often were described, as in the letter from the Mother Superior of St. Ann's, as left penniless by their families or husbands. The Salvation Army Rescue, for example, which probably took the largest share of indigent women, painted this pathetic portrait: "the poor girl (only 18 years of age) was living alone, and she was very poorly clad; no warm clothes at all, just her summer clothing, and poor thing! So sick, she was shivering with cold; she has no fire and no coal."[32] However, as this kind of description was routinely included in the institutions' pleas for financial assistance from the public, these claims of poverty should not necessarily be taken at face value.

The indirect evidence of poverty is more persuasive. Although it is possible that middle-class women came to the refuges for shelter and anonymity, these were charitable institutions that, more often than not, could not collect even modest fees from their clientele and experienced financial difficulties with some regularity.[33] Many women came to the homes for free medical care, and the unmarried mothers who bore their children there were also often ill. The sketchy figures on infant mortality are high, suggesting the inadequate prenatal care associated with poverty. In 1882, the Retreat recorded 4 deaths among 54 infants; of 88 children born in the Rescue Home in 1907, 5 died; of the 505 infants at St. Ann's in 1906—a figure that includes foundlings as well as illegitimate children—179 died, an appalling 35 percent.[34] Poverty is also indicated by the women's confinements in the two hospital facilities, St. Ann's and the Maternity Hospital. Until the 1920s most middle-class women had their babies at home; maternity and lying-in hospitals were the province of poor women who had no homes and upon whom fledgling doctors could learn and practice their professional skills in a convenient setting.[35] The vast majority of St. Ann's patients from 1888 to 1900 (201 out of 249) were charity patients.[36] According to its 1892 by-laws, the Maternity Hospital patients were to be "worthy" women, "worthy" of the charity provided by this benevolent institution.[37]

In the view of the homes' administrators, therefore, fallen women should be saved from poverty as well as from sin, and this salvation was to be achieved through training for honest employment so that women would not be tempted into prostitution or other sexual misconduct for money. All the homes taught women cooking, sewing, laundering, and child-care and, if possible, placed them in domestic service after they were released.[38] Although the illogic, or at least the irony, of placing a women in a job that had contributed to her "fall" in the first place was obvious, domestic service had certain advantages. It was available, acceptable, and sometimes made it possible for a women to take her child with her. A woman in financial straits prior to giving birth, however, was not likely to improve her situation much by taking up or resuming domestic service with a child to support in addition to herself.

This pattern, established in the 1870s, of poverty and dependence, family disorganization, and sexual victimization and the middle-class benevolent response to it, persisted into the first decades of the twentieth century as Cleveland and other cities experimented with progressive reformism. The perceptions and treatment of fallen women remained almost unchanged, despite the growing secularization and professionalization of benevolence. In 1910, Cleveland was the sixth-largest city in the country, its prospering economy resting on the manufacture of automobiles, finished iron and steel products, and textiles. Its population, swollen almost 50 percent since 1900, was ethnically diverse; only one-fifth of its citizens were native born of native parentage.[39] This growth and diversity placed great strains on the existing charitable organizations, and in 1913 the Cleveland Federation of Charity and Philanthropy, typifying the progressive desire to combine efficiency and humanitarianism, was formed to systematize the fund-raising and planning for the city's myriad charities. The Federation, renamed the Welfare Federation in 1917, responded vigorously to what it perceived as "the challenges of the city": the sharpening "contrasts between sufficiency and want . . . the noise and monotony of city life," the loss of the "spirit of neighborliness," the spread of disease, "the over-stimulating excitement and the intense city amusement."[40]

Of particular concern to the Federation was "shelter for the unfortunate woman," for "next to the child in helplessness is the weak woman," victim of a double standard that condemns her to "shame and sorrow while the man in most cases escapes censure."[41] This anxiety about female sexual delinquency, as common during the progressive period as it was in the late nineteenth century, was reflected in the lists of inmates in the Cleveland House of Correction; female offenses were almost entirely sexual, including "common prostitution," "street soliciting," and keeping or residing in a "house of ill fame."[42] City officials conducted a highly publicized antivice campaign in 1915 and temporarily closed the red-light district, proclaiming that "the policy of persistent repression of prostitution is now in effect."[43]

Women reformers took their own measures, designed less to repress than to prevent sexual delinquency and exploitation. The YWCA's Stillman Witt Boarding Home and the WCTU's Mary Ingersoll Girls' Club, where women could find respectable and inexpensive lodgings, were expanded. The Women's Protective Association was established in 1916 to provide young women with legal protection and temporary shelter in its Sterling House. The Catholic Women's League founded the Catherine Horstman Training Home for girls referred by the Juvenile Court. In 1912, the National Florence Crittenton Mission opened a home for unwed mothers in Cleveland, part of its large chain of maternity homes.

The proliferation of social agencies prompted the Federation to form a Conference on Illegitimacy, which was to coordinate the policies and practices of agencies dealing with illegitimate children and unwed mothers. These included the maternity homes as well as the probate and juvenile courts and the Cleveland Humane Society, a child-placing agency. The Conference was also a fact-finding body, and its records, particularly the several quantitative studies compiled by its members and the city's Bureau of Vital Statistics, provide further information on the city's fallen women.[44] The Conference's interest, however, was limited to women who were pregnant out of wedlock, not simply sexually delinquent. The refuges and maternity homes had already begun to specialize in obstetrical care, only occasionally providing temporary shelter.[45]

Yet case studies discussed by the Conference reveal the familiar stories of seduction and abandonment. The Florence Crittenton Home, for example, reported on a 17-year-old girl with a one-year-old child who had been at the Home for eleven months; the child's father was the girl's brother-in-law; her mother was a drunkard; the girl wished to leave the Home but had nowhere to leave the baby.[46] The Humane Society received a "neatly and modestly dressed" young woman who had left her small town in Virginia because of her "father's intemperance and general abuse of his family." She had worked first as a domestic servant and then as a marker in a laundry. The father of her child had disappeared after giving her a small sum of money, which was exhausted by the costs of her confinement. She came to the Humane Society to give her baby up for adoption.[47]

Conference quantitative studies always reported a great preponderance of pregnant single women. In 1914, for example, 65 of the 72 women whose marital status was known were unmarried. Only 2 of the 100 men named as fathers married the mothers of their children. Thirteen of the women claimed still to care for these men; only 4 women would take legal steps against them.[48] Yet some women were married, but deserted, divorced, or separated; marriage was no guarantee of support or security.[49]

Conference studies also turned up signs of family disintegration, as in this case.

> American girl, 19 years old. Employment sought. Later found to be pregnant. Had given birth to an illegitimate child 18 months previous. Child placed out and later died. Her family had been unable to account for her actions for the past 2½ years.... Her older sister also had an illegitimate child. This girl was known to sixteen agencies and had been admitted to three maternity homes as well as other institutions where she defied all suggestions.[50]

As in the late nineteenth century, families were not always disorganized or neglectful, but often simply unable to control their daughters, exposed to new customs and companions. The 1914 report showed that most of the women had become pregnant while living with their families or relatives: "A surprisingly large number of the women in difficulty were living at home at the time of their down-fall. This indicates that something is wrong with parents and home conditions," the report hazarded.[51]

Cleveland's fallen women were still poor, and likely to stay that way. Once again, as study after study revealed, these women overwhelmingly reported themselves as domestic servants. The 1914 study reported, for example, that "a surprisingly large number of the women [37 of the 85 who gave an occupation] were engaged in housework, making it by far the most dangerous occupation, morally." Other occupations listed were factory worker, waitress, clerk, dressmaker, and telephone girl. The average salary was $8.88 a week, although a servant's salary would have been less because it included room and board. This average salary actually declined after the women's release from the maternity homes when they were placed again in domestic service jobs.[52] Two years later the Conference claimed to be "astonished" at the number of unwed mothers apparently engaged in housework, 100 of the 175 being so listed. Some shift in job opportunities was apparent, however, as 17 women worked in factories or shops, and the same number in offices or stores.[53]

The sexual partners of these women seem to have been of roughly comparable social and economic status. According to a 1922 study, one of the few to include information on the fathers of illegitimate children, the largest percentage of these men described themselves as "laborers"; the next significant ranking was factory worker and machinist.[54]

Whatever the men's economic standings, they seldom took financial responsibility for their children, despite the best efforts of the Conference and its members. The Florence Crittenton Home particularly had a policy of pursuing the putative father so that he would marry the woman, or at least provide money for the child.[55] Unwed mothers also received legal assistance from the Humane Society, as in this case:

> Bohemian girl, 20 years old, Catholic, living at home. Engaged in office work at $20 a week, applied for assistance when four months pregnant, in securing prosecution of the man involved, stating that he was 22 years old, a Slovak, earning between $150 and $200 a month as a crane electrician.... The man involved was arrested and brought [to trial] where he acknowledged paternity and stated his willingness to pay $200 settlement. This was refused, and he was bound over to the Grand Jury, where he was given a sentence to pay $6 a week until the child is 16 years old.[56]

Such legal procedures, however, were expensive and time-consuming, and made anonymity for the women impossible. Even after the passage of a more stringent child support law in 1923, the fathers, when they complied, seem to have paid minimal amounts such as $5 a week.[57]

With little or no financial support from the child's father and probably limited education and job skills, the unwed mother with an infant faced an economic situation like this:

> On the question of what work girls with illegitimate children are able to find, [the Salvation Army officer] stated a case of her own experience. A most ignorant and inexperienced girl, an orphan who had not hardly any advantage in life, became a mother at 16 years of age.... After the usual stay in the Salvation Army Rescue Home, she secured a position with her baby in a private family where she remained until the baby was more than a year old. After that she boarded the baby in the Home. The child is now six years old. The mother is making $6 a week as a domestic and has a bank account. She has always paid for the baby's board at the Home.[58]

The perpetuation of poverty was revealed in the story of the "unmarried mother who did housework part time and part of the time did sewing outside," and of the woman "who worked in a rag shop and boarded the child with one of the Babies' Dispensary families. She was firm in her devotion to the child, and when she was sick, borrowed money to pay its board."'[59]

The free care provided by the maternity homes did not protect these indigent women from high maternal and infant mortality rates. The 1914 study, for example, noted that 17 of the 97 illegitimate children in the sample died, a higher mortality figure than the city's 1916 infant mortality rate of 105.4 per 1000 births.[60] In 1921 a Cleveland doctor warned that stillbirths among illegimate children were double those of legitimate births. Maternal deaths were also much higher; reported illegitimate births were 2 percent of total births, but 4.4 percent of maternal deaths were of unwed mothers. The doctor attributed the infant mortality to the diet of condensed or cows' milk distributed free at dispensaries, and maternal mortality to inadequate pre- and postnatal care. Unwed mothers also had a higher death rate from abortion, which, because illegal, was likely to be either self-induced or administered by ill-equipped amateurs.[61]

These maternity facilities, however, offered more than medical care; all viewed themselves still—perhaps primarily—as reformatory institutions where, as in the nineteenth century, fallen women could be reclaimed to virtue. As the unwed mothers were in large part the same kinds of women they had always been, the homes and hospitals employed almost the same kind of reformatory tactics. The institutions, with the exception of the Maternity Hospital, all had strong denominational links, and in all "the religious element [was] strong."[62]

All still instructed women in cooking, sewing, and other domestic skills and placed them in domestic service jobs when possible. All stressed the desirability of a home-like atmosphere and, at the urging of the Conference, made a six-month confinement period mandatory, during which time the mother's maternal instincts could be fully developed. Every effort was made to keep mother and child together, even after release from the institution and even if this meant continued subsidy by the home or a child-caring agency such as the Humane Society. Social workers warned Conference members of the dire consequences of separating mother and child:

> Eleven years ago Bertha was made to give up her illegitimate baby. This was insisted upon by her parents who had what they thought was her interest at heart.... A year or so later Bertha married the father of her baby. In a couple of years another baby came to them, but only to live a short time. Last year Bertha wrote a letter to the Humane Society to learn what had become of her first baby and to ask if she might have him for her own. Never since he was torn from her arms, had she been able to go to bed at night without thinking of him. The baby cannot be found. It is quite probable that Bertha will become a nervous wreck, if the aching void that she has carried all these years is not filled.[63]

In two respects these women differed from those of the late nineteenth century: their age and their ethnicity. Case studies described very young girls: a 13-year-old impregnated by a 24-year-old man, for example, or a 14-year-old "colored girl" with an 18-month-old infant.[64] More methodical studies, however, indicate that the average age was about 20, with a maximum age of 34 and a minimum age of 13 in 1914; the median age in 1916 was between 17 and 22.[65] By the 1920s the ages began to drop slightly, a trend that continued. In 1922 more than 25 percent of the women were of school age.[66]

The 1914 study also reported that more than half of the women studied (51 of the 98) were foreign-born, reflecting the city's heterogeneous population.[67] The 1922 report, on the other hand, found a large majority of native-born mothers, but 75 of these 311 were black.[68] By 1923 black unwed mothers accounted for slightly more than 22 percent of all registered illegitimate births, although blacks constituted only 4.3 percent of the city's total population in 1920.[69] These rising figures resulted in the Salvation Army's opening of the Mary B. Talbert Home for black women, who were not routinely admitted to any of the maternity homes except St. Ann's.

This changed ethnic and racial background of unwed mothers was reflected in a rather oblique way by the fascination of the Conference and the social work profession as a whole with "feeble-mindedness" as an explanation for pregnancy out of wedlock or any kind of sexual deviancy.[70] Because the backgrounds of these immigrant and black mothers were obviously so different from their own, it was easy for middle-class social workers to regard them as mentally deficient, equating that with sexual nonconformity. Maternity homes were urged to administer IQ tests to their inmates, and a Conference Committee on Feeble-Mindedness reported that "Rescue homes for unwed mothers generally show a larger proportion of feeble-mindedness than the population at large." And, the committee warned, feeble-minded unwed mothers produced feeble-minded illegitimate children.[71] The Conference's insistence on the use of professional social workers suggests the growing conviction that the pious middle-class volunteer of the late nineteenth century no longer had enough in common with fallen women to be effective.

In 1928 Mabel Mattingly, a graduate of the School of Applied Social Sciences of Western Reserve University, published a master's thesis illustrating many of these trends that had developed in the 1920s. The thesis concentrated on 53 mothers who had been able to keep their children, so these women apparently had more resources than most. Yet their story is pathetic and familiar. Their median age was 20, about the same as unwed mother generally. They were not prostitutes, or even promiscuous; in 95 percent of the cases, pregnancy had occurred only after long-term sexual intimacy.[72] Yet 48 of the 53 women were single, left to cope alone with their pregnancies and infants by men who often were already married.

Most of these unwed mothers had contemplated or unsuccessfully attempted the desperate step of an illegal abortion.[73] Almost half were living with family or relatives, but this had not prevented them from attending public dances and unsavory places of recreation. Half of this group were domestic servants, although only 11.8 percent of employed women in Cleveland were engaged as domestics at this time.[74] Those who had been confined in maternity homes had been trained in domestic service, and some remembered with displeasure the smells of the laundry or caring for numerous babies.[75] Mattingly also noted that in 1926, 28 percent of the recorded illegitimate births were to black women.[76]

The Great Depression did not significantly alter the pattern of characteristics that Mattingly described, but the zeal for the reclamation of these fallen women began to diminish by the mid-1930s. Like other heavy industry towns, Cleveland felt the slump early and long. Neither private nor public efforts to relieve the city's unemployed and impoverished succeeded. City- and county-sponsored public works programs employed only a fraction of those men out of work and no women. The distribution of surplus foods by private agencies could not begin to feed the hungry. The city itself had not appropriated or distributed funds for direct relief since 1922, leaving this task to Associated Charities and the Jewish Social Service Bureau, whose case workers were swamped, even with the help of scores of volunteers.[77] After 1931 the Welfare Federation's annual fund drives fell far short of their goals—by $500,000 in 1932 and $600,000 in 1933[78]—leaving its participating agencies, especially Associated Charities, to plunge deeper and deeper into debt.[79] Not until 1933 did a public agency, the Cuyahoga County Relief Agency, mandated by the Federal Emergency Relief Act, take over from the private agencies the responsibility for direct relief. By then, 31 percent of Cleveland's work force was jobless.[80]

The Associated Charities had provided jobs for a few women in its Sewing Center, and the federal Civil Works Administration set up the first public works program for women, sewing and distributing garments to families on relief and working in public offices and libraries.[81] Nevertheless, the number of women receiving Mother's Pensions more than doubled between 1928 and 1934, and by 1938 42 percent of all families on relief were headed by women.[82]

Agencies and institutions that served women suffered also. The Women's Protective Association's Sterling House closed for lack of funds. Once wealthy residences like the YWCA's Stillman Witt and the WCTU's Mary G. Ingersoll Club ran deficits, as did the Humane Society and the Catherine Horstman Home.[83] All of the maternity homes, except for Mary B. Talbert, had declining numbers of inmates,[84] and all operated in the red after 1929. By the mid-1930s both the Retreat and the Florence Crittenton Home teetered on the brink of bankruptcy.[85] In response, the Conference on Illegitimacy took a long, hard look at the role of maternity homes in the community and at the kinds of women who used them.

The unwed mothers who came to the Conference's attention during the 1930s were still likely to undergo childbirth without support from the fathers of their children. Women tended to arrive by themselves at the maternity facilities, often in the last stages of labor and in need of emergency care. Few of the fathers seemed interested in visiting the women, although the maternity homes did not encourage such visits unless the man promised to marry the woman or at least acknowledge paternity.[86] By the mid-1930s social workers seldom even pursued or prosecuted the putative fathers either because forced marriages were no longer viewed with favor or because the expense involved was prohibitive, especially when hard times made it less likely that the father would pay anyway.[87]

A 1930 study of cases handled by two child-placing agencies and the Associated Charities indicated that only 15 of the 87 women married after bearing their children, and only 9 of these took their children with them. Three of the fathers received custody, but in one instance the mother had been committed to an institution for the feeble-minded. In only two other cases was financial support secured from the fathers. The vast majority of these women either shouldered the burden of child-care alone, or with some help from their families, or placed their infants up for adoption, a trend that accelerated during the 1930s and was a reversal of the earlier policy of keeping the woman and child together.[88]

Although these unwed mothers could sometimes count on help from their families after their babies were born, families seemed increasingly unwilling or unable to provide support prior to the birth. According to this same study, women pregnant out of wedlock were referred to the child-placing agencies seldom by relatives and most often by maternity facilities such as St. Ann's, the obstetrical dispensaries, or general hospitals, by the Women's Police Bureau and Juvenile Court, or by relief agencies such as Associated Charities or Catholic Charities.[89]

As indicated by the frequent referral from relief agencies, unwed mothers, as before, were poor, their always precarious economic plight worsened by the Depression. A massive report compiled by the Conference in 1936 underscored this poverty. Of those women who were employed in 1935, more than half were domestic servants. Although only 19 listed themselves as unemployed, 80 of the 482 were on relief.[90] Less than half of the city's unwed mothers bore their children in maternity homes; the Cuyahoga County Relief Agency would not pay the costs of confinement there. The proportion of these women who had their children at home or in the charity wards of Cleveland City Hospital increased.[91]

In 1935 almost 30 percent of unwed mothers whose births were registered were black, although blacks constituted only 8 percent of the city's population in 1930.[92] More than 10 percent of all black registered births were illegitimate, as compared with 2.3 percent of white registered births.[93] These blacks were the poorest of the women, and the youngest. The median age for white women was 21, and for black women, 17.[94] Twenty percent of the black women were unemployed; of the 22 who had jobs, 21 were domestics. Almost half of the women on the relief rolls were black, as were more than half of the women whose children were born in Cleveland City Hospital.[95]

The 1936 study had been prompted in large part by the Conference's desire to discover why fewer women entered maternity homes. An obvious explanation was the declining birthrate; regular maternity hospitals also had empty beds.[96] As early as the 1930s, however, there had been criticism of the "strictness and closeness with which a girl is held both during confinement and after."[97] Conference members were even more critical of the policies that the homes felt necessary to achieve their traditional goal of reformation. Homes still kept the women in a cloistered setting, preventing most outside excursions, limited vocational training to domestic work, and insisted whenever possible on the long, expensive confinement.[98] Over the expressed objections of the maternity homes' representatives, the Conference suggested that more flexible and less costly programs, such as the placement of unwed mothers in foster homes, might be preferable to institutional care.[99]

As in the 1910s when the Conference began to stress the professionalization of services and mental testing of unwed mothers, the Conference's shift in policy—the waning enthusiasm for the homes—was a response to changed circumstances and changed perceptions of clientele. The Welfare Federation and the Conference may well have felt that in the face of the economic disaster of the 1930s there were more pressing needs than the reformation of women pregnant out of wedlock, especially as many were black, and especially as the maternity homes did not seem in fact to be reforming or reclaiming their inmates. Although the homes always liked to boast of their successes, they had always recorded occasional failures too. The Retreat board, for example, sadly noted in 1872: "Some [women] have returned to their former lives of sin, tis true, and that is the experience of every such institution [as ours]."[100] And in 1915 the Florence Crittenton Home puzzled "as to what to do with a young woman with a second illegitimate baby who shows no disposition to work or even to be of any service in the household ... and is back with her original bad companions and seems altogether indifferent."[101] Women who bore a second,—or even a third, illegitimate child after lengthly stays in maternity homes obviously weakened their claims to effect a moral transformation. One of the few case studies from the 1930s, for example, helps to explain the growing reluctance of social workers to refer women to the homes:

> This woman of good American stock, a woman of 25 years of age now, is of normal intelligence and healthy. Under proper influences her behavior is socially acceptable. She has been pregnant five times, had two miscarriages, and placed her three children up for adoption. All confinements had been in Cleveland maternity homes. The social agencies had known her ... [S]he had married the father of her first child, but he had not provided a home, and he was not the father of the other two children. The father of one child was colored, and the father of the other Jewish. While one social agency was attempting to follow her up on two separate cases reported, she was being confined in a maternity home for the second time under a different name. The case work agency never did catch up with her. At Probate Court two separate cases on her children were being investigated when it was discovered she was one and the same mother going by different names.[102]

In 1936 the city's first maternity home, the Retreat, closed its doors; its pleas to the Conference for continued support had been unavailing.[103] The surviving maternity homes sheltered a smaller and smaller proportion of the city's unwed mothers in the decades to come.[104] The Conference of Illegitimacy itself died in 1936. Some of its work was carried on by a committee of the Children's Council of the Welfare Federation, but the Conference's detailed descriptions of fallen women were not duplicated. Later studies of illegitimacy in Cleveland and elsewhere have focused almost exclusively on the race and age of unwed mothers.[105] This narrowed focus had its origins in the 1920s and 1930s, when unwed mothers became increasingly young and increasingly black. The fallen woman who now haunts the American imagination is the black, teen-aged mother of several illegitimate children, all on ADC; she is no longer viewed as a soul reclaimable by pious matrons, but as a sexually promiscuous burden on the taxpayer.

Between the opening and closing of the Retreat, Cleveland experienced dramatic changes. The city's economy shifted from commerce to heavy industry. Its native-born white population gave way to an ethnically and racially diverse citizenry as the city became a giant metropolis. The responsibility for

Cleveland's dependent people became less a private and more a public responsibility. Trained professionals took the place of the benevolent ladies who had earlier distributed material relief and spiritual salvation. Yet although her setting may have been very different. Cleveland's fallen woman in the midst of the Great Depression remained much as she had been at the conclusion of the Civil War: too often abandoned, too easily exploited, too often dependent on the charity of those from whose grace she had fallen.

NOTES

1. The title is adapted from Wendy Martin, "Seduced and Abandoned in the New World: The Fallen Woman in American Fiction," in Wendy Martin, ed., *The American Sisterhood: Writings of the Feminist Movement from Colonial Times to the Present* (New York, 1972), 257-272.

2. Young Women's Christian Association, Cleveland, Newspaper clipping, 1869, in scrapbook, Container 11, MS 3516, Western Reserve Historical Society. Hereafter this collection will be referred to as YWCA, Cleveland, although the group is called the Woman's Christian Association until 1893.

3. Egal Feldman, "Prostitution, the Alien Woman, and the Progressive Imagination," *American Quarterly* (Summer 1967), 194.

4. Ruth Rosen, *The Lost Sisterhood: Prostitution in America, 1900-1918* (Baltimore, 1982), xiii, 40-46; Mark Thomas Connelly, *The Response to Prostitution in the Progressive Era* (Chapel Hill, NC, 1980), 29-34.

5. On antebellum moral reform, see Barbara Berg, *The Remembered Gate: Origins of American Feminism: The Woman and the City, 1800-1860* (New York, 1978); Carroll Smith-Rosenberg, *Religion and the Rise of the American City: The New York City Mission Movement, 1812-1870* (Ithaca, NY, 1971); Flora L. Northrup, *The Record of a Century, 1834-1934* (New York, 1934); Kathleen D. McCarthy, *Noblesse Oblige: Charity and Cultural Philanthropy in Chicago, 1849-1929* (Chicago, 1982); and on later antiprostitution efforts, David Pivar, *The Purity Crusade, Sexual Morality, and Social Control* (Westport, CT, 1973); Rosen, *The Lost Sisterhood;* Connelly, *The Response to Prostitution.* The Salvation Army refuges are described in Herbert A. Wisbey, Jr., *Soldiers Without Swords: A History of the Salvation Army in the United States* (New York, 1955) and Edward H. McKinley, *Marching to Glory: The History of the Salvation Army in the United States* (New York, 1980); and those of the National Florence Crittenton Mission in Katherine G. Aiken, "The National Florence Crittenton Mission, 1883-1925: A Case Study in Progressive Reform" (Ph. D. dissertation, Washington State University, 1980) and Otto Wilson, *Fifty Years Work with Girls, 1883-1933* (Alexandria, VA, 1933). The Inter-City Conference on Illegitimacy is

described briefly in Fred S. Hall, ed., *Social Work Year Book, 1935* (New York, 1935), 596, and often is referred to in the minutes of the Cleveland Conference on Illegitimacy in the collection of the Federation for Community Planning, Cleveland, Ohio, MS 3788, Western Reserve Historical Society.

6. Barbara Brenzel, *Daughters of the State: A Social Portait of the First Reform School for Girls in North America, 1865-1905* (Cambridge, 1983), 107-135; Steven Ruggles, "Fallen Women: The Inmates of the Magdalen Asylum of Philadelphia, 1836-1908," *Journal of Social History* (Summer 1983), 65-82; Percy Gamble Kammerer, *The Unmarried Mother: A Study of Five Hundred Cases* (Boston, 1918).

7. Edmund H. Chapman, *Cleveland: Village to Metropolis: A Case Study of Problems of Urban Development in Nineteenth-Century America* (Cleveland, 1964), 97-150; William Ganson Rose, *Cleveland: The Making of a City* (Cleveland, 1950), 361.

8. Works Progress Administration of Ohio, *Annals of Cleveland, 1818-1935*, vol. 52 (1869) (Cleveland, 1937), 614; vol. 48, (1865), 60, 68, 83.

9. Quoted in Milred Esgar, "Women Involved in the Real World: A History of the Young Women's Christian Association of Cleveland, Ohio" (unpublished typescript, Western Reserve Historical Society, vol. 1, 41.

10. Esgar, "Women," vol., 1, 42.

11. Ibid., p. 41.

12. *The Earnest Worker*, June 1874, 5; *Cleveland Plain Dealer*, clipping, no date, but probably 1893, unpaged.

13. *Earnest Worker*, Novemer 1875, 2.

14. See Berg, *The Remembered Gate*, 177-193; Smith-Rosenberg, *Religion*, 98-113.

15. YWCA, Cleveland, *Annual Report*, 1870, 15, Container 8, Folder 1.

16. Ibid., 1872, 3, Container 8, Folder 2.

17. Ibid., "After Thirty Years" (1899), Container 10, Folder 9.

18. Salvation Army Rescue Home, Cleveland, Ohio, *Annual Report, 1893* (Cleveland, 1893), 7.

19. YWCA, Cleveland, Minutes, March 4, 1879, Container 1.

20. Salvation Army, *Diamonds in the Rough: Annual Report, Salvation Army Rescue Work in Cleveland* (Cleveland, 1905), 6.

21. Salvation Army, *Links of Love: Annual Report, Salvation Army Rescue Work in Cleveland* (Cleveland, 1904), 10.

22. Letter from Sister M. Peter, Superior of St. Ann's to Rev. Ignatius F. Horstman, August 27, 1904, Archives of the Cleveland Catholic Diocese, Cleveland.

23. Maternity Hospital, *Annual Report* (Cleveland, 1909), 17.

24. YWCA, Cleveland, *Annual Report*, 1872, 3, Container 8, Folder 2.

25. Salvation Army Rescue Home, Cleveland, Ohio *Annual Report*, 1893.

26. For another example of this technique, see Barbara Brenzel, "Domestication as Reform: The Socialization of Wayward Girls," *Harvard Educational Review* 50 (Spring 1980).

27. Salvation Army Rescue Home, *Annual Report*, 1893, 4.

28. YWCA, Cleveland, *Annual Report*, 1909, 22, Container 9, Folder 7.

29. Ibid., 1901, 17, Container 12.

30. David M. Katzman, *Seven Days a Week: Women and Domestic Service in Industrializing America* (Urbana, IL, 1981), 44; Rose, *Cleveland*, 608.

31. Katzman, *Seven Days*, 310, gives salary figures for cities comparable to Cleveland.

32. Salvation Army Rescue Home, *Annual Report*, 1893, 5.

33. For example, YWCA, Cleveland, "Minutes," January 3, 1888, Container 1; Florence Crittenton Home, MS 3910, Western Reserve Historical Society, Board of Trustees Minutes, December 15, 1913, Container 1. Folder 11.

34. YWCA, Cleveland, "Minutes," November 7, 1882, Container 1; Salvation Army, *Annual Report of the Salvation Army Home in Cleveland* (Cleveland, 1907), 19; Report of St. Ann's Infant Asylum and Maternity Hospital in Cleveland, Ohio, n.p., Archives of the Cleveland Catholic Diocese.

35. Richard W. Wertz and Dorothy C. Wertz, *Lying-In: A History of Childbirth in America* (New York, 1977), 132-177.

36. St. Ann's Maternity Hospital and Infant Asylum, Report, n.d., n.p., Archives of the Cleveland Catholic Diocese.

37. Maternity Home, Cleveland, Ohio, Constitution and By-Laws, 1892, 1.

38. The regimen in maternity homes resembled that in women's prisons described by Estelle B. Freedman, *Their Sisters' Keepers: Women's Prison Reform in American 1830-1930* (Ann Arbor, 1981), 89-96.

39. Cleveland Federation of Charity and Philanthropy, *The Social Year Book: The Human Problems and Resources of Cleveland* (Cleveland, 1913), 8.

40. Ibid., p. 9.

41. Ibid., p. 34.

42. *Annual Report of the Department of Public Safety, Division of Charities and Corrections and Cemeteries of the City of Cleveland* (Cleveland, 1910) 84-85.

43. Federated Churches of Cleveland, Ohio, *Vice Conditions in Cleveland* (Cleveland, 1916), 2.

44. City of Cleveland, Ohio, Division of Public Health, *Annual Report* (Cleveland, 1925), 118, reported that "birth registration has been a favorite subject for annual lamentations by health officials" at least since 1891; the undercount was estimated as low as 75 percent for some years, but by the late 1920s figures were thought to be about 98 percent accurate. However, if anyone got omitted, women who bore illegitimate children did. As Daniel Scott Smith has commented, "The most easily counted events in American history tend to be those belonging to people who 'counted' at the time; these are not the people most likely to conceive children out of wedlock," in "The long Cycle in American Illegitimacy and Prenuptial Bastardy," in Peter Laslett et al., eds., *Bastardy and Its Comparative History* (Cambridge, MA, 1980), 364. A contemporary study of unwed mothers in Boston whose conclusions resemble those of the Conference on Illegitimacy in many ways is Kammerer, *The Unmarried Mother: A Study of Five Hundred Cases* (Boston, 1918); Kammerer points out that "the illegitimacy rate is barely ever accurate, particularly in the United States. A certain group of the population, furthermore, is possessed of sufficient means to enable them to secure abortions which again prevent the registration of their illicit sex intercourse from the pages of birth registration" (p. 2). These records gathered by the Cleveland Conference, therefore, are incomplete, as are the records from the separate institutions, but both sets of records are the best available.

45. This specialization is reflected in the rising proportion of children to women recorded by the Retreat: YWCA, Cleveland, *Annual Report*, 1872, Container 8, Folder

2; *Annual Report*, 1891, 20, Container 8, Folder 4; *Annual Report*, 1912, 39, Container 9, Folder 10. The Salvation Army facility, like others nationally, became known as a "maternity hospital" rather than a rescue in the first decade of this century, as noted in Robert Sandall, *The History of the Salvation Army* (London, 1947), vol. 111, 1883-1953, 199.

46. Federation for Community Planning, Cleveland, Ohio, MS 3788, Western Reserve Historical Society, Conference on Illegitimacy, October 6, 1913, Container 21, Folder 516. Hereafter this collection will be referred to as FCP.

47. *Proceedings of the National Conference of Social Work, 1917* (Chicago, 1917) 285-286.

48. FCP, Conference on Illegitimacy, May 25, 1914, Container 21, Folder 516.

49. Ibid., May 9, 1921, Container 30, Folder 739.

50. Ibid., December 5, 1921, Container 30, Folder 739.

51. Ibid., May 25, 1914, Cintainer 21, Folder 516.

52. Ibid.

53. Ibid., "The Umarried Mother and Her Child." Container 30, Folder 738.

54. Ibid., "A Study of the Registration of Illegitimate Births for the Year 1922," Container 30, Folder 739.

55. Ibid., January 27, 1916, Container 21, Folder 516.

56. Ibid., December 5, 1921, Container 30, Folder 739.

57. Ibid., February 16, 1925, Container 30, Folder 739.

58. Ibid., April 6, 1914, Container 30, Folder 738.

59. Ibid.

60. Ibid., May 25, 1914, Container 21, Folder 516; City of Cleveland, Ohio, Division of Public Health, *Annual Report*, 26.

61. FCP, Conference on Illegitimacy, "The Illegitimacy Problem from the Medical Standpoint," Container 30, Folder 739.

62. Cleveland Federation of Charity and Philanthropy, *A Social Year Book*, 35.

63. Ibid., "The Unwed Mother as Deserted Wife," Container 30, Folder 738.

64. Ibid., December 8, 1913; May 3, 1915, Container 21, Folder 516.

65. Ibid., May 25, 1914, Container 21, Folder 516; "The Unwed Mother," Container 30, Folder 738.

66. Ibid., "A Study of the Registration of Illegitimate Births," Container 30, Folder 739.

67. Ibid., May 25, 1914, Container 21, Folder 516.

68. Ibid., "A Study of the Registration of Illegitimate Births," Container 30, Folder 739.

69. Ibid., June 21, 1924; Howard Whipple Greer, *Population Characteristics by Census Tracts, Cleveland, Ohio* (Cleveland, 1931), 9.

70. Rosen, *The Lost Sisterhood*, 21-23, discusses the progressive use of IQ tests on prostitutes and the not surprising results that showed these women too as "feeble-minded."

71. FCP, Conference on Illegitimacy, "The Menace of the Feeble-Minded," Container 30, Folder 738.

72. Mabel H. Mattingly, *The Unmarried Mother and her Child: A Fact-Finding Study of Fifty-Three Cases of Unmarried Mothers Who Kept Their Children* (Cleveland, 1928), 15 and 26.

73. Ibid., p. 26.

74. Ibid., p. 19; Katzman, *Seven Days*, 287.

75. Mattingly, *The Unmarried Mother*, 25.

76. Ibid., p. 7.

77. On Cleveland in the early years of the Depression, see Bing, *Social Work*, 14-26; and Florence T. Waite, *A Warm Friend for the Spirit: A History of the Family Service Association of Cleveland and Its Forebearers, 1830-1952* (Cleveland, 1960) 235-295.

78. FCP, Container 9, F. 178, disclose shortfalls until 1942.

79. Waite, *Warm Friend*, 239.

80. Rose, *Cleveland*, 912.

81. Waite, *Warm Friend*, 257-258; Bing, *Social Work*, 23.

82. Howard Whipple Greene, *Nine Years of Relief, Greater Cleveland, 1928-1937* (Cleveland, 1937), 2; Bing, *Social Work*, 23.

83. FCP, Container 8, Folders 187 and 188, records the deficits of many of the Federation's participating agencies.

84. FCP, Conference on Illegitimacy, November 30, 1936, Container 33, Folder 829. This is a lengthy joint report done by the Conference and a committee of the Federation's Children Council, which shortly thereafter took over the Conference's work.

85. FCP, Container 8, Folders 187 and 188.

86. FCP, Conference on Illegitimacy, January 23, 1943, Microfilm Reel 33.

87. Ibid., May 14, 1934.

88. Ibid., "The Unmarried Family," Container 30, Folder 741.

89. Ibid.

90. Ibid., November 30, 1936, Container 33, Folder 829.

91. Ibid.

92. Ibid.; Green, *Population Characteristics*, 9.

93. FCP, Conference on Illegitimacy, November 30, 1936, Container 33, Folder 829.

94. Ibid.

95. Ibid.

96. Ibid., October 1, 1936, Container 33, Folder 829.

97. Ibid., "Resume of the Activities of the Cleveland Conference on Illegitimacy, 1930-1931," Microfilm Reel 33.

98. Ibid., May 14, 1934, Microfilm Reel 33.

99. Ibid., Committee on Unmarried Mothers, May 2, 1935, October 21, 1935 and February 5, 1936, Container 33, Folder 829.

100. YWCA, Cleveland, *Annual Report*, 1872, 3, Container 8; Folder 2.

101. FCP, Conference on Illegitimacy, April 19, 1915, Container 30, Folder 738.

102. Ibid., June 3, 1933, Microfilm Reel 33.

103. Ibid., Committee on Unwed Mothers, February 5, 1936, Container 33, Folder 829.

104. FCP, Committee on Unmarried Mothers, "A Study of the Needs of Unmarried Mothers," 1948, Container 33, Folder 829; *Out of Wedlock: Births in the Greater Cleveland Community: Report of the Unmarried Parents Planning Committee of the Welfare Federation, 1971* (Cleveland, 1971), 13.

105. As examples, see ibid,; Smith, "The Long Cycle"; United States Department of Health, Education, and Welfare, *Trends in Illegitimacy in the United States, 1940-1963* (Washington, D.C., 1963).

TACIT ACCEPTANCE: RESPECTABLE AMERICANS AND SEGREGATED PROSTITUTION, 1870-1910

Neil L. Shumsky

During the latter half of the nineteenth century and early years of the twentieth, American cities experimented with the informal legalization of prostitution. While laws against prostitution, solicitation, and pandering remained on the books, they were selectively enforced. Women who confined their activities to certain "segregated" or "tolerated" districts were generally left alone and allowed to practice their profession. By 1900, nearly every large American city, and many smaller ones, too, possessed a recognized and well-known red-light district where prostitution flourished. San Francisco's Barbary Coast, New Orleans' Storyville, Chicago's Levee, and New York's Tenderloin may not have been household words, but few citizens of the metropolis remained unaware of such regions, their residents, and the forbidden pleasures obtainable there. Even the most naive knew about the local district.

Historians, sociologists, and contemporary observers have offered many explanations for the existence of these districts. Taking an economic view, some have suggested that prostitutes themselves chose to cluster in areas that were advantageous for business and where the greatest number of potential clients might be found. Others have argued that concentration resulted from conscious decisions by policemen and other municipal officials who believed that prostitution could not be abolished and that they could oversee it better if it was confined to a single section of town. Still others have emphasized public health considerations and claim that concern about venereal disease produced a desire to regulate prostitution and provide frequent health examinations of the women, examinations which could be more easily offered if prostitutes were limited to a particular district.

All of these explanations have merit and point to correlates of the red light district in almost every American city of the late nineteenth and early twentieth centuries. And yet, each of them, collectively and individually, fails to explain the "tacit acceptance" of respectable American urbanites for a separate zone of prostitution. None of the explanations accounts for the almost universal willingness to sanction the existence of urban prostitution so long as prostitutes confined their activities to a distinct area, usually located on the fringe of the Central Business District. Americans considered prostitution to be evil, animal, and unhealthy – but also inevitable. They tolerated it as long as they also believed that it could be segregated and restricted to a certain segment of the social order. At the same time, they saw social benefits to be derived from the existence of a separate red light district. It served, in their eyes, as a means of controlling the lower and working classes and of protecting respectable women from the supposedly rampant sexuality of immigrant men. Such a district helped establish the boundaries of proper behavior; those who accepted the sexual norms of proper society avoided the district while those who rejected propriety frequented it.

In order to develop this analysis, it is necessary to distinguish carefully between the historical study of prostitution and the historical study of the red light district. In recent years, social historians have begun to study prostitution as an indication of such important problems as social values, gender politics, reform, and class relations in a number of Western societies including the United States, England, Spain, France and Italy. However, with a few exceptions, their interest has been in prostitution generally and not in the specific phenomenon of the red light district.[1] Obviously, the two subjects are closely related. There could not be red light districts, as we generally define them, without the prior existence of prostitution; but, there can be, is, and has been, prostitution without the existence of red light districts. The red light district is a distinctive social and geographic form which sometimes characterizes prostitution and was especially prevalent in American cities during the late nineteenth and early twentieth centuries. The question of why American urban prostitution took this particular form at that particular time is a question different from, but no less important than, why prostitution existed in these cities at all.

Put in the simplest terms, the red light district was a kind of ghetto, but instead of being an ethnic ghetto, it was an economic and social ghetto meant to segregate a certain group of people. Respectable Americans accepted the red light district as long as it did not spill over into their own space. Within the red light district, thus, lived all those people whose economic livelihood depended on prostitution – not just the women themselves but also the parasites who attached themselves to prostitutes and took advantage of their activities, pimps and madames to be sure, but also merchants who profited from the fact that prostitutes were frequently not allowd to leave the segregated district and therefore had to shop locally. There were clothiers who dealt in the distinctive raiment which marked the prostitute and singled her out from other women, furniture dealers who felt justified in charging whatever the market would bear, crooked doctors who promised cures for venereal disease in an age when no such cures existed, and unscrupulous laundrymen who made tidy sums from washing large quantities of used sheets and towels.[2] But the red light district frequently did not have exclusive use of its space. It overlapped with two other important urban regions, the downtown entertainment district and Chinatown. Located in and among the cribs and parlor houses, French restaurants and hot-sheet hotels, were dance-halls, variety shows, theatres and gambling dens. Respectable restaurants and cabarets adjoined brothels and low dives. By the turn of the century, "slumming" had become a popular form of middle-class entertainment as respectable citizens sought cheap, but socially-acceptable, visual thrills. An evening on the Barbary Coast, in Storyville, or at the Levee was one of the great entertainments offered by San Francisco, New Orleans, or Chicago.[3]

These thrills of the forbidden and the erotic were frequently combined with those of the distant and the exotic because the entertainment and red light districts also overlapped with Chinatown in many large American cities. One recent study has, in fact, argued that "the Chinatown of the late 19th and early 20th centuries should be considered as a segment of the much larger red light district."[4] According to Gunther Barth, this conjunction of Chinatown, the entertainment district, and the red light district can be understood as part of the functioning of the "safety valves of the control system." Within these parts of town, Chinese immigrants were "liberated... briefly from the shackles of work which debt bondage placed on their shoulders." In particular, "the visit to a gambling hall, a brothel, or an opium den added precious hours of freedom" to the lives of indentured emigrants. In Chinatown, "they saw themselves momentarily admitted to that life of leisure which in part had motivated them to leave their native village in search of a fortune overseas."[5]

Prostitution was especially important in Chinatowns because of the gender ratios for Chinese immigrants to the United States in the nineteenth century. With the inordinately high ratio of men to women, Chinese men had the option of celibacy or patronizing prostitutes (given the contemporary attitude toward inter-racial sex), and the great tongs, or secret societies, quickly began to import girls for sexual purposes. These associations soon controlled prostitution in the Chinatowns and became rich from the business.[6]

However, the Chinatown red light district had other than Chinese clients. White men seem to have been regular patrons, and "there seems no-doubt that the dollars of white visitors enabled American Chinatowns to support many more bordellos, opium dens, and gambling halls than would have been possible solely on the basis of Chinese patronage." Chinatown prostitutes of all races seem to have had certain advantages in attracting white customers. These women, in general, sold their services more cheaply than their sisters outside this area. Moreover, white customers seem to have felt freer about asking Chinese women to perform certain acts which they would not have mentioned to white prostitutes. Finally, Chinatown provided its customers with a level of anonymity and security from apprehension not guaranteed elsewhere in the city. Whether men patronized white or Chinese prostitutes, they knew that Chinatown's underworld would provide protection from the city's police and that a complex security system allowed customers to avoid arrest if raids did occur.[7] This desire of white men for illegal sexual services helps explain why Chinese immigrants, who were disadvantaged in the general labor force, "had a motive to find compensatory livelihoods in illegal industries."[8] Taken together with Chinatown's internal demand for prostitution, the relationship between Chinatown and the red light district becomes much easier to understand.

The geographic overlap of the red light district with Chinatown was obviously one of the distinctive features which differentiated the late nineteenth-century American urban red light district from that of earlier Western cities. Another major difference was the general location of the zone of prostitution at the end of the century. Prior to this time, red light districts had frequently been located on the outskirts of cities, often beyond the city's walls. During the thirteenth century, the prostitutes of Paris were confined to certain streets outside the city's fortifications. During the Middle Ages, London, too, restricted prostitutes to a section just outside the city walls.[9] But, in American cities, the red light district was usually located in the heart of the city, frequently adjoining the Central Business District. This location created a fascinating paradox. On the one hand, by segregating all prostitutes and confining them to a single district, the city seemed to make prostitution *in*visible. Simply by staying out of this section, one could avoid taking cognizance of the business or its practitioners. But, by locating the district at its very center, the city emphasized its existence and heightened its visibility. In some cities, citizens almost had to avoid the red light district consciously, thus intensifying their awareness of its existence. By allowing the red light district to occupy such visible locations, American cities contradicted what has always been suggested as one of the major reasons for segregating prostitution, making it less noticeable.[10]

The explanation of this paradox lies in understanding the very existence of the red light district in American cities and recognizing why American urbanites tacitly accepted the district until the great crusade of the World War I era virtually wiped the district off the map. Perhaps the most obvious explanation argues that prostitutes found it economically advantageous to cluster in areas attractive and accessible to their clients. By gathering together, women could offer their patrons a range of alternative partners, and a man could shop for an appealling bedmate. Therefore, prostitutes generally congregated on the fringe of the central business district, in or near the downtown entertainment section where restaurants, cafes, dancehalls, and theatres drew men looking for amusement. Such an area also benefited from its usual location near major concentrations of hotels and boarding-houses, thereby providing access to both prospective clients and accommodations.[11]

This argument explains why prostitutes themselves might have preferred to assemble in a particular district, but it assumes that these women could freely choose their location. In fact, they could not. Municipal officials, especially the police, endlessly debated the acceptable location for prostitution, and prostitutes reacted quickly to any change in official policy by relocating.[12] Therefore, the role of the police must also be considered when accounting for the existence of the red light district. Generally-speaking, nineteenth-century police departments across the country confined prostitution to certain locations. For example, the General Superintendent of Chicago's Police Department issued a set of "Rules Governing the Regulation of Vice." Rule 10 explicitly stated that "no house of ill-fame shall be permitted outside of certain restricted districts," nor could any be established within two blocks of a school, church, hospital, public institution, or street car line. The following year, San Francisco's Board of Health, in conjunction with the Police Department, required all prostitutes to "confine themselves to... named streets and boundaries."[13]

John Warren, a New York City officer for 30 years, reflected a common view among police when he described prostitution as "a crime against the state" which "cannot be wholly eradicated." For the good of society, however, it had to be regulated by law, and this could be done most effectively if the practice was confined to specific districts. Several other New York police told the 1875 Assembly Committee on Crime "that as houses of ill-repute could not be suppressed, they should be licensed." J. Thomas Hollinberger, a District of Columbia Police Captain, testified before the Illinois Vice Commission that he favored segregation because repression could not be accomplished.[14] The police also had another motive for advocating segregation: they believed it would make their own job easier. Criminals, they thought, would flock to the crime-ridden ambiance of the red light district where cops could scoop them up with the aid of hookers acting as stool pigeons.[15]

The segregated district could not have survived without police involvement, but the fact that the police advocated segregation is not alone a sufficient explanation for its persistence. The basic problem is why the urban populace (or that part of it with power and influence) permitted the police to tolerate an activity clearly in violation of the law. None of the literature about the disappearance of the red light district suggests that the police, on their own initiative, voluntarily changed their minds and attempted to suppress prostitution. Every account of the early twentieth-century crusade against prostitution argues that the public, or some segment of it, turned against the system of segregation and forced its abandonment.

If we accept the argument that "the public" turned off the red light after 1910, we need to know why they let it burn brightly before then. Moreover, many contemporaries recognized the implicit acceptance of the system. In 1880, a New York policeman charged with neglect of duty for not suppressing brothels on his beat claimed that he had done his best but was hindered by the apathy, and even the opposition, of citizens, magistrates, and others. The Syracuse Vice Commission later claimed that the appalling conditions in that city at least partly resulted from the "indifference" and "tacit acquiescence" of the citizenry. The Charleston Vice Commission concluded that the local district reflected a "lack of united effort in demanding a change in the intolerable conditions as they now exist."[16]

Another explanation claims that American cities tolerated segregated red light districts between about 1870 and 1910, at least in part, for health reasons. During the late nineteenth century, most Americans blamed the spread of venereal disease on prostitutes who infected their patrons. Those who also believed prostitution ineradicable suggested solving the public health problem by instituting a system of medical regulation and examination. Only uninfected prostitutes would be allowed to practice their profession. Usually, this system also involved physical segregation in order to keep better track of the women and ensure their compliance with the regulations.[17]

Throughout the period, but especially in the 1870s, many Americans, and especially doctors, toyed with the idea of actually legalizing prostitution and requiring medical inspection of prostitutes. In 1867, the New York City Board of Health called for the registration of all prostitutes as a means of controlling disease, and in 1876 a city grand jury argued that legalization would stop the spread of disease. In 1874, a physician introduced a bill in the Pennsylvania legislature calling for the registration and medical inspection of all prostitutes. Three years later the Medical and Chirurgical Faculty of Maryland appointed a Committee of Five to memorialize the new legislature on the need for the medical regulation of prostitutes. On two occasions, the proponents of medical regulation actually carried the day, and systems of registration and examination were instituted in St. Louis in 1871 and San Francisco in 1911.[18]

Clearly then, a large number of Americans advocated segregating prostitutes for public health reasons. Despite 40 years of agitation, however, only two cities experimented with systems of inspection, and one of those depended largely on the support of vice interests themselves. The red light district generally existed without medical inspection, not as a reason for ensuring it.

Certainly the tendency toward "natural" segregation, together with police attitudes and public health concerns, all played a major part in the emergence and survival of the districts, but fall short of providing a completely satisfactory explanation for the phenomenon. That segregated prostitution endured in the face of constant and vociferous opposition (especially from churches and political reformers, among others), suggests a degree of acceptance by at least some segment of the population whose influence vastly outstripped the combined impact of marketing convenience, police attitudes, and public health theory. Unfortunately, there is almost no direct documentary evidence to show who countenanced the system and why. Unlike the early twentieth-century reformers who labored to extinguish the red light district, no one actively crusaded to preserve it, and no large group lobbied publicly for segregation. While there are isolated documents, quotations, and references, those who approved segregation left behind them no mountain of reports, studies, and papers. We have only the record of tacit acceptance, showing the "indisputable fact that a considerable percentage of the general adult population, both male and female... believe[d] that segregation [was] the one and only practical method of handling the social evil."[19]

However, it does seem likely that the comfortable classes of American cities generally tolerated the existence of the segregated district. As we have already seen, police departments, physicians, and municipal agencies frequently advocated the segregation of prostitutes. In addition, on three occasions, American cities formally instituted systems of legalized prostitution, and, each time, primary sponsorship seems to have had respectable origins. In 1871, St. Louis began registering prostitutes and examining them for venereal disease. The experiment lasted for four years, and, although it originated with a group of people "whose identity... is now lost in the past," John Burnham believes the plan was "backed by well-intentioned, respectable citizens (including a number of leading physicians)." Indeed, the most active public supporter of the measure was Mayor Joseph Brown, "an upstanding real estate and traction magnate."[20]

Nearly 30 years later, New Orleans made it "unlawful for any prostitute or woman notoriously abandoned to lewdness, to occupy, inhabit, live or sleep in any house, room or closet" outside of particular boundaries. Alderman Sidney Story, (hence "Storyville") "a respectable citizen and businessman," drafted the ordinance and based it on his study of European conditions. In his work, he had the assistance of Thomas McCaleb Hyman, "a prominent New Orleans attorney ...who did the legal research."[21]

Finally, in 1911, San Francisco began its own system of regulation and medical inspection. After the Fire of 1906, many citizens became concerned about the scattering of prostitutes throughout the city. The Civic League of San Francisco, an omnibus organization composed of about 90 neighborhood clubs and associations, took up the problem and asked its Committee on Education and Public Morals to study the situation jointly with its Committee on Public Health, Pure Food, and Tenement House Legislation. In 1907, after an extensive investigation, the two committees issued a report calling for the establishment of a segregated district and compulsory medical examination of all the prostitutes in the city.[22]

In addition to the experiences of St. Louis, New Orleans, and San Francisco, the European situation strongly suggests that respectable citizens generally accepted the segregation and regulation of prostitutes. This is, of course, not to say that the American and European conditions were identical. Nonetheless, we cannot disregard similarities which seem to reinforce the general pattern. In England, middle-class reformers sponsored the Contagious Disease Acts and especially favored their extension. In Italy, the urban middle class feared rural immigrants as a threat to property and political and economic stability. Administrators therefore sought to "prevent unpleasant contact between the bourgeoisie and the dangerous classes." One mechanism was by regulating prostitution.[23]

Arguing that respectable Europeans and Americans tacitly accepted the existence of segregated prostitution suggests a fascinating situation. During the last three decades of the nineteenth century, at precisely the time the red light district was flourishing, middle-class Americans and Europeans were confining their own sexuality to marriage. Perhaps the leading proponent of the historical interpretation that sexuality was being limited to marriage, Michel Foucault, has forcefully argued that during the eighteenth and nineteenth centuries sexuality became subject to social regulation and control. "The deployment of sexuality," as he calls it, "first developed on the fringes of familial institutions" and "gradually became focused on the family." The family became "reorganized" and "intensified" as "parents and relatives became the agents of a deployment of sexuality." Keith Thomas foreshadowed Foucault's argument in his study of the double standard and its decline in the nineteenth century. Thomas suggested that middle-class respectability and the heightened emphasis upon family life were major sources of attack upon the double standard, and he found that "a large body of middle-class opinion... has regarded illicit sexual activity outside marriage as equally unacceptable for men and women alike." Recently, Jeffrey Weeks, Michael Mitterauer and Reinhard Sieder have extended and developed these arguments. Weeks has shown that by 1800 sexual activity was "enshrined as a central element" in families. The idea of sexuality limited to marriage was "integrated into the bourgeois familial ideology of the nineteenth century." Mitterauer and Sieder's study of the European family has demonstrated that "middle-class standards... involved the confinement of sex within marriage" and that "a growing discrimination against pre- and extramarital [sexual] relationships" also developed among the middle class.[24]

Although Foucault, Thomas, Weeks, Mitterauer and Sieder all examined sexuality, marriage, and the family among the European bourgeoisie, other historians have recently made similar arguments about the American experience. Carroll Smith-Rosenberg has shown that a new ideology limited intercourse to marriage. Ellen K. Rothman has demonstrated that intercourse ceased to be an acceptable form of premarital sex for respectable American men and women during the second quarter of the nineteenth century. "Coitus was placed on its own continuum... as an altogether separate terrain, accessible only to married people." Finally, Robert Griswold's study of family and divorce in California has shown that, contrary to popular belief, middle-class men were not "allowed" to visit prostitutes. "To have permitted such adultery would violate the mutuality of the marriage bond and render meaningless the insistence that men and women adhere to the same sexual standard." Griswold cites numerous cases of men divorced for consorting with prostitutes and concludes that "men were subject to the same standards of marital fidelity as women."[25]

Thus, *two* problems require explanation. Why did the tolerated red light district spring up? Why did it become most important during the very era that so many Americans were becoming committed to the notion of marital fidelity and exclusive sexuality within marriage? The answers to both of these questions emerge by asking yet another. How was the new ideology spread and reinforced? By what mechanism did it come to be established and accepted? Although these historians of marriage and the family have devoted much attention and effort to explaining *why* the new system occurred, they have not spelled out *how* it occurred. It is in regard to this issue that the meaning and purpose of the red light district emerge, for it was a distinct part of the new deployment of sexuality. It elucidated for respectable Americans what the new standard had become for them – sexuality confined to marriage. Its existence helped disclose clearly and unmistakably the difference between acceptable and unacceptable behavior.

According to Kai Erikson, every group of people maintains boundaries. "Its members tend to confine themselves to a particular radius of activity and to regard any conduct which drifts outside that radius as somehow inappropriate or immoral." His theory also contains an implicit definition of a deviant – "a person whose activities have moved outside the margins of the group." Therefore, "deviant persons often supply an important service to society by patrolling the outer edges of group space and by providing a contrast which gives the rest of the community some sense of their own territorial identity." Erikson also argues that every society has its own way of deploying deviants and deviance; and he identifies three which appear frequently: special days on which rule violation is tolerated, special societies in which deviant behavior is considered normal for adolescents, and special clubs whose business it is to infringe ordinary group rules. Finally, Erikson posits a particular kind of deployment pattern characteristic of American society – "deviant behavior as the special property of a particular class of people who were more or less frozen into deviant attitudes." Americans have "generally thought it best to handle the problem by locking these people into fairly permanent deviant roles."[26]

In American cities between roughly 1870 and 1910, the segregated red light district served as another form of boundary maintenance – literally as well as figuratively. Nearly every advocate of segregation emphasized the need to avoid contaminating respectable neighborhoods and to separate moral from immoral behavior, just as traditional public health proponents had fought for the quarantine of biological plagues. The argument appeared repeatedly in New York City during the 1870s and 1880s. Letters and editorials in the *Times* questioned the desirability of police raids on disorderly houses and suggested that the major result would be to drive prostitutes into neighborhoods currently free from the nuisance. One study of Chicago's police department suggested that prostitution "be hammered and kept down" but not to the "extent of scattering it all over the city" and into the residential portions. The foreman of San Francisco's grand jury of 1913 wrote Mayor Rolph that repression would not end prostitution, but simply scatter it into respectable neighborhoods. The district gave people a choice; they could either go there or avoid it.

And this was the point. The existence of the district allowed people to declare themselves openly – to accept or reject the new standard of morality. A New York City grand jury of 1876 advocated segregation because "patronage. . . would be limited to those who are not ashamed or afraid to be seen" in the district. After a police raid in 1883, a group of citizens protested. They preferred prostitutes to be confined to an area "known and avoided by all the respectable people" rather than be in places where one's presence was no sign of shame. One doctor summed it up most fittingly. If a cesspool existed, "let it remain a cesspool." Avoid spreading its contamination everywhere. "Isolate it." People who wanted prostitutes "would go to them. Those who wished to avoid them could do so. They were well known for what they were."[27] The red light district clearly demonstrated the difference between acceptable and unacceptable behavior and thereby set boundaries for respectability.

The toleration of prostitution in a special, segregated district leads to yet another important question – where was this region to be located? The proponents never answered the question directly; they said only that it should be kept isolated from respectable neighborhoods. But even though they failed to define the difference between respectable and unrespectable overtly, it is possible to understand the distinction from the actual locations of the districts. The red light district was universally restricted to poor or marginal neighborhoods of American cities.[28]

By permitting prostitution in these areas of cities, but not in their own, respectable Americans not only developed the boundaries of proper behavior but also elaborated their own self-conception. Those citizens were distinguishing themselves from groups which had different sexual habits. As a result, prostitution was tolerable in *their* parts of the city. In other words, perceived sexual practices and ideology had become a major aspect of respectability. Jeffrey Weeks has similarly argued that in Victorian England the "prime task" of the new attitudes toward marriage and sexuality was "to articulate the class feelings and experiences of the bourgeoisie itself." During this era, the new ideology of the family "became a vital organizing factor in the development of middle-classness, and in the creation of a differentiated class identity." The domestic idea, with its attendant sexual fidelity, became "an expression of class confidence, both against the immoral aristocracy, and against the masses, apparently denied the joys of family life and prone to sexual immodesty and vice, 'fit only for sleep or sensual indulgence.' " Taking it one step further, Weeks has shown that the family not only exalted sexuality, "via the indispensable marriage bond," but also "severely regulated it. The paradox was that the more ideology stressed the role of sex within conjugality, the more it was necessary to describe and regulate those forms of sexuality which were without it."[29]

The tolerated red light district, existing near marginal neighborhoods, thus served to set boundaries and help define respectability. But it also existed to regulate the sexuality of less-comfortable Americans who presumably had not adopted or could not express the new standards of behavior. Just as in Europe, respectable Americans sought to control the sexuality of others, and the tolerated red light district was an important mechanism for doing so.[30] This idea can best be illustrated with another argument frequently presented by the champions of the segregated district. Over and over again, they claimed that without the district, respectable women would not be safe. Some who made the argument phrased it delicately. William Sanger said that the segregated district prevented virtuous women from being annoyed and insulted. James Rolph, the mayor of San Francisco, wrote that because of the system any woman could "walk all the streets of San Francisco, at any hour, day or night, without insult or embarrassment." Others were less cautious in expressing their concerns; they believed the district necessary because of the " 'passions of men who otherwise would be tempted to seduce young ladies.' " A.E. Boynton, President pro tem of the California Senate, opposed closing San Francisco's Barbary Coast because that action would lead to the "debauching of girls of good families... most of whom would preserve their virginity" otherwise. Finally, some openly expressed their real anxieties. One member of the Wisconsin Vice Commission believed in segregated prostitution because "the old Adam in man,... if denied gratification in one direction, would be certain to seek it in some other, probably more dangerous direction." As one physician told the American Medical Association in 1874, "if prostitution were abolished, crime of the most heinous and revolting character would be of incessant occurrence, and no virtuous woman would be secure from the assaults of the libertine." The Bridgeport Vice Commission said it without mincing words. "Vice is one of the weaknesses of men; it cannot be extirpated; if repressed unduly at one point, it will break out more violently and bafflingly elsewhere; a segregated district is really a protection to the morality of the womanhood of the city, for without it rape would be common."[31]

This fear of rape and seduction leads one to wonder the perceived source of the danger. Some proponents of segregation feared a general "licentiousness among men" and attributed the danger to the "many men whose passions were so violent and so ill-regulated that they would attain their gratification at any risk."[32] But others had a more restricted view of the problem and associated the danger with marginal members of society. One Wisconsin banker justified the district because of the number of sailors and lumberjacks in his town. The sheriff of Sheboygan said he kept the lights on because his town had six hundred Greeks, three or four hundred Lithuanians, and as many Austrians. Closing down the district would make the city worse than it already was. Julius Rosenstirn, the chief advocate of segregation in San Francisco, denied that laws could restrain the "mariner returning from the voyage, the miner, the woodsman, and the cowboy." Granville Price discovered that Galveston's city fathers allowed the district on into the 1930's and believed it necessary because of certain elements in the population – seamen and dock laborers, soldiers, college students, salesmen, mechanics, waiters, clerks, soda jerkers and bootleggers. Finally, the statistics of the New York City Dispensary in 1937 conveyed an "idea of the vice and disease which exist among and infect the large class who populate the overcrowded tenement districts of the city." The numbers seemed "to suggest almost promiscuous intercourse."[33]

The comfortable classes believed that large numbers of less well-to-do people had different sexual standards and feared that without the segregated district these different mores would lead to attacks on "respectable" women. In this attitude, they reflected a general belief that the poor and the immigrants were vicious, licentious, and animalistic. Witnesses before Congressional committees throughout the 1870s, 1880s and 1890s made this point reglarly and told lurid anecdotes – presumably illustrative of immigrant and working-class depravity. Henry J. Deily, representing the American Defense Association, told the House Committee on Immigration about a school teacher in Pennsylvania who had had to quit his job "because of the vile habits and practices of the Polish and Hungarian children." It was "utterly impossible to instill any sense of decency or decorum into their sex, the example of their parents and associates being too strong." The children had "no greater sense of shame or morality than a dumb brute." Adelbert Dewey, former editor of the *Journal of United Labor*, told the same committee about a building in Detroit inhabited by a "colony of Huns." Five rooms, each ten feet square, housed 127 people. In one room, five families were "sleeping in one common bed." Children "reared with such surroundings" would never make "respectable, law-abiding citizens," and Dewey especially warned his listeners who had "wives, mothers, sisters, and daughters." Did they "want to see such customs perpetuated?" Did they even "want to see it tolerated?"

In 1886, Secretary of State Bayard, concerned about the "quality" of immigrants to the United States, sent a circular letter to all American consuls in Europe and asked for information about marriage and divorce, natural and illegitimate children. The responses clearly reveal a belief that lower-class Europeans had a less refined set of sexual values. George W. Roosevelt wrote from Nantes that illegitimacy was "rarely known outside the working classes." From Dusseldorf, D.J. Partello reported an "excellent" standard of morality among the upper classes "but the contrary. . . case among the lower." Albert Woodstock, consul at Catania, found the morals of all classes "deplorable" from an American point of view, while Henry C. Crouch found that the Milanese had "a freer and broader conception of the marital relation than prevailed in the United States."[34] These beliefs produced a broadening of the groups forbidden to enter the United States. Until 1891, law had prohibited criminals, paupers, the insane, and the Chinese from immigrating. The Immigration Act of 1891 added to these classes "persons suffering from loathesome or dangerous and contagious diseases" (the widely-used euphemism for venereal disease) and "persons convicted of a felony or other infamous crime or misdemeanor involving moral turpitude."[35] Violations of proper behavior presumably originated outside the United States.

Because of their presumed immorality, some groups seemed like a threat to respectable women. They also seemed threatening because so many of them were unmarried. To Julius Rosenstirn, laws "Making the sexual act of unmarried individuals a punishable crime, while sanctifying it with a license" made no sense. The fierce call of the jungle could not be restrained, but since marriage was "impossible for the great majority of laboring men," he advocated regulated prostitution. The Medical Board of New York's Bellevue Hospital claimed that the expenses of living were a great obstacle and that a constantly increasing number of men could not afford wives. One San Francisco workingman himself wrote that he had come to San Francisco from England and been unable to marry. He was "a strong, robust, virile man" who, because of poverty, had turned in "bitter loneliness to the companionship and the caresses of the harlot."[36]

This, then, became a major concern to respectable Americans in the latter half of the nineteenth century. What should be done about what they perceived to be the rampant, uncontrolled, and uncontrollable sexuality of groups like workingmen and immigrants? They could not afford to marry, but, it was feared, if some outlet was not provided for their sexual urges, they would run amuck and attack respectable women on the streets. Obviously, because of their animality, celibacy was not an option. Because of contemporary medical belief, masturbation could not be advocated. And because of social, sexual, and religious strictures, homosexuality was not even considered. The only remaining option, if the wives, mothers, daughters, and sisters of respectable Americans were to be protected, was to provide an arena for the deployment and control of other men's sexuality. In 1874, Samuel D. Gross spoke to the American Medical Association and made this point clearly by quoting Sir William Jenner. "A large portion of the male population... are, at the age when the passions are the strongest, precluded by the necessity of their position from marriage. Under such conditions, either prostitution, seduction, or masturbation will be the prevailing vice. If by law public prostitution could be put down, the two latter of the three vices would undermine the health and lower the moral nature of the masses far more than does the present prevalence of the social evil. The inverse relation in the prevalence of masturbation, illegitimate children, and prostitution cannot be too strongly impressed on the public mind."[37]

Thus, accepting the existence of the red light district was part of the community politics of the era. American cities were becoming divided between the haves and the have-nots. There was a shifting balance of power with a disproportionate share of the resources – social, political, and economic – going to some segments of the population. Those who gained from the new distribution of resources wanted to entrench themselves further by controlling their adversaries. At the same time, they wanted to keep peace within the community and isolate themselves from the contagion of infection. One way of doing so was by providing their rivals with a separate space within which to act, a space within which to watch over, regulate, and subdue the lower, working, and immigrant classes.

The irony and the social biases inherent in the system did not escape the opponents of segregation. In 1874, Dr. J. Marion Sims addressed the American Medical Association on the subject of venereal disease and said that some scheme had to be created to prevent its importation from abroad. He proposed that a quarantine officer examine every sailor and steerage class passenger entering the country and remand syphillitics to hospitals. Aaron M. Powell, a leading advocate of repression, attacked Sims for "unjustly discriminating against the poor." If, as Sims also argued, prostitution was necessary to protect society in general and respectable women in particular, Powell sardonically observed that no home was "too sacred to furnish its offerings." If a victim class of women was inevitable, if somebody's daughters had to be despoiled, it was a Christian duty to be self-sacrificing, and the most Christian women of the community should offer themselves on the altar.[38]

Respectable women did not rush out to satisfy Powell's injunction, and Americans tolerated segregated districts for well over half a century. In this regard, they resembled their counterparts in both England and Italy where more formal systems of regulation were adopted. Judith Walkowitz has shown that in England the Contagious Disease Acts "broke new ground as domestic social measures, creating supervision of the lives of the poor." In Italy, according to Mary Gibson, the regulation of prostitution "represented an attempt by the state to extend its control over one section of the lower classes and isolate these contaminating agents as much as possible from the rest of society."[39]

Perhaps because of a lower level of class consciousness, perhaps because of a greater tradition of individual freedom, Americans never adopted a national system of regulating and segregating prostitutes, as did England, Italy, and several other European countries. But they did share with their European counterparts certain ideas about family, marriage, sexuality and the working class. In the United States, these ideas took form in the segregated districts of late nineteenth-century cities. The district helped set proper boundaries for sexual expression, reinforce the definition of respectability, and control the sexual behavior of marginal citizens. In doing so, the district became an important element in the establishment of acceptable behavioral norms.

Virginia Polytechnic Institute and State University Neil Larry Shumsky
Blackburg, Virginia 24061

FOOTNOTES

1. For a few exceptions to this generalization, see Richard Symanski, *The Immoral Landscape: Female Prostitution in Western Society* (Toronto, 1981); Neil Larry Shumsky and Larry M. Springer, "San Francisco's Zone of Prostitution, 1880-1934," *Journal of Historical Geography* 7 (1981): 71-89; Ivan Light, "From Vice District to Tourist Attraction: the Moral Career of American Chinatowns, 1880-1940," *Pacific Historical Review* 43 (1974): 367-394; Ivan Light, "The Ethnic Vice Industry, 1880-1944," *American Sociological Review* 42 (1977): 464-79.

2. Al Rose, *Storyville, New Orleans: Being an Authentic, Illustrated Account of the Notorious Red-Light District* (University of Alabama, 1974): 29-30; Sanborn Map Company, *San Francisco* (San Francisco, 1899).

3. Rose, *Storyville*; Sanborn Map Company, *San Francisco*; Herbert Asbury, *The Barbary Coast* (New York, 1933): 278-298; Light, "Ethnic Vice Industry;" Light, "From Vice District to Tourist Attraction."

4. Leonard U. Blumberg, Thomas E. Shipley, Jr., and Stephen F. Barsky, *Liquor and Poverty, Skid Row as a Human Condition* (New Brunswick, NJ, 1978): 212, 221.

5. Gunther Barth, *Bitter Strength, a History of the Chinese in the United States* (Cambridge, MA, 1964): 109-110, 126-129.

6. United States Bureau of the Census, *Historical Statistics of the United Sates, Colonial Times to 1957* (Washington, D.C., 1960); Light, "From Vice District to Tourist Attraction:" 372-373; Barth, *Bitter Strength*, 102, 107; Thomas W. Chinn, ed., *A History of the Chinese in California* (San Francisco, 1969), 67-68.

7. Light, "From Vice District to Tourist Attraction:" 370-374.

8. Light, "The Ethnic Vice Industry:" 468-469.

9. Symanski, *Immoral Landscape*, 21-22; Vern and Bonnie Bullough, *Prostitution, an Illustrated Social History* (New York, 1978): 119.

10. For a somewhat different interpretation of the visibility issue, see Symanski, *Immoral Landscape*, 2-5.

11. David R. Johnson, *Policing the Urban Underworld* (Philadelphia, 1979): 6, 152; Granville Price, *A Sociological Study of a Segregated District* (M.A. Thesis, University of Texas, Austin, 1930), 60; Walter C. Reckless, "The Distribution of Commercialized Vice in the City: A Sociological Analysis," in George A. Theodorson, ed., *Studies in Human Ecology* (New York, 1961): 52; Walter C. Reckless, *Vice in Chicago* (Chicago, 1933): 164; Syracuse, New York. Committee of Eighteen, *The Social Evil in Syracuse* (Syracuse, 1913), 15.

12. Shumsky and Springer, "San Francisco's Zone of Prostitution:" 71-89.

13. Chicago. Vice Commission, *The Social Evil in Chicago* (Chicago, 1911): 329, see also 33, 110; San Francisco. Department of PUblic Health, *Annual Report... 1911* (San Francisco, 1911): 3.

14. John H. Warren, Jr., *Thirty Years' Battle With Crime...* (New York, 1970): 39, 44; New York *Times*, Dec. 5, 1875; Illinois. Senate. Vice Committee, *Report* (np, 1911): 356; see also, New York *Times* May 26, 1880; John F. Decker, *Prostitution: Regulation and Control* (Littleton, CO 1979): 61; Robert M. Fogelson, *Big-City Police* (Cambridge, MA, 1977): 32, 70; Reckless, *Vice in Chicago*, 5; James F. Richardson, *The New York Police* (New York, 1970): 186; Robert E. Riegel, "Changing American Attitudes toward Prostitution (1800-1920)," *Journal of the History of Ideas* 29 (1968): 445; Samuel Walker, *A Critical History of Police Reform* (Lexington, MA, 1977): 98-99.

15. Thomas Byrnes, *1886 Professional Criminals of America* (New York, 1969): xvi; Mark Haller, "Historical Roots of Police Behavior: Chicago, 1890-1925," *Law and Society* 10 (1976); Reckless, *Vice in Chicago*, 235, 272.

16. New York *Times*, Feb. 5, 1880; Syracuse. Committee of Eighteen, *Social Evil*, 11; Chicago. Vice Commission, *Social Evil*, 144; Raymond B. Fosdick, "Prostitution and the Police," *Social Hygiene* 2 (1916): 15; Charleston, South Carolina. Law and Order League, *Special Report*, (Charleston, 1913): 20. See also, New York *Times*, March 5, 1874; Johnson, *Policing the Urban Underworld*, 147.

17. David J. Pivar, *Purity Crusade* (Westport, CT, 1973), 52-62; Aaron M. Powell, *State Regulation of Vice Regulation Efforts in America. The Geneva Congress* (New York, 1978): 48-49, 86; William M. Sanger, *The History of Prostitution* (New York, 1937): 693.

18. New York *Times*, Feb. 8, 1867; June 3, 1876; Powell, *State Regulation of Vice*; William L. Barrett, *Prostitution in its Relation to the Public Health* (St. Louis, 1873); Pivar, *Purity Crusade*, 51-60; John C. Burnham, "Medical Inspection of Prostitutes in America in the Nineteenth Century: the St. Louis Experiment and Its Sequel," *Bulletin of the History of Medicine* XLV (1971): 203-218; John C. Burnham, "The Social Evil Ordinance: A Social Experiment in Nineteenth-Century St. Louis," *Bulletin of the Missouri Historical Society* 27 (1971): 203-217; Neil Larry Shumsky,

"The Municipal Clinic of San Francisco," *Bulletin of the History of Medicine* 52 (1979): 542-559; Neil Larry Shumsky, "Vice Responds to Reform; San Francisco, 1910-1914," *Journal of Urban History* 7 (1980): 31-47.

19. Portland, Oregon. Vice Commission, *Report . . . to the Mayor and City Council . . .* (Portland, 1913), 207.

20. Burnham, "The Social Evil Ordinance," 204, 209.

21. Rose, *Storyville*, 193, 38.

22. George Flink, "Report of the Chairman of the Committee on Education and Public Morals of the Civic League," Red Plague Committee Papers (Commonwealth Club of California, San Francisco); Julius Rosenstirn, "The Municipal Clinic of San Francisco," *Transactions of the Fifteenth International Congress on Hygiene and Demography* IV (Washington, 1913): 93-115; Julius Rosenstirn, *The Municipal Clinic of San Francisco* (New York, 1913); Julius Rosenstirn, *Our Nation's Health Endangered by Poisonous Infection through the Social Malady, the Protective Work of the Municipal Clinic of San Francisco and Its Fight for Existence* (San Francisco, 1913).

23. Judith R. Walkowitz, *Prostitution and Victorian Society* (Cambridge, Eng., 1982), Chapter 4; Mary S. Gibson, *Urban Prostitution in Italy, 1860-1915; An Experiment in Social Control*, (Ph.D. Thesis, Indiana University, 1979): 28-29.

24. Michel Foucault, *The History of Sexuality* (New York, 1978), I, 110; Keith Thomas, "The Double Standard," *Journal of the History of Ideas*, XX (1959): 203-204; Jeffrey Weeks, *Sex, Politics, and Society* (London, 1981): 24-26; Michael Mitterauer and Reinhard Sieder, *The European Family* (Oxford, 1982): 129, 133.

25. Carroll Smith-Rosenberg, "Sex as Symbol in Victorian America: An Ethnohistorical Analysis of Jacksonian America," in John Demos and Sarane Spence Boocock, *Turning Points: Historical and Sociological Essays on the Family* (Chicago, 1978): S224; Ellen K. Rothman, "Sex and Self-Control: Middle-Class Courtship in America, 1770-1870," *Journal of Social History* 15 (1982): 415; Robert L. Griswold, *Family and Divorce in California, 1850-1890*, (Albany, 1982): 76, 117-118.

26. Kai Erikson, *Wayward Puritans, A Study in the Sociology of Deviance* (New York, 1966): 10, 11, 27-28, 196.

27. New York *Times*, April 1, 5, 1874; June 3, 1876; Nov. 26, 1883; May 25, Dec. 8, 1892; Alexander R. Piper, *Report of an Investigation of the Discipline and Administration of the Police Department of the City of Chicago* (Chicago, 1904): 15; William H. Ford to James Rolph, Jr., Feb. 28, 1913, James Rolph, Jr. Papers (California Historical Society Library, San Francisco); W.E. Whitehead, "The Social Evil," *Pacific Medical Journal* 5 (1871-72): 56-57. See also Cyrus Willoughby Waterman, *Prostitution and Its Repression in New York City, 1900-1931* (New York, 1968): 13; Reckless, "The Distribution of Commercialized Vice," in Theodorson, ed., *Studies in Human Ecology*, 50-52; William Burgess, *The World's Social Evil* (Chicago, 1914): 269; Kay Ann Holmes, "Reflections by Gaslight: Prostitution in Another Age," *Issues in Criminology* 7 (1972): 84. Marion s. Goldman has also used Erikson's theory of deviance to explain nineteenth-century treatment of prostitutes. Her interpretation focuses on the way in which "respectable" women were distinguished from prostitutes and how the categorization of the "prostitute" helped define proper behavior for other women. She thus relies on Erikson's theory of creating deviant roles as a deployment strategy. Marion S. Goldman, *Gold Diggers and Silver Miners. Prostitution and Social Life on the Comstock Lode* (Ann Arbor, 1981), esp. Chapter 7. This argument is unquestionably correct and is supported by the work of both Judith Walkowitz and Ruth Rosen. Walkowitz has found that in England, at the same time, working-class prostitutes became "a specially identified professional class." Walkowitz, *Prostitution and Victorian Society*, 210. Rosen notes that singling out "degraded" women served as an object lesson and a threat to others. "The specter of the whore was always before them as a reminder of what they might become or how

they might be treated if they failed to live up to the angel image." Ruth Rosen, *The Lost Sisterhood* (Baltimore, 1982), 6. Rosen's edition of the letters of Maimie Pinzer abounds with examples of prostitutes being labelled and differentiated from other women as a means of boundary-setting. Ruth Rosen and Sue Davidson, eds. *The Maimie Papers* (np, 1977): 10-11, 23, 273-274, 296, 328, 373. It is my contention that the toleration of the segregated red light district had functions in addition to defining and setting boundaries to women's proper sexual behavior. See also, Warren, *Thirty Years' Battle*, 145; and Reckless, *Vice in Chicago*, 54-55 on the "outcaste" nature of prostitutes.

28. Symanski, *Immoral Landscape*, 125-147; Rosen, *Lost Sisterhood*, 78; Wisconsin. Legislature. Committee on White Slave Traffic and Kindred Subjects, *Report and Recommendations*... (Madison, 1914): 26; Leonard U. Blumberg, Thomas E. Shipley, Jr., and Stephen F. Barsky, *Liquor and Poverty, Skid Row as a Human Condition* (New Brunswick, NJ, 1978): 212, 221.

29. Weeks, *Sex, Politics, and Society*, 28, 31; see also, 23, 32-33.

30. See Walkowitz, *Prostitution and Victorian Society*, 88 and Gibson, Prostitution, 31 for discussions of European middle-class attempts to control working-class sexuality.

31. Sanger, *History of Prostitution*, 652-653; James Rolph to J.C. Westenberg, Aug. 7, 1913, James Rolph, Jr. Papers; New Orleans *Mascot*, June, 1892 (quoted in Rose, *Storyville*, 37); A.E. Boynton to Miss L.H. Wall, March 24, 1913, San Francisco League of Women Voters Papers, (California Historical Society Library, San Francisco); Wisconsin. Committee on White Slave Traffic, *Report*, 185; S.D. Gross, *Syphilis in its Relation to the National Health*... (Philadelphia, 1874): 38; Rosen, *Lost Sisterhood*, 5.

32. Edmund Andrews, *Prostitution and Its Sanitary Management* (St. Louis, 1871): 21; Sanger, *History of Prostitution*, 647.

33. Wisconsin. Committee on White Slave Traffic, *Report*, 27, 149, also 116; Rosenstirn, *Our Nation's Health*, 17; Fred Franklin to Paul Smith, June 1, 1917, Paul Smith Papers (Special Collections, UCLA Library, Los Angeles); Price, Segregated District, 17, also 3, 16, 25; Sanger, *History of Prostitution*, 680. These ideas about working-class sexuality are still prevalent today. In her study of contraception, Lee Rainwater claims that the lower classes are usually assumed to be much more permissive about sexual behavior than the upper classes. "One popular middle-class stereotype of the lower-class person is that he is highly sexed. Middle-class people cherish a fantasy of the lower class as impulsive and freely self-indulgent because they are not hemmed in by prudery and constriction." Lee Rainwater, *And the Poor Get Children* (Chicago, 1960), ix, 98.

34. United States Congress. House of Representatives. 49th Cong. 2nd Sess. Executive Document 157. *Emigration and Immigration. Reports of the Consular Officers of the United States* (Washington, 1887), 45, 84, 177, 256, 274, 282, 328; United States Congress, House of Representatives. 51st Cong. 2nd Sess. Report No. 3472. *Immigration Investigation* (Washington, 1891), ii, 237, 436, 589, 604, 970; United States Congress. House of Representatives. 52nd Cong. 1st Sess. Executive Document 235. *Letter from the Secretary of the Treasury Transmitting a Report of the Commissioners of Immigration Upon the Causes Which Incite Immigration to the United States* (Washington, 1892): 1, 125. In his book on the represion of the red light district, Howard Woolston commented that "hordes" of immigrants brought with them views on sex "prevalent in their particular countries and in the social strata from which they came." Howard B. Woolston, *Prostitution in the United States* (New York, 1921), 17. Charles Rosenberg has argued that "public health advocates assumed that sexual license was characteristic of slum life and, like drink, one of those traits which kept the poor poor." Charles Rosenberg, "Sexuality, Class and Role in 19th-Century America," *American Quarterly* 25 (1973): 144. Finally, Brian Harrison refers to the "widespread assumption [in England] that working people were generally more promiscuous than other classes." Brian Harrison, "Underneath the Victorians," *Victorian Studies*, X (1967): 252.

35. 26 *Stats* 1084.

36. Rosenstirn, *Our Nation's Health*, 10-11; Sanger, *History of Prostitution*, 669; E. Teesdale, *Rev. Paul Smith Answered by E. Teesdale*, Unidentified Pamphlet, Paul Smith Papers.

37. Gross, *Syphilis*, 38.

38. Powell, *State Regulation of Vice*, 14-18.

39. Walkowitz, *Prostitution and Victorian Society*, 88; Gibson, *Prostitution*, 31.

Copyright Information

Carlisle, Marcia. "Disorderly City, Disorderly Women: Prostitution in Ante-Bellum Philadelphia." *Pennsylvania Magazine of History and Biography* 110 (October 1986): 549-568. ©Historical Society of Pennsylvania, Philadelphia, Pennsylvania, USA.

Gilfoyle, Timothy J. "Strumpets and Misogynists: Brothel 'Riots' and the Transformation of Prostitution in Antebellum New York City." *New York History* 68 (January 1987): 44-65. ©New York State Historical Association, Cooperstown, New York, USA. Reprinted with permission of the Association and the author.

Tansey, Richard. "Prostitution and Politics in Antebellum New Orleans." *Southern Studies* 18:4 (Winter 1979): 449-479. ©*Southern Studies - An Interdisciplinary Journal of the South*, Northwestern State University of Louisiana, Natchiotches, Louisiana, USA.

Best, Joel. "Careers in Brothel Prostitution: St. Paul, 1865-1883." *The Journal of Interdisciplinary History* 12:4 (Spring 1982): 597-619. "Reprinted from *The Journal of Interdisciplinary History*, XII (1982), 597-619, with permission of the editors of *The Journal of Interdisciplinary History* and the MIT Press, Cambridge, Massachusetts (USA). ©1982 by the Massachusetts Institute of Technology and the editors of *The Journal of Interdisciplinary History*."

Newman, Frances, and Elizabeth Cohen, with Patricia Tobin and Gail [Gael] MacPherson. "Historical Perspectives on the Study of Female Prostitution." *International Journal of Women's Studies: Special Issue I: Feminist Psychology* (Canada) 8:1 (1985): 80-86. ©Frances Newman, Elizabeth Cohen, Patricia Tobin and Gail [Gael] MacPherson. Reprinted with permission of the authors.

Beckman, Marlene D. "The White Slave Traffic Act: Historical Impact of a Federal Crime Policy on Women." *Women & Politics* 4:3 (1984): 85-101. ©by The Haworth Press, Inc. All rights reserved. Binghamton, NY, USA.

Hirata, Lucie Cheng. "Free, Indentured, Enslaved: Chinese Prostitutes in Nineteenth-Century America." *Signs: Journal of Women in Culture and Society* 5:1 (Autumn 1979): 3-29. "©1979 by The University of Chicago. All rights reserved." Chicago, Illinois, USA.

Goldman, Marion. "Sexual Commerce on the Comstock Lode." *Nevada Historical Society Quarterly* 21 (Summer 1978): 98-129. ©Nevada Historical Society, Reno, Nevada, USA.

Ichioka, Yuji. "Ameyuki-san: Japanese Prostitutes in Nineteenth-Century America." *Amerasia Journal* 4:1 (1977): 1-21. ©1977 by Yugi Ichioka and the Asian American Studies Center, University of California-Los Angeles, Los Angeles, California, USA.

Petrik, Paula. "Capitalists with Rooms: Prostitution in Helena, Montana, 1865-1900." *Montana: The Magazine of Western History* 31:2 (April 1981): 28-41. ©Montana Historical Society, Helena, Montana, USA. Reprinted with permission of the Society and the author.

Burnham, John C. "Medical Inspection of Prostitutes in America in the Nineteenth Century: The St. Louis Experiment and Its Sequel." *Bulletin of the History of Medicine* 45:3 (May-June 1971): 203-218. ©1971 The Johns Hopkins University Press, Baltimore, Maryland, USA.

Riegel, Robert E. "Changing American Attitudes toward Prostitution (1800-1920)." *Journal of the History of Ideas* 29 (1968): 437-452. ©*Journal of the History of Ideas*, Rochester, NY, USA.

Lubove, Roy. "The Progressives and the Prostitute." *The Historian* 24:3 (May 1962): 308-330. ©1962 by Phi Alpha Theta International Honor Society in History, Allentown, Pennsylvania, USA.

Feldman, Egal. "Prostitution, the Alien Woman and the Progressive Imagination, 1910-1915." *American Quarterly* 19:2, Part 1 (Summer 1967): 192-206. "©1973, 1985, 1986, 1965, 1966, 1981, 1982, 1980, 1979, 1967, 1974, American Studies Association, Washington, D.C., USA." Reprinted with permission of the Association and the author.

Murphy, Mary. "The Private Lives of Public Women: Prostitution in Butte, Montana, 1878-1917. In *The Women's West*, edited by Susan Armitage and Elizabeth Jameson (Norman, Oklahoma: University of Oklahoma Press, 1987): 193-205. "From *The Women's West*, Edited and With Introductions by Susan

Armitage and Elizabeth Jameson. Copyright ©1987 by the University of Oklahoma Press." Also reprinted with permission of the author. Photograph on page 287 reprinted 'Courtesy Glenn Kinnamon.'" Article first appeared in *Frontiers: a journal of women's studies* 7:3 (1984): 30-35. Women's Studies Program, University of Colorado at Boulder, Colorado, USA.

Morton, Marian J. "Seduced and Abandoned in an American City: Cleveland and Its Fallen Women, 1869-1936." *Journal of Urban History* 11:4 (August 1985): 443-469. "©1985 by Sage Publications. Inc. Reprinted by permission of Sage Publications, Inc. Newbury Park, California, USA."

Shumsky, Neil L. "Tacit Acceptance: Respectable Americans and Segregated Prostitution, 1870-1910." *Journal of Social History* 19:4 (1986): 665-679. ©*Journal of Social History*, Carnegie-Mellon University Press, Pittsburgh, Pennsylvania, USA.

Index

Bei Fragen zur Produktsicherheit wenden Sie sich bitte an:
If you have any questions regarding product safety,
please contact:

Walter de Gruyter GmbH
Genthiner Straße 13
10785 Berlin
productsafety@degruyterbrill.com